Politics in the German Democratic Republic

John M. Starrels
Anita M. Mallinckrodt

The Praeger Special Studies program—
utilizing the most modern and efficient book
production techniques and a selective
worldwide distribution network—makes
available to the academic, government, and
business communities significant, timely
research in U.S. and international economic, social, and political development.

Politics in the German Democratic Republic

Praeger Publishers   New York   Washington   London

PRAEGER SPECIAL STUDIES IN INTERNATIONAL POLITICS AND GOVERNMENT

Library of Congress Cataloging in Publication Data

Starrels, John M
    Politics in the German Democratic Republic

    (Praeger special studies in international
politics and government)
    Includes index
    1. Germany, East—Politics and government.
I. Dasbach, Anita Mallinckrodt, joint author.
II. Title.
JN3971.5.A2S78   320.4'43'1   75-23994
ISBN 0-275-01520-3

PRAEGER PUBLISHERS
111 Fourth Avenue, New York, N.Y. 10003, U.S.A.

Published in the United States of America in 1975
by Praeger Publishers, Inc.

Dedicated with gratitude
to the many friends in
both German states who
provided the understanding
necessary for the writing
of this book.

CONTENTS

Politics in the German Democratic Republic

The field of comparative communist studies continues to inch forward. Despite Robert Tucker's widely accepted assertion that methodological problems are keeping the field from the "take-off" stage, [1] scholars doggedly remain at their research in an effort to move the field ahead. In doing so, they are painfully aware of the short distance they have come and the long way they have to go in finding methodologies that facilitate the study of communist systems per se and eventually make East/West comparisons possible. The steps toward that goal are worth recounting.

In the look backward, one of the early indications of change in the until-then Western-oriented field of comparative politics is found as long ago as 1955. In an editorial foreword to a comparative government book by Roy Macridis, Richard Snyder said that while political science was passing through a period of change and reappraisal and comparative studies could profit from a thorough reexamination, it might also be useful to look at the idea that "the almost exclusive attention to the differences between democracy and dictatorship has obscured what could be learned about politics from assuming that some characteristics are equally typical of both systems." [2]

In that study Macridis charged that comparative government, in its traditional approach, was essentially parochial because it focused on democratic systems to the exclusion of non-Western systems. Such an approach, he said, had been treating nondemocratic systems as aberrations from democratic "norms." Comparative government was, essentially, a study dealing with Western political systems, excessively formalistic in its approach to political institutions and chiefly descriptive rather than problem-solving, explanatory, or analytic in method.

Comparative government could be much more than that, Macridis maintained. It could deal with major concepts, such as decision-

1

making, power, ideology, political institutional relationships. In doing so it could make use of theories, such as group theory (to examine the concept of decision-making, for example, by studying elites), the equilibrium theory (to examine concepts of power and ideology and how they are used to maintain systems' stability), or functional theory (to examine political institutions).

As the academic reevaluation of comparative politics slowly began, with few exceptions the major communist political system, that of the USSR, was still ignored. Most analysts, apparently, continued to think of it as a static totalitarian system, largely black and white, without differences and similarities that could be studied comparatively within, for instance, the East European context. Philip Mosely, who had contributed much to the area approach, for example, reminded his area specialist colleagues in 1959 that "an important task which has hardly been tackled at all is the comparative study of Communist systems,"[3] that is, intrasystem analysis. In 1960 Gordon H. Skilling joined the call for applying the comparative approach to communist political systems.[4] But a dynamic model and relevant categories for such analysis were still lacking.

A breakthrough, however, was near, for that same year Gabriel Almond and James Coleman published The Politics of Developing Areas, and in it they gave comparative political science a new semantic with which to work, that is, categories of functional analysis. In analyzing the political systems of the developing areas, which had become important to policy-makers in the postwar period, Almond and Coleman said since many of those systems lacked formal political structure, it was necessary instead to concentrate on the functions performed by the system. Thus, it would be useful to analyze developing entities as "political systems" rather than as "governments, nations, or states." Such terms had legal and institutional meanings that got bogged down in interpretation and hampered analysis. "Political system," on the other hand, "directs attention to the entire scope of political activities within a society, regardless of where in the society such activities may be located."[5] In short, Almond and Coleman saw the political system as including all interactions that authoritatively allocate values for the society. Further, they called for a substitution of the terms "functions, role, and structures," respectively, for the old formal norms of "powers, offices, and institutions." And finally, they advocated substituting the broader terms "political culture" for "public opinion" and "political socialization" for "citizenship training."

Challenged by this more flexible approach, F.C. Barghoorn in 1962 began the pioneering job of applying it to a communist political system—his was the "first full-length functional analysis of Soviet politics."[6] Another major academic breakthrough in applying

comparative methodology to communist systems came in 1964 when
Z.B. Brzezinski and Samuel Huntington published their comparative
study of U.S. and Soviet concepts and practice of power.[7]

And in 1966 the landmark work concerning interest groups in
communist societies, an article by Skilling, appeared in World
Politics. In it he pointed out that "the comparative analysis conducted
by David Easton, Gabriel Almond, and others is intended to be applicable to all types of states, including the Communist." But rather
than looking at communist societies from such points of view, Skilling
said most Western analysis was still concerned with communist politics
"outputs" without recognizing that there are "inputs," too. "Unlike
all other systems," Skilling said, "the Soviet has been often depicted
as one in which struggles over ideas and interests, or conflicts of
rival groups, are absent." Yet, he went on, Almond and Coleman had
"offered the suggestive thought that the articulation and aggregation
of interests characteristic of all systems take place within a totalitarian party, largely latently, through the interplay of interest groups
and functions."[8] This, Skilling offered in conclusion, was a good
comparative approach to Communist systems, that is, the application
of the interest-group approach.

Also in 1966 a general series on comparative governments
included, along with the old standbys of France, Germany, Great
Britain, etc., a treatment of Eastern Europe.[9] In this book for the
Crowell series, Skilling took up the concepts Macridis had called for
more than a decade ago—decision-making, power, ideology, political
institutions—and did so through the use of group and functional theory.
And at the same time Barghoorn's study of the Soviet Union appeared
as the first communist political system analysis in Little, Brown's
Country Study series in comparative politics. In it Barghoorn under-
took to examine several significant themes not ordinarily treated in
introductory studies of Soviet politics: political culture and socialization, interest-group activity, and policy-making process. Thus,
academicians had taken the first steps in analyzing communist systems
by categories they hoped eventually could be applied to East/West,
that is, cross-system, comparisons. By 1967, therefore, the Newsletter of the American Council of Learned Societies could report that
the scope of the Comparative Communist Studies field was emerging:
"In terms of timing . . . the comparative study of communism may be
thought of as being in its adolescence."[10]

By 1968 the emerging comparative communist field had pro-
gressed sufficiently for a second major conference organized by the
Committee on Comparative Communist Studies. Taking up the theme
of "How, When, and Why Communist Systems Change," the conferees
felt that they had been so surprised by post-1948 changes in Eastern
Europe because they had been tied to a static model of analysis, the

totalitarian model, which had concentrated on control rather than
change. What they felt they needed was a dynamic model, such as
that of the "mobilizing regime." And so the search for relevant
methodology went on.

    Enough individual studies had resulted from all this mental
agitation that by 1971 Roger E. Kanet could pull together 13 works
and publish a reader under the provocative title, The Behavioral
Revolution and Communist Studies. In it he traced the traditional
descriptive, policy-oriented approach to communist studies—organizational structure of the Communist party, power struggles, social
control, revolutionary change, description and explanation of specific
events—that emphasized the uniqueness of the communist system.
But "by focusing on the uniqueness of the Communist party-state,
some scholars have tended to ignore questions concerning decision-
making procedures and methods of policy implementation." Now,
Kanet suggested, the scene was changing. Increasing numbers of
scholars

> have become interested in the formation and competition
> of groups within the Communist Party . . . they have
> examined the career patterns of members of the political
> elite or have conducted detailed content analyses of
> published statements in order to discover similarities or
> divergencies in the policy orientation of various occupa-
> tional specialists in the Soviet Union and Eastern Europe.
> Others have attempted to view the Communist system as
> a means of achieving rapid modernization and have employed
> some of the insights developed in the literature on political
> and economic modernization. [11]

    The changes that Kanet referred to were reflected in Barghoorn's
1972 revised edition of his breakthrough comparative study of the
Soviet Union. In their foreword, editors Almond, Coleman, and Pye
pointed out that "in the last few years the intellectual ferment characteristic of political science in general has more thoroughly penetrated
Soviet studies, rapidly changing the novelty of five years ago into the
accepted idea of today."[12] Taking into account these recent intellectual
developments, Barghoorn's new edition incorporated systemic and
functional frameworks, interest group and pluralistic theories, developmental theories.

    It is within this slowly advancing trial-and-error methodological
context that this study of Politics in the German Democratic Republic
was undertaken. It attempts, as Barghoorn did, to use the systems-
functional conceptual model as the framework for examining a communist political system. Thus, while it is more descriptive than

analytical, the study offers readers a dynamic approach for thinking about a communist political system, one that sheds light on the processes of social change. While the study is not comparative, it is believed to be a step in that direction.

Such a study, however, has not been easy. In addition to the general problems facing comparative communist studies, an examination of the German Democratic Republic (GDR) is hampered by additional specific factors:

1. For a quarter of a century American political science has largely ignored the German Democratic Republic. Following politics, as U.S. academe is inclined to do, American scholars largely regarded the GDR as a transitory phenomenon that would disappear from the world scene when "the German problem" was solved and the two halves of the former German empire were reunified. If this was not the point of view, then scholars often ignored the GDR because it was regarded as a "satellite," insufficiently different from the mother planet, the Soviet Union, to warrant study. Or if the GDR was accorded any kind of permanency at all, American scholars often abandoned the study of it to their West German colleagues who "were on the spot," so to speak, with accessibility to information and equipped with unique motivation for studying the GDR. Recently, however, this scenario is beginning to change. With diplomatic recognition by major countries of the world and membership in the United Nations, the GDR's permanency no longer can be tenably questioned. As a result, American scholars interested in the GDR are increasing, as shown by the growing numbers of political science dissertations dealing with the German Democratic Republic.

2. A second problem complicating GDR research is the nature of the background research to which American scholars have access— it is voluminous; it is based on traditional methodologies; it often is not balanced. The reason is that it is found primarily in the Federal Republic of Germany (FRG). Understandably, West German specialists, who for 25 years have been confronted daily by the existence of a direct competitor to their political system, have had more than a passing interest in "the other half of Germany." Over the years they have, as a result, subjected every imaginable aspect of life in the GDR to scrutiny. The resulting commentaries seem unending. In Europe there is nothing to compare to this situation that has resulted from Germany's "divided nation" status—there is not a second Hungary, or Poland, or Yugoslavia studying and challenging the other. At the same time, however, most of the voluminous analyses undertaken of the GDR are not of a systematic nature. Political science has been relatively slow to develop in the Federal Republic of Germany, and so law and history have remained the traditional disciplinary approaches— or intuitive journalism—to the study of the GDR. The result,

predictably, has been constitutional and organizational analysis. A
notable exception has been the annual Report to the Federal Government and Material on the State of the Nation. [13]

However, with the signing of the Basic Treaty between the two
German states in 1973, GDR research in the FRG is being reassessed.
For instance, Deutschland Archiv, the monthly journal for GDR and
intra-German questions, said in its May 1973 issue that the time had
come for a new look at the "problems, goals and organization of GDR
research." [14] As a result, the journal opened its pages to a discussion
of these aspects.

The contributions that followed the journal's invitation were
interesting from a number of aspects. For instance, the old question
of whether research should be policy oriented was pursued with renewed vigor. The overall impression seemed to be that even if research should/could serve other purposes, GDR research in the FRG
would remain highly policy oriented because of the competitive nature
of coexistence between the two German states. A second question
concerned the aspects of sociopolitical life in the GDR that should be
studied. Here there was general agreement that the answer was
"Practically everything!" The third question, "How should the GDR
be researched?" did not produce satisfying answers. While some
called for "the development of theories and new methodological possibilities in the social and economic sciences," with emphasis on "comparative politics," "comparative sociology," and "comparative system
research," [15] others called for continuation of historical, organizational, and institutional studies. [16] The difficulties of comparative
studies of the GDR were seen in the paucity of information available
and in theoretical problems, such as the alleged tendency of comparative assessments to stress similarities rather than contrasts. [17] The
three-month-long discussion, however, contributed little to specific
methodological questions.

Thus, on the one hand in the FRG there presently is the call for
more systematic studies. In fact, the assertion that one is using a
"scientific" approach or is doing "scientific" work has become com-
monplace. As noted, the term "comparative study," too, is being
heard more and more. However, the latter often seems to mean
primarily statistical comparisons, and the willingness to try out more
sophisticated methodology is lacking.

Thus, not surprisingly, studies produced by West German
specialists frequently are based on the assumption that the political
system of the GDR is inferior to that of the FRG. Discrepancies
between theory and practice, common to all political systems, are
triumphantly pointed out as failures of the GDR "system." Assessments of performance then are made on the basis of Western standards,
rather than against the stated intentions of the GDR system itself.

Ideology is still frequently viewed as a tool for measurement rather than as a broad guideline of values and intentions. And when it is studied, ideology often is viewed in isolation from other factors.

To overcome some of these problems, this study will attempt a systems-functional examination of the GDR, despite the perhaps well-founded reservations of West German colleagues. The study will try to concentrate on describing what "is" and not what "ought" to be. In doing so, it will take into account the basic problems of communist studies: classification, model building, and data collection.

1. Agreeing that communist states are not always easy to classify, and rejecting the totalitarian or authoritarian systems types, this study accepts that the GDR, on the basis of its political culture, is an "ideological, elitist, and subject-participatory" system (the description Barghoorn applied to the Soviet Union). Equally as useful might be Peter Ludz's classification of the GDR as a "consultative authoritarian" system, [18] or Harry Rigby's "state-party system."[19]

2. Rejecting the totalitarian model, this study instead makes use of the systems-functional perspective. It is conceived of not as a specific procedure or a general theory, but rather as a suggested network of definitions applicable to communist as well as other political contexts.

By "system" we mean (a) that a political system has identifiable parts or elements—units of which it is composed—that include all those activities that bear on the formation and enforcement of authoritative policies, (b) that a political system constitutes an identifiable whole with recognizable boundaries (distinguished, for example, from the educational system, the religious system, etc.) and that the activities of the system are to some degree integrated or coordinated (one element of the system cannot operate in complete disregard of the activities of other elements without disrupting or destroying the system), and (c) that the constituent units of a political system are interdependent (each part affects and is affected by all the other parts, although not all elements play equally vital roles). This, however, is not to suggest that while the boundaries between the political and other "systems" are held to be "recognizable" in this analytical scheme, they are impenetrable. Quite the contrary is the case, and therefore a dotted rather than solid line separates the "political" from other systems in Figure 1. For instance, a clear separation between the "political" system of a state and its "economic" system is unrealistic. This is especially true when analyzing a Marxist-oriented system that claims as one of its distinctions the fact that it sees economics and politics as inseparable (calling the science of it "Political Economy") both in theory and practice.

In Figure 1 the boundaries of the political system are indicated by the dotted line, the interrelationships by the arrows, the dependence

FIGURE 1

Political Culture

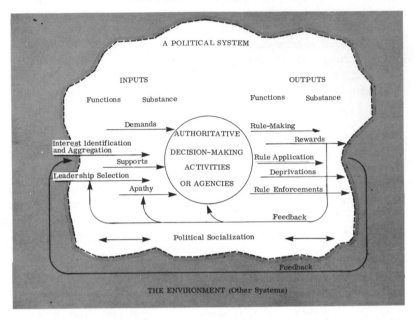

Source: "A Political System." Marian D. Irish and James W.
Prothro, The Politics of American Democracy, 4th Ed., Englewood
Cliffs, N.J., 1968, p. 9.

on the broader environment by the shaded area outside the dotted line,
its variable area by the ungeometric shape and breaks in its boundaries,
its activities by the center circle and the inputs and outputs.

These activities illustrate the nontraditional semantics used in
this type of political study. On the "input" side of the political system
(those activities that keep the system going), we refer to "leadership
selection" rather than "elections" and to "interest identification and
aggregation" instead of, for instance, to "political parties" and
"lobbying." (Since such input demands are generated largely within
the political system itself, by the Communist party, the diagram
includes feedback arrows to represent inputs on decision-makers
from within the political system as well as the nonpolitical environment. Further, the supports, including attitudes and behavior supporting the political system at every level—such as the political community, the party, and particular policies—also are indicated through
the feedback arrows, as well as apathy which gives decision-makers
room to maneuver.)

On the output side, we refer to "rule-making" activities rather than "the legislature," "rule application" rather than "the bureaucracy," and "rule adjudication and enforcement," rather than "the judicial." (In the case of a communist political system this is particularly applicable since Marxists/Leninists reject the principle of the separation of powers.) The substance of their policy outputs are indentified as "rewards" and "deprivations," for political decision-making is never neutral.

The "functions," as sketched above, are the effects or consequences of an activity. They promote the survival of the system, while "dysfunctions" refer to consequences that tend to disrupt or destroy the system. Clearly, the system must furnish general rules or policies to maintain order and satisfy demands on the system. In addition, it must carry out the rules or policies decided on, that is, apply them in actual practice. And it must settle disputes that arise among citizens and between citizens and the system. And basic to the entire system is the political culture and the major function of "political culture and the major function of "political socialization," formerly called "citizenship training." It supports the entire system, and in some respects is an output and in other respects an input: It is an output, for each political system seeks to indoctrinate children into the political processes and beliefs of their society; it is an input since it conditions the kinds of demands and supports that enter the system.

As Almond has written, "The principle advantage of the system concept is that it analytically differentiates the object of study from its environment, directs attention to the interaction of the system with other systems in its environment, to its own conversion characteristics, and to its maintenance and adaptive properties."[20] In other words, the systems approach facilitates the effort to shift from an examination of formal government institutions to examination of the basic structures—formal or informal—through which the system responds to its environment.

This model obviously is not accepted by all researchers concerned with communist political systems. However, it contains insights that we find useful. Implicit in the systems-functional model is the distinction between self-regulating systems in a state of primary equilibrium and systems guided by feedback mechanisms. The latter emphasize the activities of communication and decision-making necessary for the efficient operation of a complex society.

3. Developing a fund of comparative data is crucial in the field of comparative communist studies. However, it is difficult, for the problems of data adequacy and reliability remain nearly as serious as ever. Aggregative data (available from statistical reporting) is becoming easier to obtain, but sample survey data (obtained through

interviews and polling) remains illusive. To the extent that it is
available, it will be used in this study. However, the authors concede
that GDR research is not yet in a position to contribute toward the
advancement of comparative communist studies as a quantitative
discipline.

Finally, the authors join the younger generation of American
political scientists generally, and West German political scientists
specifically, who question claims of "value-free" analysis. Instead,
they concede that their own values are clearly implied in their rejection, scientifically and ideologically, of the totalitarian model. Further, they attempt to understand the GDR as an accepted state and,
above all, to understand it from its point of view. Within the American
context this is especially important, for although some progress has
been made since the early 1960s[21] the fact that not one political
science text on GDR affairs has been written in the United States is
testimony to an unsatisfactory situation, especially when one assesses
the robust condition of West German research in the United States.
This text is an attempt, then, to partially close the gap in our
knowledge about the GDR.

NOTES

1. Robert C. Tucker, "Communism and Political Culture,"
Newsletter on Comparative Studies of Communism, May 1971,
pp. 3-12.

2. Roy C. Macridis, The Study of Comparative Government
(New York: Random House, 1955), p. vii.

3. Cited by Robert C. Tucker in "Research Notes on the Comparative Study of Communism," World Politics, January 1967, p. 242.

4. Gordon H. Skilling, "Soviet and Communist Politics: A
Comparative Approach," Journal of Politics, May 1960, pp. 300-13.

5. Gabriel Almond and James Coleman, The Politics of Developing Areas (Princeton: Princeton University Press, 1960), p. 17.

6. Frederick C. Barghoorn, Politics in the USSR (Boston:
Little, Brown, 1966), p. viii.

7. Z.B. Brzezinski and S.P. Huntington, Politics and Power:
USA/USSR (New York, Viking Press), 1963.

8. Gordon H. Skilling, "Interest Groups and Communist
Politics," World Politics, April 1966, pp. 435-51.

9. Gordon H. Skilling, The Governments of Communist East
Europe (New York: Crowell, 1966).

10. ACLS Newsletter, American Council of Learned Societies,
January/February 1967, pp. 8-11.

11. Roger Kanet, ed., The Behavioral Revolution and Communist Studies (New York: The Free Press, 1971), pp. 5-7.

12. Frederick C. Barghoorn, Politics in the USSR, rev. ed. (Boston: Little, Brown, 1972), p. viii.

13. Prepared under the guidance of P.C. Ludz, this report is a systematic comparison of various aspects of FRG and GDR society.

14. Deutschland Archiv, May 1973, p. 485.

15. P.C. Ludz, in ibid., pp. 488-93.

16. Hermann Weber, Deutschland Archiv, June 1973, p. 588.

17. Hartmut Zimmermann, Deutschland Archiv, July 1973, p. 716.

18. Peter C. Ludz, The Changing Party Elite in East Germany (Boston: MIT Press, 1972), p. 42.

19. T. Harry Rigby, Communist Party Membership in the U.S.S.R., 1917-1967 (Princeton, N.J.: Princeton University Press, 1968), p. 2.

20. Gabriel Almond, "Political Theory and Political Science," American Political Science Review, December 1966, p. 876.

21. See John M. Starrels, "Research on East German Politics in the United States: A Research Note," unpublished manuscript (available on request).

INPUTS: DEMANDS, SUPPORTS, APATHY

Viewing political activities as a system, as described in Chapter 1, aids in seeing the interrelationship among the parts of the system. All stimuli and responses, or inputs and outputs, then, are seen as interactive and interdependent, rather than as a "cause" or "trigger" to political activities. Rather than viewing political systems as something imposed on society, the systems approach enables one to focus on the supports that sustain it. Thus, by using the systems approach, insight is gained into basic processes by which political systems generally persist, that is, the "life processes" of systems as such.

As David Easton says of the approach he devised for analyzing political systems,

> From this perspective, systems analysis of political life responds most sensitively and rewardingly when questions are posed that seek to unravel the processes through which a political system is able to cope with the various stresses imposed upon it. In its ultimate returns this mode of analysis will enable the investigator to understand more fully the way in which some kind of political system in a society manages to persist in the face of stresses that might well have been expected to lead to its destruction. [1]

If a political system is viewed in this way—as a process that persists—three input substances are of special significance.

First, for instance, the importance of the demands generated within the political system itself or from the nonpolitical environment is obvious. What citizens believe they can and should demand from their political systems is largely conditioned by the political culture and transmitted through communications. It is an integral cause/effect link in the political process. Citizens of constitutional democracies, for instance, are conditioned to articulate demands through pluralistic channels; citizens of communist systems, as we shall see, through the party.

Equally important is a second form of inputs, the supports. These are both the attitudes and behavior that support the political system. Examples might include attitudes of national identity and patriotism emerging from the political culture or, in more extreme form, nationalism, ethnocentrism, and chauvinism. Support, however, is not the same at all levels of political activity. At a lower level of government, such general supports may drop off as citizen discontent

expresses itself. Shortage of consumer goods or unemployment
diminishes appeals to patriotism. Even less uniform support may be
seen when the input is viewed at the level of specific policies, an area
where opinions and behavior may be divided sharply, for instance, as
regarding land collectivization. However, even here supports are
present, if when a controversial policy becomes law it is accepted as
legitimate by the citizenry.

A third source of input may be said to be apathy. Unlike support,
which connotes some positive activity, apathy is neutral. It suggests
acquiescence to basic governmental arrangements. Though generally
criticized for their apoliticism, citizens who feed apathy into the
political system may be credited with giving decision-makers freedom
to act. In the communist system, apathy also exists regarding the
expression of public opinion, although this should not be confused with
inactivity. As we shall see, with its emphasis on modernization, more
importance is placed on participation in a communist system, that is,
less inactivity is tolerated. But regarding apathetic public opinion,
Kadar of Hungary sounded the keynote in his statement that "he who
is not against us is with us."

Stress in a political system is not uncommon. The variety of
influences from the environment that may disturb the system is enor-
mous, judging by any single day's news in industrialized societies or
by the process of modernization in developing societies, including
Eastern Europe.

One of the two major types of stress is a change in the volume
and variety of demands being poured into the system. Authorities may
be unable or unwilling to consider the demands, or the volume and the
variety of demands may be excessive for the system itself. However,
the system has built into it ways of regulating the demand so it will
not reach this unmanageable stage. For instance, there are structural
regulators, such as political parties, interest groups, opinion leaders,
and mass media, that take up the demands and provide some satisfaction. Irate citizens are easier to satisfy if, for instance, they have
"let off steam" through an interest group than if they are expressing
dissatisfaction in open revolt. Similarly, there are cultural restraints,
or regulators, that prevent overload—such as citizens' reluctance to
become involved in politics and other related psychological inhibitions,
for the nature of man apparently is not to live constantly in an agitated
state. The system also may cope with increased demands by increasing
the channels to deal with them, as for instance through proliferation
of political structures. Appointment of a specialized commission can
take the direct heat off decision-makers by absorbing articulated discontent and demands. The system can also, of course, turn to coercion
to decrease demands. Coercion has many forms: from forbidding
newspapers to carry troublesome news, which increases public unrest

and demands for political action, to actual acts of force against the articulators of demands, such as arrests of political dissidents.

A decrease in the support being poured into the political system is the second major type of stress. Again the system has built-in ways of dealing with the problem. A radical form of attempting to renew the input of support is to change the structure and processes of the system, that is, structural regulation. Examples would be the adoption of new laws or giving nonsupportive groups a greater voice in the decision-making process, as by increasing their representation or influence in decision-making agencies and activities. A less radical change is that of increasing diffuse support, that is, encouraging sentiments of legitimacy and compliance by, for instance, emphasizing the sense of political community, patriotism, loyalty, general welfare, etc. A third means of renewing the input of support is by granting specific benefits or advantages in return for specific support, such as an improved standard of living for reduced public agitation. If people feel their minimal demands are not met, specific support declines and a political system has to rely increasingly on diffuse support, as described above. Unending appeals to patriotism, for instance, become watered down (especially in the absence of an external threat) and eventually a credibility gap between words and actions develops.

Thus, through the communications feedback process, authorities assess how much output is needed to reduce the stress. As has been seen, they may either (1) satisfy or regulate the increased demand volume and/or (2) maximize the support. The interaction of the feedback and the response thus enables a political system dynamically to regulate stress by modifying or redirecting its own behavior. This, in turn, influences public opinion anew.[2] In other words, if the demands being put into a political system, despite the regulators, outweigh the supports and apathy being put in, and the usual rule-making, rule-application, or rule-enforcement functions growing out of decision-making cannot resolve the imbalance in an acceptable way, one could say the political system were in grave trouble. A "crisis" may be said to be reached in a stress situation when the usual adaptive mechanisms (law, custom, bargaining, etc.) are inadequate to handle new issues or where old issues in conflict tend almost to overwhelm the mechanisms. A decision then must be made to undertake an adaptation.

If, however, the crisis calling for adaptation is met through an adjustment of the decision-making mechanism and its functions (as by bringing in new leadership), one could suggest that the political system was capable of handling its crises. Either "real" actions or the "impression" of actions must address the circumstances causing the input/output discrepancy.

Thus, it is clear that every government requires in varying degrees the support of its citizens. Even a tyranny, which initially may have come to power with relatively little support, to endure requires the loyalty of at least some of its people. A more broadly based political system obviously requires wider support, and a modernizing system must meet more demands.

This is the substance that results from the interplay of leadership selection and training and interest identification and aggregation to be discussed in the following pages.

NOTES

1. David Easton, A Framework for Political Analysis (Englewood Cliffs, N.J.: Prentice-Hall, 1965), p. 25.
2. Ibid., pp. 116-28.

2

The German Democratic Republic has now been in official existence for a quarter of a century. Commenting upon the meaning of this historical occasion, the head of East Germany's ruling Communist party, the SED (Socialist Unity party of Germany), made these observations:

> October 7, 1949 marked the day when we embarked on the road towards the construction of a new, socialist order of society. There emerged a state which had broken once and for all with the accursed imperialist past and, from the very first moment of its existence, made its contribution to preserving peace and putting it on a lasting basis. Today there is a greater awareness than ever before that the founding of the German Democratic Republic marked a turning point in the history of our people and indeed of the whole of Europe. . . . The twenty-five years of the German Democratic Republic have been marked by our people's entry into the age of socialism, the fundamental transformation of their social existence, the active participation of our people under the leadership of the working class and its party in the revolutionary changes taking place in the world. The finest sons of the German working class have fought for this future to make the invincible ideas of Marx, Engels, and Lenin come true. Socialism was the objective that inspired antifascist resistance in the prisons and concentration camps, in the International Brigades, in the underground and exile. . . . This is the legacy of such unforgotten revolutionaries as Wilhelm Liebknecht and August Bebel, Clara Zetkin and Franz

Mehring, Karl Liebknecht and Rosa Luxembourg, of
Ernst Thälmann, of Wilhelm Pieck and Otto Grotewohl,
Walter Ulbricht, Herman Matern and Otto Buchwitz.[1]

Given the significance of this occasion, it would have been
surprising to read an official proclamation bereft of such high-sounding
and self-congratulatory observations, a consideration bearing special
relevance to a political system that has only recently come to enjoy
the psychological and tangible fruits of worldwide diplomatic acceptance. Because East Germany's ruling political elite has been forced
to come to terms with its short history by emphasizing real or imagined patterns of historical continuity tying the GDR to the path of all
German and communist history, however, the relative deemphasis
on the impact and contributions of Walter Ulbricht, the GDR's founder,
is perhaps somewhat surprising.[2]

This chapter attempts to gain some understanding of East
Germany's brief history by an examination of its political culture,
the basis of that country's political system. While succeeding chapters
discuss specific aspects of this phenomenon in detail, this chapter
attempts to provide a general overview and understanding of the
phenomenon.

Political culture, as usually defined by analysts, "embraces
both systematic doctrine and traditional attitudes, and this includes
the implicit as well as explicit, the emotional as the rational, practice
as well as theory, all of these disparate elements existing in tension
and conflict with each other."[3] In short, political culture is that complex mix of attitudes concerning governing that arise in any nation
over a period of time and form the basis for much of the political
activity under any system of government. As such, it conditions the
inputs and outputs, as noted earlier. Further, the concept of political
culture is intimately related to socialization, that is, the process of
induction in or general orientation to political action. As a dynamic
expression of political culture, the political socialization process is
directly responsible for the creation of individuals who normally feel
it incumbent upon themselves to obey the dictates and general expectations of the social order in which they have grown up.

This chapter focuses attention on various issues and problems
surrounding East German political culture by (1) examining those
aspects of its basic philosophy touching upon the concept, (2) looking
at the historical evolution of the phenomenon from 1945 to the present,
(3) describing some of its more significant doctrines and values, and
(4) focusing upon selected aspects of the political socialization process.

THEORETICAL FRAMEWORK

Marxism/Leninism

The German Democratic Republic was formed on the Soviet pattern. Thus, its leading social and political institutions were founded on the working assumptions and beliefs located in the writings of Marx, Lenin, and to a lesser degree Engels. Appropriately enough, a general appreciation of Marxism/Leninism provides a general framework of integrated beliefs and hopes about the nature of man and the universe within which he lives. Recognizing that the fit between ideology and the operational environment is rarely perfect, it is nevertheless important to understand the basic ideological assumptions that are fundamental to the GDR's political culture (as the ruling Marxist/Leninist party defines and operationalizes these assumptions).

Specifically, this means a fusion of Marx's and Lenin's writing: While Karl Marx is awarded the distinction of being the quintessential theorist of social development, Lenin is accorded the status of revolutionary strategist, organizer, and consolidator. Thus, Marxism/Leninism consists of basic assumptions about the nature of politics and society, as well as an analysis and description of authority relations. It is the foundation upon which all other assumptions are built.

Some of the most relevant aspects of this Marxist/Leninist framework are the following concepts relating to the political culture.

Class Struggle and Revolution

Building a theory of revolution around the concept of class relations, Marx and Engels maintained that modern history—from the late eighteenth century through the late nineteenth—involved inevitable antagonism and resulting confrontation between the property-owning class (the bourgeoisie) and the working class (the proletariat). Whereas property owners represent capitalist society, and its attendant evils, the proletariat incorporates a new stage of socioeconomic, and ultimately political, development within itself. While the bourgeoisie exhibits behavior and thought patterns characteristic of a departed epoch, the proletariat's struggle against "exploitation by a capitalist class signals the dawn of a communist future." In their words, "While in bourgeois society the past reigns over the present, in communist society the present reigns over the past."[4]

Thus, Marx and Engels' theory of social revolution turns on a particular concept of property relations. On the one hand, they contend that industrial capitalism has robbed the average worker of creative identity by divorcing him from direct involvement in, and responsibility for, the creation of a product. On the other hand, Marx and Engels argue that the proletariat eventually will reach a point of evolution where their numerical strength and knowledge, plus their understanding of political processes (including the art of gaining power), will inevitably push them into armed confrontation with their oppressors. "The weapons which the bourgeoisie used to destroy feudalism are now being turned against themselves. But the bourgeoisie has not only created the weapons which will bring about their death; they have also produced the men who will use these weapons against them—the modern worker, the proletariat."[5] Once the basis of capitalist society, private property, is transferred into the hands of the proletariat, the foundations of a future communist society will have been laid.

Basis and Superstructure

Communist theory offers an overview of historical development. Beginning with "Primitive-Communal" societies, Marxism subsequently examines "slave," "fedual," "capitalist," and, finally, "socialist" systems. As a theory of history, Marxism maintains that social change is developmental and "progressive," with "socialism" representing the most advanced form of human organization within the present historical era. From "socialism" mankind gradually moves toward the most advanced, and final, stage of development, "communism," which is defined as "from each according to his ability, to each according to his need."

Though each historical epoch possesses unique characteristics peculiar to its level of development, Marxism/Leninism maintains that all epochs are defined by two types of authority relationship:

> The state of the productive forces determines, as we have
> seen, the character of men's production relations, i.e.,
> the economic structure of society. This economic structure
> in its turn constitutes the basis, the foundation, on which
> there arise many kinds of social relations, ideas and institu-
> tions. The ideas of society [political, legal, philosophical,
> religious, etc.], the institutions and organizations which
> arise on a given basis, constitute the superstructure of
> society. The theory of basis and superstructure explains
> how in the final analysis the mode of production determines
> all aspects of social life and reveals the link between the
> socio-economic relations and all other relations of a given
> society.[6]

Addressing special attention to the evolution of capitalist and socialist systems, Marxism/Leninism's concept of basis and super-structure are employed to explain the development of political systems. From their perspective, a "capitalist" system must possess the following characteristics:

> The capitalist class and the working class become the main classes of society. As before, the relations between them remain antagonistic in character, since they are based on exploitation, on the oppression of the propertyless by the possessors of property. . . . Deprived of the means of production . . . the worker is compelled to do so "volun-tarily"—under threat of death by starvation. . . . The changed methods of exploitation bring about a change in the methods of political rule. The transition takes place from the undisguised despotism of previous epochs to more refined forms of rule, to bourgeois democracy.[7]

"Eventually" a violent confrontation between the capitalist and working class occurs. "Rallying on its side all the working people, the working class overthrows the power of capital and creates a new, socialist, system free from the exploitation of man by man." Once the "basis" of society has become the property of the working class, the elemental preconditions for the erection of a new "superstructure" are satisfied:

> The socialist mode of production is based on social ownership of the means of production. The production relations of socialist society are therefore relations of cooperation and mutual assistance among workers liberated from exploitation. They correspond to the character of the productive forces, the social character of production being based on social ownership of the means of production.[8]

The Dictatorship of the Proletariat

How was political power, then, to be exercised in a socialist society? In whose hands was ultimate decision-making authority to be placed? Assuming that a revolutionary society goes through various developmental phases, what specific issues would have to be met and resolved by this new society in its march toward the final stages of communism? The answer comes from Lenin, for not only did he fashion a theory and operational strategy of armed revolution, but he developed a framework for the transformation of a capitalist society into a communist one, that is, postrevolutionary consolidation.

Confronted with the burden of turning Russia into a modern industrial society, Lenin realized that an immediate move toward full communism—"the classless society"—did not correspond to reality. Even if Marx had not spelled out a detailed blueprint for a communist society, his suggestion that a "new" order would allow individual workers to independently create their products (thereby helping them to realize their full creative potential) did not "yet" coincide with the realities facing a system that had recently divested itself of the remnants of capitalism. For Lenin, an "intermediate" stage of political development was necessary, hence the "dictatorship of the proletariat."[9]

Lenin correctly realized that revolutionary change involves long periods of time for the creation and transmission of new values. In a society that had been ruled by autocratic leaders, the challenge of modernization not only involved the ability and readiness of a tightly organized conspiratorial group—the Communist party—to grab the reins of power from the state, but the persistence of a new group of leaders in attempting to exterminate the remnants of the old order, on the one hand, and the creation of a new one, on the other hand. "The passage from a capitalist society within which communism has developed to a communist society is impossible without a 'political transition' period in which the state creates the revolutionary dictatorship of the proletariat."[10]

Role of the Party

If the working class was the inheritor of revolutionary legitimacy, it was the Communist party that was called upon to provide a structure for the administration, and direction, of sociopolitical change. From this angle, Lenin considered the Soviet Communist party to be the "organized" expression of the working class:

> The conquest of power by the working class fundamentally alters the position of its militant vanguard, the Marxist/ Leninist party. Before that, it is the party of a class fighting for power; after it is the party of the ruling class. Experience has shown that after the revolution the role of the Marxist party as leader of the working class and all the working people not only does not decrease, but, on the contrary, becomes immeasurably greater. It now becomes responsible for everything that goes on in society, for the policy of the state of the dictatorship of the proletariat, for the development of productive forces and culture, for the improvement of the people's welfare.[11]

Development of the Socialist State

A strict separation cannot be made between the "dictatorship of the proletariat" and the Marxist/Leninist concept of state power. Perhaps the easiest way of distinguishing between the two ideas is to include "state development" within the broader subject of "class dictatorship." In this vein, one can analyze Lenin's conception of state development in terms of "administrative" acts that all modern governments are called upon to initiate.

For Lenin, the norms guiding policy formation are the outcome of governmental decisions aimed at the destruction of private property and the simultaneous granting of political power to the working class. What happens once the transfer of political power has been secured, the expropriation of the basis from the hands of the bourgeoisie and into the hands of the proletariat? At this moment in time the revolutionary society, while continuing modified class warfare, since the battle for power has not been entirely won during the early phases of the dictatorship of the preletariat, begins to move toward a policy of "national integration." Though Lenin does not explicitly address himself to this issue, in large degree because he was dead before Soviet society began to move toward its integrative phase of development in the late 1940s, the concept of "Socialist Democracy" can be attributed to the influence of Leninist principles of political thought and organization.

Education of a "New" Socialist Personality

The establishment of total political power in the hands of the working class cannot take place in the absence of far-reaching psychological changes in the way individuals relate to political authority within the new socialist society. Both Marx and Engels devoted some attention to the meaning of personality transformation in a new society governed by communist morals, but it was with Lenin that a comprehensive framework for the education of large numbers of individuals in the spirit and practice of communism was developed.

Lenin supported the development of state-controlled institutions whose central task was the systematic education and training of new socialist citizens. As later parts of the chapter demonstrate, the USSR's recent historical experiences in the realm of citizenship development have been faithfully applied to meet the demands of state- and nation-building in the GDR. [12]

Functional

According to functional theory, the study of contemporary political systems begins with an appreciation, and understanding, of the environments within which they have developed. Two considerations merit attention here. First, functional theory emphasizes the importance of studying the impact of various developmental epochs within which they have developed. Two considerations merit attention here. First, functional theory emphasizes the importance of studying the impact of various developmental epochs within which political systems have evolved. Second, functional examinations of political systems tend to emphasize the significance of subjective dimensions of politics. Political culture is correspondingly defined as "internalized in the cognitions, feelings, and evaluations of its population. People are inducted into it just as they are socialized into nonpolitical roles and social systems. . . . The political culture of a nation is the particular distribution of patterns of orientation toward political objects among the members of the nation." The communication of political culture is carried out through the political socialization process. [13]

Thus Marxism/Leninism and functional theory both emphasize the importance of studying the impact of cultural and socialization variables. While Marxism/Leninism describes the evolution of societies from capitalism, to socialism, and ultimately to communism, functionalism posits the existence of various developmental challenges: state-building, nation-building, participation, and distribution. Thus, both theories rely heavily on historical progression for their explanatory power. Regarding political culture and its transmission via the political socialization process, both theories also complement each other: While Marxism/Leninism wants to create a personality structure congruent with its conception of the socialist personality, functional theory suggests that all societies, and especially socialist ones, attempt to transmit their political culture through the socialization process.

At this juncture one broad generalization emerges: Similar to Marxism/Leninism's concept that the basis determines the superstructure, so functionalists see political culture as conditioning various aspects of the political system. In the case of the GDR, this means that the attitudes, beliefs, and values of Marxism/Leninism, as well as German tradition more generally, affect the nature and form of the inputs (leadership recruitment, training, interest indentification, and aggregation), the outputs (rule making, rule application, rule enforcement), as well as decision-making and feedback. Especially in terms of inputs, what citizens believe they can and should demand from their political system is largely conditioned by the political culture and transmitted through communications processes. In this regard, a society's political culture represents a complex mixture of rights, expectations, and obligations, all of which can be appealed to by leaders and citizens alike. If political systems can develop a coherent identity, it is found within the design of its political culture, a complex symbolic world which supplies general meaning and legitimacy to political action. [14]

SITUATION IN THE GDR

The development of a political culture in the GDR, or the base for its revolutionary superstructure, has been a gradual one. The following phases mark its evolution.

The Anti-Fascist Democratic Revolution (1945-49)

In the immediate aftermath of celebrating its twenty-fifth year of official existence, it should not be forgotten that the establishment of the GDR in October 1949 was something less than a foregone historical conclusion. In the first place, SED writers have continued to argue through GDR history that it was the establishment of a "separate" sociopolitical order in West Germany during the late 1940s that played a decisive role in the founding of the GDR, almost as a defensive reaction. Thus one observer contends that

> the struggle of the KPD [German Communist Party] and
> then the SED (in the Eastern sector) and the political
> activities of the communists in the Western zones on
> behalf of democracy, represented a struggle for the
> national interests of our people in the very best of
> senses. With complete justification, our Party pushed
> to the very limit in attempting to forge a democratic and
> progressive development for all of Germany in the hope
> of frustrating the imperialist's goal of dividing the nation.
> From the very beginning, the imperialist occupational
> forces gained support from the recently defeated German
> monopoly capitalists. In common with other Anti-Fascist
> Democratic forces, the SED struggled against the subse-
> quent creation of a separate West German state and for
> the goal of building a unified Anti-Fascist Democratic

Republic. This effort remains one of its historical
services . . . (but) . . . the goal could not be
achieved. [15]

In the second place, and in line with broader currents at work
in the immediate postwar international environment, the Soviet Union
was not wholly committed to the establishment of a separate East
German polity until the early 1950s, given its hope that West Germany
might be brought into Moscow's direct sphere of political influence. [16]

Between 1945 and 1949 the foundations of East German political
culture were nonetheless laid. Not only was the Soviet occupational
administration (SMNAD) instrumental in helping its German allies
eventually gain a monopolistic foothold on all areas of decision-making,
but the destruction of non-Nazi middle-class parties during the Hitler
era created a gap within the structure of political legitimacy that only
the left found itself in the strategic position to fill. In the spring of
1946 the situation was further simplified by the "fusion" of the Eastern
zone's Communist and Social Democratic parties into the Socialist
Unity party, or SED (Sozialistische Einheitspartei Deutschland). [17]

This period signals the transformation of the SED from a
"catchall" to what Marxists/Leninists call a "party of the new type,"
that is, a highly centralized organization controlled by communists.
While the immediate aftermath of World War II dictated a policy of
accommodation for German communists, the consolidation of Soviet
authority in Eastern Europe in the late 1940s dictated a fundamental
shift in SED policy:

In the period of the struggle for power, several working-
class parties may exist side by side. The struggle of the
working class, however, is seriously hampered by this if
there is no unity of action among them. After the victory
of the working class, consolidation of the new power and
unanimity of will in the government of society requires,
as a rule, the establishment of a single Marxist-Leninist
party. That, for instance, was the path taken by Communist and Social Democratic Parties in Czechoslovakia,
Poland, the German Democratic Republic and other People's
Democracies, where united Worker's Parties were founded
on the basis of Marxist/Leninist ideology and organization
principles at the beginning of the transition period. [18]

Thus, by late 1949, this transformation in the party system was
translated into the government when the German Democratic Republic
was officially proclaimed.

In applying the teaching of Marx and Engels on class struggle and revolution to the GDR during this period, the link between ideology and political practice appears to be close. Private property was largely abolished between 1946 and 1949 in both the industrial and agricultural sectors, and within official East German historiography this opening historical epoch additionally brought to light the existence of "class struggle."[19] Although the proletariat, acting under the guidance and leadership of German communists, did not take "official" power until October 7, 1949, the foundations of what became East Germany's version of the "dictatorship of the proletariat" grew out of the experiences supplied by Marx and Engels's conception of expropriation and class warfare.

During this period the foundations of East Germany's evolving political culture were given institutionalized expression by the promulgation of far-reaching reforms in the areas of education and justice, undertakings that tended to appropriately highlight the new leadership's commitment to substantive societal transformation. As one regime source characterizes the period: "The task confronting the anti-fascist democratic forces not only existed in the clearing away of rubble, setting the economy into motion, dealing with war criminals and Nazi activists, but no less with the surmounting of imperialist norms and values and the creation of a humane way of life."[20]

Transition to the Construction of Socialism (1950-61)

From the early through the late 1950s, East Germany's political history was characterized by the existence of intra- and extraparty opposition to SED rule. The era, in this conflict-laden sense, was highly fluid:

> In general, this stage was characterized by the so-called class struggle within and by a continuous reorganization in almost all areas of party, state, economy, and society. Not only did the SED leadership systematically try to place its loyal cadres in all these areas; it also methodically destroyed the remnants of private property and of the older social structure in commerce, the small crafts and trades, agriculture, and industry. . . . on the whole . . . the political, economic, and in particular, the psychological achievements of the SED in these years were relatively limited.[21]

If the psychological "achievements" of the SED were limited, however, Marxist/Leninist theory provides an explanation for why this invariably appears to be the case for all systems undergoing revolutionary transformation:

> By taking care of the purity in their ranks, the Communist Parties create the conditions necessary for strengthening their unity. In the conditions of the dictatorship of the proletariat, Party unity plays a still greater role. Since the class struggle does not cease but assumes more complicated forms, the Party constantly experiences not only the pressure of the remnants of the capitalist classes, but also the waverings of the unstable elements among the working people.[22]

From the middle through the late 1950s the GDR experienced a period of relative stabilization. In contrast with the first period, the population began to extend a degree of legitimacy to the SED. Perhaps the people were not prepared to grant the new regime the kind of unqualified effective support all governments crave—democratic pluralist or communist—but they were at least prepared to wait upon events before making final judgment. Though economic growth, and the standard of living more generally, continued to lag behind that of West Germany, a period of normalization had apparently arrived.

From late 1959 through August 1961 the picture changed dramatically. After publicly disclaiming any intention to apply force in the collectivization of private agricultural holdings, the SED suddenly reversed itself by launching a campaign to complete collectivization on December 13, 1959. By the early 1960s large segments of the prewar middle classes in private industry were once again pushed into a defensive posture in their dealings with the regime, a consideration most dramatically reflected in the upsurge of refugees who left the GDR for the Federal Republic via West Berlin.[23] Responding to the sharp increase in population outflow, the SED cordoned off West Berlin on August 13, 1961, and the construction of the Berlin Wall was begun. With the last remaining escape route to the West, via West Berlin, closed off, the SED signaled a definitive end to contested sociopolitical legitimacy in the GDR. Subsequent economic and administrative reforms then made it possible for the regime to forge a bond of limited unity with the mass population. By the early 1960s the role of the socialist state within the GDR had begun to change from an oppressive apparatus to an agent of social integration.

Developing Socialism (1962-75)

The erection of a viable political culture not only demands an atmosphere of consensus on the major issues and challenges facing society, it no less demands a government that can ensure social and economic stability. While the early years of SED rule had been characterized by the absence of these factors, the middle 1960s and beyond represent a dramatic, and seemingly permanent, change in the direction of social and political change as mirrored in the stabilization of party authority, both internally and within the society more generally. (One significant indicator of this reality was mirrored in the fact that the SED had not purged its ranks since 1957.)

With the erection of the Berlin Wall, the SED found itself in a new position, one that argued for a relaxation of oppressive rule. This hardly meant, or means, an end to the "dictatorship of the proletariat," though it has meant a gradual emergence of sociopolitical consensus between regime and society.

A number of additional factors become increasingly important over this time period. One, the memories of the immediate postwar era began to grow increasingly dim as new generations of East Germans arrived on the adult scene. By 1965—a mere two years after the New Economic System had been launched—the GDR could boast the highest standard of living in the socialist camp and the ninth highest level of industrial production in the world.[24] Two, the GDR's integration into the Soviet-led alliance system, and particularly its cultivation of "special relations" with the Soviet Union, had become institutionalized and incorporated into the September 27, 1974 revisions of the East German Constitution as follows: "The German Democratic Republic is allied for ever and irrevocably with the Union of Soviet Socialist Republics. The close and fraternal alliance with the Soviet Union guarantees the people of the GDR further strides forward on the path to socialism and peace." Shifting toward relations with other socialist countries in Eastern Europe, and the world more generally, the document goes on to state that "the GDR is an inseparable component of the socialist community of states. True to the principles of socialist internationalism it contributes to the strengthening of the community, and fosters and develops friendship, all-round cooperation, and mutual aid with all states of the socialist community."[25] Finally, and in response to Soviet sponsorship on the world diplomatic scene, especially after the change of leadership from Ulbricht to Honecker in the spring of 1971, the GDR was able to break out of diplomatic isolation. This pleasant new state of affairs recently terminated with the signing of protocols between themselves and the United States on September 4, 1974.[26]

SYSTEMATIC DOCTRINE AND VALUES

In the absence of reliable public opinion polls it is impossible to determine to what extent the mass population supports the Marxist/ Leninist principles that are basic to the GDR's evolving political culture discussed above. However, even if we lack the available means of probing popular attitudes, indirect evidence does suggest that many elements of communist ideology have indeed taken root in the GDR, especially within the consciousness of the younger genera- tion, which has only had the opportunity to grow up within the geo- graphic, psychological, and political boundaries of East Germany.[27]

In addition to the general traditional principles and values of Marxism/Leninism discussed earlier, the GDR has highlighted some, and developed others, to meet its specific political cultural needs. National consciousness, collectivism and the socialist personality, and "love for the GDR" seem especially significant.

National Consciousness

Throughout its history the SED has emphasized the necessity of implanting a "GDR consciousness" (DDR Bewusstsein) within the mass population. But although the GDR did not officially abandon reunification until the VIII Party Congress of the SED in the spring of 1971, few would argue that a "national" consciousness was a real possibility until the middle 1960s. By this time, however, a number of West German observers were forced to conclude that the goal of reunification—tenaciously held by Bonn at this time—had become academic and increasingly unrealistic. Thus the West German political-sociologist Ralf Dahrendorf characterized the situation with the remark that "while the two Germanies may still debate the aca- demic, or rather diplomatic, question of whether they are two states, they have already become two societies."[28] The resulting decade has, if anything, deepened the cleavages separating the GDR and the FRG, though one can still argue with some conviction that neither German state has yet to develop an operative "national" identity. In order to gain some additional insight into the SED's definition and application of the national consciousness phenomenon, some preliminary observa- tions are in order.

At the outset it is important to realize that the SED's under- standing of national consciousness rests on a Marxist/Leninist con- ception of nationhood more generally. From this vantage point it is of some interest to realize that the SED's position is not based so much

on a legalistic definition of nationhood, despite frequent public asser-
tions by the party during the prerecognition era on legalistic formulas
to undergird its argument that it was legitimate, but on socioeconomic
and historical determinants. Thus Hermann Axen has asserted that

> . . . nations are dominantly a result of fundamental
> economic and social processes of development and
> historical class struggles. In this sense nations do
> not have an "actual content," as ideologists of the Great
> Bourgeoise and Social Democracy contest. They are
> necessary manifestations of social development whose
> content is determined by socioeconomic development
> and social classes.[29]

Without explicitly making note of the fact, he then goes on to link the
existence of these above attributes with the development of national
consciousness in the GDR. Thus,

> the socialist revolution in the GDR . . . led to a funda-
> mental change in the thought, feeling and behavior of the
> working people, a phenomenon which we refer to as a revo-
> lution in the area of ideology and culture. The creation of
> a socialist nation in the GDR has been accompanied by the
> creation of a socialist consciousness—viewed as a dominant
> ideology, and is a process which has developed itself con-
> tinuously, and over a long period of time, in struggle against
> the influence of bourgeoise ideology. As our Party has con-
> tinuously explained, socialist patriotism and proletarian
> internationalism constitute the crucial content of socialist
> consciousness.[30]

With these general considerations in mind, some mention should be
made of how Walter Ulbricht, the departed chief of the SED, and his
successor, Erich Honecker, conceived of national consciousness.

When Walter Ulbricht died in August 1973 an era of German
communism ended. Perhaps death is the only occasion when political
ironies gain their vigor, but one of the more amusing considerations—
or ironies—surrounding Ulbricht's passing was the apparently spontaneous realization that perhaps the departed head of the SED was as
much of a German nationalist as a Moscow-trained communist. Within
the 16-month period that was left to him after separation from the top
party slot, Ulbricht's image dramatically transformed itself from
that of a Moscow satrap, ever willing to sacrifice the GDR's interest
when the Kremlin so demanded,[31] into something resembling a
"Founding Father." An examination of the Ulbricht concept of national
development sheds some interesting light on this apparent paradox as
it has been mirrored in East German political culture.

National development in the Ulbricht era (1949 to early 1971) is
characterized by a double tendency. First, despite his willingness to
subordinate the GDR's domestic interests to the dictates of Soviet
foreign policy, Ulbricht remained a supporter of German nationalism.
As head of the "National Committee for a Free Germany," an organization of ex-Wehrmacht officers and Moscow-exiled German communists,
Ulbricht, among others, supported the idea of a unified socialist
Germany once the war was concluded. When the SED seized power in
East Germany after the war, he subsequently began to introduce a
series of confederation proposals to the West German government,
albeit without success. When the lines of national division began to
permanently harden in the early 1960s, he still felt duty-bound to
demonstrate the "superiority of the innate Germanness" of GDR
socialism over the "bourgeoisie," and in his and the SED view,
un-German, West German capitalism.

Second, in fashioning an image of East German national development and national consciousness, Ulbricht devised a three-dimen-
sional cultural formula. From the eighteenth century he synthesized
the "Spirit of Potsdam," with its emphasis on military-bureaucratic
authority, and with the "Spirit of Weimar" and its embrace of German
classicism in the written and performing arts. Out of the nineteenth
century, Ulbricht sought to develop a pattern of ideological consistency
capable of linking SED authority with the recent all-German past.
While Marx and Engels were used to provide the foundation stones
upon which party authority was to be presented to the people, Karl
Liebknecht, Rosa Luxembourg, and Ernst Thälmann were presented
as contemporary, as well as German, expressions of SED legitimacy.
Finally, the all-German past was integrated into the world of technological change by the former head of the SED. Indeed, by the late
1960s the ideal East German citizen was no longer epitomized by the
worker clothed in coveralls, but by the young scientist who had internalized the political doctrine of the SED, on the one hand, and the
demands of the technological-scientific revolution, on the other hand. [32]

If Ulbricht's demise can be directly traced to his intransigence
toward the Soviet Union, and especially toward Moscow's detente
policies with the Federal Republic, one should be especially careful
not to overemphasize the relevance of personnel changes within the
leadership cadre of the SED. By the late 1960s the GDR was moving
in a direction that made even Ulbricht's lip-service support of reunification increasingly untenable. Indeed, despite his public commitment to the symbolic value of reunification, at least until 1970,
Ulbricht can be seen as the individual chiefly responsible for initiating
those changes within East German society that made the reunification
discussion extremely difficult to translate into practical reality. From
this vantage point, then, Erich Honecker's assumption of supreme

political power in the spring of 1971 represented a smooth changing
of the guard—probably overdue by several years in any case—as well
as a final Soviet response to Ulbricht's intransigence. It should always
be remembered in this regard that at the time of leadership change,
Walter Ulbricht was 76, his successor, 59. As one result, Honecker's
superficially new conception of "separate national development,"
announced officially at the VIII Party Congress of the SED a few weeks
after Ulbricht's departure, can be seen as an official East German
response to what more than 25 years of sociopolitical transformation
in both German societies had made increasingly obvious. His remarks
dealing with political and social development within the GDR are
nonetheless interesting for the light they shed on the phenomenon of
national consciousness. Having wiped the all-German past clean, at
least to his, and assumedly the SED's, satisfaction, he noted the
following changes at work within the domestic environment that have
taken place within East Germany since the end of World War II:

> With the socialization of the crucial means of production,
> with the victory of "socialist-production-relationships,"
> a new social and economic foundation for society has been
> created. In place of capitalist anarchy and rivalry, has
> stepped the socialist-planned economy. Socialist society
> in the German Democratic Republic possesses a funda-
> mentally new class structure. Under the leadership of
> the working class, there exist amiably aligned classes and
> strata within the population who possess socialist char-
> acter traits. In the course of socialist development in
> our Republic, socialist ideology and a new socialist
> national culture—which has integrated all the humanistic
> traditions of the German past within it—have become
> dominant. [33]

If the creation of a "new" socialist national culture represents
one of the more important, as well as lasting, achievements of the
SED, Honecker has also emphasized the degree to which the GDR
shares in the all-German past, albeit in a highly selective manner.
In this the present head of the SED is imitating the eclectic predilec-
tions of his former mentor. Thus at the SED's 9th Plenum, he was
moved to remark:

> The German Democratic Republic is the political
> embodiment of the best traditions in German history—
> the peasant uprisings of the middle ages, the struggles
> for a revolutionary democracy in 1848, the founding by
> Marx and Engels, Bebel and Liebknecht of the German

workers' movement, the heroism of the anti-fascist
resistance struggle. In the German Democratic
Republic a socialist nation has developed itself under
the leadership of the working class. In the socialist
national culture of our Republic there is a new blossoming, a blossoming which in the past would have been
engaged in the creation of cultural riches. From those
aspects of history, culture, and speech which are worth
retaining, from those elements which reflect upon the
humanistic and revolutionary traditions of our society,
no price for their retention is too high. [34]

Thus the many years of GDR efforts to develop political culture
concepts reflecting a national consciousness have reached a stable
plateau under Honecker. Given the dramatic increase in intra-German
contact since he has come to power, it will be interesting to study
whether the "national" image will be forced to change in response to
the impact of outside influence and opinion.

Collectivism and the Socialist Personality

Collectivism refers to life-style. In a perceptive essay on
East German society written a decade ago, Ralf Dahrendorf has
argued that "public virtues" have triumphed in the GDR. He notes
in this regard that "a large part of the life of people takes place in
public."[35] Honoring Engels' thesis that "man is the ensemble of his
social relationships," the GDR has created a social ethic that emphasizes both the desirability and necessity for individuals to jointly act
and plan together. Accordingly, one notes the constant exhortation
for citizens to internalize such commands as "be concerned for the
well-being of others," "carry social responsibility on your own
shoulders!," and, of course, the most famous of them all, "Work
With! Plan With! Rule With!"
    The SED's belief in a rigorously developed standard of public
ethics may have something to do with the earlier tradition of authoritarian training that gained its fame in the eighteenth century empire
of Prussia and its celebration of royal authority. But the most important intellectual influence on the GDR's conception of public virtues
undoubtedly stems from the impact of Soviet educational theory and
practice that was transported to East Germany at the end of World
War II. In this particular regard, the work of the Soviet educational
theorist, A.S. Makarenko, is of crucial significance for the contributions he made to the traditions of collective education, first in the
USSR, subsequently in postwar socialist systems, especially the GDR.

For Makarenko the primary challenge facing Soviet society in
the middle to late 1920s had to do with the relative absence of viable
authority structures in the new revolutionary state. While Makarenko's
experiments with errant young children during this period can hardly
be credited with making the USSR a stable political system in the
absence of numerous other historical, economic, and military factors,
there is hardly any question that his contributions have greatly en-
hanced the impact and effectiveness of the political socialization
process in the USSR. Central to his theoretical and practical writing
is the "collective," that is, "a free group of working people, possessing one goal, bound together by a unified pattern of behavior; it
is an organized group with directive organs, discipline, and a sense
of responsibility. The collective is a social organism in a healthy
human society."[36]

Within the GDR the concept of collective training and education
(Bildung und Erziehung) has been applied to every conceivable form
of social experience that involves the attention and activities of individuals. Flowing from these experiences is the hope, as well as
assumption, that increased social interchange will make individuals
learn to think of their own well-being in group-related terms to the
point where boundaries separating individual from collective consciousness become increasingly hard to draw, as well as irrelevant.
"The step from 'I' to 'we'" begins with the entrance of East German
children into nursery school life at the age of one or two, and continues up through the unified ten-class school system. By the time
individuals enter adult occupational and political roles, the impact of
collective working, and most particularly decision-making, experiences must undoubtedly be great. The ultimate result should be the
development of what East German educational theorists call the
socialist personality.

If a collectivist society is to be developed in the GDR, the
"socialist personality" is the psychological vehicle employed to
achieve it. As East German educational theorists see it,

> the Socialist cultural ideal is the free person, the
> person as a conscious sovereign over nature, one's
> social life, and over oneself. . . . When the person
> is a conscious creator of one's whole life, when one
> exercises many-sided forms of control (physical and
> intellectual) over nature, over social life and the self,
> one must master all means and forms through which
> the world can be mastered and changed. . . . [37]

In view of the mammoth social and political tasks the SED has set
itself for the transformation of East German society, perhaps the

most important and enduring characteristic associated with the development of a socialist personality is a contemporary variant of stoicism. Hence, "a human being proves himself as a socialist personality when he refuses to resign himself in the face of a difficult situation, when he resolutely and persistently struggles to master a problem by relying upon his power and that of the collective. One's personality is evaluated by one's ability to meet the demands of the day, rather than running from them."[38]

"Love for the GDR"

The SED has attempted to win not only the passive consent of East German citizens; it has in no less measure attempted to win their hearts and emotions. In the early developmental period (1945-49), the SED adopted a strategy of identifying itself with postwar reconstruction. Not only was this appeal meant to galvanize the individual behind the emerging regime for the purposes of material reconstruction, but the use of such an expression as "the step from I to we" was meant to communicate an appeal for psychological reconstruction as well. From the early 1960s to the present, the SED has given attention primarily to the following means of generating loyalty and affection within the population toward the GDR. First, it has tried to make citizenship a contractual relationship between individual and regime. This phenomenon is strikingly apparent within the occupational world where individual and group premiums are distributed when production norms are fulfilled and overfulfilled. The SED has apparently decided that psychological reinforcement based on the allocation of material rewards, or the distribution of social status (in the form of medals, public citations, etc.), can be translated into political legitimacy. Second, the GDR has long been noted for its cultivation of an ingroup psychology, one that effectively distinguishes East Germans from West Germans. Until recently this conception was given tacit reinforcement by the Federal Republic in its penchant not to recognize, or even talk with, the GDR. As intra-German contacts have broadened over the past several years, and especially since the Basic Treaty between the two governments made it possible for large numbers of West Germans and Berliners to travel East, the SED has found it more difficult to cultivate this exclusive image.

Since "Love for the GDR" underlines the development of subjective orientations toward East German social and political institutions, it is not possible to say how widespread and deep this phenomenon is within the consciousness of the mass population. Nonetheless, an impressive record of economic performance (especially since the early to middle 1960s) and continuing success in international athletic competition (the GDR came in third behind the Soviet Union and the United States in the 1972 Olympics) suggests the existence of positive orientations, and feelings of identification, with those elements of East German society capable of supplying individuals and groups with tangible material and symbolic rewards. Whether performance-based legitimacy, as some Western observers refer to this phenomenon, is helping to create a solid foundation of effective support for the regime and its purposes is extremely difficult to determine at this time.

Productivity and Performance

In the GDR, as in other socialist countries, the development of socialism involves not only the role of the state and party in the planning and production process, but the understanding and acceptance of the population. In short, the regime has made socialism on the "economic" level synonymous with the pursuit of "rationality" and "scientism." Marx, with his commitment to the reintegration of the worker into the production process, and Lenin, with his belief in making economic modernization an integral part of communist political development, are combined within the SED's program to improve conditions within all areas of the economy, thereby increasing production and worker satisfaction.

This emphasis on productivity and performance has placed a heavy burden on the GDR to constantly improve the image it has created within Eastern Europe of being an economic dynamo. The relevance of these values for the development of a viable political culture necessarily makes it incumbent on the regime to constantly exhort individuals to actively and enthusiastically participate in the production process so that personal and social well-being will be improved. In this way, the GDR will be strengthened on the material (production) and psychological (the socialist personality will be perfected) levels.

The resulting relationship between rationality, planning, and political legitimacy has already been examined by Thomas Baylis.[39] As he sees it, the SED has invented a "legitimacy formula" which "involves a dialectic of economic planning and its symbolism of rationality, hierarchy, and control, and popular participation with its suggestions of individuality, equality, and spontaneity."[40] From this angle, the values of productivity and performance are used as a means of catalyzing human energy behind the plans of the regime—in so doing they create the foundation of political legitimacy through the medium of the work place. On practical, if not ideological, grounds the appeal makes sense.

In summarizing the evolution of East German political culture, Jean Smith's exposition on "Red Prussianism" catches at least part of the spirit of contemporary development in the GDR when he suggests that the SED relies "on the traditional form of the administrative state; the Reichstaat of Bismarck and the Emperor. And in this way, socialism in East Germany merges into the traditional pattern of Prussia. The citizen obeys, but he does so freely. And growing economic prosperity—plus a genuine belief in many of the new norms—makes the graft seem permanent."[41]

SOCIALIZATION

The political socialization process within the GDR attempts to transmit socialist political culture to the mass population. From this vantage point, and in partial contrast with earlier observations, this side of the problem shifts attention to subjective aspects of political culture in East Germany. Hence, the emphasis is now placed on questions dealing with how individuals and groups respond to political and social stimuli, how they emotionally feel about these elements, and how they are ultimately compelled to act upon the images of reality they receive. Thus, from the SED's standpoint, the final test of political legitimacy rests on the ability of the political socialization process to instill a sense of voluntary support for regime goals within all strata of the population. Given the newness of political institutions and social values, this means that the SED has had to make a special attempt to implant the foundations of socialist legitimacy within the consciousness of youth. So an ever-increasing effort has been made by the regime over the past two decades to "win" the young generation for socialism through a variety of incentives extended by the educational and occupational structures. Appropriately, the main thrust of discussion devotes attention to the transmission of political culture via the political socialization process to East German youth. (How it is further reinforced more generally, through leadership training and political communications, is discussed in Chapters 3 and 8, respectively.)

Primary School

After some preliminary definitional matters are taken care of, attention is devoted to the unfolding of political socialization processes within the East German primary school. Discussion begins with an

elaboration of important East German educational principles employed
within the classroom, being terminated with an overview of leading
conceptual aspects of the process.

David Easton and Jack Dennis define political socialization as
"those developmental processes through which persons acquire
political orientations and patterns of behavior."[42] In terms of educational institutions and their role within the political socialization
process, another group of writers note that

> in modern societies a major portion of political learning
> takes place in the classroom. It is through this agency
> that the most comprehensive and deliberate efforts are
> made by modern and modernizing polities to shape the
> political outlooks of new citizens. Within the classroom
> the formal curriculum of instruction, various ritual
> activities, and the activities of the teacher all help to
> shape the political development of youngsters.[43]

Within the environment of the classroom, perhaps the most important
influence within the political socialization process emanates from the
intellectual experiences children, and pupils more generally, have
with literary presentations dealing with the nation's past, present,
and future evolution. Thus, "the use of literature reflects favorably
on the nation's past and forecasts great things for its future. Such
portrayals are presented for citizenship training. Generally, political
leaders and educators explicitly view the curriculum as the appropriate agency for transmitting knowledge and values conducive to good
citizenship."[44]

The significance of viewing political socialization processes
from the vantage point of educational institutions is that formalized
learning situations provide a necessary element of structure and
direction that would be notably—and in the GDR fatally—absent if only
informal processes of opinion transmission were relied upon for the
communication of a society's political culture. These various factors
are strikingly mirrored in the conduct of socialization processes
within the strategically important East German primary school, the
first, and most crucial, step in the path leading toward socialist
citizenship in the GDR. An examination of leading educational principles within the primary school follows.

In terms of the East German primary (elementary is used
interchangeably) school, children enter the Unterstufe, or lower
level, at age 6, grade one, and leave at age 9, upon successful completion of the third grade. Curricular offerings—despite allowance
for regional differences (city versus country distinctions are especially

significant*)—possess two outstanding characteristics: (1) a "balance"
between cultural (humanistic instruction, especially in the German
language), social scientific (civics or <u>Heimatkunde</u>), and technical
education is consistently striven for. (2) the "unity" between political,
moral (self-comportment in public and private settings), and ideological (civics) education is adhered to strictly. Regarding both sets
of general curricular requirements, a tightly organized alliance of
classroom instructors, youth group leaders, parent-teacher councils,
and, to a lesser degree, the family, is expected to perform the task
of translating formal principles into concrete educational practice,
maximally geared to the development of young socialist citizens by
the time the child is expected to move from the primary to the middle
school, grade four, level.

The following three educational principles perform crucial roles
in the socialization process within the elementary school of East
Germany.

Association with One's Neighborhood and the "Socialist Fatherland"

The first three school years are crucial ones in the life of the
East German child, for it is during this period that individual orientations toward SED conceptions of authority are formed. This means
a number of things.

In the first place, children are expected to acquaint themselves
with the visible objects of community life. Local economic units
(such as factories or agricultural collectives), the mayor, policemen,
and historical monuments are the main, and most visible, elements
of community life that provide rudimentary conceptions of regime
authority to the child. These objects are meaningless unto themselves,
however. The crucial issue revolves around how they are presented
to the child. GDR educational theory is clear on this point in its
admonition that each object within the local community is to be integrated into the ideological framework of Marxism/Leninism. This
task involves teachers in the ambitious task of weaving present-day
events into a historical fabric underlining the continuity and legitimacy
of SED since the end of World War II, and communist authority within
the broader expanse of German history as previously discussed.
Curricular materials are especially helpful to the teacher since they
provide children with reading materials devoted to human-interest
accounts of the local community. In many of these accounts a strong
emphasis is devoted to how the most mundane attributes of local

---

*Despite intensive efforts by the regime to overcome qualitative
differences separating urban from rural schools in the GDR, important
distinctions continue to persist.

existence have been made better for the common people by the SED.
One of the more effective means of communicating this fundamental
insight is through depictions of conversations taking place between
young school children and older members of the community who
possess vivid memories of how things were before socialism came
to the GDR.

Secondly, and in a manner reminiscent of studies done on
political socialization in the United States, East German educational
theory presents political leaders with an eye for soliciting diffuse
responses from children. Public authorities are invariably described
in the humanest of terms as the following depiction of Walter Ulbricht's
birthday demonstrates:

> Walter Ulbricht occupies the pinnacle of authority in the
> German Democratic Republic. He is especially dedicated
> to the working people, especially to its children and
> youngsters. Even as a pupil, he wanted to learn in order
> to improve the lives of working people. As a member of
> the Party of the working class, as a trade union member
> as well, he fought against the factory and landowners.
> Today he works tirelessly as President of the State
> Council for the improvement of living conditions for
> the working people, for socialist development in the
> GDR, for the maintenance of peace. [45]

Along with the presentation of authority figures come methodological
guides that the teacher is expected to employ in the classroom: "At
the outset, it is important to make Walter Ulbricht's personality
relevant to children. Class reports, letters to him, pictures of the
man, assist in this task. Additionally, episodes from his childhood
up through the teenage years should be given in class. The overall
impression that children receive should be heavily affective."[46]
Though the influence of the former SED chief has been on the wane
since his departure from the top party post in the spring of 1971,
the methodological and conceptual emphases attached to the presentation of authority figures remain consistent over time.

Love toward Learning, Work, and the Working Class

The cultivation of a particular life-style is not unique to the
East German primary school. All educational systems attempt to
imprint a particular social identity on the consciousness of children.
In socialist political systems, however, the ambitiousness of such
efforts highlights the degree to which such regimes are committed
to the transmission of a "new" political culture in line with the

ideological goal of creating a socialist personality structure as previously discussed.

An emphasis on learning, work, and the working class is reflected in the nature of group learning processes within and outside
of the classroom. In the GDR the elementary school involves the
pupil in numerous such experiences. Normally organized under the
auspices of the Young Pioneers, the initial secondary organization
children are expected to join upon entrance into the first grade,
numerous visits to local industries, historical monuments, and talks
with leading personalities are organized. Appropriately enough,
children are expected to develop a social consciousness that sensitizes
them to the centrality of the work world and the role of the working
class within it.

As the child begins to learn about the world of work experience,
the expectation is communicated to him that young socialist citizens
should emulate the working class: Discipline, willingness to assist
others in the conduct of group-dependent tasks, and an admiration
for applied technology are some of the more important traits that
should flow out of frequent contact with the work world. As the child's
range of contacts with the industrial and/or agricultural environment
increases over time in terms of curricular—polytechnical instruction
being of crucial importance here—and extracurricular experience,
the depth of individual and group identification with the world of work
and the working class should increase accordingly. Since the assumption of supreme political leadership by Erich Honecker, the SED has
tended to intensify its public commitment to the symbols of proletarian
consciousness.

Friendship with the Soviet Union

The emulation of the Soviet Union in all phases of cultural and
political life has been a marked characteristic of SED rule since the
late 1940s. Within the political socialization process, the East
German primary school unceasingly emphasizes the impact of Soviet
political, ideological, and technical achievements. Exploits in space
exploration are given special attention. As one primer for elementary
teachers appropriately phrases it, "Friendship toward the Soviet
Union must become a need for children."[47]

Concepts and Socialization

Established social systems are not called upon to devote large
amounts of attention to the transmission of political concepts and
behavior patterns to their youth. In England, to choose one obvious

example, established ways of doing things, plus the weight and
legitimacy of tradition, make it unnecessary for the society to directly
engage itself in this aspect of the political socialization process. The
sheer momentum of past historical development allows English society
—for better or for worse—to carry out a political socialization process
accenting a low-key approach to the job of training individuals for
future entry into activist citizenship roles. In relatively new social
orders, however, the regime cannot expect its citizens to be aware
of the symbolic world it wants to create, a consideration bearing
special relevance for socialist orders and their emphasis on creating
alternative value structures, and accepted models of behavior, on the
wreckage of the old and discredited political culture.

In the East German primary school an impressive list of concepts must be learned and internalized by the child during the first
three school years. Flowing directly out of the classroom environment,
some of the more important ones are: the German Democratic Republic, its ideological, economic, and political foundations; the Soviet
Union, why it is the most important "friend of the GDR," and why it
possesses initial revolutionary legitimacy; visible political actors—
Erich Honecker (chief of the SED), Horst Sinderman (chairman of the
Minister Council), Willy Stoph (chairman of the State Council); frequently employed terms that are used to describe sociopolitical
change—revolution, strike, and war; socialist conceptions of East
German society—socialism, the working class, people's concerns
(nationalized industries), and agricultural collectives (collectivized
agriculture); antagonistic social concepts—capitalism, a capitalist,
and private property.[48] In order to impart a taste for how such
concepts are described within elementary school texts, two additional
ones come into view:

Love of Country (Heimatliebe)—Young pioneers love our
GDR. Our GDR is a beautiful country. The factories,
the fields, the forests and the seas belong to the people.
In our country, the working people rule. We must defend
our Republic. When one loves one's country, one must
also be ready to defend it.

Socialist Countries (Sozialistische Länder)—Countries
where the factories and fields belong to the people. The
working people rule here. These countries want peace.
We are bound in intimate friendship with them. The GDR
belongs to this community. Among them, the Soviet Union
is not only the largest and richest member, it is also the
strongest and most powerful country in the world. Socialist
countries support each other. They live in friendship
together. They have good trade relations.[49]

Seen within the tight organizational framework supplied by several important educational principles, the above concepts are fitted into live contexts for school children in the elementary school environment through the provision that teachers and youth group leaders, among others, are expected systematically to acquaint young pupils with the most salient political and social institutions, personalities, and symbols within their local community. In making the attempt to politicize children during the first three years of school, it should be kept in mind that only limited results can be gained. While research on political cognition and activism in the GDR has yet to be made available to the West in sufficient quantity and quality, there is every reason to assume that the impact of its political socialization process on the broad mass of young school children does not begin to make itself felt in system-supportive ways until the individual is called upon to perform a responsible political role at an advanced point within the educational structure. Nonetheless, the intensity of the political socialization process within the elementary school should not be underemphasized for the possible impact it has on the consciousness of young school children: At the very least, the first three years of engagement with political concepts has laid the foundations of passive support for the goals of the SED. This is an important achievement in itself.

POLITICAL CULTURE AND POLITICAL PERFORMANCE

Throughout its 25 years of official existence the SED has attempted to create a political culture congruent with its ideological goals and aspirations. Because the GDR was created in the midst of a broader pattern of confrontation between two power blocs, and because the SED's conception of domestic legitimacy was consistently challenged by the actions of a larger and stronger German counterpart to its west, East Germany's ability to develop a viable political culture has been compromised. Even in the wake of unparalleled diplomatic triumphs over the last several years, the SED still feels itself threatened by external forces emanating from the Federal Republic specifically, from the capitalist, or bourgeois, world more generally. For this reason alone, the SED's heightened emphasis on generating an independent East German political culture within the boundaries of the GDR has to come to terms with the realization that the status of socialist values and goals has yet to be secured. In this sense, the GDR has yet to create a viable political culture. As already discussed, however, the regime has made an ambitious effort to create one.

The regime has set ambitious goals for itself. In doing so, it has implicitly accepted the risk that its inability to achieve them will result in a withdrawal of confidence from a population it is anxiously committed to winning for the goals of socialist development within the present historical epoch. The following discussion attempts to highlight some of the present and future problems facing the regime in its attempt to win the broad population for the goals and purposes of the SED.

Sense of Involvement

Standard accounts of one-party systems tend to assume that mass participation within the political system and social order merely reflects the impact of repressive mechanisms that are geared to elicit public displays of enthusiasm for the goals of the regime. In terms of the GDR, one should not lightly dismiss the strong possibility that the obligation to participate within many phases of social life— running the gamut from occupational activity to the undefined, yet omnipresent, realm of "voluntary" work on weekends and holidays— reflects a widespread feeling within the population that "going along" with the party is preferable to resistance. While it is not possible to determine the degree to which individuals and groups perceive themselves to be coerced into participatory roles, it is probably true that large numbers of East German citizens are "indifferent" to the obligation of publicly involving themselves in the affairs of society. As one observer notes in this regard, when questions are posed to youths regarding "their level of interest (in social affairs), as measured by the degree to which they participate, indifference is the normal response. Or in terms of adults: to be sure, one attends trade union assemblies (Gewerkschaftsversammlungen), but it is a normal habit to look forward to their speedy conclusion."[50]

Surrounding this sense of indifference to the "role" of self in East German society is a general feeling of personal malaise, not rebellion, or for that matter even dissatisfaction.

If there is an aura of indifference, and in many cases even smugness, within large sectors of East German society, there is also little question that few political systems have addressed more attention to the task of engaging their members in their daily operation than has the SED. Indeed, despite the fact that many East Germans do not feel themselves to be involved in the running of their society, the regime's effort to broaden the base for social and political participation is impressive. The condition of youth in general, and women in particular, is worthy of some mention in this regard.

Today every second East German citizen is less than 35 years old and, thus, has spent most of his life under the influence of its form of socialism. While it would stray from the mark to argue that every person born and raised within the boundaries of the GDR is completely at ease within the political and social confines of this new society, there is every reason to believe that the most durable centers of proregime sentiment reside within those sectors of the population who have spent their formative—if not all—years under the direction of the SED. At least this is the conception that has guided the behavior of the party in its dealings with the generation that was born after 1939. Appropriately, a whole range of participatory opportunities are provided young people in the GDR. This consideration begins with Article 22 of the East German Constitution, which provides that "every citizen . . . is enfranchised to vote if 18 years of age on the day of an election."[51] Within the same article, revisions approved by the People's Chamber on September 27, 1974 (Section 2) now allow citizens of 18 the right to stand for election to the GDR's highest legislative chamber.[52] In terms of participation within all levels of the East German political structure, one document supplies the following picture: "More than 41,000 young people between the ages of 18 and 30—20 percent of all representatives—are engaged in the activities of the most important organs of socialist state activity."[53] Additionally—as of mid-1973, 61 representatives within the People's Chamber fell within the age range stretching between 21 and 30; 607 representatives within the District (Bezirk) Assemblies are between 18 and 30 years old; on the district assembly level, 4,525 representatives fall within this age group; finally, within city assemblies, city-county assemblies, and communal representative organs, some 36,567 individuals are active below the age of 31.[54]

The situation of women in the GDR is an interesting one. Given the fact that East Germany's working population will not appreciably increase over the next several years, the SED's plans for economic modernization have unavoidably been compromised. Under these sober circumstances, the party and state apparatuses have made ambitious attempts to induct women into all areas of public life in an effort to at least ameliorate unfavorable population growth rates. As of late 1974 this meant that almost 80 percent of East Germany's adult women were working either full or part time. In terms of political considerations, the SED has tried to make entrance into the party attractive for women, though aggregate figures on their representation within the SED since the VIII Party Congress are not especially impressive: As of mid-June 1971, there was a total of 28.7 percent women out of a total membership of 1,845,280;[55] in the aftermath of the 1973-74 party elections, the percentage had grown by .7 percent out of a total membership of 1,902,809.[56]

Along with a provision for generous maternity leaves for working
mothers having children, as well as the extension of liberal credit
terms for families wishing to refurbish or purchase a dwelling, the
regime has also attempted to galvanize women behind programs aimed
at the improvement of educational attainments within the work force.
Under the bulky slogan, for an "Improvement in the Occupational-
Technical and Political-Ideological Qualification of the Women," the
regime has since 1971 energetically encouraged working-age females
to advance themselves up the educational ladder. A recent sociological
study attempted to measure and evaluate the attitudes of working
female respondents within East German factories and industrial combines. From of total sample of 3,375, opinion researchers interviewed
two broad occupational categories: 2,461 on-the-job trainees, 914
technical employees who had already completed training for their
present occupation. While the results of the study left researchers
in some doubt about the different motivational structures at work
within various occupational categories—no visible correlation was
found that could relate type of work with varying degrees of readiness
to undertake further educational training—the "strongest motive"
working in favor of a positive attitude toward upward educational
mobility had to do with the recognition that (1) additional education was
generally necessary, and (2) that an increase of income was strongly
dependent upon an improved educational profile.[57] In terms of regime
efforts to interest working women in improving their educational
positions, another, and somewhat troubling, conclusion was that
women expressing a disinterest in further educational advancement
saw a contradiction between their familial (toward husband and children
in many cases) and occupational responsibilities.[58] The study concludes that an improvement in women's attitudes toward furthering
their educational attainments, and thereby "qualifying" for more
prestigious and better paying jobs, rests on the society's ability to
link the furtherment of education with political issues, such as the
SED position that the advancement of women into ever-increasing
levels of public responsibility serves the interests of socialist development in the GDR.[59]

In another study addressing attention to the question of female
"qualification" for higher paying and more prestigious jobs within the
industrial sector, a sample (the kind of sample was not specified)
of 100 male and 100 female production workers yielded these interesting conclusions: From the original male sample, 78 respondents
possessed a complete occupational degree, while for females the
number was 52. While the study unfortunately does not provide
supportive data, it does preliminarily conclude that for those male
and female respondents who "grew up under the conditions of Socialist
construction" no discernible differences between educational attainment

could be detected. Indeed, women tended to predominate over men
in their educational attainments on both the university and advanced
technical school levels.[60] Not surprisingly, differences between the
two samples become increasingly evident as the age of respective
male and female respondents increases. Thus, in the age group
falling between 30 and 50 years of age, 20 percent of men and 47
percent of women have failed to complete their occupational training;
within the over 50 age group, 28.4 percent of the men and 67 percent
of the women have not received a full complement of occupational
education. Concluding on an optimistic note, the study notes that
women are becoming increasingly involved with further qualifying
themselves, albeit in undefined ways, in the work place: By 1973 the
GDR's official trade union organization, the FDGB (Free German
Trade Union Association) announced that 1,500,000 women had participated in the movement for "Socialist work, learning, and living,"
or 45.1 percent of the entire movement. By August 1973 every fourth
member of factory-supported "Work and Research Groups" was
female. In contrast with 1963, when 5.8 percent of female industrial
workers participated in "innovator movements," party-sponsored
campaigns to voluntarily enlist individuals and groups behind programs
aimed at increasing industrial productivity and the conservation of
raw materials, the percentage had increased to 16.5 percent by
1972.[61] As with the first study cited, the political ramifications behind
party-sponsored "qualification" programs lie with the hope and
assumption "that with an increase of educational qualifications (for
women) an understanding of broad social relationship will emerge,
and the subsequent readiness by individuals to exercise socialist
Democracy beyond the realm of the factory and into the local community, within schools and local representative bodies."[62]

Individual Satisfaction

        Large numbers of average East German citizens may feel
uninvolved in the public affairs of their society. In part this may be
attributable to the possibility that many individuals believe that the
SED's monopolization of public affairs effectively removes any possibility for dynamic and creative change. Certainly within those
elements of the population who have grown up under conditions favoring
pluralist politics, as was the situation during the Weimar era (1919-
33), this sense of resignation may be justified. Additionally, there
are certainly elements of the population 35 years old and younger who
believe that (1) the SED has preempted effective political participation
within many areas of social and political activity, and (2) that the very

nature of East German political culture, with its emphasis on mass
public participation, is simply unattractive. While a decade is a long
time within the life of established political orders, this period of time
covers vast amounts of social and political change within the GDR.
Nonetheless, two responses taken from an interview study undertaken
during the early 1960s by Hans Apel, a naturalized German-American,
are at least instructive. In both cases, the author was talking with
university students:

> Material matters do not interest me: I am interested in
> literature and simply cannot understand why books from
> the West are not allowed. This restriction on personal
> freedom is simply intolerable. I would not travel to the
> West, even if it were allowed because my entire family
> lives here and I have, alternatively, no one in the West.
> If I had the opportunity to vote between the two systems,
> however, I would unconditionally support the abolition of
> Socialism. It is abundantly clear that the GDR is backwards
> in the economic sphere because we lack competition. For
> us there is only one solution—Reunification on the basis
> of free elections. [63]

The other student continues this line of thinking in a pessimistic vein:
"The hope for reunification no longer exists. The lack of freedom is
an integral part of this system. As long as this condition exists,
nothing else will change. . . . Among us pedagogues there are more
fellow travelers than in other disciplines. In medicine, for example,
there are very few. I believe that 80 percent of all students are
opposed to the SED regime, at least 60 percent are."[64] Perhaps the
root cause of the problem—to the degree it exists—lies within the
content and presentation of information dealing with aspects of citizenship training in the GDR. Another writer notes in this regard that
"Staatsbürgerkunde—civics—has been a source of problems; it has
not been very effective as an instrument of socialization. Part of the
responsibility must be attributed to the dullness of civics instruction
and its repetitiveness. One student told me that he had been through
it all so often by the time he had reached the university that it was
excruciating to have to continue."[65]

For the SED the question of individual satisfaction is appropriately tied to specific social contexts within which the party has
invested large amounts of time and effort to make its influence felt.
In this regard one of the most significant areas of research activity
within the GDR surrounds the work environment and the degree to
which individuals identify with it. This concern on the part of the
party and state apparatus is understandable for at least two elementary

reasons. One, the ideological foundations of Marxist/Leninist authority rest upon the belief that "material," that is, productive, factors
determine individual and group perceptions of politics. If people feel
alienated from the world of material production, this suggests for the
SED that problems of political authority and leadership are not being
handled effectively. This consideration has proven especially significant in the regime's conduct of relations with the working class, an
issue played upon with increased frequency since the resumption of
supreme political power by Erich Honecker in the spring of 1971.
Two, and in line with the party's commitment to the achievement of
publicly announced growth plans at the VIII Party Congress of the
SED, the further development of socialism rests upon the willingness
of the working population to devote all available efforts to the fulfillment of economic programs. Unhappiness within the work place works
against this commitment.

Information on the attitudes of workers within the industrial
environment is relatively plentiful, though the results are invariably
mixed. On the negative side, a study done by a former East German
citizen on the attitudes of assembly workers supplies a picture of
dissatisfaction with various conditions in their factory environment.
Without attempting to synthesize all of his findings, several of the
most germane ones coming out of his 1965-66 study are that out of
a total interview sample of 911, (1) 74.1 percent (675 individuals)
did not believe that the FDGB represented their interests within the
work place; (2) 29.9 percent of the sample (273) "absolutely did not"
believe that they possessed decision-making latitude in their work
section; (3) recruitment into the higher reaches of the factory apparatus
was dominantly oriented toward individual political, rather than
occupational, activity on the order of 59.6 percent (543). [66] Given
the length of time that has elapsed—a full nine years—since this study
was completed and the incontrovertible fact that the analysis rivets
attention on one category of industrial worker only, additional sources
of information are clearly necessary. A number of East German
studies dealing with various aspects of group satisfaction and dissatisfaction within the industrial environment supply a different image.

In late 1966 an East German sociologist interviewed a sample
of "young innovators" within an East German industrial combine.
Within this group of 200, two questions were of special significance:
(1) Are you convinced that the socialist social order will triumph on
a world scale? and (2) Are you proud to be a young citizen of our
socialist state? The first item netted the following response: I am
very certain, 59 percent, I believe it to be so, 34.2 percent, No
opinion at this time, 3.0 percent, I doubt it, 1.2 percent. For the
second item the results are: very proud, 40.1 percent, proud, 50.9
percent, somewhat proud, 3.7 percent, not very much, 2.5 percent. [67]

A year later a similar type of analysis was performed by another
East German sociologist who posed the following question to 123
"young innovators"; "Today there is much talk about the technical
revolution's ability to substantively change the nature of production
in the GDR through the introduction of automatic assembly lines,
cybernetic steering and regulatory systems, and electronic data
analysis. What are your opinions on this issue?" The two most
important responses were that (1) Within the next ten years production
in the GDR will have reached this level, 31.5 percent, and (2) I am
convinced that this development will occur, but it will take a longer
period of time before it reaches the GDR, 59.7 percent.[68] Linking
these positive findings to their own occupational roles, the respondents
were then asked about whether they felt their participation would contribute to the successful carrying-through of the scientific-technical
revolution in the GDR: 72.4 percent answered in the affirmative,
14.4 percent responded with an "I'm not sure," while 11.6 percent
answered in the negative.[69]

Given the degree of disparity separating the last two from the
initial study, it is not possible to argue strongly in a positive or
negative direction regarding the degree to which East German respondents within the industrial order are satisfied with their occupations.
Perhaps the best answer is that negative and positive responses to
various questions dealing with individual satisfaction in the industrial
world fluctuate according to the kind of group being studied—young
innovators are highly motivated, and specially trained cadres, for
example—and the nature of the questions posed. Studies dealing
specifically with the motives behind occupational choice within the industrial world should be able to provide some additional insight into the
broader question surrounding whether individuals are deriving a
sense of satisfaction within East German society.

One study done in the GDR during 1971 supplies some significant
insight into the general question of occupational satisfaction within
a sample of on-the-job trainees. While the authors do not provide
specific data (including sample size) to support their basic generalizations, the general conclusion of this study is illustrative:

> Regarding the question on satisfaction with occupational
> choice, only a very small number provided a negative
> answer; the largest part responded with answers running
> from "complete" to "partially" satisfied. The largest
> portion of those who expressed only a "partial" degree
> of satisfaction cannot be explained in terms of the
> acquired occupation itself but in terms of the level of
> work organization. This finding is confirmed by the fact
> that three-fourths of the trainees want to achieve higher

qualifications within their own occupation. . . . The
largest portion of respondents feel themselves to be
insufficiently challenged, and a majority recognizes
the value of innovator-work for the good of society, the
factory, and their own personality development: They
would gladly participate in this activity except for the fact
that the innovator-system is insufficiently developed in
their factory.[70]

Carrying along this tradition of research a bit further, a later
study attempted to isolate and evaluate the crucial factors lying behind
career choices for 418 individuals in the industrial world. According
to the authors, four special factors played key roles in this descending
order: (1) an orientation toward the content of the occupation (whether
the work is interesting, creative); whether intellectual abilities could
be employed on the job—the relevance of the occupation for the future;
(2) whether the individual could feel a sense of responsibility toward
society within this occupation (endeavoring to make the job socially
useful; the need of our state for good technical workers); (3) the
personality-forming nature of the occupation as well as the degree
to which the occupation encouraged cooperative traits within people
(the possibility for further education; whether the job could provide
a foundation upon which marriage and a family could be pursued;
whether the job involved work within a collective); (4) the satisfaction
of material needs (above all this means favorable earning possibilities).[71] Given the amount of emphasis the regime gives to the
element of career choice, especially for the younger strata of East
Germany's employable population, it is not surprising that this study
concludes with the assertion that the most important motivation behind
occupational choice "is decisively influenced by the socioeconomic
structure of society."[72]

Do partial insights into the nature of career choice, or the
broader question of job satisfaction, provide answers to the questions
of whether the SED has given the population a sense of individual
satisfaction with socialist political institutions? No one answer can
suffice, but the general impression does suggest that the growing
material well-being of the GDR, combined with the fact that every
year brings larger numbers of young people into positions of responsibility, has significantly narrowed the "legitimacy" gap for the SED
in its relations with the mass population, a conclusion that gains
added meaning in the careful observations of one West German student
of national development within the GDR and the FRG that in both
societies, "the younger generations appear to be tied much stronger
into their system than the older generations. . . . The movement
towards nation-statehood seems inevitable; the German Question
appears to have been answered."[73]

In searching for answers to the questions of whether individuals and groups feel themselves a part of East German society, one should not ignore those elements of life in the GDR that have unavoidably pushed the SED in ways that have forced the party to extend a certain degree of trust in the natural instincts and emotions of the broad population. Seen from this vantage point, the most impressive aspect of change in the GDR lies in the realm of international affairs. Thus, East Germany has become a transnational society, perhaps Europe's first. In this an irony of sorts must undoubtedly perplex the SED, for while the party has officially embarked upon a campaign of separate national development, its contacts with the Western world, and particularly the Federal Republic, have dramatically broadened over the last several years. Thus, while East Berlin was called upon to receive 25,646 guests from foreign countries on the occasion of the Tenth Youth Festival (July 28-August 5, 1973), this event also played host to some 1,556 accredited journalists from the press, radio, motion picture, and television organs.[74] Though the party made impressive efforts to provide rigorous ideological training for all of the 500,000 members of the Free German Youth (FDJ) who were present during the festival so that their conversations with foreign visitors, especially those from West Berlin and the FRG, would not result in unpleasant and confusing experiences for the GDR's youth, there were numerous indications that conversations were invariably characterized by free and open exchanges of opinion for the most part. The FDJ "easily held up their side." Regarding its successful experience with the Tenth Youth Festival, and subsequent contacts since then, the most encouraging result for the SED lies in the fact that increased interchange with the outside world, particularly the FRG and West Berlin—between January 1, 1973, and May 1, 1974, 4,414,506 visitors came from the FRG, while visitors to the GDR from West Berlin numbered 4,056,805 over this same period[75]— did not engender a sense of doubt within the East German population about the legitimacy of their social order, but instead tended to demonstrate the degree to which the party's authority had become accepted by large segments of East Germany's strategically important younger generation.

To suggest that East Germany's social and political system has become increasingly legitimate within the mass population does not, in itself, mean that all segments of society are wholeheartedly in support of SED rule. Invariably, the level of support depends upon such general factors as age, education, occupational status, and more generally the quality of treatment various groups and individuals have received at the hands of the regime. In this last regard there is little reason to question the general proposition that the working class has fared better than traditional elements of the middle class, though the

SED's ambitious wooing of the former since the VIII Party Congress strongly suggests that the regime had taken the support of the working class for granted.

Viability and Political Culture

Perhaps the biggest challenge facing the SED in its on-going attempt to gain effective support within the population lies in its apparent disinclination to trust the broad population's better instincts. Many aspects of this problem have been examined by GDR scholars in the West, but certainly one of the more interesting sides of the problem resides in the realm of popular culture. Here the changes that have been gradually introduced since the assumption of supreme authority by Erich Honecker are notable for the degree to which the party has begun to allow relatively open and free discussions of cultural matters that would have elicited firm reprimands a decade ago. Indeed, with the single exception that performing artists may not call the "achievements" and main ideological assumptions of Marxism/Leninism into question, there is no area of public or private life that is considered taboo for East German performing artists. Again, this hardly means an end to regime oversight of the arts, nor does it suggest a permanent change in the party's conception of cultural politics, but at least for the forseeable future the SED has decided that a relatively free airing of controversial issues—from wages to sexual mores—no longer represents an implicit threat to the regime's authority. Indeed, given the GDR's impressive entrance into the world of diplomatic respectability, combined with its undoubted preeminence in sports competition, and capped off by the fact that ever-increasing numbers of its citizens have grown up within the environment of socialist values and institutions, the party has evidently concluded that the time has come for a more candid relationship with the society over which it rules, and upon whose trust and support it ultimately depends.

Within the forseeable future, however, the SED will continue to search for support within the mass population. A variety of complicated reasons stand behind this reality. In the first case, the regime believes that West Germany continues to work for its inclusion into some kind of broader, and invariably Western-oriented, entity that would effectively exclude the party from dominantly influencing the conduct of politics within a "new" German nation. The SED is strongly committed to the proposition that the FRG will be frustrated in this goal and has made every attempt to make this intention known to Bonn. While the Federal Republic has made impressive strides toward a more accommodating posture toward the GDR since the late 1960s, there is abundant evidence to support the SED's fear in this regard, a consideration that is strikingly illustrated by the fact that even now the Federal Republic continues to define citizenship as extending automatically to all individuals currently living within the GDR. As long as the regime perceives itself threatened by West Germany, it will feel itself compelled to conduct a "loyalty campaign" within the mass population. Formal declarations that the GDR constitutes a socialist nation, therefore rejecting the FRG's contention that the two parts of Germany continue to maintain a "special relationship" with each other, cannot ignore the weight and influence of geographic circumstances that place the GDR within the direct line of influence from a more-powerful German neighbor to its west. Second, aside from the SED's perception of threat from the Federal Republic, the party will continue anxiously to look over its shoulder at the population over which it rules, given the traditions of distrust and secretiveness within which the SED has evolved. The revolutionary conception of "marginality," a hallmark of all Marxist/Leninist parties, invariably creates a chasm between itself and the population. At least for the next decade or so, there is little if any indication that the relationship between regime and population will dramatically change in this regard.

At this juncture the party's dedication to the creation of a viable political culture is directly related to the challenge of gaining larger amounts of voluntary support within the population, for in the absence of an accepted tradition of ruling norms, only the elements of personal and group opportunism and the application of raw force can maintain the hold of the SED within the GDR. On the basis of this and preceding discussions, there is impressive evidence to suggest that the party has every intention of building a socialist political culture capable of generating the kind of effective support upon which all regimes depend. Given the "special," and highly unfavorable, conditions surrounding the creation of the GDR, the generation of a "new" socialist value system has not been easy for the SED to successfully engineer. With the passing of time, however, East German citizens of a new generation are coming into political and occupational maturity. Their continuous entrance into adult East German society will not signal a permanent end to the problems that have burdened party and population in their attempt to adapt to each other, but there is every reason to believe that the long-term prospects for the development of a durable and viable political culture are good.

SUMMARY AND CONCLUSIONS

The creation and extension of East German political culture
has dominantly revolved around several key factors. First, there is
a tradition of Marxist/Leninist principles that provide historical
relevance and legitimation to the exercise of power and authority by
the SED. Along with these principles has come a tradition of Prussian
statecraft, which the SED has selectively employed in the design of
relationships between itself and the population. Second, the step-wise
evolution of East German society has provided an immediate social
context within which the GDR's political culture has progressively
evolved. Even allowing for the obvious tendency to "retrospectively
redefine" history in line with current interpretations of reality,
alterations in the party's definition of East German postwar history
still fit within the formative experiences that have made the GDR
what it is today. Third, and in response to the impact of ideological
and historical forces, a complex of doctrine and values has gradually
provided the GDR's political culture with a unique, albeit Marxist/
Leninist, identity. In this vein, national consciousness, collectivism,
"love for the GDR," and productivity and performance constitute the
main building blocks. Finally, and most prominently, the link between
political culture and political socialization has been emphasized given
the close relationship between the creation of socialist values and
norms and their communication within the environment of public
institutions, especially the educational system. While the GDR's
political culture has undergone various transformations over the
last several decades, and while the SED continues to experience a
sense of insecurity in its relations with the broad population, the
existence of a viable East German political culture is no longer in
doubt.

Beyond the immediate impact of the political socialization
process upon the development of a socialist political culture in the
GDR, one should not lose sight of the broader picture that ties the
extension of this phenomenon into the political communications process
(see Chapter 8 for an exposition of this subject). From this angle
the generation of a socialist value and normative structure cannot be
divorced from the performance of the GDR's communications media,
running the gamut from large-scale advertising campaigns in preparation for an important holiday, such as May 1 or October 7, to intimate
conversations within the smallest cells of the SED. Moving beyond
structural considerations, it is of perhaps greater importance to
realize the degree to which the communications media provides a
necessary element of continuous feedback, enabling the political culture to adapt itself to the changing problems and challenges facing
East German society.

Of immediate significance is the relationship between political culture and the processes of political recruitment, training, and leadership selection, topics to be dealt with in Chapter 3. From this vantage point the impact of governing values and norms on these interrelated processes alluded to above cannot be underemphasized. Indeed, the recruitment, training, and leadership selection processes are direct outgrowths and expressions of Marxist/Leninist political culture in the GDR. To choose one of many examples in this regard, it is self-evident that the criteria for the selection of SED members from the candidate to the propagandist level is crucially dependent upon the manner by which the party defines and applies its conception of where the GDR is moving in an ideological and political sense. Additionally, the content of systematic doctrines and values invariably tends to supply the party with operational criteria that can be employed during various phases of the leadership selection process. These particular considerations are reflected at various points in the upcoming discussion.

Beyond the impact of political culture on recruitment, leadership selection, and training processes, it should finally be noted that the significance of a society's reigning values and norms is manifested in literally every phase of political activity. In this vein the GDR is not excluded. As subsequent discussions dealing with various input and output dynamics should easily demonstrate, the relevance of political culture across the entire range of political behavior in East Germany becomes increasingly clear. Indeed, there is no phase of political activity in the GDR that is not amenable to the influence of this constantly evolving structure of legitimized norms and values that give daily and long-run meaning to the actions and thoughts of public authorities.

NOTES

1. Democratic German Report, October 23, 1974, p. 149.

2. Hermann Weber, "25 Jahre DDR-Kontinuität und Wandel," Deutschland Archiv, October 1974, pp. 1031-35.

3. Gordon H. Skilling, The Governments of Communist East Europe (New York: Thomas Y. Crowell, 1966), p. 200.

4. Marx/Engels, Manifest der Kommunistischen Partei (Berlin: Dietz Verlag, 1966), p. 45.

5. Ibid., p. 50.

6. Clemens Dutt, Fundamentals of Marxism/Leninism (Moscow: Foreign Languages Publishing House, 1963), p. 123.

7. Ibid., p. 132.

8. Ibid., p. 133.

9. Ibid., Chapter 21, pp. 509-38.

10. V.I. Lenin, "Der Übergang vom Kapitalismus zum Kommunismus," in Staat und Revolution (Berlin: Dietz Verlag, 1970), p. 93.

11. Dutt, op. cit., pp. 524-25.

12. See for additional information, A.S. Makarenko: Eine Auswahl (Berlin: Volk and Wissen Verlag), 1967.

13. Peter Merkl, Modern Comparative Politics (New York: Holt, Rinehart and Winston, 1970), p. 149.

14. For an interpretive treatment of political culture and its significance for the political order, see Gabriel Almond and Sidney Verba, The Civic Culture (Boston: Little, Brown, 1963).

15. Hermann Axen, Zur Entwicklung der sozialistischen Nation in der DDR (Berlin: Dietz Verlag, 1973), p. 9.

16. J.P. Nettl, The Eastern Zone and Soviet Policy in Germany (London: Oxford University Press, 1951), p. 282.

17. See Thomas A. Baylis, "East Germany's Rulers," MA thesis, University of California, Berkeley, 1961, pp. 87-94.

18. Dutt, op. cit., p. 525.

19. For the SED standpoint on this period, see Geschichte der Deutschen Arbeiter Bewegung (1945-1949) (Berlin: Dietz Verlag, 1968).

20. Lebensweise und Moral im Sozialismus (Berlin: Dietz Verlag, 1972), p. 104.

21. Peter Christian Ludz, The German Democratic Republic from the 60's to the 70's (Cambridge, Mass: Center for International Affairs, Harvard University, 1970), pp. 5-6.

22. Dutt, op. cit., p. 527.

23. Hermann Weber, Von SBZ zur DDR (Hannover: Verlag fur Literatur und Zeitgeschehen, 1968), p. 147.

24. See Karl Heinz Kahrs, "The Economic System of Socialism in East Germany," Ph.D dissertation, University of California, Santa Barbara, 1970. This analysis covers the rise and consolidation of the GDR's economy over this period more than competently.

25. Democratic German Report, October 9, 1974, p. 142.

26. "E. Berlin, U.S. Ties Set Up," Washington Post, September 5, 1975, pp. 1 and 15. For a recent elaboration of the SED delineation of historical epochs within the GDR, see Author Collective, Klassenkampf, Tradition, Socialismus (Berlin: VEB Deutscher Verlag der Wissenschaften, 1974).

27. See Gebhard L. Schweigler, "The Development of National Consciousness in the German Democratic Republic," paper delivered at the 1973 Annual Meeting of the American Political Science Association, New Orleans, September 4-8, 1973.

28. Ralf Dahrendorf, Society and Democracy in Germany (New York: Doubleday, 1967), p. 398.

29. Hermann Axen, Zur Entwicklung der sozialistischen Nation in der DDR (Berlin: Dietz Verlag, 1973), p. 16.

30. Ibid., p. 32.

31. See Peter Christian Ludz's observations on this matter in "Continuity and Change Since Ulbricht," Problems of Communism, March-April 1972, p. 58.

32. For a good "period piece" on the SED's conception of cultural politics, see Elmar Faber and Erhard John, Das Sozialistische Menschenbild (Leipzig: Karl Marx Universität, 1967).

33. Erich Honecker, "Der Kampf gegen den Imperialismus," in Protokoll des VIII Parteitages der SED Vol. 1 (Berlin: Dietz Verlag, 1971), pp. 56-57.

34. Erich Honecker, Zügig voran bei der weiteren Verwirklichung der Beschlüsse des VIII. Parteitag der SED (Berlin: Dietz Verlag, May 1973), p. 21.

35. Ralf Dahrendorf, Society and Democracy, p. 407.

36. A.S. Makarenko: Eine Auswahl, op. cit., p. 15.

37. Wolfgang Eichhorn, Von der Entwicklung des Sozialistischen Menschen (Berlin: Dietz Verlag, 1964), pp. 170 and 178.

38. Lebensweise und Moral im Sozialismus (Berlin: Dietz Verlag, 1972), p. 200.

39. Thomas Arthur Baylis, "Planning, Participation and the Search for Authority in the GDR," paper delivered at the 1971 Annual Meeting of the American Political Science Association, Chicago, September 7-11, 1971.

40. Ibid., Introduction.

41. Jean Edward Smith, "Limitations of Political Persuasion: The German Democratic Republic: Soviet Policy in Central Europe," paper delivered at the 1966 Annual Meeting of the American Political Science Association, New York, September 10, 1966, p. 12.

42. David Easton and Jack Dennis, Children in the Political System (New York: McGraw-Hill, 1969), p. 17.

43. Richard E. Dawson and Kenneth E. Prewitt, Political Socialization (Boston: Little, Brown, 1969), p. 147.

44. Ibid., p. 149.

45. Paul Klimpel, Zur Begriffsbildung in der Unterstufe (Berlin: Volk und Wissen, 1969), p. 117.

46. Ibid., pp. 117-18.

47. Die Erziehung des jüngeren Schulkindes (Berlin: Volk und Wissen, 1969), p. 124.

48. Klimpel, op. cit., pp. 93-140, contains a full listing of relevant socialization concepts.

49. Ibid., pp. 105 and 135.

50. Peter Heilmann, "Die Deutsche Demokratische Republik nach 25 Jahren-Versuch einer Bilanz," Korrigiertes Tonbandmanuskript eines Vortrages vom 2. Oktober 1974 in der Evangelischen Akademie Berlin, pp. 10-11.

51. Dokumentation: "Verfassung der Deutschen Demokratischen Republik-Synopse der Fassungen vom 9.4. 1968 und 7.10. 1974," Deutschland Archiv, November 1974, p. 1198.

52. Ibid., p. 1199.

53. Redaktion: DDR-Staat der Jugend (Dokumentation) (7; pp. 43-48).

54. Ibid.

55. Protokoll der Verhandlungen des VIII. Parteitages der SED Vol.1 (Berlin: Dietz Verlag, 1971), p. 101.

56. Fred Oldenburg, "Informationen über die SED. Aus Anlass der Parteiwahlen 1973/74," Deutschland Archiv, January 1974, p. 52.

57. Wulfram Speigner, "Soziale Bedingungen und Motivation der Einstellung von Produktionsarbeiterinnen zur Qualifizierung," Berufsbildung, March 1974, pp. 111-13.

58. Ibid.

59. Ibid.

60. Herta Kuhrig, "Zur gesellschaftlichen Bedeutung der Aus- und Weiterbildung der Produktionsarbeiterinnen," Berufsbildung, March 1974, pp. 107-10.

61. Ibid.

62. Ibid.

63. Hans Apel, Ohne Begleiter: 287 Gespräche jenseits der Zonengrenze (Cologne: Verlag und Politik, 1965), p. 84.

64. Ibid., p. 93.

65. Arthur M. Hanhardt, Jr., "Political Socialization in the German Democratic Republic," paper delivered at the 1970 Annual Meeting of the American Political Science Association, Los Angeles, September 1970, p. 34.

66. Dieter Voigt, "Montagearbeiter in der DDR: Eine empirische Untersuchung über IndustrieBauarbeiter in den volkseigenen Grossbetrieben," Ph.D dissertation, Justus Liebig-University Giessen, 1971, pp. 158, 159, and 184.

67. Werner Hennig, "Zur Psychologie des Jugendlichen Neuerers," Jugendforschung, March 4, 1967, pp. 7-29.

68. Werner Gerth, "Verhaltensweisen und Einstellungen Junger Neuerer," Jugendforschung, August 1968, pp. 27-46.

69. Ibid., p. 40.

70. Fritz Macher/Karoline Macher, "Arbeits-und Berufszufriedenheit bei Lehrlingen," Berufsbildung, No. 12 (December 1971), pp. 535-38.

71. Kurt Ducke, "Motive und Faktoren der Berufswahl,"
Polytechnische Bildung und Erziehung, No. 4 (April 1974), pp. 141-44.

72. Ibid., p. 144.

73. Gebhard L. Schweigler, "The Development of National
Consciousness in the German Democratic Republic," paper delivered
at the 1973 Annual Meeting of the American Political Science Association, New Orleans, September 4-8, p. 17.

74. Heinz Lippmann, "X. Weltjugendfestspiele im Geist der
Volksfrontpolitik," Deutschland Archiv, August 1973, p. 788.

75. Neues Deutschland, June 4, 1974, p. 3.

3

POLITICAL RECRUITMENT, LEADERSHIP SELECTION, AND TRAINING

THEORETICAL FRAMEWORK

Marxism/Leninism

The theories of Marxism/Leninism relevant to political recruitment, leadership, and training are based on a fundamental concept regarding the role of the masses in history. Briefly put, the masses make history: "Marxism/Leninism shows that historical necessity finds its main expression through the masses, the force that plays the determining role in social development."[1] The masses make history because of their productive activity that creates all material value, their creative role in times of revolution and national liberation, their influence on the ruling class while that remains dominant, and their creation of culture.[2]

While the masses make history, the other side of the Marxist concept is that "history makes me." In fact, Marx apparently never wearied of reasserting this principle and its corollary that all leaders are replaceable. As Engels wrote, "That such and such a man and precisely that man arises at a particular time in a particular country is, of course, pure chance. But cut him out and there will be a demand for a substitute, and this substitute will be found, good or bad, but in the long run he will be found."[3] This, then, logically rules out "cult of personality." As Marx said,

> . . . because of aversion to any personality cult, I
> have never permitted the numerous expressions of
> appreciation from various countries, with which I

was pestered during the existence of the International, to reach the realm of publicity, and have never answered them, except occasionally by rebuke. When Engels and I first joined the secret Communist Society, we made it a condition that everything tending to encourage super- stitious belief in authority was to be removed from the statutes.[4]

Similarly, contemporary standard works on Marxism/Leninism point out that

the cult of the individual is therefore alien to the whole spirit and requirements of the socialist movement and incompatible with Marxism-Leninism. It was no accident that Marx, Engels, and Lenin always fought against any manifestation of this cult, were incapable of tolerating flattery and adulation, and more than once warned the working class and its Party against the practice of mag- nifying and over-praising its leaders.[5]

Nevertheless, despite this warning, Marx saw individual leadership as key to the historical process. While he ultimately envisioned a society free of social control and viewed institutionalized political leadership as anathema, at the same time he considered revolutionary leadership important—it would organize the party of the proletariat, which was the vanguard of the working class. As Engels wrote about revolutionary leadership:

It is the specific duty of the leaders to gain an ever clearer understanding of the theoretical problems, to free themselves more and more from the influence of traditional phrases inherited from the old conception of the world, and constantly to keep in mind that Socialism, having become a science, demands the same treatment as every other science—it must be studied. The task of the leaders will be to bring understanding, thus acquired and clarified, to the working masses, to spread it with increased enthusiasm, to close the ranks of the party organizations and of the labor unions with ever greater energy.[6]

The working class party that such leaders would organize was not, however, seen by Marx and Engels as an elite organization leading the working class. Rather, it was part of the labor movement itself, a means to an end:

> The Communists do not form a separate party opposed
> to other working class parties. They have no interests
> separate and apart from those of the proletariat as a
> whole. They do not set up sectarian principles of their
> own by which to shape and mold the proletarian movement.
>   The Communists are distinguished from other
> working-class parties by this only: (1) In the national
> struggles of the proletarians of the different countries,
> they point out and bring to the front the common interests
> of the entire proletariat, independently of nationality.
> (2) In the various stages of development which the struggle
> of the working class against the bourgeoisie has to pass
> through, they always and everywhere represent the interests
> of the movement as a whole.
>   The Communists therefore are, on the one hand,
> practically the most advanced and resolute section of the
> working-class parties of every country, that section which
> pushes forward all others; on the other hand, theoretically,
> they have over the great mass of the proletariat the advan-
> tages of clearly understanding the lines of march, the
> conditions, and the ultimate general results of the pro-
> letarian movement.[7]

Thus Marxism provided the key to recruitment (the masses who make history), leadership (produced by history, to lead the working class), and training (theoretical study by leaders who raise mass conscious-ness).

     Lenin, however, gave the concepts new emphasis, for in his time the Communist party was a ruling party, not fighting to gain power. That, obviously, called for refinement of Marx's and Engels' leadership concepts. Whereas Marx and Engels saw the workers' party as representing interests of the workers as a whole, Lenin saw it as a militant elite party. Whereas Marx and Engels had envisioned a loosely structured party as part of the working-class movement, Lenin saw it as a party of highly disciplined professional revolu-tionaries leading the working class movement.[8]

     These changed concepts are spelled out in great detail in Lenin's work "What Is To Be Done?" written in 1901-02. It was based on the recognition that "we have no people, because we have no leaders, no political leaders, no talented organizers."[9]

> I assert: (1) that no revolutionary movement can endure
> without a stable organization of leaders maintaining
> continuity; (2) that the broader the popular mass drawn
> spontaneously into the struggle, which forms the basis

of the movement and participates in it, the more urgent
the need for such an organization, and the more solid
this organization must (for it is much easier for all
sorts demagogues to side-track the more backward
sections of the masses); (3) that such an organization
must consist chiefly of people professionally engaged
in revolutionary activity. [10]

Clearly then, while recruitment remained the same (the broad masses),
Lenin changed significantly the concepts of leadership (elite and
selected), as well as training (specific programs designed to make
revolutionaries out of workers). The latter became especially important within the context of Lenin's rejection of the idea that class
consciousness would come automatically to the proletariat. Instead,
agitation and propaganda were essential, that is, training.

For instance, as early as 1900 he wrote: "Our principal and
fundamental task is to facilitate the political development and the
political organization of the working class. . . . It is being pushed
into the background . . . by those who restrict the content and scope
of political propaganda, agitation, and organization."[11] In 1902 he
defined agitation a bit further: "All-sided political agitation is a focus
in which the vital interests of political education of the proletariat
coincide with the vital interests of social development as a whole, of
the entire people, that is, of all its democratic elements."[12] And
that this political education was necessary for everyone was spelled
out in "What Is To Be Done?": "We must 'go among all classes of
the population' as theoreticians, as propagandists, as agitators, and
as organizers. No one doubts that the theoretical work of Social-
Democrats should aim at studying all the specific features of the
social and political conditions of the various classes."[13] In short,
propaganda was in the forefront so long as, and to the extent that,
the question was (and insofar as it still is) one of winning over the
vanguard of the proletariat to communism. [14]

Once the revolution had arrived, the training tasks of both the
masses and the leadership were different. Then, as will be seen
later, the public social consciousness had to be guided toward stabilization of the revolution and construction of socialism, and eventually,
communism. This meant, specifically, developing attitudes and skills
necessary for economic development, as well as the psychological
development of "the new socialist man."

In synthesizing the contributions of Marxism/Leninism with a
theory of socialist political recruitment, training, and leadership
selection, several things are obvious. First, while Marx and Engels
devote attention to "restructuring" the base, economic relationships,
Lenin builds a theory of political superstructure upon it. In developing

a highly organized party capable of seizing, then consolidating, power,
Lenin's writing represents nothing less than a theory of socialist
state-building that was tested in the Soviet Union and subsequently,
with a few modifications to be sure, applied within Eastern Europe
after 1945. Second, an understanding of contemporary aspects of
political development, especially recruitment, training, and leadership selection, lies with an appreciation of Lenin's theory on these
questions, and not those of Marx or Engels. Finally, in perhaps no
other country, aside from the USSR, has Lenin's theory of leadership
been employed more diligently and successfully than in the GDR, as
will be seen.

Functional

Functional theory makes little attempt to separate recruitment
and leadership selection. It examines aspects of training in terms
of the political socialization function. Because we are examining
the "formal" sides of these phenomena, however, the functional
definition of political recruitment will apply to all three variables:

> The political recruitment function takes up where the
> general political socialization function leaves off. It
> recruits members of society out of particular subcultures
> and trains them in the appropriate skills, provides them
> with political cognitive maps, values, expectations, and
> affects. In other words, it consists of the special political
> role socializations which occur in a society "on top of"
> the general political socialization function. [15]

Functional theory views recruitment, training, and leadership
selection as interrelated processes that, in sum, provide the polity
with an ability to sustain, or maintain, itself in the face of various
shocks and challenges. In modern industrial societies, functionalists
assert that all three processes become increasingly complex as the
tempo of social, economic, and political demands rises. On this
particular issue, Marxist/Leninists easily agree. However, in the
case of a communist political system with a mass political party, it
seems justified to consider recruitment as the function of drawing
socialized citizens into the party selection process, whereby leaders
are recruited from its base, and improving the training process in
which leaders learn their roles.
  Functional and Marxist/Leninist theories are complementary.
On the one hand, both of them are directly involved with the tasks of

explaining how modern industrial societies maintain themselves. Though Marxism/Leninism posits the "irreconciliability" of capitalist and socialist societies, the theory does not in principle argue that problems of system maintenance cannot be examined by the use of analytical categories developed from functional theory. At the very least, they are used by them. Functionalism, on the other hand, looks upon training, recruitment, and leadership selection processes in socialist systems as manifestations of how one type of polity responds to challenges and opportunities within its environment.

SITUATION IN THE GDR

Recruitment, training, and leadership selection vary according to the demands and capabilities of different societies. In revolutionary systems—those that have recently developed out of an old system, say autocracy—the political elite normally attempts to build a political culture radically different from the one preceding it. As the revolution becomes "institutionalized," greater attention is given to the improvement of the recruitment, training, and leadership selection processes. Both sides of this issue are reflected in the political history of the GDR.

The following discussion examines the development of recruitment, training, and leadership selection in the GDR over the last quarter century. Each period of change is discussed in terms of how these variables were reflected in it. Of central interest will be the role of the SED and its direction of these processes.

1945-49

The aftermath of World War II left the Eastern part of Germany in disarray. In terms of political authority, this meant that East Germany's future communist elite had to start from scratch in attempting to build a foundation for the development of a socialist ideology. That meant, above all, leadership, but also building or recruiting a party.

Leadership was an especially acute problem. As one who was involved in leadership recruitment at that time has reported,

the Party in 1945 had only a few leading cadres available and almost no functionaries at the middle or lower level. The cadre core consisted almost exclusively of functionaries

returned from Soviet or Western emigration or who had
survived the Nazi regime in illegality, prisons, or
concentration camps. The exact number was never
determined, but it was fewer than 5,000. [16]

While the majority of KPD functionaries had been killed in the concentration camps, and because a large portion of the pre-1933 membership had compromised themselves with National Socialism, young
members were especially a problem:

Above all, the important generation born from 1912 to
1920, who belonged to the most active forces, the
communist children's or youth organization, had been
killed in the Spanish Civil War or World War II. Further,
the terror and spy system of the Nazis had hindered even
those committed to communism, the illegal remnants of
the KPD [German Communist Party] had to immunize
their own children against fascism out of security
reasons. [17]

Soviet perceptions of German communists also posed leadership
problems. Thus, "The Soviets considered the 'old communists'
Germans—to the extent that they had not come out of Soviet emigration—as principally untrustworthy. The Communists who had remained
in Germany during the Third Reich were considered by the Soviets
to be co-guilty, and those emigrants from capitalist countries were
suspected of unreliability." [18]
        Thus, the youth organization, the FDJ (Free German Youth),
became an essential "cadre forge for the party," as Stalin said.
Furthermore, there was room at the top for young members of the
FDJ because the "radical denazification of the faculty of schools and
universities, justice and police, and all other institutions of public
life, demanded a rapid education of successor personnel
[Nachwuchskräften]. This mass demand for young cadre would
be overcome by different types of schools, short courses, and
special schools."
        From 1945 to 1947, East German communists were able to
effect a fusion of the "zonal" KPD with its counterpart, the SPD
(Socialist Party of Germany), thus creating the potential for a mass
party. Though contemporary SED writers attempt to argue that a
strong line of ideological continuity, extending from the early postwar
years to the present, exists, accounts of ex-SED members strongly
underline the "catchall" nature of the SED's early appeal. In terms
of recruitment, this meant that

the Party was to include the best men and women of
all classes in the active population, and all sincere
opponents of Fascism. Ulbricht was critical of the fact
that in many areas comparatively few Party members
had been admitted, and in many cases the Party leadership had set up impossible conditions for admission to
the Party: This was a grave mistake. Unmistakable
sounds of astonishment were to be heard in the hall as
Ulbricht declared: "In admitting people to the Party,
it must not make any difference at all whether the
anti-Fascists are Catholic, Evangelical or Jewish in
their religious affiliations."[19]

This apparent abandonment of ideological criteria within the
recruitment process is explained by J.P. Nettl in his examination of
staffing problems at all levels of the governmental and political
apparatuses. In light of the fact that trusted cadres were not yet
available in sufficient number, Ulbricht and the Soviet authorities
opted for a pragmatic answer to the recruitment dilemma:

Matters of personnel were decided on the basis of two
simple questions: (1) Was a man useful, and (2) had he
been a Nazi? The materialist conception of a man's
usefulness as a general basis of approach has been
used for a long time in Russia, and though strongly
embodied in Marxist ideas is by no means exclusive
to that philosophy. In Germany it was much in vogue
during the Nazi period, and remains a relic of that
heterogeneous philosophy. To-day (1951) it is a
leitmotif of government in the Eastern zone.[20]

Perhaps the most spectacular, yet understandable, response to
staffing problems was the relatively nonideological approach taken
toward military recruitment. Commenting on this selected aspect
of the broader phenomenon, another analyst focuses on how the
staffing problem was temporarily resolved within the first generation
of the future East German military system:

The educational level of most individuals who became
officers in the KVP [Kasernierte Volkspolizei or
People's Police Quartered in Barracks] was abysmally
low. But little effort was expended to correct this
situation. This is not to suggest that the Russians were
oblivious to the need for military technicians to operate
the equipment they supplied to the East Germans. But

instead of investing time and money in educating these
individuals, they decided to rely on the services of
former Wehrmacht officers who were sympathetic or
at least neutral toward their cause.[21]

In 1948 events within the newly established Soviet bloc pushed
the SED into a harder ideological mold that affected the nature of
recruitment as well as leadership selection. Principally responding
to the expulsion of Marshall Tito, the Yugoslav premier, from the
councils of the socialist camp, Ulbricht shifted the orientation of the
SED away from a pragmatic and into a "Party of the New Type."
Directing attention to the impact of these alterations on the noncommunist elements of East Germany who had previously been courted
by the recently established SED, one writer notes:

> Already assailed by doubts . . . the former Social
> Democrats on the Central Committee [of the SED]
> now saw themselves confronted with the choice of
> either becoming servile instruments of a militant
> Communism or of quitting the party and losing all the
> prestige and benefits attendant on their positions. The
> choice could not have been an easy one. . . . In January
> 1949, the party principle was finally and officially
> abandoned, and a Politburo with a Communist majority
> elected [reference is being made to the mutual "power
> sharing" responsibilities given to the KPD and SPD
> when the SED was formed in the spring of 1946]. . . .
> Shortly thereafter, the first verbal assaults against
> "social democratism" began. (Though assaults against
> Social Democrats were commonplace during the Weimar
> Republic as well, there is little question that the new
> attacks represented a sharp turn away from ideological
> conciliation).[22]

1950-61

With the establishment of official political power in East
Germany, the SED was able to begin its program of sociopolitical
change in earnest. Perhaps there would continue to be challenges
from noncommunist groups, that is, unreconciled Social Democrats
and elements of the prewar middle classes more generally, but the
scientific nature of Marxism/Leninism, as defined and applied by
the SED, could not be put into daily and long-term practice. Such

was the SED's new position. Three characteristics of this period are
worthy of attention:

1. The SED transformed itself into a streamlined organization,
a "party of the new type." As one consequence, the necessity for
purging elements of the lower ranks not fully committed to the goals
of the SED elite was complemented by the attempt to create a foundation of future political authority within the party apparatus. The
carrying out of these dual processes involved the following:

> It was proposed [by the SED's Politburo] that all members
> be required to turn in their membership books and that
> new ones be issued only after a careful examination and
> interrogation. The Parteiüberprüfung was to serve two
> purposes: to cleanse the party's ranks further of un-
> desirable members, and to uncover capable and reliable
> cadres for assuming key tasks in the organization.
> Accordingly, some 6,000 "examining commissions"
> were set up and between January and October 1951 each
> member was thoroughly questioned on his ideological
> orientations, party records, and personal background.[23]

By late 1950, "only 65,000 further members were stricken from the
rolls of the party by the commissions, but many more, perhaps
300,000 seem to have resigned in anticipation of or as a result of . . .
interrogations. Around 70,000 [SED members] . . . were declared
eligible for new and more important jobs or advanced party schools."[24]

While the party was recruiting new members capable of making
the SED an effective agent of Marxist/Leninist social and political
transformation, the top of its hierarchy was being consolidated, an
event that was crystalized in 1952 when Walter Ulbricht moved from
the post of general secretary to the commanding position of first
secretary of the SED's Central Committee.[25]

During this early period the SED was called upon to withstand a
popular rebellion against its economic programs in June 1953, an
event that culminated with the active intervention of Soviet troops and
the purging of two important dissidents within the SED's Politburo,
Wilhelm Zaisser and Rudolf Herrnstadt, who had voiced criticism of
Ulbricht's policies. Perhaps the existence of a communications gap
between the SED, on the one side, and the nonparty masses, on the
other side, supplies the best explanation of this traumatic event. In
writing about the career of the present SED chief, Erich Honecker,
one observer makes this specific point by arguing that "the 'Construction of Socialism' was so fascinating to Honecker that he hardly was
aware of the feelings of the people under him. He did not want to
comprehend the fact that the weak party apparatus, attributable to the

demand for centralized decision-making in all phases of administration, was overextended. The concept of centralized planning simply left little room for flexibility. Honecker appeared to possess little feel for these realities."[26]

2. The middle 1950s up to the early 1960s (1961) are watershed years within the history of this second period of SED rule. Having purged its ranks of unreliable and dissident members (mass membership and party elites, respectively), Ulbricht was once again called upon to respond to challenges from party insiders in 1957—led by Wolfgang Harich—who wanted to, (1) improve living standards in the spirit of limited economic reforms initiated after the June 1953 revolt, (2) dissolve agricultural collectives and support the existence of an independent peasantry, (3) restore intellectual freedom and university autonomy, (4) reform the electoral system so that voters could "really choose" between parties, (5) conduct a more independent GDR foreign policy. Harich's reformist appeal, as well as those voiced by other members of the SED's hierarchy, was answered negatively. In his case, a period of imprisonment was prescribed, with others getting off less harshly.[27]

3. If the SED experienced challenges to its authority during this period, one should not ignore "positive" developments. On the one hand, the party had finally begun to create a pragmatic economic order. Rationing, which had been in effect since 1945, was abandoned in 1958. By the late 1950s the GDR was on its way to becoming the number-two economic power in the socialist camp. On the other hand, the party was attempting to put steam behind its economic modernization effort by recruiting large numbers of individuals with advanced degrees in public administration, economics, and the hard sciences into the ranks of the governmental bureaucracy where the important decisions on economic policy increasingly were being made.[28]

The erection of the Berlin Wall made it easier for the SED to maintain this initial recruitment momentum by effectively sealing off the intercity borders in August 1961. Speaking in terms of East German society as a whole, and elite recruitment in particular, one writer explains the "impact" of the Wall by asserting that

> the resulting halt in the exodus to the West forced many
> of the groups within the population to "integrate" them-
> selves into the social, though not necessarily into the
> political, process. Numerous groups, especially the
> party itself and the workers, were thus compelled to
> make more allowances for each other than heretofore. . . .
> It was true that the professionally ambitious man who
> aspired to a leadership position in business and society

had to be a member of the SED. But party membership
per se was often accepted as sufficient proof of party
allegiance. For their part, many of the people no longer
saw in every party measure some form of terroristic
coercion.[29]

1962-75

In functionalist language, the first 12 years of the GDR's
existence highlighted the challenges of "state building," with its
emphasis on the SED's ability to gain the acquiescence of the mass
population. The Berlin Wall epitomizes the outcome of that struggle.
From the early 1960s onward the SED has gradually shifted attention
to the next challenges that underline the importance of building a
sense of effective loyalty and devotion to the GDR. "Nation-building"
accents and gives meaning to this goal.

Political recruitment, leadership selection, and training have
increased importance within this latest epoch. Perhaps the most
obvious explanation of this development is that the GDR has been able
to develop a foundation of legitimacy within the society as a whole.
Longevity has its own rewards, irrespective of the regime involved.
One forgets how "it was" before the SED took over power. Secondly,
the demands of a modern industrial society make the recruitment,
leadership selection, and training processes increasingly complex in
the GDR. Commenting on the attributes of East Germany's "technical
intelligentsia," Baylis indirectly highlights the yawning differences
existing between this new stratum of elites and the old communist
apparatchiki:

They are young, talented, and, although most are
members of the SED, scrupulous in avoiding the
tortured phrases of "party Chinese," or Kaderwelsch,
as an East German word play has it. They speak the
language of the technical revolution, of cybernetics,
data processing, and sophisticated uses of mathematics;
they talk realistically about the needs and shortcomings
of their industries, and are willing to listen to and
acknowledge the correctness of many criticisms of past
policies; they are energetic workers willing to take
initiative and exhibit a kind of daring that the timid
bureaucrats who often preceded them would not have.[30]

POLITICAL RECRUITMENT

The political recruitment function takes up where the
general political socialization function leaves off. It
recruits members of society out of particular subcul-
tures and inducts them into the specialized roles of the
political system, trains them in the appropriate skills,
provides them with political cognitive maps, values,
expectations, and affects. In other words, it consists
of the special political role socializations which occur
in a society "on top of" the general political socialization
process. [31]

For any political system the implications of studying recruitment
are several. In the first case, the political recruitment process is
powerfully conditioned by the existing political culture. Laws, mores,
modes of approved social behavior, indeed, the way in which individuals are chosen for employment, are traceable back to the political
culture of a society and the recruitment process that has grown up
within it. Secondly, although we speak of a political culture and
recruitment as something tangible, slow to change, an examination
of these phenomena involves an appreciation, and understanding, of
change: Especially in modern industrial societies—capitalist or
socialist—the rates of change within their political cultures and recruitment processes are impressive. Finally, an examination of
political recruitment provides some insight into the general expectations, needs, and demands, which the ruling elite places on the broad
society. From this angle, the study of political socialization is an
important means of understanding the recruitment process. While
political socialization roughly corresponds to (or at least includes)
educating the public to political responsibility, political recruitment
is the obvious counterpart of the selection of leaders. [32]

Mass

As a mass party, the SED possesses the following socioeconomic
characteristics: As of mid-1974 it contained 1,907,719 full members
and 46,411 candidates; from this latter figure, 75.7 percent (21,858)
were classified as workers; 82.5 percent of these party candidates
were 30 years old and younger. [33]
At the VIII Party Congress of the SED, Honecker notes the
following characteristics of the Party: "28.7 percent of all members

are women. The social origins of men and women cadres stem from
the working class, 76.8 percent of the total. Out of our leading cadres
in all areas of social life, 75 percent come out of the working class
and peasantry. Almost half, 45 percent, of the members and candidates are younger than 40."[34]

The SED's Statute (1972) lists the selection requirements in
some detail, though the most general consideration is the question
of entry:

> It is a great honor to be a member of the Socialist Unity
> Party of Germany. Membership in the Socialist Unity
> Party involves great obligations. Any working person
> can be a member of the Socialist Unity Party who
> recognizes the Program and Statute of the Party, who
> actively takes part in socialist construction, who is
> active in a Party organization, who subordinates oneself
> to, as well as carries out, Party decisions [Beschlüssen],
> and who regularly pays the agreed upon membership dues.
> (Statute 19)[35]

Narrowing this general requirement down to an important aspect of
recruitment into the SED on the mass level, entering members are
called upon to consistently recognize that

> in all situations, the Party's instructions regarding the
> correct choice and advancement of Party workers is to
> be made in terms of their political and technical capabil-
> ities, with the realization that all aspects of Party life
> involve a necessary degree of vigilance against the
> existence of heartless and bureaucratic behavior on the
> part of SED members.
>
> Formally, these specific entrance requirements
> must be met by aspiring members: In order for a candi-
> date to be accepted as a Party member, the following
> conditions are to be met: (a) A candidate wishing to
> become a member of the Party, and whose candidate time
> has expired, must submit a membership application in
> his basic organization which must be accompanied by a
> supporting statement signed by two Party members. These
> supporting statements must be submitted by members who
> have been in the Party for at least two years and who have
> known the candidate for one year on the basis of experi-
> ences with him in the areas of occupational and societal
> activity. These individuals shoulder a great responsi-
> bility for the Party in their ability to supply an objective
> and unbiased evaluation of candidates.[36]

   Additional considerations are relevant in dealing with selection
questions. Though SED documents do not explicitly say it, there is
abundant evidence that the selection of workers, especially individuals
engaged in the realm of industrial production, is the most important
consideration for the recruitment of SED membership on the mass
level. On ideological grounds, Honecker has emphasized this concern
on numerous occasions, as for example at the VIII Party Congress:
"The decisions of the Central Committee on the strengthening of the
class basis of the Party will be subsequently realized. [As of mid-
1970] among the 296,720 who have been accepted into the Party during
the time this report was being prepared, there are 211,899 workers
within our ranks, 71.4 percent. This path, which corresponds with
the character of our Party and is congruent with the growing role of
the working class, will be deepened by us."[37] As of mid-1974 the
SED has continued to make good on the commitment to swell the
party's ranks with this essential class.

   Because it is a Marxist/Leninist party, the SED is constantly
vigilant to the danger of "opportunism" and "infiltration," both problems being concomitant with the selection of too many (of the wrong
sort) for membership. In this vein the concept of mass party membership in socialist systems is radically different from the concept of
"catchall" electoral organizations found in Western Europe and the
United States. In brief, the SED believes that it must maintain a
critical "distance" from the broader society if it is to preserve its
ideological sense of identity and long-range sociopolitical mission.

   How does a socialist system control the behavior of its number-
one party? While this is not an easy question to answer, one consideration deserves attention: Though the SED does not provide hard data
on the number of weekly, monthly, or yearly expulsions from its
ranks, its Statute unambiguously states those conditions that can
endanger, if not utterly compromise, the membership status of
errant individuals:

       Members and candidates who do not pay their membership
       dues, or do not pay them according to their established
       level, and who do not supply adequate reason for this
       neglect, must answer to the Party leadership or the
       membership assembly of their basic organization if
       this neglect of responsibility has extended over three
       months; Members and candidates not displaying the will
       and commitment to support the Party's binding obligations
       can, with the confirmation of the regional [Kreis] leader-
       ship, be stricken from the rolls by the membership
       assembly of the basic organization; Individuals who violate
       the unity and purity of the Party, who break Party discipline

and fail to adequately perform the functions stemming
from membership, and who do not behave in a worthy
manner in public and private life, are to be held to
account by the basic organization or by a higher Party
organ. According to the nature of the offense, the following
disciplinary measures can be taken: (a) simple censure,
(b) harsh censure, (c) expulsion from the Party. [38]

At least during periods of relative social and political stability, there
is good—albeit no more than hypothetical—reason to believe that the
SED is somewhat lax in its exercise of disciplinary measures, even
to the point where some members are occasionally moved to remark
that the ranks of the party have become far too large for the maintenance of revolutionary "distance" from the larger, and nonparty,
society.

Elites

Elite recruitment in the GDR has changed in response to broad
patterns of change at work within its social structure and political
system. From a society run by old-line communist functionaries,
East Germany has gradually turned into a system that heavily emphasizes the importance of drafting highly trained specialists into its
elite organs. This hardly means the triumph of "technocrats" over
"ideologists," as some students of convergence theory were prone
to argue in the middle-1960s, though it does suggest that the SED
continues to be genuinely concerned about developing a system of
social control run by individuals well versed in all phases of socialist
construction—running the gamut from highly trained and sophisticated
party cadres, graduated from the party university, "Karl Marx,"
to more technically oriented individuals who have received training
in the fields of applied physics, mathematics, organization science,
cybernetics, and computer programming. Perhaps the central assumption behind elite recruitment in all these varied cases is "cooptation." [39]

The impact of cooptation on the Soviet Communist party has
obvious relevance for an examination of recruitment into East
Germany's elite organs on the party and state levels. Thus as one
student of the Soviet system has argued:

A major aspect of cooptation has always been to draw
leaders of particular groups into the official centers of
decision-making, thereby giving them access to the

principal party and government leaders and reducing
the chances of their developing into an active opposition.
But increasingly this device is also used to bring in
persons who are not so much group representatives as
interpreters of some mass of specialized information
that must be assimilated if the most effective decisions
are to be made. Cooptation . . . is a means of political
recruitment that has considerable relevance for the study
of political parties, for the parties are the principal
instruments through which personnel are selected for
decision-making centers of government.[40]

Peter Christian Ludz and Ursula Hoffmann convincingly demonstrate
the relevance of this quotation for the analysis of elite recruitment
in the GDR.

Central Committee Elites

Ludz argues that East German society has evolved from a rigid
Stalinist system, with its appropriate emphasis on coercion and
systematically directed terror against real and imagined opponents,
into a "consultative authoritarian" one. In this vein, Ludz suggests
that the party's concern with recruiting individuals capable of interpreting complex bodies of information relates back to the SED's
general commitment to successfully engineer broad-scale social and
political change, a commitment that cannot be successfully pursued
in the absence of highly trained personnel within all levels of the
party apparatus. The SED's Central Committee plays an especially
important role in this regard:

. . . Central Committee members always have and still
do participate in meetings of commissions and committees
of the Politburo and the Central Committee apparatus. In
addition, since the V Party Congress in 1958—but more
so since the beginning of 1963—scientists, technocrats,
managers, and leading functionaries of the central
Bezirk [district] and Kreis [regional] party apparatuses
have been invited by the SED leadership for repeated or
occasional consultations. This is an institutionalized
expression of the party leadership's stated goal of
"expertization" of social planning and control. . . . The
Central Committee, as the "parliament" of the party,
now constitutes a true representation of society's
currents, one different from that projected by the party
in the 1950's.[41]

Ludz's analysis of the SED's Central Committee not only involves an examination of recruitment, however, but a more general study of social system change as well, especially in terms of how broader dynamics are inevitably reflected in the elite recruitment process over time. Regarding the Central Committee, he pursues these interrelated goals by describing and subsequently analyzing the biographical characteristics of Central Committee members most generally: "Our study includes all 275 full and candidate members of the Central Committee in 1954, 1958, and 1963. . . . A personal file was established for each full and candidate member, which contains notes on his membership in the Central Committee, the Central Committee Secretariat, and the Politburo in 1954, 1958, 1963."[42] The following attributes are then focused upon:

> Sex; Place of Birth (Country); Father's profession; Completion of education or professional training; Acquired profession; Date of entry into the KPD/SED or other parties; Political training; Residence in the Soviet Union; Politically relevant activity or residence between 1933-1945; Membership in the People's Chamber (1954, 1958, and 1963); Membership in the Council of Ministers (1954, 1958, 1963, and 1965); Membership in the State Council (1960 and 1963); Actual occupation [primary function] during comparable periods: 1954, 1958, and 1963.[43]

The analysis moves in a developmental direction as Ludz then traces change in Central Committee "from an exclusively acclamatory and declaratory organ to a cooperative, transmittable and—above all—consultative assembly (to the Politburo)" from the early 1950s through the early 1960s. Though he arrives at a number of conclusions, two central propositions emerge. (1) in terms of internal structure, the Central Committee is increasingly characterized by the "replacement of the older generation (60 and above), a rise in the number of trained party functionaries, and an increase in professional mobility."[44] (2) with a decrease in the number, if not direct influence, of older Central Committee members, "the existence of a process of 'professionalization,' and a clear separation in functional areas of party and state apparatus has occurred. This is accompanied by an advance of younger, more highly qualified party functionaries."[45]

Minister Council Elites

Since the departure of Walter Ulbricht from the post of SED first secretary, the Minister Council has become the supreme economic planning and coordinating instrument in the GDR's governmental

structure. Previous to mid-1971, the State Council, created and
headed by Ulbricht until his death in late summer 1973, had played
a superior role. Since his passing from the scene, however, the
Minister Council has continued to gain power and influence in the
GDR, a reality given institutional legitimization on September 28,
1974, when revisions in East Germany's 1968 Constitution were
formally announced by Erich Honecker. Regarding the status of the
Minister Council he notes that its responsibility in the carrying out
of the "whole complex of state activity is codified in the (new) legal
draft."[46]

Ursula Hoffmann's study of elite recruitment into the Minister
Council does not provide one with insights into the evolution of this
organ into an increasingly important policy actor in the GDR. In a
more modest vein, it does provide some understanding of personnel
fluctuations over the first two decades of its official existence (1949-
69).[47] Gathering data on biographical attributes of 139 members,
the following variables are analyzed: age; social origin ("what
class does the individual come from?);* party membership (SED or
bourgeois party?); occupational training; career pursuit after 1945;
position held immediately before and immediately after leaving the
Minister Council; position (status) in the Minister Council; length of
time in the organ; simultaneous member in the People's Chamber
(the GDR's parliament), Central Committee, and Politburo (the
supreme political organ in the GDR).[48]

On the basis of her findings, which diverge slightly from those
of Ludz, the conclusion emerges that a "fusion" has taken place
whereby personnel on the Minister Council are increasingly to be
found on the Central Committee and Politburo.[49] Noting the growth
of policy-making autonomy within the Minister Council, Hoffmann
apparently believes that Ludz's proposition on the decline of positional
changes between various sectors of party and governmental activity
does not hold for this one particular organ.†

---

*Even when class is known, what conclusions can be drawn
from this knowledge? This question is especially significant when
one considers the fact that members of elite organizations come from
families that, in many cases, lived before socialism had come to
the GDR.

†Hoffmann also might have noted that the Minister Council,
consisting of no more than 50 individuals, is less bulky, personnel-
wise, than the Central Committee, with a membership fluctuating
between 110 and 130 full-time members.

SELECTION

Within all socialist systems, the SED considers itself to be the leading force (die führende Kraft) in East Germany's drive toward national development. At the VIII Party Congress of the SED, Erich Honecker attempted to describe the relevance of this role:

> Comrades: The assignment facing the SED, as a
> Marxist/Leninist Party of the working class, is the
> political leadership of socialist society. The Party
> awakes and challenges the citizens of the GDR in their
> desire to enrich our socialist order. In the twenty-five
> years since it was founded by Wilhelm Pieck and Otto
> Grotewohl, our Party has energetically engaged itself
> in the consistent and successful pursuit of unity. As a
> revolutionary party of the working class and the working
> people more generally, the Party has been able to accom-
> plish things in the face of complicated historical circum-
> stances. The victory of the anti-fascist-democratic
> revolution, the construction of a solid foundation of
> socialism, and the successful development of a mature
> socialist society proves this: Our Party is right about
> what the objective demands of our epoch are. The SED
> leads the people on the correct, and on a sure, course.
> Those goals, founded on the teachings of Marx, Engels,
> and Lenin, and pursued within the revolutionary workers'
> movement, are being realized. [50]

If the SED has pursued the goals of socialist construction successfully since its founding in 1946, it has required the efforts of single individuals and groups within all parts of the hierarchy. Since we now know something about general considerations attached to the recruitment of elite and mass membership into the SED, some specific aspects of this process governing the general treatment of several strategically important groups are now covered. Selection procedures for elites, cadres, and propagandists are dealt with below.

Elites

Elites in the GDR refer to various groups actively involved in the direction and exercise of public authority. While one West German writer breaks the East German elite into four broad

categories—party apparatus, mass organizations (leaders and sub-
leaders), the state apparatus, and the economic leadership—another
analyst makes a finer discrimination: the "Old Guard," the "Young
Guard," First County (district) Secretaries (15 in all), the tech-
nologists, ideologists and social scientists, the "Exponents of Sanctions and Demonstrations" (security and military organs), "Men
Standing at the Peripheries of Power" (deposed elites), the young
elite (individuals between 40 and 50, and those in their thirties).[51]
A third categorization suggests a partial integration of the first two
categorization schemata. Thus, Baylis, while ignoring the impact
of political organs narrowly conceived (the SED Central Committee,
its Secretariat and Politburo), emphasizes six broad categories of
social elite who play a role in East German political life: "They
include (1) the chief governmental planners and economists; (2) bureaucrats with important economic, technical, or scientific responsibilities; (3) industrial managers on all levels; (4) physical scientists
and mathematicians; (5) engineers; and (6) educators and journalists
in scientific, technical, and economic fields."[52]

     Without denying the importance of these subgroups, there is
still little question that examinations of elite selection criteria
ultimately begin with an analysis of the "top" strata of the SED
hierarchy. Thus our observations on elite selection begin with a
look at how these criteria are developed and employed in the choice
of members for the Politburo and Central Committee.

     However, elite selections are hard to come by. For example,
we are not clear about how the SED's leading organ, the Politburo,
evaluates the performance of its members and candidates. Furthermore, there is little direct evidence about how criteria are developed,
and subsequently applied, in choosing individuals for inclusion into
lower levels of the party apparatus. If there is a paucity of codified
rules and guidelines, however, enough indirect evidence supplies the
following picture.

     For the top elite strata, several factors are key:

     1. Ability to perform the job. In a society undergoing the pains
of sociopolitical development, one born in the aftermath of war,
national division, and unremitting competition with its West German
counterpart, the competence of the SED leadership elite is taken very
seriously. This consideration hardly contradicts the obvious fact that
the Ulbricht years, especially between 1950 and 1961, did not always
award individual merit when questions of loyalty to the SED came up.
Thus the purges of 1953 and 1957 had to do with his objection to the
political stances of some Politburo colleagues, not their abilities or
loyalties to socialism per se. Since the early 1960s, however, the
selection of candidates and members to the Politburo and Central
Committee are increasingly based on performance criteria: Can the

person do the job assigned? As one student notes in this particular regard: "It can be definitely stated that there has been a recognition of the priorities of technical and economic progress and an awareness of processes of differentiation and on-going dynamic changes in the GDR's society, coupled with the vision of a permanent increase in productivity. These developments provide the prerequisites for further processes of rationalization of the new elite's outlook, which could facilitate its further attunement to the needs and realities of GDR society."[53]

2. Loyalty to the principles of Marxism/Leninism. As with party members in general, membership in the SED's elite structure necessarily calls upon individuals to fully support the principles of "socialist patriotism" (loyalty to the GDR) and "proletarian internationalism" (unqualified support for the foreign policy of the Soviet Union). In terms of elite obligations and roles (in contrast with the mass membership of the party), however, the application of these principles in the conduct of public affairs is more intensive, fraught with greater consequences. The case of Walter Ulbricht comes to the forefront here: Because he apparently violated the canons of proletarian internationalism by opposing certain elements of Soviet detente policy, he was accused of "nationalism" by Moscow. From this vantage point, and especially since the change in leadership within the post of first secretary occurred immediately prior to the VIII Party Congress, the obligation and duty of elites in the GDR to work closely with the USSR is not subject to public or private challenge.

3. Personal connections. No political system, and certainly no selection process, runs entirely on universalistic criteria. During the Ulbricht era, for example, it was acknowledged that his former associates from Saxony were gaining immediate access to luxury apartments on Stalin (later renamed Karl Marx) Allee. Of perhaps greater relevance was the existence of old and trusted SED members in what Ludz calls the "strategic clique," composed of men who had spent World War II in the Soviet Union, or who had become prominently associated with the Ulbricht brand of socialist soon after the end of the war.[54] (In another section, attention is devoted to Honecker's penchant for individuals who served under him in the Free German Youth.)

Cadres

The backbone of the SED is the cadre. Not only are these 195,000 individuals expected to support the basic principles of Marxism/Leninism, but unlike the mass membership, they are also

called upon to take the lead in providing new applications, and interpretations, of these concepts in daily life. In the work place—
especially the factory—this involves the cadre in the job of drawing
meaningful and practical relationships between SED ideology, as
spelled out during party congresses and plenums, and the production
schedule for a specific plan or agricultural collective. Thus, in the
eyes of the SED, cadres "carry personal responsibility, as for example
in the role as leaders in a collective, for the carrying through of
decisions made by the party of the working class, and the laws and
decrees of state organs."[55]

Of equal importance, the SED specifically calls upon the cadre
to bring "new cadre blood" (Nachwuchskadern) into the party. In other
words, they perform a crucial recruitment function within the society
by providing the SED with new members, though one must be careful
in noting that, as with all communist parties (a point previously
touched upon), the danger of bringing in too many individuals can
result in a loss of party elan. Even here one notes the fact that the
SED possesses the highest member/nonmember ratio in Eastern
Europe. In the words of Honecker, "one out of every sixth citizen
over 18 years of age belongs to our Party."[56]

Selection Procedures

SED training literature discusses cadre selection procedures
at great length. Beginning with a listing of specific criteria considered important by the SED in making choices about the suitability,
or nonsuitability, of individuals aspiring to become cadres, attention
is then shifted to more general, or judgment, considerations applied
to the evaluation of candidates:

> The existing supply of cadres and a determination of
> whether new blood [Nachwuchs] is needed should be
> based upon the following criteria: (1) The existing
> supply of leading cadres (what we have, what we should
> have), and their relevant attributes—political and
> technical qualifications; leadership experiences and
> abilities; proportion of women; the existing age break-
> down; general health conditions. (2) Forseeable elimina-
> tion of the existing supply, due to undertaking of a higher
> function; study; delegation to a social organization;
> personal reasons (age, family, no longer capable of
> meeting educational requirements). (3) Future develop-
> ment of the cadre supply should be based upon a con-
> sideration of the following—changing task areas; changes
> within the organizational structure of the Party apparatus;

the need of central and superior gains . . . for new
blood, for example the need for reserve cadres, taken
out of the existing cadre supply, by state organs."[57]

In discussing central criteria applied to the selection of cadres
several considerations are important:

Firstly, socialist cadre work [Sozialistische Kaderarbeit]
is the realization of the Leninist principle that working
cadres should be developed from politically and technically
qualified workers from the socialist economy. They should
be individuals who, as production workers, have acquired
outstanding levels of performance, having attained distinction through their active involvement in social work
and who have demonstrated in their thought and behavior
a socialist personality, thereby enabling the development
of a socialist worker collective.

Secondly, socialist cadre work demands that strict
attention be given to the criteria used in the selection and
placement of the cadre.

Thirdly, it follows that cadre must be carefully
chosen, tested, and entered into the work process. As
Lenin wrote, "We must endeavour to find patient and
genuine organizers, individuals possessing a sober understanding and a practical mentality—men who are bound
loyally to socialism, who without alarm will perform
solid and organized work for the large number of human
beings within the organizations of Soviet society."

Finally, the choice and placement of cadre must
correspond with correct age categories for leadership
and cooperative work collectives: This means a correct
relationship between old and young forces, and in line
with the directives of the VIII Party Congress, a greater
degree of attention being devoted to the choice and placement of women for leading positions within the state
apparatus.[58]

In examining these selection criteria, the crucial one appears
to be the first: The cutting point of SED selection procedure lies in
the ability and willingness of the cadre structure to integrate party
doctrine with the demands of real life, particularly in the sphere of
industrial production. Thus, the cadre performs the vital function
of consolidating the economic base of socialism by unstintingly
engaging him- or herself with problems of leadership in the work
place.

Because the SED understandably places great importance on the role of cadres within the party, training literature emphasizes the role of personal judgment in the evaluation of cadre performance, not only when they have been initially selected, but at all times when evaluations by superiors must be made. The "judgment" (Beurteilung) is the method employed in this regard:

> A crucial foundation for the selection and development of functionaries [Nomenklaturkader] lies in the regular evaluation of their performance, abilities, and personal characteristics. The leadership is often faced with the task of making evaluations or drawing up a profile. This activity must be performed very carefully. What must be contained within it? At the outset, these considerations should always be kept in mind: The essential strengths of the comrade; in what areas he is seeking to fulfill himself; in what measure does his performance go beyond the normal demands placed on him; where do his outer performance limits lie; and what is the appropriate developmental path for him.[59]

Within this complex, the "head" of a factory (topped off by the party leader and production manager) or government section (that is, in city, regional, or district government—Stadt, Kreis, Bezirk, respectively) must be able to remark critically upon relevant individual characteristics that either improve the quality of work and group morale, or alternatively, contribute to difficulties in these areas. It must be stressed: For the SED it is the cadre who represent the programmatic intentions and goals of the party in the real world.

The following questions normally accompany the making of a judgment:

> Importance criteria for the evaluating of a comrade are:
> Does the comrade feel personally responsible for the realization of the policy of the Party and the interests of socialist society in his daily involvement? How are his political convictions [politische Überzeugungen] reflected in his behavior and deeds?
>
> Does he feel himself anchored in the work collective, and does he provide a good example for his colleagues by his political presence as measured in work performance?
>
> Does he continuously keep himself well informed about the decisions of the Party? Does he pay attention to real political events and does he try to win others for the great cause of socialism?

> Does he behave as a proletarian internationalist,
> and is he intimately bound with the CPSU and the Soviet
> Union?[60]

As a final consideration relating to selection, cadres must also
meet the following standards to be considered for selection: "It is
crucial to select comrades who will engage themselves as leadership
functionaries. They must be members of the Party for a minimum
of three years, and must not have passed their forty-fifth birthday."[61]
In light of the amount and intensity of work laid upon their shoulders,
this last item does not come as a surprise.

Elections

While main attention has been devoted to the process whereby
cadres gain entrance into the appropriate levels of party organization,
party functionaries who are not popular with the population face some
degree of accountability at election—when Honecker calls upon the
party membership "to test through the free articulation what has been
accomplished in fulfilling the resolution of the VIII Party Congress,"
unpopular functionaries can be criticized and even voted out by the
electorate when it is concluded that "with Comrade X we cannot fulfill
the 'Main Tasks' of the 5-Year plan."[62]

This form of accountability is used as an instrument for stabilization and selection within the party organizations; it is a method of
cadre development, for when superiors are present at election meeting
discussions, they register carefully the behavior of the various candidate speakers.[63] In turn, the role of the leading cadre (Führungskader)
in using party elections as a control instrument was emphasized in
all basic documents concerning the 1973-74 elections. For instance,
"die Wahldirektive des ZK der SED" made it clear that the party
leadership (leading cadre) themselves should decide with what comrade
it was necessary to have personal conversations.[64] Further, the
directive exactly described who should be newly elected to party
membership:

> Class conscious comrades . . . who possess a good
> knowledge of Marxism/Leninism and understand how
> to put it into practice. These are members of the Party
> who have, through devotion to it, been able to develop
> relationships of trust with the working people. Among
> these individuals are found battle-tested workers from
> the area of material production, and young male and
> female comrades who have proven themselves in their
> work performance and social activities. Within the new

leadership structures of the Party, members must be
chosen who demonstrate in their whole personality a
commitment to the realization of the policies spelled
out at the VIII Party Congress, and who will be able to
engage themselves by word and deed in the carrying
through of the Party's policies. [65]

Thus, Honecker made it clear that the purpose of the election included
the "political maturity of the Party organization" and the "further
improvement of the political composition of the Party and the right
selection of cadre."[66] As a result, the local-level party elections
resulted in some personnel changes, though not many.

In fact, the 1973-74 party elections demonstrated the stability
of the SED's cadre corps. Out of the 263 first secretaries at the
Region (Kreis) level, all but 16 were returned to their posts. Some
were voted out because of reasons of age, illness, or because they
took over other functions. At the District (Bezirk) level, the picture
was much the same. Each County leadership group includes 6 secretaries (first and second secretary, a secretary for economics,
agriculture, agitation/propaganda, science, education, and culture),
and the leadership group at Wismut has 5—out of these 95 secretaries, 24 lost their seats. In addition there are 124 leading members
of the County Secretariats (such as the chairman of commissions)—of
these, 39 were replaced.

Despite the fact that women make up 29.4 percent of the SED's
membership (in 1974), that proportion was not reflected in the 1973
elections. Only 4 out of the 95 County first secretaries are female,
and only 9 of the 263 Regional counterparts represent this group.

The relatively long time in office of the party's regional first
secretaries demonstrates the stability of the SED's cadre policies.
About a third of the Regional secretaries have been in those party
positions longer than 10 years, the overall time being 8 years. [67]

Propagandists

Propagandists are the "avant garde" of a larger category of
party member, the cadre. From this angle, there is little if any
apparent difference between the more specialized and broader group,
with perhaps one significant exception: Official party literature
leaves no doubt that propagandists have to be more active, more
involved, in both an intellectual and emotional sense, than the rest
of the SED leadership group found within the cadre stratum. This
particular consideration is especially significant because it lies with

the propagandist to educate large parts of the SED and nonparty masses in the spirit of Marxism/Leninism. Thus, as one training manual states, "If our Party now has access to ten thousand propaganda cadre, who possess a solid Marxist/Leninist education, as well as understanding how to powerfully link revolutionary science with life in their dealings with Party members, candidates, and nonaligned working people, the teacher-collectives at the Party universities deserve a large degree of the credit."[68]

Within the SED, propagandists supply a necessary air of elan within the ranks of the party rank and file, at least in theory if not in practice. As a training manual asserts in this particular regard, "the propagandist is the best informed man." Flowing from this general obligation, one specific task orientation evolves:

> The Party's axis of rotation turns on the initial and further training of propagandists as cadre of the Party who have been selected to help increase the effectiveness of the entire Party in light of new demands made at the VIII Congress. The weight of this responsibility lies in the area of Party work where propagandists are called upon to perform the most important obligation the Party can vest in its membership: to unceasingly engage itself in the struggle for the affairs of the working class, the attempt to educate them [the working class] in the thought and behavior of proletarian internationalism and socialist patriotism. [69]

As seen above, then, propagandists must be the decisive catalyzers that make the SED perform its routine functions of interest articulation, aggregation, communications (as will be seen in Chapter 8), socialization, and political recruitment. The frequently employed phrase, "Where there is a comrade, there is the Party!" has special meaning for the work of propagandists who constantly must be aware of their ideological obligation to the SED within a variety of daily, and invariably challenging, circumstances. Commenting on one criteria used in the selection of these elite cadre, the ability to acquire political and ideological skills in the performance of their routine duties is certainly essential. As the SED sees this, it means that

> the observance of the Leninist principles for cadre selection are based upon a foundation stressing many-sided considerations attached to the acquisition of political-ideological abilities which are employed in the areas of Party work and mass propaganda. Propagandists of our Party are only able to perform

their tasks if they are carefully selected and well
prepared. Having acquired a solid knowledge of
Marxist/Leninist theory, they are then able to communicate its scientific foundations, out of which flow
the strategy and tactics of our Party.[70]

TRAINING

Once individuals have been selected by the SED for the cadre,
propagandist, or general membership level, a period of training then
ensues. Depending upon the individual's rank within the party hierarchy, the training program varies according to such factors as
duration of study, the intensity at which various subjects are taught,
and the nature of the experience as a whole. If the training process
is varied, however, this should not blur the fact that all members
of the SED are expected unconditionally to support the principles of
membership contained in the party statutes.

Cadres

Despite a number of changes introduced in cadre training
procedures since the middle 1950s, the following account of an ex-SED
functionary still contains the essential elements of the process:

> Curricular materials for the Party University
> [Parteihochschule] and the central schools for front
> organizations were similar in their basic orientations.
> The basic courses being offered were: history of the
> international workers' movement (especially the history
> of the CPSU); dialectical and historical materialism;
> political economy; history; party development
> [Parteiaufbau]; political and economic geography;
> political principles; military science; art and literature;
> Russian.
>   [The writer then goes on to note that the] essential
> characteristic of Party education involved the demand for
> criticism and self-criticism on the part of the student,
> education in unconditional Party loyalty, unconditional
> belief in the perfectness of the Party, belief in the
> leading role of the Communist Party of the Soviet Union
> (CPSU) and a belief in the victory of socialism. The

atmosphere of the Party University [where SED cadres were, and are, being trained] was directed toward the acquisition of an elite consciousness by the students as an essential part of their preparation for leadership functions.

Party functionaries are required to undergo extended periods of training. Indeed, a perusal of official training manuals suggests a never-ending process of formal and informal training for the party activist. In a modern industrial society, elites are required to "stay on top" of masses of literature, running the gamut from popular journals to the most detailed instructions concerning the conduct of a job. In the GDR, two considerations have made the life of the cadre especially demanding from the learning end of the spectrum: On the one hand, there has always been a scholastic mentality attached to the teaching and learning of Marxist/Leninist concepts. Appropriately enough, party activists are constantly expected to "further qualify" themselves in their ability to attain ever-higher levels of formal training. On the other hand, East German society has become increasingly complex, thereby making the tasks of political administration, planning, and coordination more difficult and unwieldy. Under these changing, and interrelated, circumstances, some issues specifically related to cadre training merit attention.

The operative rationale behind the training process is immediately significant. Thus, "Party schools offer courses of instruction geared toward the education and training of comrades in Marxism/Leninism. They will become acquainted with the basic questions of Marxism/Leninism, and armed with the new theoretical and practical challenges posed by the VIII Party Congress, will help in the further organization of developing socialist society, especially the fulfillment of the "Main Task" [die Hauptaufgabe] which was assigned at the Congress."[72] Assessing the progress of various cadre training programs, Honecker reported at the VIII Party Congress that the program for the "education and further-education" of the party cadre had been completed since the VII Party Congress. "At schools and institutes of the party 100,000 male and female comrades carry out their studies."[73]

These educational opportunities are available for cadres:

- Factory (Betriebschulen) and regional (Kreis) schools of Marxism/Leninism—length of study is one year, beginning in september and terminating in July.
- District (Bezirk) party schools (Bezirksparteischulen)— length of time, three months.
- One year of Direct Studies. "It is crucial to select comrades who wish to serve as head administrative functionaries," as one training catalog asserts.

- Correspondence Study—length of study, two years.
- The Party University "Karl Marx" offers these possibilities—
  Direct Study, three years [at graduation the individual
  receives a diploma of social science]; Correspondence
  Study, five years [a diploma of social science is also
  awarded at the end of this period]; Direct Study, offering
  individuals the chance to "further qualify" in their attempt
  to become a leading cadre (no degree offered).
- Finally, there are various possibilities left open for participation in special lecture series (Vortragszyklen), as well
  as evening courses offered by educational institutions on
  the regional (Kreis) levels. [74]

The question, "On what basis is a person selected for cadre
training?" is answered in this manner by an SED functionary responsible for such situations in the early period: "The induction of students
into various courses of instruction was determined by the following
factors: (a) according to the function the individual was performing
prior to entrance, (b) from his behavior at school, (c) test results
of the individual supplied by the teacher collective, (d) results of
examinations administered the individual by the Central Committee
(educational) commission, (e) existing occupational needs, (f) on the
basis of the student's personal wishes."[75]

Propagandists

The training of propagandists varies. Running the gamut from
special programs and weekend seminars to more ambitious programs
carried out within the "Propagandist Academies," the SED is continuously attempting to improve on the quality of educational preparation acquired by its most active, and assumedly committed, members.
Of special significance in this regard has been the gradual proliferation of various programs on the District levels. Corresponding
roughly to the West German state system, District Party Schools
have taken over a large part of propagandist training. Working
closely with the County leaders of the SED, these institutions have
performed valuable service for the party:

> The Party School, and special schools operating under
> the auspices of their leadership, provide an important
> contribution to the further training of cadre propagandists
> for the Party. Between the time of the VIII Party Congress
> and the beginning of May 1972, over 240 short courses,
> extending over one- to two-week periods and involving

16, 000 participants, took place. Of this number,
more than 50 percent were composed of propagandists. . . . At present, some 3, 000 propagandists
are in the process of "qualifying" on the regional
and factory school levels. [76]

On the Regional (Kreis) level, training processes continue
within various kinds of special seminars and discussion sections
organized by local universities in cooperation with the SED regional
leadership. Two kinds of educational experiences are of particular
interest in this regard. First, special days are set aside for presentations dealing with important "pedagogical-methodological" themes
bearing directly on the daily work of the propagandist. These events
are called the "Day of the Propagandist" and are normally designed
to improve the "overall educational advancement of propagandists in
terms of an introductory thematic complex."[77] Second, in relation
to the Marxist/Leninist qualification of the propaganda cadre, "a
program of lectures is provided with the purpose of relating theoretical-ideological problems with the experiences of Party work, as
well as linking these various consequences with further aspects of
theoretical, political-ideological, and organizational work germane
to the Party organization."[78] Close cooperation between county and
regional leadership organizations is invariably necessary in this
particular regard.
    In sum, the following training programs are available for
propagandists: lecture series, organized propaganda gatherings, short
courses, work with lecture groups in specific areas, "consultations
and argumentative discussions with propagandists and agitators
regarding actual questions of strategy and tactics facing our Party
as it fulfills its obligations within the communist world movement,
as well as dealing with new questions generated out of Marxist/
Leninist theory." Presently, there is also a new three-year course
of instruction geared to the training of new propaganda cadres
administered by the County leadership of the SED. [79]

Comrades

    The "Party Study Year" (Partei Lehrjahr) is the backbone of
the SED's training program for rank-and-file members. Within this
program, the party provides candidates with basic concepts and
interpretations of Marxism/Leninism. Organizationally, the Study
Year turns on the ability and willingness of program leaders to
cooperate with propagandists in the ongoing administration of the

course of study: While instructors are expected to supply candidates
with fundamental positions of the SED on politics, ideology, and economics, propagandists are called upon to selectively introduce themes
dealing with practical aspects of party life that must then be integrated
with the broader perspectives developed by the instructor.[80]

Addressing attention to rank-and-file members and candidates,
the following statement mirrors the basic goals and assumptions of
the Study Year:

> The basic task to be accomplished during the Party
> Years 1971-1975 is involving participants in the
> acquisition of advanced theoretical competence in the
> theory of Marxism/Leninism, as well as helping one to
> thoroughly understand the determined strategy and
> tactics in our struggle for the further strengthening of
> the GDR. The Party Study Year should additionally
> attempt to supply members and candidates with
> greater technical knowledge and an increased desire
> to engage themselves in the implementation of the
> Party's decisions, seen from the spirit of proletarian
> internationalism.[81]

Though various training opportunities also exist for rank-and-file
members—in almost all cases they parallel options provided cadres
and propagandists—the basic text used in the Study Year is the same,
with provision made for implementation of additional subjects when
deemed necessary throughout the year.[82] Titled Study Material for
the Marxist/Leninist School for Candidates of the SED, its listing
of subject matter areas provides some general insight into what the
new SED member is expected to know and accept as a precondition
for entry into the party:

> Theme 1: "Manifest of the Communist Party," dealing
> with the historical mission of the working class and its
> scientific world view. I. The "Manifest" focuses atten-
> tion on the founding documents of scientific-communism;
> II. Justification of the world-historical mission of the
> working class as contained in the teaching of Marx and
> Engels.
>
> Theme 2: Marxist/Leninist teaching about the
> Party of the working class. V.I. Lenin, founder of a
> Party of the New Type.
>
> Theme 3: The Great Socialist October Revolution—
> the passage of humanity from capitalism to socialism.
> The general viability of socialism's laws and teachings.

Theme 4: The VIII Party Congress of the SED—
the further organization of the developing socialist
society in the German Democratic Republic.

Theme 5: Leninist principles of Party construction
and its anchoring in the Statute of the SED.

Theme 6: The meaning of proletarian internationalism for the unity of the international communist
movement. The struggle against anticommunism and
reactionary bourgeoise nationalism.

Theme 7: The youth policy of the SED and the tasks
of members and candidates of the Party regarding the
Marxist/Leninist education of the young generation.[83]

At the conclusion of each chapter there are at least two "control"
questions that are posed by the instructor to the student during class,
or that are supposed to be posed by the student to himself when reading
alone. Two sample questions provide appropriate flavor to this pedagogical device. Thus, at the end of Theme 7 comes the following:
(1) Why is it considered the basic task of a Marxist/Leninist party
to provide socialist education for youth, especially those stemming
from the working class? (2) What tasks are to be performed by
members and candidates in the socialist education of youth?[84]

Two concluding points should be made here. First, since the
Free German Youth, the youth organization of the GDR, is the main
jumping-off point for new candidates—it is the most important training
ground for future entry into the SED—most students already will have
been exposed to these materials. The Party Study Year simply
attempts to deepen knowledge attained in earlier phases of the recruitment process (see earlier recruitment discussion). Second, because
the SED is the "vanguard party" of the GDR, new candidates and
members are expected to make personal efforts to acquire the necessary intellectual rudiments of Marxism/Leninism. Indeed a training
manual asserts that the "persistent private study of Marxist/Leninist
classics, as well as involvement and understanding of SED decisions
and those aspects of the international workers movement considered
important—above all the activities of the CPSU—is and will remain
the basic method for the acquisition of revolutionary theory."[85]

LEADERS AT THE TOP

Ulbricht: Performance and Efficiency

Almond and Powell assert that the first challenge facing new
polities lies with "state-building," or the problem "of penetration and

integration."[86] When Ulbricht passed from the scene in August 1973,
the Tenth Youth Festival was taking place in East Berlin. These
two disparate events were not unrelated to each other since it was
the Ulbricht era that created the essential political, social, and
economic preconditions that lay behind the subsequent staging of the
festival in an atmosphere of surprising openness and spontaneity.

The hallmark of the Ulbricht era was performance and efficiency.
These particular characteristics were especially evident in the
middle and late 1960s when the former chairman of the SED began
to make a fetish of "scientism" and economics in the pursuit of
legitimacy for his society. Though he never said so directly, there
is little doubt that his last years as party leader led to the neglect
of what Marxists/Leninists call "subjective" factors, meaning
ideology. Nonetheless, and with special regard for recruitment,
selection, and training processes, he was the person who, more
than any other party figure, was responsible for the entrance of a
new generation of leaders. Subsequent changes within various phases
and aspects of these processes have not brought about fundamental
changes in the theory or criteria applied to the entrance of coming
generations of party leaders into East German society.

Honecker: The Successor

The assumption of power by Erich Honecker in the spring of
1971 went smoothly. Perhaps Ulbricht's anger over Soviet detente
policies led to the final demise of the old leader, thus making it
easy to get rid of him, but two additional, and perhaps weightier,
items should not be neglected in this regard. At the outset, when
power passed from Ulbricht to his eventual successor, the former
had already reached his seventy-sixth birthday, while Erich Honecker
was awaiting his sixtieth. Second, Honecker had secured the final
trust of Ulbricht over the years when he had loyally served as the
number-two man of the SED chief. Heinz Lippmann, Honecker's
biographer, makes this point nicely when he asserts: "That Honecker
should succeed Ulbricht as leader of the Party was the logical sequel
of the development we have described. Since the VI Congress of the
SED it had been clear that Ulbricht had selected him and was systematically grooming him for this position."[87]

Honecker, if anyone, is the individual called upon to meet the
"second" challenge facing political systems. If Ulbricht, somewhat
in the manner of a Saxon Leviathan, had created the "foundations"
of socialism in the GDR, thereby guaranteeing it a stability grievously
lacking during the early years, Honecker has attempted to "win the

loyalty and commitment" of East Germans. In short, "delimitation" as nation-building.

Reflecting the attitudes of a different, and younger, generation, there are two special characteristics of the Honecker leadership style worthy of attention.

Openness

The production of the movie "The Legend of Paul and Paula" created excitement in the GDR. Generally speaking, the SED was not impressed with a film that successfully purported to describe the more somber, and inescapable, realities of East German life. Though Western audiences are used to such displays, the liberal use of language and the highly suggestive scenes involving men and women were something new and exciting for the GDR's mass population. Somewhat ironically, the film was criticized in the party press but continued to play without let-up through the summer and fall of 1973.

Without a new attitude at the top of the SED hierarchy, this new approach toward "socialist reality" in the performing arts would not have been possible. This change of attitude is reflected in these statements made by Honecker at an SED plenum:

> Starting out from firm socialist positions developed
> around a variety of themes, and which invariably reflect
> various means of expression, there is a broad field open
> for artistic creativity. Only on the basis of these firm
> positions—and this clearly includes socialist ethics—
> can these forms of expression fully evolve. It is only
> possible for artists to find persuasive answers to the
> questions of life which citizens in our Republic pose to
> them through an acceptance of these positions. Many
> aspects of our life need time to mature. This con-
> sideration holds with equal relevance for the flowering
> of culture and art. The intelligent, courageous, and
> openness of artistic design during the socialist present
> and future demands, as we all know, a nearness to life,
> feelings of identification with the people, partiality. In
> this spirit, a broad spectrum of literature, visual art,
> and music offers a wide array of colorful answers to the
> problems, inclinations, and needs of people. [88]

As of late 1974, the pursuit of artistic creativity in the GDR has apparently been able to move forward in an unaccustomed manner, notwithstanding the obligation to support the general policies of the SED, albeit in an increasingly liberal manner (see Chapter 2).

The FDJ Connection

If there is a key to the behavior of the Honecker regime, it lies with an understanding of his socialization experiences within the Communist Youth Organization before World War II and his successful attempt to build a strong youth organization as first secretary of the Free German Youth. Whether 61 years of age is considered young for a political leader invariably depends upon the nature of the individual in question and the kind of political culture being examined. In the case of Honecker, however, few would argue that the direction, content, and style of his personnel selection practices is strongly oriented toward the needs and expectations of youth.

Writing about Honecker's penchant for selecting colleagues from the FDJ days, his biographer notes that "at least five of the new appointees [to the Politburo] came up through the ranks of the FDJ while Honecker was First Secretary. Four of them held high positions and were among Honecker's close associates. . . . "[89] This trend toward the selection of youth for elite positions in the party hierarchy has continued up to the present. Indeed, the entrance of new membership into the prestigious Politburo is graced by individuals substantially younger than the youth-oriented SED chief as the following quotation tends to suggest:

> Every new member of the Politburo (16 full members, 10 candidates), with the exception of Heinz Hoffman, range approximately fifteen years younger than Honecker and were substantially influenced by the Stalin era after 1945. This situation provides Honecker with a natural authority over the new recruits, thus heightening his leadership role. At this point, more than half of its members and candidates (13 of 25) are substantially younger (between ten and fifteen years) than Honecker, thus having no experiences stemming from the workers movement of the Weimar Republic or the years of illegality during the Third Reich. Old communists are already spoken about with some irony from the FDJ-side of the Party.[90]

SUMMARY AND CONCLUSIONS

In this examination of the political recruitment, leadership selection, and training processes, it has become clear that the GDR's political culture provides insight into the operation of these interrelated

processes. Though it is impossible to trace the exact, and authoritative, origins of various rules, values, and evaluative standards used
in the selection and training processes, the political culture certainly
provides a general "context" within which these elements have been
fashioned. Saying these things does not mean that the carrying-through
of recruitment, leadership selection, and training processes, is
unfolding without difficulty in the GDR. It would be surprising, as
well as unbelievable, to assume otherwise given the complexity of
these processes. Some recent problems surrounding the carrying-out
and design of these dynamics are briefly touched upon below.

     1. The choice of people. By European standards, the German
Democratic Republic is a "young" political system. The foundations
of political authority laid by the SED have finally begun to meet
acceptance within the mass, and particularly the under-35, population,
but there is certainly little question that the party must continue
successfully to attack the challenge of "nation-building" if it hopes
eventually to gain the unqualified support of the people. Given the
GDR's success in the realms of economic modernization and social
integration—as seen in terms of mass participation within many areas
of public life, such as sports competition—the regime has good reason
to believe that its goals of socialist nation-building in East Germany
will be achieved. Nonetheless, the party has placed itself in a position
of being forced to "publicly" make good on the promises it has made
to the larger society, and in this regard has yet to fulfill some of the
obligations it has set itself. The condition of women in East German
society represents one important aspect of this concern, especially
as it is mirrored in the recruitment, training, and leadership selection
processes.

     As previously noted, the entrance of women into the upper
reaches of the SED hierarchy has yet to occur, despite the commitment of the party to female emancipation in East German society.
The entrance of females into the organs of state and social authority
(People's Chamber, 31.8 percent out of 159 members are women;
County Assemblies, 35.9 percent out of a total of 1,021; Regional
and municipal assemblies in urban districts, 36 percent out of
6,208; municipal assemblies and village assemblies, 29.8 percent
out of a total of 53,883; borough assemblies, 35.2 percent out of a
total number of 1,057) is reasonably impressive. As of August 1974,
there were no women members in the Politburo, 2 out of 10 located
in the candidate category (Ingeborg Lange and Margaret Müller), 1
out of 11 in the Politburo's Secretariat (Ingeborg Lang), a mere 18
out of a total Central Committee membership of 135, or 13.3 percent,
and 6 out of a total of 46 Central Committee candidates, 13 percent.[91]
As a report dealing with the 1973-74 party elections additionally
points out, the representation (and hence their recruitment, selection,

and training) of women in the County party organizations is not
impressive on the executive level. Thus, while the SED's mass
membership is composed of 635,000 women, or 29.4 percent, there
are only 4 women in the 95-position SED county-party Secretariat
structure. [92] Since the party has made impressive efforts to raise
the status of women in East German society ever since the GDR was
founded, and especially since the coming to power of Erich Honecker
in the spring of 1971, there is every reason to believe that the regime
will make honest attempts to bring more qualified female party
members into the SED's executive apparatus. At the present, however,
the leadership recruitment, selection, and training processes have
yet to reflect the presence of qualified, and deserving, women cadres.
To this extent, then, the SED has failed to complete the development
of socialism in the GDR.

          2. Cadre problems. The SED depends on the cadre, including
the propagandist, to lend an air of dynamism to the carrying-through
of party programs within the broad society. For this reason, the
recruitment, selection, and training of this subelite represents one
of the most important aspects of socialist construction in the GDR.
While this select group has been able partially to meet the demands
of social and political change that have dramatically transformed
East German society over the last 30 years, various difficulties
continue to plague the performance of the cadre apparatus. A recent
study listed the following areas of official concern: (1) young industrial workers (males) were not being brought into the apparatus in
sufficient number; (2) the recruitment of females for "leading positions"
in the state and economic bureaucracy continued to be inadequate,
(3) leading cadres (perhaps propagandists) had failed to set up an
appropriate cadre-reserve and had, more generally, failed to carry
through an adequate level of cadre-work; (4) of perhaps greatest
significance in terms of long-run developmental goals, leading cadres
had apparently become sloppy in the administration of cadre activities,
had failed to apply appropriately rigorous standards in the "selection"
of new blood. In general, cadre leaders were strongly encouraged to
develop better relations of trust (Vertrauensverhältnisse) between
themselves and the lower rungs of the organization. [93]

          Within the realm of cadre problems, one of the most important,
if not the key, issue revolves around the content and overall design
of the training process. At the outset it should be noted that an
approach to what Marxist/Leninist's call "subjective," or ideological,
factors cannot ignore the obvious difficulties facing Western analysts
in their attempt to fully appreciate and comprehend the impact of
education in a socialist system. Nonetheless, there is some reason
to believe that a gap exists between the SED's conception of political
training—what it should consist of, and what personal results it should

bring about in the thought and behavior patterns of members generally, cadres more particularly—and the empirical result. Thus, in a recent statement, Erich Honecker once again called for a renewed emphasis on cadre education. In his words, "the Politburo views the ideological tempering [Stählung] of the cadre, on the firm foundation of Marxism/ Leninism, as the decisive precondition for the further raising of the Party's battle readiness. Hence, it must be repeated that all levels of the leadership must be aware that further improvements in the education and further training of the cadre at Party schools, study circles, and seminars, demands increased attention."[94] The problem does not lie with Honecker's general concern about the level of cadre education, but with its content. In this vein, the dilemma may lie in the SED's penchant to overorganize, thus bureaucratize, the political socialization process, thereby undermining the degree to which individuals are able to learn emotionally relevant responses from their ideological and political training once they begin to participate within the ranks of the party. In a word, "they've heard it all before," a concern voiced in the following manner:

> Staatsbürgerkunde—civics—has been a source of problems; it has not been very effective as an instrument of sociali- zation. Part of the responsibility must be attributed to the dullness of civics instruction and its repetitiveness. One student told me that he had been through it all so often by the time he had reached the university that it was excruciating to have to continue. The repetitiveness results in part from the fact that the material presented in civics is covered in several other courses permeated by the world view that civics is supposed to impart. Moreover the content of civics courses is frequently so incredibly stereotyped that little sophistication is required to "unmask" them as ridiculous.[95]

In this regard, there is a high probability that ideological training within various levels of the SED's hierarchy tends to overlap, thus adding to the problem of making topical ideological and political prob- lems personally relevant to individuals participating in the educational process.

Because the SED is certainly aware of curricular problems, it would be incorrect to assume that no one is giving serious thought to the further improvement of the training process specifically, and recruitment and selection processes more generally. Nonetheless, there continues to be some question whether the party will be able to develop the kind of activist and revolutionary personality it believes necessary for the construction of socialism in the GDR given the obvious, and unalterable, fact that East Germany has moved away from its revolutionary past.[96] Indeed, the "new" generation may be less revolutionary than the last one. While this possibility does not mean the deterioration of the SED's recruitment, selection, and training processes, it does mean that the regime must continue to meet the challenge of complacency in a society that has come to enjoy a decidedly nonrevolutionary way of life. (In this regard the tendency of the SED to equate "participation" with effective political socialization is especially obvious.) Especially within the realms of political culture (Chapter 2) and political communication (see Chapter 8), the important challenges and opportunities surrounding these processes will be posed and ultimately answered.

NOTES

1. Fundamentals of Marxism-Leninism (Moscow: Foreign Language Publishing House, 1963), p. 175.

2. Ibid., pp. 175-79.

3. Karl Marx and F. Engels, Selected Correspondence (Moscow: Foreign Language Publishing House, 1956), p. 550.

4. Karl Marx and F. Engels, "Letter to W. Blos, 11/10/1877," Selected Works (Moscow: Foreign Language Publishing House, 1955), p. 687.

5. Fundamentals of Marxism-Leninism, op. cit., p. 186.

6. F. Engels, The Peasant War in Germany (New York: International Publishers, 1926), Pref. 2d ed.

7. Karl Marx and F. Engels, Selected Works, Vol. 1 (Moscow: Foreign Language Publishing House, 1962), p. 46.

8. V.I. Lenin, Selected Works, Vol. 1 (Moscow: Foreign Language Publishing House, 1960), p. 230.

9. V.I. Lenin, Selected Works, Vol. 2 (Moscow: Foreign Language Publishing House, 1960), p. 221.

10. V.I. Lenin, "The Urgent Tasks of our Movement," in Collected Works, Vol. 4 (Moscow: Foreign Language Publishing House, 1960), pp. 366-71.

11. V.I. Lenin, "Political Agitation and 'The Class' Point of View," in Collected Works, Vol. 5 (Moscow: Foreign Language Publishing House, 1961), p. 341.

12. V.I. Lenin, "What Is To Be Done?" in Collected Works, Vol. 5, op. cit., p. 425.

13. Ibid.

14. V.I. Lenin, "Left-Wing Communism, an Infantile Disorder," in Selected Works, Vol. 3 (Moscow: Foreign Language Publishing House, 1961), p. 438.

15. Gabriel Almond and James Coleman, The Politics of Developing Areas (Princeton, N.J.: Princeton University Press, 1960), pp. 31-32.

16. Heinz Lippmann, "Zum System der Erziehung und Auswahl sowie des Einsatzes der kommunistischen Kader in der DDR und der BRD" (Cologne: Private Manuscript, 1969), p. 3.

17. Ibid., pp. 3-4.

18. Ibid., pp. 4-5.

19. Wolfgang Leonhard, Child of the Revolution (Chicago: Henry Regnery, 1958), pp. 237-38.

20. John Peter Nettl, The Eastern Zone and Soviet Policy in Germany (New York: Oxford University Press, 1951), pp. 69-70.

21. Dale R. Herspring, East German Civil-Military Relations (New York: Praeger, 1973), p. 44.

22. Thomas Arthur Baylis, "East Germany's Rulers," M.A. thesis, University of California, Berkeley, 1961, pp. 105-06.

23. Ibid., pp. 103-104.

24. Ibid., pp. 105-06.

25. Ibid., p. 110.

26. Heinz Lippmann, Honecker: Porträt eines Nachfolgers (Cologne: Verlag Wissenschaft und Politik, 1971), pp. 144-45.

27. Baylis, op. cit., pp. 153-60.

28. Thomas A. Baylis, "Communist Elites & Industrial Society: The Technical Intelligentsia in East German Politics," Ph.D. dissertation, University of California, Berkeley, 1968, and Ursula Hoffmann, Die Veranderungen in der Sozialstruktur des Ministerrats der DDR 1949-1969 (Dusseldorf: Droste Verlag, 1971).

29. Peter Christian Ludz, The German Democratic Republic from the 60's to the 70's (Cambridge, Mass.: Center For International Affairs, Harvard University, 1970), p. 11.

30. Baylis, "Communist Elites," op. cit., p. 172.

31. Almond and Coleman, op. cit., pp. 31-32.

32. Michael Gehlen, The Communist Party of the Soviet Union: A Functional Analysis (Bloomington: Indiana University Press, 1969), p. 11.

33. Dokumentation, "Die 12. Tagung des ZK der SED (I)," Deutschland Archiv, 8/74, p. 876.

34. Erich Honecker, Protokoll die Verhandlungen des VIII. Parteitages der SED (Berlin: Dietz Verlag, 1971), p. 101.

35. Statut Der Sozialistischen Einheitspartei Deutschlands (Berlin: Dietz Verlag, 1972), p. 19. (Hereafter SED Statute.)

36. Ibid., p. 29.

37. Erich Honecker, Bericht des Zentral Kommittees an den VIII. Parteitag der SED (Berlin: Dietz Verlag, 1971), p. 83.

38. SED Statute, op. cit., pp. 32-33.

39. Gehlen, op. cit., pp. 19-20.

40. Ibid.

41. Peter Christian Ludz, The Changing Party Elite in East Germany (Cambridge, Mass: MIT Press, 1972), pp. 126-27.

42. Ibid., pp. 187-88.

43. Ibid.

44. Ibid., p. 410.

45. Ibid.

46. Dokumentation, "Honecker zur Verfassungsrevision," Deutschland Archiv, 11/74, p. 1227.

47. Ursula Hoffmann, Die Veränderungen in der Sozialstrucktur des Ministerrats de DDR 1949-69, (Dusseldorf: Droste Verlag, 1971).

48. The overlapping of recruitment processes in modern industrial society is a phenomenon known outside of the GDR. See C.W. Mills, The Power Elite (New York: Oxford University Press, 1957).

49. Hoffmann, op. cit., 69-70.

50. Honecker, Protokoll die Verhandlungen, op. cit., pp. 99-100.

51. Hermann Weber, Von SBZ zur DDR (Hannover: Verlag für Literatur und Zeitgeschehen, 1968), p. 214; and Ernst Richert, Die DDR Elite (Hamburg: Rowholt Verlag, 1968).

52. Baylis, "Communist Elites," op. cit., p. 14.

53. Ludz, The Changing Party Elite, op. cit., p. 412.

54. Ibid., pp. 35-43.

55. Kleines Politisches Wörterbuch (Berlin: Dietz Verlag, 1973), p. 389.

56. Honecker, Protokoll die Verhandlungen, op. cit., p. 100.

57. Günther Liebe, Entwicklung von Nachwuchskadern für die ortlichen Staatsorgane (Staatsverlag, 1973), p. 61.

58. Ibid., pp. 28-32.

59. Der Parteiarbeiter: Handmaterial für den Parteisekretär (Berlin: Dietz Verlag, 1972), p. 109.

60. Ibid., pp. 110-11.

61. Ibid., p. 108.

62. Erich Honecker, "Interview zu dem Begin der Parteiwahlen," in Neues Deutschland, 1/11/73.

63. Heinz Lippmann, Die SED Parteiwahlen als Instrument der Abgrenzung und innenpolitischen Festigung (Bonn: Gesamtdeutsches Institüt, 28/11/73).

64. "die Wahldirektive des ZK der SED," Neuer Weg, 15/73, pp. 693-700.

65. Ibid., pp. 698-99.

66. Erich Honecker, op. cit.

67. "Wenig personelle Veränderungen in den Sekretariaten bei den Kreis und Bezirkswahlen" (Bonn: Bundesminister für innerdeutsche Beziehungen, 2/74.

68. Der Parteiarbeiter: Aufgaben und Erfahrungen der Partei- und Massenpropaganda nach dem VIII. Parteig der SED (Berlin: Dietz Verlag, 1972), p. 83.

69. Ibid., p. 77.

70. Ibid., p. 80.

71. Lippmann, "Zum System der Erziehung und Auswahl," op. cit., p. 29.

72. Der Parteiarbeiter: Hand material für den Parteisekretär, op. cit., p. 107.

73. Honecker, Protokoll die Verhandlungen, op. cit., p. 107.

74. Der Parteiarbeiter: Handmaterial für den parteisekretär, op. cit., p. 106.

75. Lippmann, "Zum System der Erziehung und Auswahl," op. cit., p. 32.

76. Der Parteiarbeiter: Aufgaben und Erfahrungen, op. cit., p. 85.

77. Ibid., p. 88.

78. Ibid.

79. "Langfristige Aus- und Weiterbildung der Propagandisten," pp. 21-22 in Was und Wie: Methodischer Ratschlag für Agitatoren und Propagandisten, Heft, 2/73.

80. Der Parteiarbeiter: Handmaterial für den Parteisekretär, op. cit., p. 50.

81. Ibid. p. 20.

82. Studienmaterial für die marxistisch-leninistische Schulg der Kandidaten der SED: Parteilehrjahr der SED 1972/73 (Berlin: Dietz Verlag, 1972).

83. Ibid., pp. 269-71.

84. Ibid., p. 248.

85. Der Parteiarbeiter: Aufgaben und Erfahrungen, op. cit., p. 33.

86. Gabriel Almond and G. Bingham Powell, Comparative Politics (Boston: Little, Brown, 1966), p. 35.

87. Heinz Lippmann, Honecker, trans. Helen Sebba (New York: Macmillan, 1972), p. 217.

88. Erich Honecker, Zügig voran bei der weiteren Verwirklichung der Beschlüsse des VIII. Parteitages der SED (Berlin: Dietz Verlag, 1973), pp. 62-63.

89. Lippmann, Honecker, op. cit., p. 226.

90. Heinz Lippmann, "Die personellen Veränderungen in den Machtzentren der SED als Ausdruck kollektiver Führung," Deutschland Archiv, 12/73, p. 1267.

91. Staats- und Parteiapparat der DDR (August, 1974) (Bonn), pp. 26-29.

92. "Wenig personelle Veränderungen in den Sekretariaten bei den Kreis- und Bezirkswahlen der SED," Informationen (Bonn: Bundesminister für innerdeutsche Beziehuggen, No. 5, 1974), p. 11.

93. Rudolf Schwarzenback remarks on Edition 8 of Staat und Recht in Deutschland Archiv, 11/74, p. 1143.

94. Erich Honecker, "Aus dem Bericht des Politbüros an die 13 Tagung des Zentralkomitees der SED," Neues Deutschland, 12/13/74, p. 8.

95. Arthur M. Hanhardt, Jr., "Political Socialization in the German Democratic Republic," a paper delivered at the 1970 Annual Meeting of the American Political Science Association, Los Angeles, September 1970, pp. 34-35.

96. Note Honecker's continual underlining of "intellectual" activism when speaking about the future behavior of cadres. See Honecker, "Aus dem Bericht," op. cit., p. 8.

4

INTEREST
IDENTIFICATION
AND AGGREGATION

THEORETICAL FRAMEWORK

Marxism/Leninism

Proceeding from the theoretical assumption that the organization of the working class, that is, the Communist party, represents the "real" interests of the people as a whole, Marxist/Leninists traditionally have regarded so-called interest groups negatively. Theorists denied the possibility of fundamental conflicts of interest within the society—thus "interest groups" did not exist. The party could, and should, speak for all.

While "fundamental," that is, "antagonistic contradictions," would disappear from socialist society, this was not held by Lenin to be the same as "nonantagonistic contradictions." Those, indeed, would remain under socialism. Thus, for instance, an antagonistic contradiction, such as that between the proletariat and the capitalists, would disappear; but a contradiction such as between the niveau of the countryside as opposed to the city would remain for some time.

Since about the 1950s, however, a debate has developed in the Soviet Union, and so spilled over into Eastern Europe, concerning the definition of such "antagonistic" and "nonantagonistic" contradictions. Within the context of this discussion, it generally has been conceded that divergent opinions and conflicting interests do indeed exist and are to be taken into account by the party. Further, some groups have been permitted to express their special opinions and interests, of course within the limitations of the concept of "the leading role of the party."[1]

It is significant, therefore, to find the following discussion of
interests published in Moscow in 1972 and in the GDR in 1973:

> The fact that the basic interest of all social groups and
> social cells of the socialist society are the same does
> not exclude differences between their specific group
> interests and personal interests. The productive forces
> and production relationships of the communist formation
> in their first development phases—under the conditions of
> socialism—have not yet reached such a degree of maturity
> that there no longer would be grounds for disagreement
> between the personal interest of individuals, between
> group interests (the specific interest of various social
> groups or various collectives), and the interests of the
> total society.
>
> In other words: the social analysis of society must
> also advance to the individual strata [Schichten] or groups
> which exist within the class context. Be their peculiarities
> more or less defined, they in no case may be ignored and
> may not remain disregarded. Since the socialist society
> knows no antagonistic contradiction between classes, it
> is of special importance that the ways of life of the groups
> and strata within a class, their relations to each other,
> their peculiarities, etc., be attentively followed and in
> connection to their growing proximity to classes, be
> constantly analyzed.

The varying interests, says the Soviet author, are characteristics of (1) production branches (differences between industry,
agriculture, construction, transportation, defense, education, administration, science, art, regarding resource allocation), (2) professions
(criterion for performance and, therefore, wages), (3) nationality,
(4) territory or region, and (5) psychology (sex, age, health). These,
in the opinion of the author, are "the basic characteristics on the
basis of which the social groups, or more precisely said the social
levels (Schichten) can be divided. What is involved is that the concept
'group' has greater stability, clearer limitations, and indicates
definite interests and, therefore, is closer to the concept of 'class.'"
An analysis of such social interests is "extraordinarily complicated,"
says Schachnasarow, stressing the issue-orientation of many interest
groups:

> Only in the rarest cases are we concerned with a
> completely clearly defined social strata [Schichten]
> which unanimously makes known its specific interest.

In the predominant number of cases the social strata
have no definite limits. Frequently they form themselves around and group themselves around newly
arisen interests—including only for a definite period
of time.

In addition, there are examples that a social strata
at first exists only as a potential. It "rests" as long as
it remains untouched by the not yet conscious general
interest. However, if it unexpectedly is touched by
economic or social processes, then this strata "awakens"
and surely engages itself with it [the general interest].[2]

A Polish contribution to this discussion goes much further. It
says there are different interests among classes, social levels,
groups, and persons concerning national resource allocation:
"Especially in the phase of industrialization contradictions clearly
appear between consumption and accumulation."[3] Further, the
party's task of aggregating those interests is also seen as admittedly
difficult by party theoreticians:

It certainly is difficult to analyze exactly the interests of
social strata—how much more complicated it is for Party
and state power to coordinate these interests and in their
decisions to have to make a selection among equally
founded, legitimate, and justified interests.

If it concerns measures which influence the material
condition of people in two significantly similar social
strata, the decision will depend on two factors: which
strata needs such measures soonest and which strata
deserves precedence in view of usefulness to the total
society. To answer these questions is not easy, but
nevertheless significantly easier than the solution of
many tasks in the practice of government.

The state budget, after all, is decided only once a
year. But problems which concern the coordination of
social interest must be solved daily and hourly, for today
and in view of the coming years and occasionally also for
a decade. . . . On what are all these decisions based? . . .
Every decision demands above all a firm scientific
basis—scientifically founded, factual, realistic analysis
of the problem, with consideration of all the factors
which we today can identify and assess through social
sciences. . . . However, this politics itself can be the
concern only of a political organization which the society
entrusts with leading the country and which enjoys a high

authority in the working class, the collective farmers,
the intelligentsia—a concern of the Communist Party.[4]

In addition to comprehending the party's view of interests, it
also is necessary to understand the Marxist/Leninist theory of communications (communications used in the broadest contemporary
sense, not as Lenin conceived of it as primarily "press") and the
role it plays in the function of interest articulation/identification and
aggregation. And that theory about how the mass media shall operate
in socialist societies is very specific.

According to Marxism/Leninism, the transition from capitalism
to socialism is a gradual process. While the economic change from
a capitalist to socialist system is being made on one level, the social
transition from spontaneous development (under capitalism) to conscious guiding of progress is being made simultaneously at other
levels. The revolutionary party is the only institution that can carry
out this conscious guiding of social progress, that is, the accumulation and sorting out of demands and claims. The party has this
responsibility because, as the conscious, progressive, and organized
front ranks of the working class and working people, it presumably
knows the objective developmental laws of the society. From this
knowledge it deduces its claim to leadership, that is, interest aggregation.

Further, according to the concept of the party, the masses have
a need for constant education and persuasion regarding their interests,
even in the socialist phase that precedes the realization of a communist society. The need for this constant education arises because
the socialist consciousness does not develop spontaneously and simultaneously just because the economic production relationships have
been changed from capitalist to socialist. Further, socialist consciousness does not develop equally in all social groups, and progressive forces are opposed by residual ones. (The superstructure
lags behind the base.) Additionally, bourgeois influences on demands
and interests continue to penetrate from the outside, as well as to
exist among parts of the population inside the system. However, even
if this unevenness did not exist, the process of developing consciousness would never be complete, for social development is a never-
ending process. Therefore, in this long process of developing consciousness, the party feels the people need the permanent educational
and persuasive work of the party in order to be able to fulfill their
social tasks.

Since the people have to be constantly educated, schooled, led,
and controlled, the party has concluded that the mass communications
media are a decisive instrument for instruction. The mass media,
therefore, are not to be private property, but rather collective organs

of the party, the mass organizations, or social institutions that are
working to realize a socialist/communist social order.

According to Lenin, within this context the media are collective
propagandists, agitators, and organizers. As propagandists, the
media shall disseminate Marxism/Leninism among all groups of the
population as a context for their demands and claims; as agitators
they shall mobilize people for the fulfillment of party-set goals arising
from the aggregation of interests; as organizers they are to lead and
control the political, economic, and cultural interests given priority
by the party. Thus, information disseminated by the mass media is
selected on the basis of how it furthers these three major tasks as
the party sees them at a given point in time. (Just to report "news"
is inadequate—it must have relevance to the current situation and
phase of social development, that is, be agitation through deeds.)

Functional

According to functionalists, "the process by which individuals
and groups make demands upon the political decision-makers we call
interest articulation." Such a process exists in every political system
because

> Political decisions involve advantage or disadvantage
> for various individuals and groups in the society,
> including the political elites themselves. Some sort
> of demands, even if only individual goals or desires,
> or even if stemming predominantly from the elites
> themselves must be brought to the attention of the
> decision makers to form the basis for political choice.[5]

So-called authoritarian systems are not an exception in this process,
for "there will probably be some amount of group activity, and
therefore some degree of pluralism, in any political system."

However, the process in communist systems will "differ pro-
foundly with regard to the types of political groups present and active,
their nature and strength, their relationship with each other, and
their correlation with leadership. They will, that is, vary in the
degree and kind of political pluralism present in each of them. A
Communist system, it may be assumed, will never be fully totalitarian,
nor will it be fully pluralist."[6]

Furthermore, while some Western specialists argue that
Communist parties in the post-Stalin period had to give more attention to competing policy views, others point out that within every

Communist party there always has been serious conflict regarding
policy—when it did burst into the open it usually was identified with
leading personalities and was seen in the West as a "personal power
struggle," rather than also an "issue conflict." Thus, the "interest"
approach provides the observer with a means for getting beyond such
purely personalized politics and for understanding the issues crucial
to a communist political system in its various stages of development.

In short, it may be suggested about all communist political
systems, as about the Soviet system, that

> politics has always been characterized by group conflict,
> but that the conflict has differed in successive periods in
> the relative importance and influence of particular groups,
> in the size and composition of the groups themselves, in
> their style and methods of action, in the degree of oppor-
> tunity for overt articulation, and in their ability to exert
> an influence on the course of politics.[7]

Thus while functionalist specialists in communist affairs do not
assume that interest groups are the principle feature of the communist
system—rather, the leadership—they do, however, agree that political
interest groups are an important element that cannot be overlooked.

Within this context, the functionalists apply the following definitions:

1. Interest Group: "A group of individuals who are linked by
particular bonds of concern or advantage, and who have some awareness of these bonds."[8]

2. Political Interest Group: An aggregation of persons who
possess certain common characteristics and share certain attitudes
on public issues, and who adopt distinct positions on these issues
and make definite claims on those in authority.[9] In short, political
interest groups in communist political systems are made up of
specialist elites who have group self-consciousness (are conscious
of themselves as a distinct entity), who are ascribed group status
(are perceived as groups by other elites), and who possess a set of
shared values (which distinguishes them from other elites).[10]

3. Interest: "An expressed attitude on the matters of concern
. . . an articulated claim for some kind of public action in this
respect."[11]

4. Political Articulation: "An act of communication in which
an expectation about the authoritative allocation of a value or set
of values is conveyed by one political participant to another. For
articulation to occur, the expectation transmitted must also be
received in some form."[12]

Further, according to functionalists, the process of interest articulation involves different <u>types of groups</u> and <u>types of access channels</u>. According to Almond, for instance, there are (1) anomic interest groups who more or less spontaneously penetrate the political system through riots, demonstrations, assassinations, etc., (2) non-associational interest groups, such as kinship/lineage, ethnic, regional, status, and class groups who articulate their interests intermittently, but lack continuity and organized procedures, primarily through personal connections, (3) institutional interest groups, such as political parties, legislatures, armies, bureaucracies, churches, etc., who have formal organizations and use primarily the access channel of elite representation, and (4) associational interest groups, such as trade unions, organizations of businessmen or industrialists, ethnic associations, religious associations, and civic groups who rely on formal and institutional access channels. [13]

Applying this context to communist political systems, especially to the Soviet system, functionalists have found that interest articulation takes place primarily through institutional interest groups who use the informal techniques of personal connection and elite representation. [14] Influence is brought to bear by communicating expert judgments to top-level leaders who, in turn, can influence decision-making. [15] While groups such as the police, military, and "apparatchiki" have been institutionalized as government or party agencies, others have used informal procedures such as conferences and communications media. This indirect approach to policy-makers has involved open debate on questions such as cultural policy, economic or legal reforms, or military strategy. The debate is designed to affect public opinion, especially of relevant groups. Such debate takes place

> mainly in the conferences and the publications of
> professional and scholarly associations, and in the
> newspapers and magazines generally . . . in the
> specialized publications of scholars. . . . Letters to
> the newspapers and speeches on public occasions also
> play a significant role. Although the party's monopoly
> of the media of communication and the normally one-
> directional nature of communications set severe limits
> on freedom of expression, this has not prevented sharp
> confrontations of conflicting opinions, sometimes quite
> openly, sometimes in veiled and Aesopian form.

In short, "whether organized or not, group action usually takes the form of statements or deeds of a few outstanding individuals, who arrogate to themselves the authority to express group interests and

are not selected by or authorized to act for the group."[16] While
articulation itself does not guarantee success, as Almond cautions,
on the other hand "to fail to gain articulation even through sympathetic
elite members is to forego any chance of shaping political decisions."[1]

At the same time it generally is the assumption of Western
functional specialists that major decision-making power remains in
the hands of a few top leaders and that "the making of policy is not
the automatic result of the pressures and counterpressures of rival
groups. Decisions may be made by the ruling elite, on their own
initiative, without reference to group pressures, or in defiance of
the attitudes expressed by important groups. Leaders may also
manipulate the elite groups, using them in their own struggle for
power and controversies over policy." Thus it is the Politburo that
is seen as the target of interest groups within communist political
systems, for that is where the power of ultimate decision-making
lies. Logically, then, pressure is brought to bear on party and
state administrative agencies, for they, in turn, influence the top
leaders.[18]

Within communist societies, therefore, the key political interest
groups are felt to include (1) the leadership group or factions that
play key decision-making roles, (2) official or bureaucratic groups,
such as the party apparatchiki, state bureaucrats, and managers who
have close contact to the top group, (3) the intellectual groups—
writers, journalists, scientists, economists, scholars—who have
influence because of their expertise, (4) broad social groups, such
as workers, farmers, nationalities, and religious groups who lack
expertise and direct access to decision-makers, or communications
media.[19]

These, then, are the groups within the GDR context that will
be surveyed briefly. They will be described in terms of issues and
influence channels, without attempting to assess their effectiveness.

The gathering together of the demands of such groups and their
conversion into policies occurs in all political systems—it is known
to functionalists as the process of "interest aggregation." Aggregation
may be achieved "by means of the formulation of general policies in
which interests are combined, accomodated or otherwise taken account
of, or by means of the recruitment of political personnel, more or
less committed to a particular pattern of policy."[20] In other words,
the function of interest aggregation is to accumulate and compromise
the interest claims introduced through interest articulation. Different
party systems obviously have different aggregating processes.

In a communist political system, this occurs through the party
structure based on the theory of the party's "leading role." Or, as
Almond says, in a centralized political system, the aggregation
process may be managed successfully by a small elite, or ruling

party, "in a manner similar to that of a large bureaucracy."[21] Thus, structures and organizations close to the party and state are important vehicles of interest aggregation, as will be seen.

Within this functional context of interest articulation and aggregation, special attention must be paid to the mass media, for, as has been noted, the entire communications network is at the disposal of the party. Furthermore, since a communist political system sees itself as a revolutionary sociopolitical entity evolving over time, it seems reasonable to view the communications structure within a developmental context. For instance, in linking communications and politics within a developmental framework, the functional political roles of communications may be seen as:

1. Establishment of order—helping to organize vast numbers of random actions that make up men's pursuit of power in a society (politics) into relationships viewed as being acceptable parts of a new social process.

2. Amplification of man-sized to society-sized acts—placing individual actions into a perspective that enhances national development by showing that what the individual does is important to economic/ political development.

3. Provision of the essential basis for rationality and standards— making available and understandable a common fund of knowledge and information needed for sensible debate of collective actions and for judging the wisdom and validity of leaders and their actions.

4. Establishment of a common framework regarding consideration of the future.

In other words, communications assists a revolutionary society to establish new rules of political causality and to define the realm of plausible demands. Thus, it is suggested that "the basic processes of political modernization and national development can be advantageously conceived of as problems in communication."[22] Further, and especially relevant to newly established communist systems, communications essentially can be seen as acting to establish a climate in which economic and social development of a country can take place. Communications can, for instance, (1) create the idea of "nation-ness" and counter centrifugal tendencies, (2) implant and extend the idea of change so the aspirations of the people would be raised, (3) teach the new skills necessary to achieve the desired changes, and (4) act to guide and control the process of change.[23] This perspective of (a) seeing communications as an integral factor in the economic and political development, or modernization, of a nation, and (b) viewing communist societies as nations in varying stages of the process of modernization, gives communications a new context. Rather than being seen only, or chiefly, as a means of maintaining the Communist party in power, as was the view of the so-called totalitarian model, communications can be seen from this point of view as an instrument of modernization or nation-building, as an effective tool of the interest articulation/aggregation process.

Thus in the early phases of national integration, following the revolution, the mass media concentrate on information to the people— to convey political authority and to create political consciousness and identity. In short, the media reflect the party. When the common identification has been largely achieved, as the party sees it, the media also begin to reflect society—that is, to serve as a forum of interest identification, or information from the people. At this stage the party can begin to use the mass media as a means of accumulating the demands and claims of the various interest groups.

SITUATION IN THE GDR

As noted above, the role of interest groups in traditional Marxism/Leninism was a negative one, overshadowed by the leading role accorded to the party. This same development is found in the GDR. For instance, the SED's party Statutes leave no question about the leading role of the party:

> The Party is the leading force and in unity guides the total social life of the Republic. It is responsible for the total complex of political-ideological, scientific, technical, economic, and cultural work. This political leadership consists above all of working out scientifically founded policies, goal-oriented scientific leadership, and coordination of all state and social forces toward a united execution of the tasks of the comprehensive construction of socialism, as well as control over fulfillment of resolutions. [24]

And as SED chief Honecker said in 1971, "the more comprehensive the socialist construction . . . the greater the role and responsibility of the Party." [25]

This principle, as will be seen, is also anchored in the Constitution of the GDR and in its laws, as well as in the party's statutes and programs. Furthermore, in all the statutes of the state organs, the party's decision-making authority is underlined, as well as in the mass and social organizations.

Until recently the existence of conflicts between the party's interpretation of social needs and those of the citizenry was largely denied.

But in recent years in the GDR the subject of interests, the conflict between them, and the party's role in aggregating those interests has been of great interest. For instance, the GDR called specifically upon its social scientists to engage in a more creative, open discussion, especially through professional journals, of problems facing the society.[26] Their research should concern, "stronger than previously," the "real processes of social life, including the concrete working and living conditions and the contradictions in the establishment of the developed socialist society."[26]

And so the discussion, especially of "social contradictions," has gone forward. The forums for the discussion were primarily the journals Deutsche Zeitschrift für Philosophie, Forum, Wirtschaftswissenschaft, and Sinn und Form. As noted for the Soviet context, the view of previous years that contradictions did not exist in the socialist society was set aside—contradictions now were seen as unavoidable, natural characteristics of the socialist phase of a society on the way to communism:

> Today there no longer are antagonistic classes in the
> GDR. Exploitation of people by people is overcome;
> socialist production relations have been victorious.
> Yet among the still existing classes and strata [Schichten]
> there are differences and definitely differentiated interests.
> As long as there are such differences, the leadership of
> the society must be exercised through one class; and that
> can, in the total process of the construction of the socialist
> society, only be the working class with the power of its
> historic mission, and its Party.[28]

There are, of course, differing views in the ongoing discussion. Some GDR writers express the view that the antagonistic contradictions are the result of a class society and when all the class differences (in the Marxist sense) are overcome in the GDR, the antagonisms will disappear. Others, however, say that the capitalist legacy causes contradictions in socialism that are antagonistic or could become antagonistic. What is especially interesting, however, as careful observers of the GDR press point out, is that there is elbow room for open discussion and controversy in the press concerning whether or not contradictions are antagonistic or nonantagonistic. Further, regardless of which kind they are, they no longer are seen as elements disturbing a priori harmonious social development. Rather, they are seen as "systemimmanent" (systemically determined), which the state and Party must deal with.[29] Much of the open discussion in recent years concerning whether new dramas and movies and books are "good" or not centers around this question of how the artistic work

deals with the conflicts, the contradictions, of present-day life in the
GDR and the citizenry's right to comment and criticize through various
channels of interest articulation.

One of the interesting results of the interplay between (1) the
theoretical discussion over conflicting interests within the socialist
society and (2) the practical situation in the GDR of increasing consumer demands, has been the attempt to define for the public what
the legitimate demands of the various groups may include and how
the party will aggregate those demands. Thus, for instance, the
discussion often centers around the differences between Bedarf
(material needs) and Bedürfnisse (nonmaterial needs).[30] Within this
context, the party secretary responsible for agitation and propaganda,
Werner Lamberz, gave the following explanation:

> But already there arises the question, what are "the"
> needs of "the" workers? Doesn't every person, every
> group of workers, have really quite different wishes
> and expectations regarding the improvement of the
> niveau of life? The basic orientation exists: In the first
> place we are concerned with the needs of the leading
> class of our society, the working class; but that does
> not mean that the needs of other classes and strata
> [Schichten] are considered unimportant. The working
> class is the most conscious and revolutionary part of
> our population, and it constitutes a majority. Its needs
> are in many respects signposts for all workers. That
> results because the interests of the working class
> simultaneously express the interests of all workers,
> that the qualitative characteristics of the leading class
> increasingly influence the character of the total society.
> It is the workers in whom the need for peace has
> been implanted most deeply because of their class
> situation and historical experiences and whose need
> for developed socialist relationships always drives the
> tempo of things forward.

Thus Lamberz made it clear that the interests of the workers would
be met first. But which interests? To this he said:

> Therefore when we here speak of needs which arise
> from society itself, we mean the socialist society on
> its way to its mature phase of development. We have
> to keep in view the aim to satisfy and develop exactly
> those needs which have arisen from this our society.
> Then naturally there also arise daily spontaneous needs

in our life which do not originate in the socialist society, but rather have their origins in the bourgeois tradition and oppositional influences. For their satisfaction we have exactly as little interest as for their stimulation. [31]

Groups singled out by the GDR as "representing the specific interests" of "the differing population schichts (levels)" in the present phase of socialist construction were the trade unions, youth and women's organizations, cultural and sports organizations, scientific and technical societies. [32] Thus, for instance, sociological research has been undertaken concerning the situation of women (as a specific social group) who either study or are working. [33]

INTEREST ARTICULATORS: ACCESS, CHANNELS, ISSUES

Party Leadership

Clearly one of the major demands of the SED leadership, as for any political leadership group, is that of maintaining the power of the system. Not only are most leaders convinced of its ideological "rightness," but it is the basis of their personal power (defined here primarily as sociopolitical influence and material gain).

Although the demands of the party leadership (beyond system maintenance) are not clearly discernible, as far as can be ascertained there seems to be a general demand "to get the society moving again." Socialized to revolutionary concepts, and wedded to the concept that social change is possible through centralized leadership and planning, party leaders apparently experience the frustration of persons once they are in power—so much effort is demanded by pure administrative duties that the possibilities for innovation are limited. This perhaps explains the repeated demand of party leaders on themselves for more and more education, application of science, and general involvement.

In terms of education, the 16 full Politburo members have completed the following:

- 1 University degree: Mittag (economics)
- 3 Party University (Parteihochschule) programs: Honecker (CPSU), Lamberz (Komsomol School, Moscow), Mückenberg (SED)
- 1 Advanced military school: Hoffmann (Moscow)

2 Abitur degrees (classical German high school diploma for
university admittance): Hager, Norden

4 high school (Realgymnasium, Oberrealschule, Mittelschule):
Axen, Ebert, Sindermann, Verner

5 grammar school: Grüneberg, Krolikowski, Neumann, Stoph,
Warnke

The candidate members' education has been:

1 university degree: Jarowinsky (economics)

2 technical university diplomas: Kleiber, Felfe (engineering)

6 Party University diplomas: Lange, Müller, Tisch (SED,
in social science), Schürer (CPSU, social science), Naumann
(Komsomol School, Moscow, teaching)

2 high school: Hermann, Mielke

In terms of specific interests represented by Politburo members,
some clues may be found in their areas of specialization. Of the 26
members (16 full, 10 candidates), the "all-around politicians," with
experience at the central and regional levels and general responsibility in the Politburo, number 10: Honecker, Stoph, Sindermann,
Neumann, Tisch, Felfe, Ebert, Warnke, Müller, and Naumann.
Those representing economic functional specialization total 5:
Brüneberg (agriculture), Schürer (planning), Jarowinsky (trade and
supplies), Kleiber (machine and vehicle construction), and possibly
Krolikowski (who is believed to have taken over the position of secretary for economics formerly held by Politburo member Günter
Mittag, an economist). Three Politburo members are specialists for
security (Verner, Mielke, Hoffmann), 1 for foreign policy (Axen), 1
for science culture, and ideology (Hager), 3 for agitation and propaganda (Norden, Lamberz, Herrmann), 1 for women's affairs (Lange),
and 1 for party control (Mückenberger).[34]

Official/Bureaucratic

Below the top party leaders are the official or bureaucratic
groups. They may themselves constitute an interest group. In fact,
it long has been contended by critics of the communist political system that this group, seen monolithically as the "new class," was the
group that counted most in a communist society. Being close to those
in power, and themselves having the power leverage that comes from
being part of the governing process, it was felt that they could and
did make their own interests prevail. And it was presumed that this
interest was primarily that of supporting the political structures that
they had learned to use and that gave them influence and prestige

within the society. If political factions evolved within this official or bureaucratic group, they were thought to be motivated by the wish for increased power or power maintenance.

Now, however, some specialists believe that factions often are a matter of institutional relationships. That is, a kind of "alumni spirit" may have evolved among the increasingly educated official/ bureaucratic group that motivates many of them to identify primarily with others who have studied at the same school, under the same professor, or worked in the same research institute. Other specialists, however, believe such ties are not too important because of the "nominally common ideology" that the political (and economic) elite share—that is, elites usually are members of the SED, have been and are exposed to a never-ending process of socialization, are recruited from above (a value-conservatizing recruitment system), and enjoy career continuity (though the party personnel system favors frequent position changes). [35]

In addition to generally representing its own interests (be they power or institutional relationships), the official/bureaucratic group also represents specific departmental or ministerial functional interests. For instance, the state Ministry of Culture logically would represent the demands of the literary community; the State Planning Commission, those of the managers and planners; the Ministry of Defense, those of the military leaders. Furthermore, Agitprop, the party's communications department, logically would have to take into account the interests channeled to it from the Ministry of Culture; the party's Central Committee Secretary for Security would have to take up the interests coming to him from the Ministry of Defense; and the party's Secretary for Economics the interests of the State Planning Council.

Party Apparat

The party's 195,000 functionaries who work within state or Party institutions, [36] have logical channels of access to the top echelons of decision-making of the party. And there they usually have good connections, for many top-level leaders once were apparat men themselves. Party chief Eric Honecker, for instance, spent years running the party organization and its personnel policies as Central Committee Secretary for Party Organs and Cadre Questions.

One of the common interests that ties these "apparatchiki," or official functionaries of the party, together as an interest group is that of adherence to certain political principles, such as that of the one-party system. While that is true, on the other hand the related assumption that the functionaries therefore also have a mutual interest in defending the top leader has been shown to be questionable—

there is always the possibility that the party apparat would oppose
a first secretary who kept too much power for himself because that
would leave less power to lower-level party functionaries.

Aside from the common interests, there are many diverging
interests and opinions within the apparat itself. Not surprisingly,
for instance, criteria of age, education, experience, and department
of employment result in varying opinions. Not only are there conflicts
between the specialists in the central and in the local secretariats,
but also within these branches themselves. Specialized party officials,
for instance, may frequently clash with strictly administrative party
functionaries. Young apparat men, while advocating just as selfishly
as the "old-timers" maintenance of the one-party system and the
leading role of the party that secures their positions, may, because
of relatively more education and specialization, also favor certain
reforms. In addition, those at the lowest level, in contrast to those
at the top, may be for economic decentralization, since it would
increase their influence. Further, since they are in close contact
with their geographic areas, those at the bottom may have other
priorities, as for example more investment in agriculture, or in
consumer goods, or housing.

On the other hand, if apparat men are at the top of the hierarchy,
functioning in a control capacity for state ministries, they may support
ministerial priorities. This identity develops through frequent and
close contact between the party and state personnel involved in a
particular branch of the economy. For instance, officials of the Central Committee and other party functionaries attend meetings of
ministries and probably also work together to formulate major decisions, along with scientific and academic specialists. Thus, at resource allocation time such party functionaries will favor development
of the industrial branch for which they are responsible, and thus may
conflict with other functionaries responsible for branches competing
for the funds.

Thus the party faces the problem of diverging interests within
its own ranks. But since the party needs functional experts, it no
longer can insist on ideological "purity" alone, although that might
make its job of administration easier. And, further, it has produced
many of these specialists itself within the apparat's academic institutes, such as the Central Committee's Institute for Social Sciences
and the Central Institute for Socialist Economic Management. Thus
it is clear that the party faces continuing diverging interests within
its apparat. In addition to the usual organizational channels for
expressing these interests, the party apparat also has its communication channels for interest articulation. The major one is Neuer Weg,
a monthly magazine published by the Central Committee for Questions
of Party Life.

Some clues as to the interests represented within the party apparat may be found in statistics concerning the Central Committee:

1. Age. According to analyses of the Central Committee, it was found that increasingly younger specialists were recruited into the party's top levels. For instance, from 1954 to 1967 the number of Central Committee members (full and candidate members) between the ages of 30 to 50 rose significantly.[37] But after the VIII Party Congress of 1971 the trend to youthfulness slowed a bit—a total of 113 members (69 full and 44 candidate members) out of the total Central Committee of 189 members (135 full, 54 candidates) were between the ages of 30 to 50, or nearly 60 percent.

2. Professionalization. In the Central Committee in 1971 some 120 members (84 full, 45 candidates), or 68 percent, had completed university or trade school educations (contrasted to 61 percent in 1967).

3. Functions. Of the 189 members of the Central Committee, 72 represented the so-called party apparat, that is, the Secretariat, its departments, regional functionaries, and institutes. (Here it is interesting to note that the directors of the Central Committee's Institute for Marxism-Leninism, Institute for Social Sciences, the Party School, and the Institute for Opinion Research were represented, but not the Central Institute for Socialist Economic Management.) In addition, 50 members of the Central Committee represented the state apparat, including 27 members of the Minister Council (out of a total of 41). (Of the 50 state apparat representatives, 35 have university or technical school educations, and nearly half of them are younger than 50.) Among the 50 state representatives in the 1971 Central Committee are 13, all with higher education, who are among the country's management leaders, from VVBs (Volks Vereinigte Betriebes, large industrial combines) and VEBs. (The average age of these representatives of the economic sector is 43.) One of them is the general director of a VVB (out of a total of 90 such directors) and 6 are directors of Kombinats. In addition, 15 Central Committee members represent mass organizations (18 for science and culture and 13 for local level affairs), and 8 are so-called party veterans.[38]

State Bureaucracies

As in the case of party functionaries, functional interests are among the primary demands of state bureaucrats. Thus, interest group articulation can be expected to reflect the professional status of their ministerial and official functions. For instance, about 79 percent of the top state functionaries (state secretaries, chief section directors, and section directors) had university, college, or professional school backgrounds in 1963. In that same year, 57 percent of the executives in the central state apparat had this type of education (a significant increase over the 38 percent in 1958).[39]

This increasing specialization of state bureaucrats is demonstrated by another study. It was found, for instance, that the number of area chiefs (Fachressortchefs) within the Minister Council who were specialists in their fields increased from 30 percent in 1961 to 79 percent by the end of 1969. These were persons who had completed a trade school or university education. Clearly, then, functional expertise, especially in the technical-scientific and social-sciences fields is increasing,[40] and, one may assume, professionally motivated interest articulation as well. On the other hand, however, the fact that two of the top economists in the state apparat—the chairmen of the State Planning Commission and of the Agricultural Council—do not have specialized training might indicate that the party leadership is still reluctant to turn the important area of domestic economics over to experts.

That which has been suggested about party apparat functionaries and their interests in keeping and enlarging present positions of power logically would apply also to state bureaucrats. As seems endemic in such hierarchical structures, change is seen as threatening and so maintenance of the status quo has top priority.

One of the major channels of interest articulation for state bureaucrats at the regional level is the publication Stadt und Gemeinde. In addition, various ministries have their own publications, as for instance, Kooperation, the magazine for agricultural and foodstuff production; Deutsche Leherzeitung, published by the Ministry for Education; and Neue Justiz, published by the Supreme Court of the GDR.

Managers

One of the issues on which the GDR's managers can logically be expected to express their views is the old question of economic centralization versus decentralization, as well as the priorities accorded heavy industry, light industry, and agriculture. As in other communist countries, past periods of forced industrialization probably made GDR managers more supply-oriented, whereas now, with increased economic development and consumer articulation, their priorities may reflect demands more.

As a result, there seems to be some conflict within the manager group between the "old-timers," who still think primarily in terms of meeting quotas, and junior members, who also may think in terms of meeting needs and demands. On the other hand, this difference probably to a large extent has been overcome by programs of continued education for older hands.

Although in communist political systems managers as a group do not have access to the Politburo, they are believed increasingly to have elite representation. For instance, Politburo member Günter Mittag was held to be spokesman for the production priorities of the younger managers as long as he was Central Committee Secretary for Economics. Now Gerhard Schürer, State Planning Commission chief, who became a candidate member of the Politburo in October 1973, is thought to fill this role. This personnel change could be seen as significant since the managers receive their "guidance" through the Planning Commission and, logically, therefore have access to it.

Also logical seems to be the suggestion that the managers' demands to the Planning Commission probably include proposals for greater enterprise autonomy (or less "direction" from ministry and party) and demands for greater participation in decision-making generally. Logical too, from well-trained managers, would be demands for accelerated application of expertise and the setting of efficient and realizable economic goals.

As suggested, the GDR's managers have a major channel of access in the State Planning Commission, as well as the ministries responsible for overseeing the enterprises in which they work. Through regional party secretaries they also have access to central party authorities in Berlin.

Military/Security

What the military/security interest group in the GDR (in common with such groups generally) seems to demand is status, resources, and influence to undergird its sense of professionalization. It is not unreasonable, for instance, to suggest that, as in other communist political systems, the military/security group on the issue of resource allocation would come out on the side of heavy industry, since that sector of the economy is basic to military needs. Even more obviously, it would favor high-level military budgets. And, it is suggested, the military/security group tends to be "hawkish," that is, not displeased by international political tension, since that provides a rationale for the large budgets with which the military wishes to undergird its demand for status and influence. However, it is difficult, at best, to separate individual interests from national ones, for the former are intimately linked with those of the political system as a whole, especially those of system maintenance and growth.[41]

Furthermore, the military/security group cannot be seen as a monolith. Naturally there is interservice rivalry, plus differences between young technical experts and "old-timers," between political workers and military professionals. Although not much can be said concretely about the military/security interest group, there probably are disagreements on matters of military strategy, which, in turn, would be reflected in varying opinions on resource allocation. Further, it may be assumed that differences exist between "old-timers," who may have come out of a background of pre-World War II underground and conspiratorial work, and younger members, who might fit more into the "technocrat" group. Members of the regular police, too, may differ in their attitudes toward use of extreme coercion (terror) and guarantees of legality.

Members of this military/security interest group include the army (Volksarmee) which numbers 171,000 men (of which 90,000 are land forces, 25,000 air force, 16,000 sea force, and 40,000 border guards). In addition, there are 16,000 emergency police (Bereit-schaftspolizei), 8,500 transportation police (Transportpolizei), 4,500 troops of the Security Ministry, and 40,000 regular police. Another segment of the population that might be included in the military/security interest group is the 350,000-member militia, organized on the basis of enterprises (Betriebskampfgruppen).[42]

The demands of this military/security interest group in the GDR stand a good chance of top-level hearing since the Minister of Defense, Heinz Hoffmann, is a full member of the Politburo (as of October 1973) and Erich Mielke, State Security Service chief, is a candidate member (since June 1971). In addition, the Central Committee secretary responsible for security questions, Paul Verner, is also a full Politburo member. Finally, because of the GDR's geographic proximity to the West, that is, common border with the Federal Republic of Germany, internal and external security questions are bound to have top priority.

That does not, however, mean that the GDR is a "militarist" state, in the usual sense of the word. The basic political values and ideology of the political culture are relatively antimilitaristic— Marxist/Leninists distrust professional military men because of their potential war power. Thus, while they are clearly essential for the maintenance of a political system seen as still relatively insecure (because it is perceived as the object of undermining external tactics), the military men are, nevertheless, kept at an arm's length and under civilian control.[43]

Intellectuals

There is continuing ambivalence in the SED regarding the exact definition of "intellectuals," as they differ from "workers" and "farmers," the mainstays of the political system.[44] Nevertheless, the system clearly needs its intellectuals, especially in the present period of renewed ideological delimitation (Abgrenzung) from the class enemy, capitalism, particularly as it exists in the Federal Republic of Germany. And out of this need may come increased interest group influence.

Within this so-called intellectual group, scientific and technical experts clearly are materially privileged. For instance, the scientific intellegentsia is represented in the 189-member Central Committee with 7 members, while no university is represented in this influential body.[45] Obviously, therefore, one of the interests of those who have influence and privilege is to keep it and, indeed, to increase it, if possible. On the other hand, along with intellectuals in all political systems, those who do not yet have influence want it.

This may be particularly relevant to social scientists—in fall 1971 the party officially "invited" GDR social scientists to bring a more "creative approach to scientific work" and especially to further the "development of opinion controversies." Thus, the future perhaps will bring increasing articulation of divergent opinions, for, according to the SED, a climate of open opinion did not exist everywhere. As SED ideological chief Kurt Hager said,

> Not infrequently is a real difference of opinion avoided
> out of differing motivations. In this connection, bourgeois
> behavior often plays a role. Positions of dogmatism,
> subjectivism, and arrogance hinder scientific discussion.
> We must also be very careful that the authority of various
> scientists and establishments does not tend in a false
> direction. It does not help us one step farther when
> certain research results and publications from the
> beginning are considered taboo, if it becomes custom
> no longer to discuss publications. In this way scientific
> conflicts of opinion will choke.

Especially to be avoided were inhibitions to open discussion resulting from "falsely understood collegiality." And that seemed to apply to social scientists "where polemics are almost completely missing." This could be corrected, suggested Hager, if journals would fulfill their important function as opinion forums and if critical reviews were increased in all publications. Furthermore, textbooks in the social sciences should be improved, both in quality and quantity.[46] This seemed to confirm the observation already noted that intellectuals in a communist political system exert their group influence through institutes and associations, special conferences, and the media of newspapers and scholarly journals.

In this context, then, it is interesting to note the wave of discussion begun in 1972 when Prof. Dr. Jürgen Kuczynski opened a debate about the nature of social contradictions in the Deutschen Zeitschrift für Philosophie,[47] starting a wave of articles in that publication among university philosophy professors.[48] Other publications, too, picked up on the theme. For instance, Forum, published by the Central Council of the FDJ as a "newspaper for the intellectual problems of youth," also opened its early 1972 numbers to a discussion of the issue of social contradictions.[49]

Members of the intellectual interest group also exercise their influence through professional congresses. For instance, the GDR's historians used the occasion of their V Congress in Dresden in December 1972 to debate the question of the content and stages of the transition from capitalism to socialism in the GDR. Esoteric sounding enough, this question, as noted at the beginning of this chapter, has practical implications of great significance to the everyday life of the GDR—the phase that a society built on Marxist/Leninist principles believes to find itself, and the characteristics believed to mark that phase, determine the goals, short- as well as long-range, of the society. Thus, at the historians' conference, for instance, there were those who said the 1945-49 period was the antiimperialist-democratic phase within the transitional period and that in it important elements and the first basis of socialism resulted; others saw the significance of measures and processes in this early period as already more or less socialist in character.[50]

The intellectual interest group also uses institutes to articulate their interests. Thus, it is interesting to note that the influential Academy of Science was upgraded in a new regulation of January 1, 1973.[51] The regulation not only called for coordination between the academy and the universities, but provided more funds for the work. This was in keeping with a Politburo resolution of October 22, 1968, calling for further development of Marxist/Leninist social sciences in the GDR.[52] In the GDR's present phase of socioeconomic development, the academy and universities were asked to increase their emphasis on the practical application of research. Thus their future influence may be increased. Furthermore, that intellectuals and their contribution to the GDR society are given a high priority is also suggested by the number of institutes newly founded in recent years. For example, in the field of government and law a significant new group was founded in 1972 by the Academy of Science—the Institute for Theory of State and Law. A similar institute through which intellectuals in this area of specialization find a channel of interest articulation is the German Academy for State and Legal Science.

Economists

The GDR has some 27,000 university graduates in the field of economics, employed in various sectors of the society, and 46,000 university teachers of economics. Thus, about 9 percent of all workers have higher economic education. As a group they are relatively young (less than 40, and if directors, or Werkleiter, then less than 30), mostly males, are from the working class, and had practical work experience before higher education.

Most of them are dissatisfied with their jobs. They rarely are employed in the area of their academic specialization, work long overtime hours, are paid less than engineers/technicians (but at the same time earn on the average twice as much as production workers), and have relatively limited social prestige. The latter is because of the predominance of technical, rather than economic, problems in the GDR. Further, economists are still identified with the state and bureaucracy as it existed in Prussian times. Then, too, the public has an unclear image of what an economist is (1) because the educational path followed is less clear (relative to medicine, for instance) and so less prestigious and (2) because there are few VIP images.[53] Thus, the primary demand of economists would seem to be for influence (which equals prestige). It is interesting, therefore, to note that within the Central Committee economists are represented by about 30 of the total 189 members,[54] an underrepresentation vis-a-vis their significance.

As an interest group, economists apparently have several channels for making their interest known. One is the public meetings and specialized journals in which they carry on debates. A second is influential leaders, within the Politburo or close to it, whom the economists persuade to support one or another policy alternative. In addition, economists, like scientists, also are called before party and state officials and commissions to give expert opinions that are influential in the decision-making process. Further, some economists have slots in leading planning and administrative units. Thus, theirs is a purely persuasive influence, exercised largely individually, for they do not have an association of their own. In the communist political systems, however, some economists are bound together in academic institutes that give them a basis for interest articulation. This does not, however, mean that economists have a monolithic interest. As all other interest groups, they, too, differ in their views and resulting demands on the basis of age, specialized training, and perhaps institutional affiliation.

Some of the institutions through which economists may express their interests are the Academy of Science, institutes of economics, the State Planning Commission (as noted, its chairman became a candidate member of the Politburo in 1973), ministries, and higher educational institutions. Major communications forums for interest articulation by economists are the publications Wirtschaftswissenschaft, Die Wirtschaft, Sozialistische Finanzwirtschaft, and Die Handel. Another publication, Sozialistische Aussenwirtschaft, formerly a channel for economists which advocated isolation of the GDR economy, has been discontinued.

Scientists

Among the demands of scientists is that of increased consultation in scientific questions as well as in allocation of funds and personnel for research (not yet experiencing significance increases in industrial and research institutes). The opportunity for international exchange of information that facilitates research is also a demand. In the case of the GDR scientists, this international aspect of their demands poses interesting problems.

After 20 years of increasing scientific-technological cooperation, the East European countries in July 1971 passed a resolution to further intensify that cooperation and to make it truly international, but within a regional setting, for the next 10-20 years.[55] Thus by 1972 already about 80 percent of the GDR's research and development tasks of the State Plan for Science and Technology were of an international character. At the beginning of 1973, for instance, the GDR and the Soviet Union alone had signed 100 agreements, and about 25,000 GDR scientists and engineers were to cooperate directly with Soviet colleagues.[56] Further, the work of the Institute for Scientific Theory and Organization of the Academy of Science if to be coordinated with the Soviet Academy of Science. Also it is to coordinate the internationally oriented natural scientific basic research with the domestically oriented special social science research of the GDR. Universities, in addition to their bilateral international relations through friendship treaties, now are to act as partners of the academy in its international research cooperation.

Thus, as this process develops, more scientific functions will be taken over by intra-East European organs; more decisions regarding research will be taken in international bodies and made binding on the GDR. For GDR scientists this poses real interest problems. For instance, the use of the Russian language probably will be intensified, and yet it apparently is a fact that despite many years of such language training (and the fact that 5,000 GDR scientists completed overseas studies in the USSR in the past 20 years),[57] GDR scientists still concentrate on Western languages, since Russian has not become the international language of science.

Another increasingly important related interest group issue in the GDR among scientists will be their support of internationally oriented projects vis-a-vis their advocacy of more nationally oriented undertakings. The matter of resource allocation and priorities may become a serious point of disagreement among scientists concerned about keeping their field free of Soviet domination. The issue may be further heightened by the unevenness of scientific development within Eastern Europe—GDR scientists may be more willing to cooperate with certain East European states, because they can learn from them,

and less willing to work with others where the level of development
is lower and GDR scientists would act more as "development helpers."
Another aspect of the issue that surely will bring controversy is to
what extent GDR scientists should give up plans for increasing their
East-West cooperation while concentrating instead on intra-East
cooperation.[58]

Especially affected by these diverging opinions will be the
interest articulation of the prestigious Academy of Science, the
technical academies, universities, technical universities, and the
SED party institutes. In 1970-71 that included 54 universities and
colleges (Hochschulen), with 21,000 teachers and 139 million students,
plus 15 academies of science with 71,000 employees.[59] One of the
newer channels for interest group influence is the Scientific Council
for Social Science Research, set up by the Academy of Science in
April 1972.

Further, as an interest group, scientists probably have relatively more direct channels of access to decision-making levels than
other intellectuals because of their expertise. In addition, scientists
may use as a channel those state agencies dealing with technological
and scientific affairs. Furthermore, they frequently are called in
for top-level consultation by party and state committees and commissions of all kinds. In the Central Committee, for instance, science
is represented by seven members selected from the Academy of
Science, the Academy for Agricultural Science, the Academy for
State and Legal Science, the Academy for Pedogogical Science, the
Construction Academy (Bauakademie), and the Academy of Medicine.[60]

Writers

The primary issue motivating GDR writers to articulation is
that of so-called freedom of discussion, or creative elbowroom. This
became an especially acute interest after the VIII Party Congress
where party chief Honecker said that no topics or forms were taboo,
in his opinion, if writers and artists proceeded from "firm socialist
positions." That left open, of course, the question of what "firm"
and "socialist" meant. One school of thought was that problems do
exist in society and so should be presented in artistic works. The
other view was that the criticism of daily life must not be too negative,
but must be balanced by the positive.

Between the time of the Party Congress in June 1971 and the
VII Writers Congress in November 1973, the debate over these two
points of view raged in scholarly journals. At the same time, numerous previously unaired themes found their way into print and onto the
stage and screen. Sometimes party spokesmen criticized the authors
and works by names, other times indirectly.

Those from the artistic community who responded pro and con, including leading intellectuals as well as the writers themselves, used various communications channels. Included were the journals Sinn und Form, Weimarer Beiträge, the newspaper Sonntag, Theater der Zeit, and Neuen Deutschen Literature. Professors for culture and art, as for instance from the Central Committee's Institute for Social Sciences, [61] got into the act, as well as the economic-historian, Dr. Kuczyniski. As one of the leading spokesman in the literary debates, his background in philosophy and the U.S. trade movement in the late 1920s has given him an unusually broad perspective of social developments.

Apparently the more "liberal" view among these intellectuals had the greater influence as 1973 ended, for there was no official censoring of this wing of the intellectual community at the Writers Congress. While it was true that some progressive writers were not invited, on the other hand others were. [62]

In addition to the mass communications media and the voices of influential individuals, the writers also have more direct organizational channels for expressing their group interests to decision-making levels. For example, 11 of the 189 members of the Central Committee represent culture and education, including 4 for theater and 4 for literature. [63]

While it is difficult to ascertain which Politburo members are most receptive to the writers' demands, it is felt that the main leverage is that of public opinion generally. In a population educated for more than two decades to art and literature appreciation, a kind of unofficial "fan club" has developed for writers and artists producing quality work. This apparently gave the interest group a source of influence to bring to bear, as reflected in the VIII Party Congress' "softer" line toward the artists and its continued permissiveness, as expressed at the Writers Congress. Thus, while the Writers Union does not serve as a lobby to protect or defend creative elbowroom, its meetings do serve as a forum of interest articulation. And in that its proceedings are given coverage, the interest articulation reaches many segments of the public.

At the present then, GDR writers seem to be bound together by their interest in a common "professional" standard and the wish to promote the interests of society as they interpret them. Thus, their social and personal interests are interrelated.

Broad Social Groups

In addition to the association groups discussed above, there are broad social groups whose members loosely relate to each other on the basis of common issues: such as workers, farmers, youth, women, and religious persons. The channels through which they express their interests are usually the mass organizations, such as the FDJ for the youth, the FDGB for workers, the DFD for women, or forums such as conferences for farmers and publications for religious believers.

Some of the members of these broad social groups also view the four noncommunist parties of the GDR as channels for expressing interests—Christians, for instance, often feel the CDU (Christian Democratic Union) speaks for them, while professional and middle-class people identify with the LDPD (Liberal Democratic Party of Germany), moderate nationalists with the NDPD (National Democratic Party of Germany), and the farmers with the DBP (Democratic Farmers Party). As will be seen, within the context of the "leading role" of the communist party, such non-Marxist parties are "echoes" of the SED. However, they sometimes serve as ventilators, as do the mass organizations, for the issues that move the broad social groups discussed below and thus gain support for the existing political system.

Workers

Naturally one of the trade-union interests is higher pay for workers. Another is more accessibility to holiday travel (2 million reduced-rate holidays are available) and cultural opportunities. Among the other fringe benefits that the workers demand, and to a large extent have won, are increased pensions and increased medical insurance. Also in the works are lower rents, cheaper railroad transportation for families with many children, and improved housing. [64]

However, one of the more unusual demands of the GDR's hard-pressed workers is for what they call kontinuierliche Produktion, that is, realistic work goals that are not stepped up suddenly to meet export tasks or slowed down when materials are lacking. Thus, it is not surprising that the party has promised "realistic plans" and has done much to smooth out the ups and downs of work demands.

Another of the significant interest group issues of the workers, who make up 85 percent of the GDR's population, [65] is the demand for consumer goods and improved "quality of life." In this they are typical of the total society, which until recently has had to make do with rather austere living conditions. Today, however, the GDR has the highest standard of living in Eastern Europe, and the people want more.

While GDR consumers (average four-member family) spend only 1.4 percent of their income for transportation and communication (newspapers, radio, television), 3.2 percent for culture and recreation, 16.5 percent for clothes and shoes, 5.8 percent for rent, gas, electricity, and heat, they would like to see the 48.2 percent of their income spent for food reduced, as well as the 24.9 percent GDR consumers spent for other goods and services. While basic foods such as bread, potatoes, prepared foodstuffs, vegetables, and fish are relatively cheap, automobiles, gas, TV sets, refrigerators, and luxury items (coffee, chocolate, cigarettes) are relatively expensive. [66]

GDR workers also are especially articulate in their demands for better housing and consumer service. Although housing construction has been a constant project in the GDR (1,240,000 units built from 1949 to 1970), a serious shortage remains, especially for young married couples. Thus the goal of 500,000 new dwellings has been set for the period 1971-75 and the housing shortage is to be solved by 1990. [67] In addition, such appliances as refrigerators, washing machines, and televisions are to be produced in increasing quantity. A program also is underway to make life easier—and emancipation more of a reality—for working women. Thus, more kindergartens are planned, as well as improved services such as laundries, dry cleaning, and small electric appliance repair. [68] Medical care, too, is a top priority. As SED chief Erich Honecker said in his concluding remarks at the 12th plenary session of the Central Committee (July 4-5, 1974), while availability of many goods has increased (fruit, for instance, up 33 percent), supply was irregular, choice sometimes limited, and the quality of repairs and services far behind that which the public wishes. [69]

About 95 percent of all workers in the GDR are organized into trade unions, or a total of 7.2 million members. [70] The importance to the political system of their mass trade union organization, the FDGB (Freie Deutsche Gewerkschaftsbund) is seen in the fact that it is the only mass organization whose special rights are included in the Constitution of the GDR. Article 44 says:

> The free trade unions, organized in the Confederation
> of Free German Trade Unions, are the all-embracing
> class organization of the working class. They safeguard
> the interests of the workers, office workers and intelli-
> gentsia through comprehensive co-determination in the
> state, the economy and the social sphere.

Along with other mass organizations, the FDGB once was seen simply as a "transmission belt" for the party. However, specialists feel the FDGB's influence as active articulator and implementor of the interests of the workers is increasingly growing, as seen for instance, in the pages of the FDGB journal, Die Arbeit. The FDGB, for instance, can play an active role in improving working conditions, for it is in charge of implementing the social insurance system and is responsible for labor protection, labor hygiene, [71] and holidays. At the VII Congress of the FDGB it was made clear that the organization is to be given even greater representation rights of this kind. As the FDGB chairman said, the trade unions do not want to be under the suspicion of being the right hand of the work bosses (Werkleitung), but rather the organization of the workers themselves.

At the same time, however, the FDGB's status as an arm of the party is clear. Thus, although the unions on the one hand are responsible for carrying out goals set by the party, on the other hand they are to advocate the needs and rights of the workers—these two goals, however, are not necessarily always seen as identical. While the FDGB is not a federation of relatively independent individual unions, the articulation possibilities, for criticism and participation, are supposed to take place in the small trade union groups of 10-20 members in the various enterprises. [72] There, some 2 million volunteer FDGB functionaries are active in the enterprises of the GDR and 75 percent of the trade union functions are carried out by nonparty members. [73]

One of the channels for the articulation of their primary interest is the mass communications media (these will be discussed in detail in Chapter 8). Newspapers, such as the Volksstimme in Magdeburg, for instance, have special columnists who handle the demands of consumers. Since the VIII Party Congress gave top priority to the improvement of material and cultural living conditions, workers have increasingly exercised (and been given) the opportunity to articulate their demands. State agencies have been brought under extensive pressure by party spokesmen to exert every effort to meet this promise.

Youth

Certainly one of the most significant of the broad social groups within a communist political system is the youth. The mass youth organization is one of the primary channels of political socialization and leadership recruitment, as has been shown, as well as an interest group on which the party concentrates much of its articulation efforts. Youth, in short, are the future of the system.

The role of the FDJ in the GDR is of special importance when one recalls that it was the "cadre forge" of the postwar period—through recruitment and training programs the FDJ molded most of the GDR's present-day leadership. [74] Thus, the GDR was not left without leaders in its early years, despite the fact that it radically purged whole professional classes—such as educators, jurists, professional military, etc.—who were tainted by Nazism.

Today the role of the FDJ, with 1.9 million members, or 70 percent of the youth, is no less important, but quite different. For members it now provides, among other advantages, political "acceptability," and so professional mobility and a channel for interest group articulation. For the party leadership, the FDJ is a channel for tapping youth interests and implementing the resulting political socialization programs.

GDR youth, confronted with the challenges of a scarcity society and having no remembrances of the really lean postwar years are (in the view of some party leaders) too frequently inclined to privitization, apoliticism, and "egotistic individualism." Thus, they demand consumer goods (especially a choice of chic clothing), but by far their primary current demand is for freedom to travel to the West. That, however, is not the same as the wish to emigrate. Further, youth want creative work and a meaningful role in society, as the famous but controversial play, "The New Sorrows of Young W.," by Ulrich Plenzdorf showed. Another major demand, of course, is that of employment in areas for which they have been trained, as well as that of creative employment generally. With increasing frequency young people tell of being assigned "Mickey Mouse" jobs that fulfill the state's pledge to offer them employment but that do not meet the individual need of fulfilling activity. SED chief Honecker referred to this when he said,

> Responsible quarters, in particular the industrial ministries and the works managements, often do not pay enough attention to these young forces; often they are not properly utilized to help solve those problems which they have been trained to solve. We cannot be satisfied with the present situation. Education is a valuable possession, for the individual and for the community; it must be utilized in a manner which contributes to the creative force of the team in the further shaping of developed socialist society.[75]

The major channel for interest group articulation among youth is the FDJ daily newspaper Junge Welt and numerous magazines, the best known of which are Junge Generation and Forum. All give considerable space to publication of letters to the editors, many of which discuss youth problems.

Farmers

Through a process of gradual collectivization, the agricultural industry of the GDR—involving about 12 percent of the population and

58 percent of the total territory—today is largely collectivized. Of
the land, 86 percent is organized into agricultural collectives (LPGs,
or Landwirtschaftlichen Produktionsgenossenschaften). Each LPG
elects a board of directors, a chairman, and various commissions.
Monthly membership meetings are held where work norms, division
of profits, and use of investment funds are decided. At least 80 percent
of the LPG's income is paid out in the form of wages. The remaining
20 percent is paid to members for the land they brought with them
into the collective. In addition, some 8 percent of the GDR's tillable
land is organized into VEGs (Volkseigenen Güter), or state farms.
The remainder is market gardens, allotments, and church-owned
land. [76]

Thus GDR farmers work within a context that could be an agricultural reform model for other industrial countries, for the GDR is
seeking to radically change historical agricultural production relationships from a social as well as economic point of view. [77] Specifically, the goal of GDR agricultural policy is to overcome lags in
economic, cultural, and social achievements in rural areas: Farmers
should enjoy the same quality of life as do workers in the cities, and
they should be able to use industrial production methods. Farm
children should have access to a good basic as well as polytechnical
education while their parents pursue adult education. Farmers should
have social security and health care as good as that in cities, and
they should enjoy more cultural opportunities, such as movies,
theaters, cultural houses with libraries, village clubs, organized
dance evenings, and amateur theater. Rural people should be helped
to develop a collective Weltanschaung to replace the individualistic
thinking traditional in agricultural areas, and finally they should see
their interests as compatible with those of the larger society.

The advances in many of these areas have been significant. GDR
farmers earn relatively good wages, enjoy 12- to 15-day annual
vacations, send their children to ten-year polytechnical high schools,
etc. The educational achievements have been significant. The proportion of all citizens in rural areas holding full-time jobs who have
completed a university or a technical school increased from 1.4
percent in 1960 to 5.4 percent in 1973; those with a master craftsmen
certificate rose from 1.4 percent to 6.3 percent; and those having
passed a specialized worker examination (Facharbeiterprüfung)
increased from 6.2 percent in 1960 to 60.7 percent in 1973. [78] In
addition, some models are underway for establishing settlement
centers (Siedlungszentren), which would provide these services in
one larger town connected to smaller outlying villages. These,
however, are costly undertakings and are moving slowly. [79]

Despite the progress, the demands, or interests, of the villagers
and LPG members are numerous. One problem is the long hours they

have to work because of the shortage of employees—as in most
industrialized countries, the youngsters trek to the cities, leaving
more and more old people to carry on the everyday work of agricultural production in the villages. (At the top level, among agricultural management, the personnel shortages are not so acute.)

Another interest of the farmers is that of retaining organizational elbowroom. Until now they were primarily organized in individual regional cooperatives, or Genossenschaften. These are to be
further organized horizontally into cooperative unions, or Koopera-
tionsgemeinschaft, according to products. (This reflects the old
issue within communist political systems of territorial versus functional organization.) These would have not only advisory and coordination power, but decision-making and application as well, thus cutting
into the autonomy of the lowest production units. [80]

Organizations that may be seen as influence channels for the
articulation of agricultural group interests are the Union for Mutual
Agricultural Aid (Vereinigung der gegenseitige Bauernhilfe), the
Farmers' Congress (Bauernkongress), and the Democratic Agricultural German Party (DBP). The Farmers' Congress is a meeting
of elected delegates of the various agricultural cooperatives who
come together to decide how the party's resolutions regarding agriculture can best be implemented. The DBP (equivalent to the Christian
Democratic Union, West) is one of the bloc parties coordinated through
the National Front (to be discussed later). It publishes the newspaper
Bauern-Echo and a newspaper for agricultural functionaries called
Die Pflüger. Agricultural interests also are represented in the Central Committee through seven chairmen of agricultural cooperations
(LPGs). [81]

Women

From earliest Marxist theory to the present, the equality of
women has always been seen as a goal of socialism, for without that
human emancipation would be impossible. Therefore it is not surprising that women are a significant interest group in the GDR and
have been since the founding of the state.

In 1950, for instance, the GDR passed a law that called for the
establishment of child day-care facilities so that women could take
advantage of employment opportunities. Since 1952 there have been
special plans for promoting equality of women in enterprises. Then
in 1956 the Code of Family Law was passed, which reformed the
institution of marriage: husband and wife should have equal right to
work; the woman's family name might be taken by the husband, as
well as vice versa; divorce procedures were freed of the "guilt"
principles; marriage was to be seen as an institution for mutual care

and not one of the possession of the wife by her husband. In 1968 the new Constitution of the GDR incorporated these principles in that it said in Article 20, 2: "Men and women have equal rights and have the same legal status in all spheres of social, state and personal life. The promotion of women, particularly with regard to vocational qualifications, is a task of society and the state." And in 1972 abortion was legalized.

What women in the GDR have achieved under these conditions is significant. They make up 54 percent of the population and 49 percent of the work force. Among all workers who have completed university education, 28 percent are women; of all workers who have completed a technical school, 38 percent are women. Further, 37 percent of all university students and 50 percent of all technical school students in 1971 were women.[82] In short, 76 percent of all women of working age were either studying or working in 1970.[83] But despite these achievements, only 1 out of 17 university-educated women reached leading positions, while 1 out of 3 men did.

Politically the achievements are mixed. Although 29.4 percent of all SED members are women,[84] there are only 2 female candidate members of the Politburo (out of a total of 16 full and 10 candidate members), Inge Lange and Margarete Müller; 2 among the Central Committee Department heads (out of more than 30), Lange for Womens Affairs and Giesela Glende in the Bureau of the Politburo; 1 among 5 institute directors, Hanna Wolf, Party School; and none among the first secretaries of the SED's District (Bezirk) organization.

Among the mass organizations there is only one chairwoman, Ilse Thiele for the DFD (Demokratischer Frauenbund Deutschlands), the mass organization for women. Among the numerous professional organizations there is only one woman president, Anna Seghers, of the Writers Union.

In state positions, there is 1 woman member of the 41-member Minister Council, Margot Feist Honecker, minister for education. Grete Wittkowski, former president of the State Bank, resigned in April 1974.) But no woman sits on the Presidium of the Minister Council. In the State Council there are 5 women as opposed to 20 men. In the Presidium of the Volkskammer there are 2 women,[85] and about 31 percent of the entire body are women. The Foreign Ministry has assigned no women diplomats to foreign posts. Similarly, there are few chairwomen of the agricultural collectives.[86] At local levels of government some 62,300 women fill elected positions, and 18 percent of all mayors are women. 160,000 women work in various commissions of the Volksvertretungen (local peoples representative bodies). In the trade unions there are 1.8 million women members (or a total of 96 percent of all working women), and 30 percent of them hold elected positions there. By the end of 1970, 35 percent of all judges were women and 45 percent of all jurors (Schöffe).[87]

One explanation for the relatively few women in leading positions in political and social organizations, as contrasted to their presence in the work force is, of course, that it takes time to accumulate sufficient education and experience to fulfill such tasks—and women in the GDR have had only 25 years of such encouragement. On the other hand, there are still conditions that impose on working women a so-called double burden—that is, while they are professionally employed, they also remain primarily responsible for caring for homes and families and society does not provide them with enough help. For instance, by 1969, 24 percent of all children up to the age of three and 66 percent of all children to the age of six could be cared for in day-care centers. Despite great efforts, those facilities are inadequate to meet the demand. Further, services such as laundry, cleaning, repairs, etc., that lighten the job of home management also are lacking. And then there is, of course, the matter of attitude. Although the entire GDR population for 25 years has been educated toward accepting the equality of women, all too many persons still interpret that as meaning relieving them of washing the dishes. Thus, the Academy of Science in 1967 held a critical conference on the topic, "The Social Position of Women in the GDR and the Responsibilities of Science."[88] But the progress continues to be problematic. For instance, Inge Lange, Politburo candidate member, Central Committee Secretary, and leader of its Department for Women, called the results of a survey concerning time spent on house work by women as "disappointing." Her assessment was based on data showing that attitudes were in large part responsible for continuation of traditional roles, and that making more services available would not alone change the situation.[89]

Out of this background, it is then not surprising that among the major demands of women as an interest group in the GDR there are the matters of increasing child-care and service facilities, financial provisions for easing the double burden of women generally and specifically those who study, work, or are pregnant, as well as continued improvement of the image of women as communicated in textbooks, literature, and the mass media.

One of the major channels for articulating such interests, as already has been suggested, is the mass organization, the Democratic Women's Organization of Germany, with its 1.3 million members. It articulates the interests of women not only within its own organizational units but also through its fraction in the Peoples Chamber and in all other local governmental units. Still another communications channel is the International Women's Day, March 8, as well as the various women's publications.

Religion

While the membership in churches of the GDR has steadily decreased (from nearly 15 million in 1946 to nearly 12 million in 1973 out of a population of 17 million) and the number of pastors and priests is about 6,410, it nevertheless remains an interest group of significance. Predominantly Protestant (8.5 million), the church members are primarily interested in pastoral training, publication rights, and religious education rights. However, the primary demand of church members is that of nondiscrimination against them as practicing Christians by the officially atheistic state. For instance, in November 1974 the Catholic bishops in the GDR in a pastoral letter publicly protested the attitude of the GDR government toward Christians. The bishops were especially critical of the educational monopoly of the government. Further, they said the life of Christians was made difficult through "positions and actions which force people to leave the church, consequences which separate Christians from the life of the church and the congregation, and required actions which offend love for fellowman and lead to hate toward other people."[90]

From the party's point of view, the key to the relationship between GDR churches and the state is found in a 1964 statement of Walter Ulbricht, then party chief, that "Christianity and the humanist goals of socialism are not opposites." This was generally seen as an invitation to the church to seek a new course within the context of socialism, rather than to merely conform to it.[91] However, this context also means a continued effort on the part of the Marxist/Leninist state to reduce the influence of the church in public life, to limit it to a kind of ghetto existence and to await its eventual disappearance. And in October 1972, Politburo member Albert Norden spoke of "socialist citizens with Christian belief." Referring to the mutual resistance against facism of socialists and Christians, he said that action had led religious people to the side of the working class and laid the basis for the cooperation of progressive Christians with the SED.[92]

One of the channels through which practicing Christians in the GDR express their group interests is the Christian Democratic Union (East) (CDU) political party. It serves as a kind of ventilator for certain group interests and publishes a newspaper, Neue Zeit, and a monthly magazine, Union Teilt Mit.

Already in the early postwar period the CDU was a rather "left-wing" movement, calling for religious instruction in schools but demanding state ownership of natural resources and state control of monopolies. In 1951 the East German CDU declared its support for socialism based on "Christian responsibility." Among its members today are primarily intellectuals, but also a goodly proportion

of collective farmers. They do not see themselves as a party of the
church or as a political arm of the church. Rather, they support
social and political stands arising from their acceptance of socialism
as a sociopolitical system and Christianity as a religious belief.[93]
As the chairman of the CDU wrote in spring 1973, the "socialist
citizen with Christian belief" is one who

- is motivated in his social wishes and behavior
  above all through the gospel and through the social
  consequences of the commandment "love thy
  neighbor"
- is also included in the political-moral unity of our
  people as a citizen with the same rights and duties as
  everyone else
- is co-responsible for the whole[94]

In the second point the primary interest of churchgoing GDR citizens
becomes clear.

INTEREST AGGREGATION

As has already been noted, the aggregation of the differing
group interests in the political system of the GDR takes place primarily through the ruling political party, the SED, legitimized by its
ideological tenet concerning the "leading role of the Party."
According to the SED, "realization of the objectively necessary
unity of politics, economics, and ideology is possible only through
the Marxist/Leninist party's leadership and guidance of all political-
ideological, technical-economic, and spiritual-cultural processes."[95]
Furthermore, as will be seen, this role of the party is legalized
in the Constitution of the GDR, as well as in statutes regulating the
work of the state ministries, etc. Thus, the program and resolutions
of SED organs are binding on state organs, mass organizations, as
well as the state laws based on such resolutions. (Laws of the Peoples
Chamber, for instance, or resolutions of the State Council and the
Minister Council, usually are based on resolutions of the SED party
congresses, party conferences, Central Committee plenary sessions,
and Politburo meetings.)
Thus, crucial for a Marxist/Leninist party in its interest
aggregation process is its view of where it is on the developmental
spectrum of communism, for this determines the general direction
in which the social interests must be aggregated at a given time.

For instance, it was assumed by classical Marxist theoreticians that there were two phases of development—first there was socialism, a transitional phase, and then communism, the ultimate phase. But the historical experience of implementing theory in practice brought Soviet theoreticians face to face with the necessity for breaking socialism into subperiods—the developmental process did not go exactly according to original plans. The updated time plans, in turn, have become subjects for controversy and discussion in the other East European socialist states as well.

One view prevalent in the GDR is that the phase of socialism consists of two subperiods: (1) formation (Herausbilden) of the developing socialist society, and (2) the developed, or mature, socialist society. Only the Soviet Union has reached subphase two. In the GDR, on the other hand, that phase first began in the 1960s and is still in process.

According to the GDR view, mature socialism includes external, as well as internal, conditions. Specifically, the external conditions must be such that the system of socialism is ultimately secured—obviously the GDR feels that because of its continued contention with the FRG this is not yet a fact of life for it, whereas the Soviet Union has secured its future through its position as a nuclear superpower. The internal conditions, too, are still being developed by the GDR: a powerful material-technical economic base, a stable and high rate of economic growth and work productivity, total socialization of property, elimination of every element of exploitation, and stabilization of the sociopolitical and ideological unity of society. When all of that is reached, mature socialism is at hand. And, next, when sources of wealth are adequate to satisfy all needs, socialism will be completed and communism at hand. That period, too, probably will be further subdivided as it becomes a reality.[96]

This, then, is the context within which the party considers the Bedürfnisse and Bedarf referred to earlier and sets priorities, that is, aggregates the interests of the various groups. The question next arises of the mechanisms through which the ruling party in a communist political system carries out its aggregative role vis-a-vis these demands within the society.

Party Structure

Party Organization

According to the SED, "the Party is where the comrade is." And as of December 31, 1972, there were a total of 1,902,809

members and 47,612 candidate members of the SED. (Candidates
have the same responsibilities as full members but lack voting rights.
The candidate period usually lasts a year.) Organized according to
the territorial and production principle, the SED consists of 15
district (Bezirk) organizations, 262 city, city-regional (Stadtbezirk),
and regional (Kreis) organizations numbering more than 54,000 basic
(Grundorganisationen) units. Each of these units reports up the ladder
concerning the demands of various groups, as discussed in the preceding section.

        Within the SED itself interests are aggregated, for the member-
ship consists of 56.6 percent workers, 5.7 percent collective farmers,
17.9 percent intellectuals, and 12.8 percent employees (Angestellte).
In addition, 29.4 percent of all members are women, and nearly half
of all members and candidates are younger than 40. They are becoming increasingly educated—and so, one might expect, more sophisticated in their roles—24.7 percent of all SED members and candidates
have completed university or technical school education.

        Further, they are well-educated in party affairs: 18.4 percent
of all members, 35.4 percent of the leading members, and 51.6
percent of the party secretaries attended a party school of 3 months
or longer. (In the case of the party secretaries in the large industries it was 90 percent.) Annually about 100,000 members study
at the party's schools and institutes. Additionally, the Party Study
Year (Parteilehrjahr), conducted on the job, involved more than 1.3
million members during the 1973-74 course. Another 226,000 nonparty members also took part. The party further has 530 educational
centers (Bildungsstätten), which support the educational/mobilization
work of the propagandists and agitators (as will be further discussed
in Chapter 8).[97]

        All of these members, each of whom is responsible for carrying
out party guidelines and reporting back to the leadership, are found
in the party structure in Figure 2.

        The Central Committee (135 members and 54 candidates) is
elected at the Party Congress, usually held every four years, but
at the VIII Party Congress changed to five years. The Central Committee then meets at least twice a year. Meanwhile, the daily work
of the party is carried out by the Politburo (decision-making) and the
Secretariat (implementation) of the Central Committee, in which
about 1,500 people are employed.

Party/State Personnel Fusion

        The oldest and probably most effective method used in a
communist political system to guarantee the Communist party its
"leading role" in interest aggregation is that of the personnel union

FIGURE 2

Organization of the Socialist Unity Party of Germany

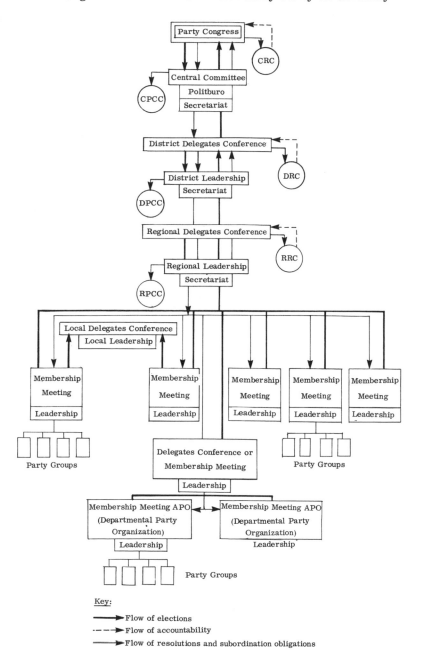

Key:

⟶ Flow of elections

--⟶ Flow of accountability

⟶ Flow of resolutions and subordination obligations

between party and state. Specifically, this means that leading party
functionaries at the same time fill top state functions—that is, members of the SED constitute sizable majorities in the Peoples Chamber,
the State Council, the Minister Council, the mass organizations, and
social institutions. Thus, their power and influence can be brought
to bear at many points to promote the party's view of which interests
shall be given priority in the aggregating process.

For instance, 36 of the 41 members of the Minister Council
are SED members and 27 of those 36 are members of the SED's
Central Committee. In all 28 ministries, the top positions are filled
by party members. In the case of the Ministry of Defense and the
Ministry for State Security, the ministers are Politburo members.
In the State Council, 15 of the 25 members belong to the SED—6 of
them are Politburo members and 10 are members of the Central
Committee. In the 12-person Presidium of the Peoples Chamber are
4 SED members, 3 of whom are in the Politburo. Further, the SED,
with 125 representatives, is the largest fraction within the 483-
member Peoples Chamber (158 represent the mass organizations
and 200 the noncommunist political parties). Of the 26 Politburo
members, 25 are also members of the Peoples Chamber. Most
chairmen of the 9 major mass and 14 professional and social organizations are SED members. And, in addition, 8 mass organization
chairpersons are Central Committee members.[98]

To assure this system of personnel fusion, there is the
nomenklatura. Taken over from the Soviet political system, the
nomenklatura is somewhat like a civil service register—it is a list
of persons who, because of their professional work or political
function, are important to the system. The personnel department at
each level of the party has such a list of party functionaries and
intellectuals for which it keeps detailed personnel files. For instance,
the Central Committee is responsible for the editorial staff of Neues
Deutschland, for heads of party institutions, the central administrators
of mass organizations, directors of the most important plants, etc.
Scientists, artists, and professors, too, are on the party's nomenklatura. Their hiring and firing, etc., can occur only within the
context of the nomenklatura provisions. Thus, the nomenklatura
provides exact limitations for the responsibilities of the different
personnel departments. At the same time it assures that personnel
acceptable to the party will be placed in key positions.

Party/State Cooperation

Further, the technical-bureaucratic cooperation between the
party and state apparats is close and interwoven. For nearly all
major units and levels of the state apparat (ministries, departments,

etc.) there are corresponding party units (departments, committees, commissions, etc.) that interpret party guidelines, pass along decisions, supervise implementation, and feed back to party officials reports concerning the interests of state agencies. This, combined with the fact that the leading positions in the state apparat are filled by party members who feel obligated to exert optimal effort toward securing effective understanding of party thinking, gives the party a double-barreled mechanism—personnel and structure—for realizing its leading role in interest aggregation.

In addition to such individual efforts, there also are basic party units, or groups, organized in all state organizations for the purpose, among others, of reporting upward. As the SED puts it, the task of all party organizations is to help the party members working in state organs to become more capable, more responsible, and more creative—this is done by providing them with a clear orientation regarding the party's priorities and major tasks.[99]

Party Elections

The party also uses its elections to further aggregate the interests of the society within the party structure. (State elections, to be discussed later, are used for similar aggregative purposes.) Party elections are an occasion when the party brings its past achievements and future plans, as well as its own leadership, before its members for endorsement, criticism, and suggestions. As noted in the previous chapter, in the 1973 party elections in the GDR, party members were especially encouraged to freely articulate their views of their organization's past accomplishments, in terms of implementation of party resolutions. In so doing, it is logical to assume that the personnel changes that resulted in the party at all levels gave the top leadership some indication of interests as reflected within the party itself.

In the SED's last party elections, those group interests might have found expression in the more than 150,000 election meetings held between November 1973 and February 17, 1974 at all party levels. The elections usually were held at annual membership meetings.

In practice, each party unit proposed candidate lists which had been approved by the next highest leadership level. The Central Committee, for instance, approved the lists for the Bezirk, the Bezirk leadership proposed lists for the Kreis, and the Kreis proposed for the Basic Party Units. Only those names confirmed by the upper-level leadership were proposed at each election meeting; this applied also to substitute candidates.[100] Abrupt changes, therefore, in the aggregative function are rare. Nevertheless, the top levels of the party can hardly be expected to ignore entirely the interests of the

level just below it when "approving" its candidates—after all, it is
that level which will or will not exert optimal effort to fulfilling goals
handed down by the level above, and that exertion depends to a large
extent on leadership.

In reporting the overall results, Neuer Weg, the monthly publication for party functionaries, said that in the 1973-74 party elections,
"About 70 percent of the comrades who were members of a leadership
unit were reelected. Many comrades, who because of their age or
health reasons, left their functions, were thanked for their many
years of active voluntary Party work. Thousands of new, young functionaries took their places . . . among them 16, 000 new secretaries
of basic organizations."[101] At the higher levesl of the party there
also were changes, but fewer. About a third of the members of
Bezirk party administrations were newly elected, including 24 of the
95 secretaries, 39 of the 124 members of the Bezirk secretariats,
two of the 15 first secretaries, and five of the second secretaries.
In the elections at Kreis, Stadt-, and Stadtbezirk levels, a third of
the leaders also were newly elected.[102]

Social Organizations

National Front

In Leninism, a "people's front" was a coalition of communist
and bourgeois democratic groups for the purpose of jointly opposing
fascism or the outbreak of war. Since the advent of socialism in the
East European countries, this old "people's front" idea has been
given a new form and new substance. In the GDR, for instance, it
has become the National Front, an organization through which
various organizations within the socialist society (such as political
parties and mass organizations) along with nonparty members work
together to implement the policies decided upon by the ruling party,
the SED.

In the view of the GDR, the National Front exists to give the
party a channel through which it can collect the various interests and
later explain its priorities, or aggregation results:

> The socialist People's Front plays an important role in
> the development and steady completion of socialist
> democracy. It is the organizer of comprehensive public

articulations and discussion of important state works of
law, background materials, and other documents of
overall social meaning. The Peoples Front is the
bearer of the elections to the socialist popular representative bodies [Volksvertretungen] at all levels. It
publishes the common election program of the parties
and organizations unified in it and has a significant role
in formation of the candidates list, election preparation,
and election execution. During the legislative period it
also works closely together with the popular representative bodies and their organs and organizes the constant
relationships and cooperation of deputies with their
electors.

But the National Front also plays a key role in mobilizing
citizens for implementation of party priorities, that is, decisions
already made:

Characteristic for the socialist Peoples Front is its
social breadth and great circumference. It attempts to
include the politically organized and nonorganized
members of all classes and strata [Schichten]
in accomplishing the goals of the total society, to win
every citizen for responsible social activity.

This role of the National Front is anchored in the Constitution
as "the alliance of all powers of the people" for the development of
the socialist society (Article 3). Further, the role of the SED within
the National Front is clear:

The democratic parties and organizations united with
the SED in the National Front and in the democratic
bloc have given their complete agreement to the SED's
program and thereby recognize without qualifications
the leading role of the Marxist/Leninist party in the GDR.
In the committees of the National Front, the SED acts as
political educator and organizer.[103]

The GDR's National Front holds a congress of elected delegates
that, in turn, selects a National Council and its president. This
council carries on the work of channeling, coordinating, and mobilizing through about 17,000 committees involving more than 335,000
citizens.[104]

Other Political Parties

In four East European countries, parties other than the ruling Communist party exist. They include the GDR where they are called "allied parties" (verbündeter Parteien), denoting their subordination to the SED.

The GDR's four such allied parties are the Christian Democratic Union (CDU), the Liberal Democratic Party of Germany (LDPD), the National Democratic Party of Germany (NDPD), and the German Farmers Party (DBP). Together they are believed to have between 70,000 and 110,000 members.[105]

According to the GDR, the existence of these parties reflects "the social differentiation of the socialist society and especially the historically influenced political structure of the single states. It is a specific, supplementary form for realizing the alliance of the working class with the farmers, the other employment groups, and the religiously affiliated population groups."[106]

In other words, these allied parties play a role in the interest aggregation process in that the SED acknowledges that they represent classes and groups in socialism that have different levels of development (that is, do not want to identify with a Marxist party) and so specific interests. In the long process of eventually bringing these interests into harmony with its own, the SED must, of course, take into account, or aggregate, present interests of the allied parties' members. Through that process of aggregation, coupled with the daily process of persuasion, the SED hopes to gain new support for its view of how to develop socialism. Meanwhile, however, it continues to exercise overall political leadership over the allied parties that sometimes are described as "echoes of the SED."

Mass Organizations

The interests of the masses of the GDR population are tapped and aggregated through the social and mass organizations that draw many thousands of persons into active social participation and articulation. Among the most significant of these mass societies, as we have seen, are the trade union organization (FDGB), the youth organization (FDJ), and the women's organization (DFD). Through them the party can show how it is incorporating the individual group interests into its overall priority list. Further, since GDR citizens, as members of these mass organizations, take part in the society's advisory and control organs (for instance, in the universities, parents' councils, conflict and arbitration commissions, industrial collectives, etc.), they spread views of party priorities gathered in mass organization meetings among many other interest groups.

Further, the party feels that through their work in such mass and social organizations average citizens in time learn to exercise the many opportunities for forming and articulating collective opinions and to develop their group interests. Thus, to the extent that it encourages free discussions (and that apparently is increasing) the party supports the evolution of the mass organizations from mere "transmission belts" of mobilization to relatively significant forums within the interest aggregation process.

Mass Media

In the case of the GDR, the SED has a sizable mass media network over which it exercises a dominant influence (within the theoretical context discussed earlier). The total daily newspaper circulation reported in 1974 was 7.8 million (the party press alone, including the central newspaper, Neues Deutschland, and the regional newspapers, account for probably about 5.5 million circulation). And the weekly circulation (including illustrateds) was 8.5 million. Magazines and professional journals totaled 16.9 million.[107] According to party chief Honecker, "In every household of the German Democratic Republic at least one daily newspaper and a weekly newspaper or illustrated magazine is read."[108] The two television channels reach 4.5 million TV watchers (80 percent of the homes have TV). And nearly all homes have a radio, with more than half of all households having two radios.[109]

All of this communications structure is directly or indirectly responsible to the party's Central Committee Departments for Propaganda and Agitation. Its administration is a state function—the licensing of the press is carried out by the Press Office of the chairman of the Minister Council. (It also is responsible for the news agency ADN). Radio and television are guided by the State Committee for Radio and State Committee for Television of the Minister Council.

As noted in the earlier part of this chapter, various interests may use such public communications media to articulate demands. The party, in turn, uses the media to accumulate the demands and claims. While it is true that the party is capable of influencing the press so that the demand articulation is regulated and the aggregation process thus perhaps simplified, it often is not in its interests to do so—the very fact that demands are articulated may take the heat out of them and at the same time give the Party a "reading" of public demands.

This apparently is the case in the GDR at present, for, as will be seen in Chapter 8, the SED in 1972 set into motion a renewed campaign to increase the effectiveness of communications. This not only included the party's agitation and propaganda work, but also that of the public mass media, seen as the "fastest and most immediate tie to the masses."

Further, that the press increasingly is seen as an aggregative mechanism, and not just a mobilizing one, seems indicated in the party spokesman's statement that

> of principal meaning is that the workers themselves,
> with their ideas, suggestions, stimulus, experiences,
> and critical directions, increasingly have a say in press,
> radio, and television and increasingly perceive better
> the function of the mass media as the tribune of socialist
> democracy.

That this is not an easy task in a revolutionary society, which is attempting to bring into being and keep going a new sociopolitical system, is clear in the party spokesman's caution that the press' role is carried on "against resistance, difficulties, laziness, despondency, or negligence; passionate argumentation for social necessity, which we help to a breakthrough, which we want to see applied and victorious everywhere."[110]

State Elections

Elections in a communist political system fill primarily the function of interest aggregation (and political communication, to be discussed later) rather than leadership selection. Clear alternative choices of leaders or of issues are not available. Instead, elections primarily offer an opportunity for the citizenry to make suggestions regarding party policy they are being asked to endorse—thus, the party is able to use the occasion to accumulate public demands and claims.

This is done through the vast communications campaign that surrounds state elections—thousands of agitators meet with collectives to nominate candidates (and hear their assessments of their capabilities) and millions of people gather to hear the candidates pledge their determination to carry out the party's program (and hear comments on problems involved in implementing that program). The entire population is involved, not only as agitators, but as members of election commissions, who take the final decisions on the acceptance/rejection of nominations, and the electoral committees, who organize the ballot and announce the results. Meetings are held at places of work and residence, as well as in schools and institutions. Official biographies are circulated and discussed and candidates personally answer questions.

Although many candidates are not members of the SED, few are nominated without its approval. For instance, SED leaders meet ahead of time with the allies' parties to agree on "acceptable" candidates for the People's Parliament. Similarly, the nominations of social and mass organizations are checked out ahead of time with the SED. (Many times the nominations are a reward for model behavior and outstanding work performance.) Further, the proportion of social groups, such as women, workers, youth, etc., is prescribed.

On election day the choice is relatively limited (and interest identification restricted). One can protest only by crossing off the single name that usually appears on the ballot, or by abstaining from voting. Very few voters choose either course, and so the SED reported 98 percent participation in the 1974 local-level elections in the nearly 9,000 GDR cities and communities and 98.4 percent in the 1971 parliamentary elections for the People's Chamber. Interesting, however, is the fact that the number of nonvoters increased, from 156,919 in the 1965 local-level elections to 246,622 in the elections of 1970. Similarly, the "No" votes in these elections rose from 15,786 in 1965 to 20,511, or 0.17 percent, in 1970, and then dropped to 0.08 percent in 1974. In the People's Chamber elections, those negative votes almost doubled—from about 9,500 in 1967 to about 17,000 in 1971. [111]

The last People's Chamber election (1971) also suggested some other new trends in the party's use of state elections as an instrument of interest aggregation. For instance, 584 candidates were proposed for 434 seats, so that more choice was available than previously. It also was reported that the election meetings often were very lively, including criticism from the voters about faulty economic planning and production problems. Too few kindergartens, playgrounds, and supplies of clothing and other consumer goods were among the complaints. Also innovative was the fact that a candidate's private life and his family were fit election topics, [112] in terms of how close the candidate came to the socialist ideal.

The last round of local elections for district and municipal assemblies (at Kreis, Stadt, Stadtbezirk, and Gemeinde levels) on May 19, 1974 showed similar trends. In the 1,090 cities and 7,757 communities of the GDR, 191,000 offices (plus successor candidates) were filled. A total of 230,000 candidates were proposed. [113] Theoretically, a candidate on the unified, or consolidated, ticket of the National Front could lose only if more than half of the voters opposed him. The name next in line on the ticket then wins. This order of the candidates on the ballot is decided by the conference of voters' representatives or voters' meetings whose members in turn have been elected, usually at their place of work. [114]

For the 1974 elections, the principle of nomination and examination of the candidates by their electorate was considerably extended. According to a Politburo decision, priority was to be given

> to have candidates nominated in the first place by teams
> of workers who personally know their future deputy from
> work within an enterprise. Such meetings should not bear
> a representative character but serve, above all, to
> thoroughly discuss the nominations and to ascertain what
> conclusions result from the nomination for the workers'
> team. This method will result in a firm link between the
> deputy and his team and in increasing the leading role of
> the working class within the people's representative
> bodies and in the enterprise itself. Thereby, at the same
> time, the basis will be laid for the deputy's awareness
> that he is, in his activities, assured of the support and
> the advice of the members of his team which he informs
> continually about his work as a deputy and gives account
> for his activities. [115]

In addition, election districts were made smaller to facilitate "more effective accounting by the deputies toward their electorates."[116]

Not surprisingly, 99.92 percent of the votes cast were for the unified ballot of the National Front. Although not relevant in the same sense as in elections in noncommunist political systems, the economic "goodies" offered the voters of the GDR several weeks before the May elections were interesting: increases in the minimum number of paid vacation days (from 15 to 18) and in wages for some types of work, as well as a decrease in the price of some synthetic fabrics. [117]

Example of Aggregation

The aggregative role of the party, the accumulating of demands and claims through its structure and through the mass media, is exemplified in the case of the new Youth Law:

Since the founding of the GDR, two Youth Laws have been passed, one in 1950 and one in 1964. In 1973 the third was proposed. First there was a decision of the SED's Politburo that a new law was needed, based no doubt to a large extent on the demands of youth reported to it from lower party levels. Then the FDJ, in consultation with the

Minister Council and the leadership of the FDGB, on June 14, 1973,
made public the proposed law and opened it to public debate. At the
VIII Conference of the FDJ, where the proposal was announced, the
first secretary of the youth organization described in unusual detail
the interest articulation and aggregation process that would take place:

> How shall the public discussion of the Youth Law
> proposal be led? We propose to the Minister Council
> to form, under its chairmanship, a mutual commission,
> of the Minister Council of the GDR and the Central
> Council of the FDJ, which examines and works out
> all suggestions for change in the proposed Youth Law,
> assesses the overall discussion, and prepares the
> reworked proposed law for resolution form. The
> constitution of this commission should result from a
> common resolution of the Minister Council of the GDR
> and the Central Council of the FDJ and the vote of the
> participating mass organizations. . . .
>
> The public discussion shall be concluded in
> November; in December the reworked proposal will be
> finished; and in the beginning of 1974 the Youth Law will
> be passed on to the supreme popular representative body
> of our Republic—the People's Chamber—for delibera-
> tion and passage.
>
> The public discussion of the proposed Youth Law
> will not be a dry discussion of paragraphs; rather we
> lead a discussion rich in substance and with rewarding
> goals. . . .
>
> We lead the discussion of the law so that with it and
> through it a living example of our socialist democracy
> will be given. It concerns a broad articulation regarding
> the responsibility of all citizens for the socialist develop-
> ment and class-conscious rearing of youth, from the
> peoples' representative bodies and the state leadership to
> the social organizations as well. . . .
>
> Concerning the organizational life of the Free
> German Youth, we propose to place the September
> membership meetings in all basic organizations and
> units uniformly under the motto "Our Youth Law and
> Us." . . .
>
> Simultaneously we challenge all our FDJ leadership
> units to apply the entire store of political mass work in
> order to engage the entire youth and all workers in con-
> versation regarding the proposed law, to learn their
> opinions and suggestions and to set into motion their
> willingness for realization.

In concert with the committees of the National
Front, the FDGB, the DTSV [German Gymnast and
Sport Organization] and the GST [Society for Sport and
Technic], as well as other social organizations, discussions with youth shall be used, round-table discussions, "Youth Law" meetings, parents' gatherings,
and other forms of public discussion. Our FDJ delegates
in the People's Chamber carry a very special responsibility, as well as the more than 22,000 youth delegates
in the local popular representative bodies. The time of
discussion of our Youth Law is a time of great activity
and special test for them. For everyone in the residential
areas of cities and villages, in the youth clubs and
dormitories—everywhere where young people meet—our
young delegates should elaborate and deliberate the
proposed Youth Law in multitudinous articulations, discussion evenings, at FDJ and youth meetings. . . .

From our friends in the press, radio, television
and film we ask a favor—to also support us in a
confirmative manner in the popularization and discussion of the proposed Youth Law. In doing so, for
the most part the youth themselves should speak up
in our organs of publications and all who take part in
the education and training of youth. . . .

Our press was always friendly to the FDJ and
the FDJ constantly friendly to the press. In leading the
public discussion of the Youth Law proposal, our mass
media and our youth organization also will be good
partners and the best allies.[118]

By early November 1973 the leader of the Central Committee's
Department for Youth could report that nearly 3 million citizens had
taken part in different discussions of the proposed youth law. Of these,
1.6 million were young people taking part in the FDJ membership
meetings dealing with "Our Youth Law and Us." By the time the law
was passed in early 1974, more than 5.4 million citizens had taken
part in more than 240,000 meetings. Suggestions for changes numbered 4821. In the reworking of the proposed law, some 200 changes
were made.[119]

The proposed changes may have included suggestions from
teachers, trade unionists, parents' councils, cultural personalities,
etc., for the nine major provisions of the proposed youth law concern
the development of the socialist personality, challenge to work
initiative, challenge to educational initiative, role in national defense,
cultural development, development of physical education and sport,

work and living conditions of youth, free time and travel, and implementation of measures to benefit youth.[120]

SUMMARY AND CONCLUSIONS

Thus it has been seen that interest identification and aggregation
in the GDR is a two-way process—the SED communicates to the people
its goals of socio-economic development that from the parameters of
public demand organizes and influences the institutional and associational channels through which those demands are identified, aggregates
the various interest group claims through the party structure, social
organizations, and mass media, and communicates to the citizenry
the party's adopted priorities. Further, it has been shown that party,
official/bureaucratic, intellectual, and broad social interest groups
participate in the input function in the GDR, using channels such as
the mass media, conferences, and elite representation.

In the discussion of this process it is assumed that there are
differences of interests not only among the groups—as among military/
security interest group members who may tend toward "hawkish"
international political views and intellectuals who may favor international contacts—but within them, as well, as between older interest
group members, who frequently may hold more political than professional priorities, and the younger ones who probably approach their
work relatively more pragmatically. Further, it has been seen that
it is not possible to make a sharp distinction between someone who
identifies with an intellectual interest group because of his training,
as for instance an economist, and one who at the same time holds a
party position and thus comes under the "party apparat" interest-group
rubric. The classification, therefore, does not necessarily represent
real divisions in the population but rather offers a tool of analysis.

Further, a really adequate interest-group analysis would seek
to determine how the various "opinion groups" within the overall
interest group—broadly described as the "liberals" and the "conserva-
tives"—form opinion coalitions on specific issues, as for instance
"liberal writers" and "liberal party apparat" members versus "conservative writers" and "conservative party functionaries" on the issue
of creative "elbowroom." That, however, is beyond the scope of this
chapter. The issues in communist political systems that would most
clearly demonstrate such varying views would include resource
allocation, structure of decision-making, and intellectual "elbowroom."

At the same time it is worth noting how this input function
relates to the other functions of the GDR's political system. For
example, interest identification and aggregation is directly related

to the GDR's political culture, which conditions the channels and content of interest articulation and aggregation. The interest function relates also to leadership recruitment and training, for, as has been seen, those persons recruited by the party into elite and leading cadre positions turn up again as interest identifiers and aggregators. The relationship to the rule-application function, too, is significant (as will be discussed in detail in a later chapter), for the party and state rule-application apparats are deeply involved in filtering out, reporting, controlling, and aggregating interest group demands.

One can, of course, criticize the GDR for not encouraging more spontaneous interest articulation, as indeed many GDR citizens do—they feel the party's "guiding" role in interest identification is too all-pervasive and that many of the structures set up for aggregation are too expensive (in terms of bureaucratic personnel and costs) relative to their achievements. On the other hand, for developing political systems there are advantages to its specialized structure. As Almond says,

> The development of specialized structures for the aggregation of a wide range of interests into a limited number of policy alternatives tends to increase system capability in several ways. It becomes easier for decision-makers to take account of all elements in the society and to respond to them. It also means that a wide range of voices can be heard without overwhelming the decision-making structures by the sheer volume of demands and thus rendering them helpless to construct effective and consistent policy. The development of specialized interest aggregation structures thus creates a potential for greater system responsiveness and effectiveness. [121]

Whether these structures present the GDR's decision-makers with enough policy alternatives is unclear. What is clear, however, is that a one-party system can become increasingly more open and responsive to interest-group demands than long was assumed.

NOTES

1. The Soviet discussion, see Grigori Glasermann, "Wiedersprüche der gesellschaftlichen Entwicklung im Sozialismus," Probleme des Friedens und des Sozialismus, No. 3 (1972), p. 381 ff. and "Dialektitk des Fortschritts," Probleme des Friedens und des Sozialismus, No. 4 (1973), pp. 451 ff.

2. G. Ch Schachnasarow, Die sozialistische Demokratie, in the series Der sozialistische Staat: Theorie, Leitung, Planung (Berlin: Staatsverlag, 1973), pp. 41 ff.

3. Adolf Dobieszweski, "Eine die Gesellschaft zementierende und umgestaltende Kraft," Probleme des Friedens und des Sozialismus, No. 4 (1974), pp. 466-71.

4. Schachnasarow, op. cit.

5. Gabriel A. Almond and G. Bingham Powell, Jr., Comparative Politics (Boston: Little, Brown, 1966), p. 73.

6. H. Gordon Skilling, "Group Conflict and Political Change," in Change in Communist Systems, ed. Chalmers Johnson (Stanford, Calif.: Stanford University Press, 1970), p. 216.

7. H. Gordon Skilling, "Group Conflict in Soviet Politics," in Interest Groups in Soviet Politics, ed. H. Gordon Skilling and Franklyn Griffiths (Princeton, N.J.: Princeton University Press, 1971), p. 399.

8. Almond and Powell, op. cit., p. 75.

9. David B. Truman, The Governmental Process, Political Interests and Public Opinion (New York: Alfred Knopf, 1951), pp. 33, 37.

10. Milton Lodge, "'Groupism' in the Post-Stalin Period," in Communist Studies and the Social Sciences, ed. Frederic J. Fleron, Jr. (Chicago: Rand McNally, 1969), p. 255.

11. Skilling in Interest Groups in Soviet Politics, op. cit., p. 27.

12. Franklyn Griffiths in Change in Communist Systems, op. cit., p. 360.

13. Almond and Powell, op. cit., pp. 74-85.

14. Frederic J. Fleron, Jr., ed. Communist Studies and the Social Sciences (Chicago: Rand McNally, 1969).

15. Joel J. Schwartz and William R. Keech, "Group Influence and the Policy Process in the Soviet Union," in Communist Studies and the Social Sciences, op. cit., p. 308.

16. Skilling, Interest Groups in Soviet Politics, op. cit., pp. 43, 382.

17. Almond and Powell, op. cit., p. 88.

18. Skilling, "Group Conflict in Soviet Politics," op. cit., p. 40-42, 392.

19. Ibid., pp. 216-17.

20. Henry Ehrmann, ed., Interest Groups on Four Continents (Pittsburg: University of Pittsburg Press, 1958), p. 38.

21. Almond and Powell, op. cit., pp. 100-02.

22. Lucien Pye, ed., Communications and Political Development (Princeton, N.J.: Princeton University Press, 1963), pp. 6-9.

23. Daniel Lerner and Stuart R. Schramm, eds. Communication and Change in the Developing Countries (Honolulu: East-West Center Press, 1967).

24. Richard Herber, "Die wachsende Führungsrolle unserer Partei," Einheit, 1/65, p. 3.

25. Protokoll der Verhandlungen des VIII Parteitages der Sozialistischen Einheitspartei Deutschlands. 15-19 Juni 1971 (Berlin, 1971), Bd. 1, S. 100.

26. Kurt Hager, Die entwickelte sozialistische Gesellschaft: Aufgaben der Gesellschaftswissenschaften nach dem VIII Parteitag der SED (Berlin: Dietz Verlag, 1971), pp. 69-78.

27. Kurt Hager, "Die entwickelte sozialistische Gesellschaft," Zur Theorie und Politik des Sozialismus (Berlin: 1972), pp. 165-66.

28. Friedrich Ebert, Der VIII Parteitag der SED über die Entwicklung der sozialistischen Demokratie. Die Aufgaben zur Erhöhung der Rolle der örtlichen Volksvertretungen (Berlin: Dietz Verlag, 1973), p. 36.

29. Hans-Jürgen Fink, DDR Report, No. 60 (1973), pp. 261-62.

30. According to the GDR's Little Political Dictionary, Bedarf is "an economic category of merchandise production [Warenproduktion]. It appears on the market as demand. . . . Constantly improving the satisfaction of it is a direct goal of the socialist society."
And Bedürfnise is

> the specific relationship of people, of human groups
> (classes) or the society as a whole, to their natural and
> social conditions of existence, which arises through the
> effort to serve these appropriate and human goals. The
> Bedürfnise are always determined concretely and
> historically by the present economic social forms,
> through their productive power and production relation-
> ships, as well as the resulting class interests. . . .
> The Bedürfnise of people take many forms. They run
> from development of productive forces and production
> relationships, improvement of working and living
> conditions, development of social relationships and
> personal capabilities, the sphere of individual consump-
> tion, deepening of knowledge, development of cultural
> and spiritual life, to meaningful leisure time, among
> others.

Kleines Politisches Wörterbuch (Berlin: Dietz Verlag, 1973), pp. 101-03.).

31. Werner Lamberz, "Die wachsende Rolle der sozialistischen Ideologie bei der Gestaltung der entwickelten sozialistischen Gesellschaft. Aktuelle Probleme des ideologischen Kampfes der SED." In series Vorträge im Parteilehrjahr der SED 1971/1972 (Berlin: Dietz Verlag, 1972), pp. 23-24, 27.

32. Die politische Organisation der sozialistischen Gesellschaft, in series Problem des wissenschaftlichen Kommunismus (Berlin: VEB Deutscher Verlag der Wissenschaften, 1973), p. 30.

33. Forum, 3/73, pp. 4-5; Arbeit und Arbeitsrecht, 4/73, pp. 99-103.

34. Namen und Daten: Biographien wichtiger Personen der DDR (Berlin and Bonn-Bad Godesberg: J.H.W. Dietz, 1973); Handbuch der Volkskammer (Berlin: Staatsverlag, 1972); Deutschland Archiv, 1/1974, pp. 49-59.

35. Thomas A. Baylis, "Elites and the Idea of Post-Industrial Society in the Two Germanies," paper delivered at the 1973 American Political Science Association annual meeting, New Orleans.

36. Einheit, 10/73, p. 1189.

37. Peter C. Ludz, "Governmental Organization and Elite Formation: The Case of the GDR," International Political Science Association Congress, Munich, August 1970.

38. Frankfurter Allgemeine Zeitung, September 10, 1971.

39. Peter C. Ludz, The Changing Party Elite in East Germany (Cambridge, Mass.: MIT Press, 1972), p. 183.

40. Ursula Hoffmann, Die Veränderung in der Sozialstruktur des Ministerrats der DDR 1949-1969 (Düsseldorf: Droste Verlag, 1971).

41. For a typical statement of this view, see article by Heinz Hoffmann, minister of national defense of the GDR, in German Foreign Policy, 4/1974, pp. 407-08.

42. Zahlenspiegel: Ein Vergleich Bundesrepublik Deutschland/ Deutsche Demokratische Republik (Bonn: Bundesminister für innerdeutsche Beziehungen, June 1973), p. 8.

43. M. Donald Hancock, "The Bundeswehr and the National People's Army: A Comparative Study of German Civil-Military Policy," (The Social Science Foundation and Graduate School of International Studies, University of Denver, Monograph No. 2, 1972-73).

44. Kurt Hager, Sozialismus und wissentschaftliche-technische Revolution (Berlin: Dietz Verlag, 1972), pp. 11-13.

45. Frankfurter Allgemeine Zeitung, op. cit.

46. Hager, Die entwickelte sozialistische Gesellschaft: Aufgaben, op. cit. pp. 69-76.

47. Deutsche Zeitschrift für Philosophie, No. 10 (1972), pp. 1269-79.

48. Deutsche Zeitschrift für Philosophie No. 3 (1972), pp. 326-43.

49. Forum, 1-6, 1973.

50. Zeitschrift für Geschichtswissenschaft, No. 3 (1973), pp. 357-62.

51. "Verordnung über die Leitung, Planung und Finanzierung an der Akademie der Wissenschaften und an Hochschulten," vom 23 August 1972, Gbl. II Nr. 53 vom 16 September 1972.

52. Einheit, 11/68, p. 1458.

53. Frank Grätz, "Wirtschaftliche Führungskräfte in der DDR," Berichte des Deutschen Industrie Institut zu Politik, Nr. 4, 1972.

54. Frankfurter Allgemeine Zeitung, op. cit.

55. "Kommunique über die XXV Tagung des RGW," Neues Deutschland, July 30, 1971.

56. "Bericht des Politbüros an die 6 Tagung des ZK der SED," Neues Deutschland, July 7, 1972.

57. Ralf Rytlewski, "Zu einigen Merkmalen der Beziehungen der DDR und der UdSSR auf den Gebieten der Naturwissenschaft und Technik," Deutschland Archiv Sonderheft, 1973.

58. Burrichter, Förtsch, Mann, "Probleme der sozialistischen Wissenschaftskooperation und Integration," Deutschland Archiv Sonderheft, 1973.

59. Rytlewski, op. cit.

60. Frankfurter Allgemeine Zeitung, op. cit.

61. Einheit, 3/73.

62. This relatively undogmatic cultural-political climate seemed confirmed by the openness of the discussions held at the 7th Congress of the Society of Plastic and Graphic Artists the end of May 1974.

63. Frankfurter Allgemeine Zeitung, op. cit.

64. Was der Parteitag beschloss, wird sein (Berlin: Verlag Tribune, 1972).

65. Die DDR-Entwicklung, Probleme, Perspektiven (Frankfurt: Verlag Marxistiche Blätter, 1972), p. 114.

66. Zahlenspiegel, op. cit., p. 39.

67. Wolfgang Junker, Das Wohnungsbauprogram der Deutschen Demokratischen Republik für die Jahre 1976 bis 1990 (Berlin: Dietz Verlag, 1973).

68. Staat und Recht, 10/11, 1972, pp. 1616-29.

69. Neues Deutschland, July 6, 1974.

70. Die politische Organisation der sozialistischen Gesellschaft (Berlin: VEB Deutscher Verlag der Wissenschaften, 1973), p. 85.

71. Die Arbeit, 3/73, pp. 14-15.

72. Hartmut Zimmermann, "Probleme der Mitbestimmung in der DDR," Kommunität (Berlin: Evangelische Akademie), 1973.

73. Die politische Organisation, op. cit., p. 87.

74. See Heinz Lippmann's biography Honecker (New York: Macmillan, 1972) for a first-hand account of the GDR's efforts in this direction in the immediate postwar period.

75. Democratic German Report, July 31, 1974, p. 106.

76. Democratic German Report, October 9, 1974, p. 145.

77. Hans Immler, "Die Landwirtschaft in der DDR" (Berlin: Institut für Angewandte Agrarpolitik und Agrarstatistik an der Technischen Universität Berlin, October 1971).

78. Neuer Weg, 19/1974, p. 913.

79. Hans Immler, Agrarpolitik in der DDR (Cologne: Verlag Wissenschaft und Politik, 1971), pp. 187-88, 196.

80. Immler, "Die Landwirtschaft in der DDR," op. cit.

81. Frankfurter Allgemeine Zeitung, op. cit.

82. DDR: Material zur politische Bildung, op. cit., pp. 77-88.

83. Die DDR-Entwicklung, op. cit., 169.

84. Einheit, 10/73, p. 1189.

85. Staat-und Parteiapparat der DDR (Bonn: Gesamtdeutschen Institute, Bundesanstalt für gesamtdeutsche Aufgaben, August 1974).

86. DDR: Material zur politische Bildung, op. cit.

87. Die DDR-Entwicklung, op. cit., pp. 166-68.

88. DDR: Material zur politische Bildung, op. cit.

89. "Die Beziehungen zwischen Ideologie, Hausarbeit und beruflicher Tätigkeit der Frauen—Referat bei der Gründung des Wissenschaftlichen Rates für Sozialpolitik und Demographie," Die Wirtschaft, No. 22 (May 1974), pp. 12-13.

90. Reprinted in Informationen (Bonn: Bundesminister für innerdeutsche Beziehungen, No. 24, 1974), pp. 15-18.

91. For an example of this discussion within the contemporary church, see the Catholic magazine Begegnung, 6/73, pp. 8-11, and the Protestant magazine Standpunkt, 6/73, pp. 141-43.

92. Neue Zeit, December 10, 1972.

93. DDR: Material zur politische Bildung, op. cit , pp. 144 ff.

94. Union Teilt Mit, April 1973, pp. 8-11.

95. Die politische Organisation, op. cit., p. 47.

96. Otto Reinhold, "Die entwickelte sozialistische Gesellschaft historischer Platz und Kriterien," Horizont 9/1973.

97. Einheit, 10/1973, p. 1198.

98. Staats- und Parteiapparat der DDR, op. cit; Die Volkskammer der DDR; VK 6. Wahlperiode (Berlin: Staatsverlag, 1972); Neues Deutschland, June 20, 1971.

99. Ebert, op. cit., p. 41.

100. Although this selection system assuring party control is not specifically stated, it is found in party statute requirements that "all members of leading Party organs must justify in their overall activity the great trust the Party has placed in them" and that "elections will pay attention to the systematic renewal of the leading Party organs through guaranteed politically and expertly qualified members of the Party." (Parteistatut, III/28). The control element in elections is further guaranteed in that the statute says party members have

the responsibility to see "that the will of an insignificant minority is not forced upon the Party majority." (Parteistatut III/32).

101. Neuer Weg, 8/1974, p. 342.

102. Richard Ebeling, "Neuwahl der SED-Bezirks- und Kreisleitungen," Deutschland Archiv, 6/74, p. 595 ff.

103. Die politische Organisation, op. cit., pp. 98-99, 58.

104. Kleines Politisches Wörterbuch (Berlin: Dietz Verlag, 1973) pp. 576-77.

105. Rüdiger Thomas, Modell DDR (Munich: Carl Hanser Verlag, 1972). p. 38.

106. Die politische Organisation, op. cit., p. 91.

107. Neue Deutsche Presse, 19/74, p. 5.

108. Erich Honecker, Bericht des Zentralkomitees an der VIII. Parteitag der SED (Berlin: Dietz Verlag, 1971), p. 100.

109. Elisabeth Noelle-Neumann and Winfried Schultz, eds., Das Fisher Lexikon: Publizistik (Frankfurt: Fischer Taschenbuch Verlag, 1971), pp. 241-45.

110. Agitation und Propaganda nach dem VIII Parteitag der SED (Berlin: Dietz Verlag, 1972), pp. 58-59, 84.

111. Deutschland Archiv, May 1970, p. 555, and Neues Deutschland, November 17, 1971.

112. Heinz Lippmann, "Volkskammerwahlen mit neuen Akzenten" (Cologne: Deutsche Welle Dokumentation, Nr. 208/71, December 1971).

113. GBl 1, 1965, S. 143.

114. Dieter Hösel, "Elections in the GDR," German Foreign Policy, 14/1974, p. 433.

115. Friedrich Ebert, Starke Volksvertretungen in engem Kontakt zum Leben (Berlin 1973), p. 46.

116. Hösel, op. cit., p. 434.

117. Neues Deutschland, April 30, 1974.

118. Junge Generation, 7/1973, pp. 14-18.

119. Einheit, 4/74, p. 423.

120. Junge Generation, 7/1973, pp. 21-42.

121. Almond and Powell, op. cit., p. 105.

OUTPUTS: REWARDS, DEPRIVATIONS

In examining functionally the output side of a communist political system, one is forced to give special attention to the "mix" of coercion/persuasion/specific benefits found in the rewards and deprivations allocated by the decision-making activities and agencies. Just as a communist political system, like all other systems, seeks a balance between inputs and outputs to regulate demands and supports, so communist decision-makers, too, seek a balance among the various forms of outputs available for coping with stress.

And such potential stress situations do exist since, as has been shown, there is an apparent trend toward increasing demands trying to find their way to the decision-making centers of communist political systems. Thus to prevent overload, coercion and the willingness to use it as an output apparently remain significant. In fact, the proportion of compulsion/persuasion is held by many students of communist affairs to be one of the distinguishing characteristics of communist political system output.

But reliance primarily on coercion as an output is an expensive proposition for a political system, more costly than, for instance, a national television address by political leaders who persuade citizens to accept and obey a decision for reasons of national interest. The ultimate aim is to turn "power" into "authority," that is, to gain the public acceptance that legitimizes a system and makes loyalty and obedience voluntary. Thus, in the case of the communist political systems of Eastern Europe one in recent years has seen an increased reliance on persuasion and material forms of output.

Communications output, for instance, is especially significant in generating diffuse support, as through the manipulation of ideology. In any political system ideology provides much of the cement that glues together the diverse groups and interests within the society. But it is even more vital in a relatively new and radically different political system, such as the communist system. Indeed, ideology serves to legitimize the system and the regime. Actions are taken in the name of Lenin and Marx. Indeed, sometimes the names of national communist leaders are invoked. In this way supports are motivated and a sense of dedication and mission is inspired. For instance, it is said that "the foreign policy of the socialist countries rests on the firm foundation of the Leninist principle of peaceful coexistence" or that calls for higher productivity of labor are "to be achieved through continuous technical progress, economic planning, strict observance of the Leninist principle of providing material incentives and moral stimuli to work for the good of society." A hardening line frequently is justified on the basis of Marxism/ Leninism, while the charge is made that principles of a period of liberalization were "counterrevolutionary," "opportunism," etc., that is, against the faith. The following chapters will again and again present examples of communications being used as an output to generate diffuse support.

Another output means, that of granting specific benefits to generate specific support, also will be illustrated. For instance, increasing demands for more consumer goods are met, at least in part, by an output of new economic reforms that produce the additional goods the people want. In modernizing societies a major problem of the ruling elite is to determine how much output of such specific demand fulfillment is necessary to gain the needed amount of specific support.

Crucial in determining the nature of the outputs is the decision-making center of the communist political system. As will be seen, this center is conceived of by most contemporary scholars of communist affairs as consisting of not just one man but the entire Politburo. Within that group of about a dozen, the first secretary of the party and several of his confidants are believed to hold the key to influence. Further, as shown in the discussion of interest aggregation, it is felt that the Politburo is a kind of forum in which the demands of the various aggregated interests are represented by sympathetic individual Politburo members. While the conflicts then are intense, diverging usually along issue lines and between modernizing and status quo views, or on the basis of resource allocation, they remain within the control of the party. Specifically, they are controlled by the party faction holding power at the moment. (However, while it is true that the change of leadership is a constant process, it is essential to keep in mind that the system itself is not challenged by such changes.)

Also crucial to the output process are the full-time party workers, the "apparatchiki." Their function is to carry out orders and communicate back reports of their implementation. Hundreds make up the leading cadre, thousands the middle cadre, and tens of thousands the "activists," that is, part-time volunteers of the rank and file membership. Among all these groups involved in output functions, communications is as crucial as among the employees of a giant corporate structure with its house organs.

Thus, using all the adaptive mechanisms available within their political systems, the communist political system in most cases has proved able to alleviate stress situations through output before they get out of hand. Although the unrest glimpsed in communist political systems often is described as "seething" by perhaps overwishful

Western observers, it is not yet, in most cases, manifested as an input of increased demand and decreased support that cannot be coped with through the regular output functions of the system.

5

DECISION-MAKING /
RULE-MAKING

The conversion of the inputs into outputs of a political system is the task of the decision-making agencies and activities, indicated by the circle in the center of the systems-functional graph presented in Chapter 1 (Figure 1, p. 8). In constitutional democratic systems the circle is usually thought of as involving primarily the executive branch of government, while the formal rule-making function is primarily exercised by the legislature.

In communist political systems, however, with their provision that arrogates "final" political power to the party over the state (or governmental apparatus), these two functions merge to an extent not found in other systems. Decisions and rules are formulated and initiated by the party's executive agencies (the Politburo, Central Committee, the Secretariat of the Central Committee), with the upper levels of the state bureaucracy (Minister Council, State Council, the People's Chamber, and local elected assemblies) serving as legitimizing and declarative agencies. Because decision-making and rule-making are merged in communist systems, both functions will be treated within the context of this chapter.

THEORETICAL FRAMEWORK

Marxism/Leninism

As noted in previous chapters, Marxist/Leninist concepts concerning who shall make authoritative decisions and rules within communist political systems are clearly spelled out. Although some of these principles previously have been alluded to (see Chapter 1, for example), the following are especially relevant within the decision-making/rule-making framework:

Leading Role of the Party

In all systems ruled by a Communist party, its "leading role" is a reality not subject to challenge. As has been discussed, the party leadership feels that the party not only is the repository of political insight, but simultaneously represents, as well as speaks authoritatively for, the most advanced forces in society. In the aftermath of a successful revolution, thus, the Communist party is expected to adapt itself to the giant tasks of revolutionary change it has set for itself:

> The conquest of power by the working class fundamentally alters the positions of its militant vanguard, the Marxist/Leninist party. Before that, it is the party of a class fighting for power; after that it is the party of the ruling class. Experience has shown that after the revolution the role of the Marxist party as leaders of the working class, and all the working people, not only does not decrease but, on the contrary, becomes immeasurably greater. It now becomes responsible for everything that goes on in society, for the policy of the state of the dictatorship of the proletariat, for the development of productive forces and culture, for the improvement of the people's welfare. [1]

If these ambitious requirements justify the extension of party rule into all areas of social life, there is an even stronger justification growing out of the Marxist/Leninist concept of historical mission: "The role of the Marxist party in the system of the dictatorship of the working class is not the usual role of a ruling-class party. Its position in the state is determined not only by elections, but by the historic mission of the working class as the natural leader of society in its advance to communism." [2]

Collective Leadership

At the time of "de-Stalinization" in the Soviet Union, this Leninist principle of collective leadership (noted in Chapter 4) was emphasized and continues to play a role in theoretical Marxist/Leninist concepts. For instance, Pravda offered the following explanation of collective leadership during this period (1953-64):

One of the fundamental principles of Party leadership is
collectivity in deciding all important problems of Party
work. It is impossible to provide genuine leadership if
inner Party democracy is violated in the Party organization, if genuine collective leadership and widely developed
criticism and self-criticism are lacking. Collectiveness
and collegial principles represent a very great force in
Party leadership. The principle of collectivity in work
means, above all, that decisions adopted by Party committees on all cardinal questions are the fruit of collective
discussion. No matter how experienced leaders may be,
no matter what their knowledge and ability, they do not
possess and they cannot replace the initiative and experience of a whole collective. In any collegium, in any
directing collective, there are people who possess
diverse experience without which leaders cannot make
correct decisions or exercise qualified leadership.

Individual decisions are always or almost always
one-sided decisions. Hence, the very important requirement that decisions must rest on the experience of many,
must be the fruit of collective effort. If this is not so, if
decisions are adopted individually, serious errors can
occur in work. Insofar as each person is able to correct
the errors of individual persons and insofar as Party
agencies in the course of practice reckon with these
corrections, the decisions which result are more correct.[3]

In terms of the GDR's leading party, the SED, it, too, has
emphasized the necessity for collective leadership:

The supreme principle of work in the leading Party organs
is collectivity. All levels of leadership dealing with Party
problems consult about and then decide on the planning
of work in the collective. The principle of collectivity
does not annul personal responsibility. The personality
cult, and the related violation of inner-party democracy,
are unreconciliable with the Leninist principle of Party
life and cannot be tolerated within it.[4]

In a word, while a person is expected to exercise individual responsibility in the execution of specific assignments, within the context of
larger decision-making environments, he is expected to play a
different role, namely that of a member of a collective.*

---

*As Chapter 2 attempts to demonstrate in its discussion of the
political socialization process, the requirement for individuals, and

Democratic Centralism

A key concept in decision-making and rule-making theory within communist political systems is found in democratic centralism. In formulating it, Lenin felt he had discovered a means by which decisions could be made efficiently, quickly, and harmoniously. For him, the most important consideration was to develop a party capable of concerted action.

Decisions were to be arrived at "democratically" within the Leninist schema, that is, through open and free discussion. Once they were made, however, they were expected to be accepted and acted upon: In all cases, decisions would be made at the "top" of the party hierarchy—after a suitable amount of discussion within lower levels of the apparatus—and (uniformly) applied by lower-ranking organizations within the party: "freedom to criticize," in Lenin's words, was permitted, "so long as this does not disturb the unity of a definitive action; it rules out all criticism that disrupts or makes difficult the unity of action decided upon by the Party."[5]

In adapting democratic centralism to the tasks of party leadership, a GDR specialist in party affairs explains the relevance of this concept, and the practical uses to which it is put:

> What does democratic centralism mean? (1) Our Party
> is democratic because the Party member, and the
> organizational components, is the supporting force out
> of whose experiences and political activities Marxist/
> Leninist theory is continuously extended and ultimately
> actualized. The politics of a Marxist/Leninist Party
> serve the interests of the people as no other Party can.
> Members determine its politics, actively work in the
> realization and choose leaders who enjoy their trust.
> (2) At the same time, our Party is centralized in that
> all of its members undividedly work from the foundation
> of Marxism/Leninism under the leadership of a unified
> center, the Central Committee. Accordingly, there is
> an inseparable relationship between centralism and
> inner-party democracy, thus guaranteeing that the
> Party will operate as a unified and organic whole.[6]

---

party members especially, to subordinate oneself to the collective is considered to be a natural "role-shift" consonant with the development of socialist personality structures in the GDR.

The operational meaning of the concept is then elaborated upon:

> Democratic centralism signifies that: (1) A unified Party
> program, decided upon by the highest Party organ, the
> Party Day, is enacted. Between Party Days the elected
> members of the Central Committee are supreme; (2) De-
> cisions made by higher organs are unconditionally binding
> on the next lower organ of the Party. Lower organs are
> placed under the control of higher ones; (3) All leading
> organs from top to bottom are elected; periodic accountings
> by Party organs are given by their Party organizations;
> (4) Strict Party discipline and the subordination of the
> minority to the majority. Conscious Party discipline is
> equally binding for all members. Through the broad
> unfolding of inner-party democracy, centralism in the
> Party will not be weakened but strengthened.[7]

Functional

Functionalists stress, as Figure 1 (Chapter 1) indicates, that
decision-making is a matter of "agencies and activities," not just
people. The point is that some political activity within the decision-
making process may not represent authoritative behavior (as described in Constitutions and Statutes), but is rather an outcome of
various efforts to influence other decision-makers (as Politburo first
secretary "lobbying" among fellow members to form a majority consensus before a pending decision). Instead of one neat circle, then,
the graph can easily be broken into subsets, each representing
different party and state departments, each connected to the others
by crisscrossing arrows representing various policy inputs and outputs.
In sum, however, these various subsets can still be viewed as representing the most important decision-making activities at work in
communist political systems.

Aside from organizational issues, functionalists are vitally
involved with problems of political control and political order, a
theme nicely touched upon in Samuel Huntington's cross-national
study:

> The most important political distinction among countries
> concerns not their form of government (pluralist vs.
> Marxist/Leninist), but their degree of government. The
> differences between democracy and dictatorship are less
> than the differences between those countries whose politics

embodies consensus, community, legitimacy, organization, effectiveness, stability, and those countries whose politics is deficient in these qualities. [8]

Within the context of order and control, functionalists are additionally interested in discovering, describing, and explaining, "how" complex political systems attempt to make authoritative public choices regarding particular policies:

> Goal specification is implicitly a part of the integrative process. When effective, it contributes to the development of political consensus. Whether good or bad, effective or ineffective, goal specification is an element of political articulation that derives in significant measure from the directive role of the political party. The question of what goals are specified must be supplemented by the questions of who sets them, through what processes they are arrived at, and how they are articulated to the public. . . . [9]

Though all polities necessarily specify goals, perhaps the crucial distinction between democratic-constitutional and Marxist/Leninist systems has to do with the degree to which the latter centralizes the process within the party and state apparatus. This consideration is especially important in examining decision- and rule-making in the GDR.

Despite obvious differences, functional and Marxist/Leninist concepts of political organization possess several commonalities that allow us to fruitfully integrate them in the analysis. In the first instance, both theories emphasize the importance of "goal specification" by political elites. Second, both theories heavily underline the necessity of making viable policy decisions, though Marxist/Leninists contend that communist systems are superior to capitalist ones in their ability to arrive at scientifically "correct" policies for society. Third, both theories emphasize the complexities of policy-making in highly industrialized societies, and from this vantage point also devote parallel amounts of attention to the challenges of social and political coordination. Finally, Marxist/Leninist and functional concepts of decision- and rule-making place appropriate stress on the phenomenon and necessity of leadership on all levels of the social and political system. [10]

SITUATION IN THE GDR

The "Catchall" Period (1945-49)

The early postwar years made it necessary for East German communists to dispel, if not extinguish, traditional assumptions of party dominance in the policy-making and rule-making processes. This consideration simultaneously touches on tactical and ideological questions.

From the tactical side, the communist group under Walter Ulbricht was not in the initial position of being able to enforce its will on noncommunist elements in East German society. Not only were the lines of cleavage separating the Western powers from the Soviet Union within divided Germany—and especially Berlin—yet to be drawn with finality, but the population had yet to become convinced that socialism was an inevitable alternative in the East to capitalist development in the West. For these reasons, the communist "appeal to the population in the Eastern zone was vague as well as muted." As one Western observer of this critically important epoch notes,

> Wilhelm Pieck [future president of the GDR] arrived from Moscow at the beginning of June 1945 and brought with him the new KPD Gründungsaufruf . . . "completed to the last comma." The Aufruf . . . was astonishingly mild in tone and substance. It insisted that "it would be wrong to force the Soviet system on Germany, for that does not correspond to her present conditions of develop-ment." Rather, those conditions demanded an "anti-fascist, democratic regime, a parliamentary republic with all democratic rights and liberties for the people." Only the most moderate of economic reforms were pro-posed: Land reform and the socialization of public utilities on the Land [state] and communal levels. So mild, in fact, was the Aufruf that many of the former members of the underground resistance, who had anticipated the immediate construction of the new order, protested audibly. 11

From the ideological side, there was no contradiction with tactical considerations since Marxist/Leninist theory is very specific in its emphasis on historical timing. The expulsion of Marshall Tito from the Soviet bloc and the Berlin crisis and the subsequent per-manent division of Germany played historical roles in the transforma-tion of East Germany into a communist system by the late 1940s.

"Building Legitimacy" and "New Work Styles"
(1949-75)

The early years of official SED rule were characterized by a
certain degree of harshness (see Chapter 1). Perhaps the party could
have avoided the kinds of decisions that led to the progressive alienation of the urban and rural middle classes, but the SED's concept of
historical role clearly made it difficult for the new elite to identify
with, much less understand, the problems facing social strata who
suddenly felt themselves out of tune with the far-reaching changes
being put into operation by a Marxist/Leninist party. In either case,
the GDR was gradually able to develop a political system capable of
generating a high rate of industrial growth and social mobility for all
strata after an initially unstable and turbulent beginning. Thus, by
the middle 1960s, the SED could boast that its decision-making and
rule-making processes had acquired legitimacy within the mass population.

Since the departure of Walter Ulbricht from the scene, a number
of tendencies have been added to this general picture of forward
movement that began to transform the SED's relationship with the
broad population during the last several years of his rule. In all
cases, corresponding changes in the conduct of decision-making and
rule-making should be noted.

In the first instance, the accentuation of personal power within
the governmental apparatus has been halted. As will be discussed
later, this means a relative loss of power and influence within the
State Council, and a corresponding increase in the visibility and
rule-making latitude of the Minister Council.

Further, though membership in state organs, from the People's
Chamber (the GDR's Parliament) to the local people's representative
bodies (Örtliche Volksvertretungen), continues to be regulated by the
principle of "democratic-centralism," the SED has nonetheless
attempted to introduce an atmosphere of administrative initiative
within all levels of the governmental structure. Commenting on the
contemporary role of these last-named entities, one official source
remarks that "local authorities are increasingly becoming involved
in defining basic issues of government policy."[12]

Finally, and perhaps most significantly for the long run, the
style of decision-making within the SED has been markedly altered:

The most striking innovation in the SED since Honecker
took office is a conspicuous change in working style in
the widest sense, including a refocusing of domestic
policy. The new style is characterized by a more

objective attitude and stronger emphasis on the
practical aspect. There is more sober analysis and
less formulation of permanent long-term projections
than there was in the last few years under Walter
Ulbricht. One of Honecker's first official actions as
First Secretary is said to have been to commission a
group of economists and other experts to analyze certain economic miscalculations objectively, openly and
quickly. [13]

In regard to the second change previously noted, the observer goes
on to remark that "immediately after the VIII Congress of the SED,
the party organizations, especially in government, mass and cultural
organizations, took their stance on questions of the new working style,
utilizing the resolutions of the VIII Congress."[14]

STRUCTURES

Party

The Socialist Unity Party of Germany (SED) is a creature of
two interrelated dynamics. In the first case, it styles itself in the
tradition of a Marxist/Leninist party. Not only does this suggest a
historical obligation to realize the "objective" laws of socialist, and
ultimately communist, development as it conceives of them, but in
the short term it also commits the SED to a continuous program of
political education and decision-making. Secondly, because the party
rules over, as well as directs, a society that is highly educated and
occupationally diversified, it necessarily is called upon to develop
numerous participatory structures capable of exercising decision-
and rule-making authority. In relation to both sets of dynamics, the
SED has increasingly felt the need to rationalize its mode of operation,
on the one hand, while developing a subordinate system of government
—the socialist state—capable of translating authoritative decision
into binding rules of public conduct, on the other hand. Questions of
rationalization within the party are dealt with first, while rule-making
(that is, ogvernmental) phenomena are examined later.

Decision-making cannot be understood, much less appreciated,
without examining those structures standing behind the making of
authoritative public commitments. Students of decision-making in the
United States, for example, have attempted to study this phenomenon
by tracing policies back to their points of institutional origin. The

question of "who governs" thus inevitably involves an attempt to
uncover sources and patterns of influence and power that shape the
content and direction of public policy issues. In the GDR this consideration involves a description of the SED's self-concept in the
decision-making realm.

As with other Marxist/Leninist parties, the SED asserts that
it alone is the single-most important force guiding the development
of socialist values, institutions, and policies in the GDR. The party's
Program is very explicit on this point:

> The program of a Marxist/Leninist Party is the
> fundamental theoretical and political document for
> an entire period of social development. As an authori-
> tative program for the undivided behavior of its members,
> it reflects the highest and most general will of the entire
> membership. It creatively applies the general laws of
> Marxism/Leninism to the conditions of the GDR after the
> triumph of socialist production relationships as well as
> drawing generalizations from the experiences of 120
> years of struggle in the German and international
> workers' movement. . . . Contained within the Program
> are the basic tasks [Hauptaufgaben] directed toward the
> progressive strengthening and consolidation of the Party,
> toward the progressive development of socialist state
> power and socialist democracy, toward the organization
> of the economic system and socialist economic leadership,
> toward the development of socialist ideology, toward
> culture and the educational system, as well as toward
> other areas of society. [15]

The complexity of these tasks necessarily forces the SED to
develop a division of decision-making labor within its ranks. In this
vein, four basic structures come into play.

Politburo

Official party documents create the impression that the SED
Congress (previously held every four years, now held every five
since the VIII Party Congress), runs the political system of the GDR.
Operational reality dictates otherwise, however. As in constitutional
democracies, the demands on political leadership inevitably push
decision-making responsibilities into the hands of small numbers of
strategically placed individuals and groups. From this vantage point,
the SED's supreme policy-making organ is not an assemblage of
delegates, called together once every several years, but a cohesive
body of individuals who meet together on a weekly basis, the Politburo.

The Politburo has fluctuated between 14 and 26 people, if full members and candidates are combined. With one exception (1967), this body has continued to grow consistently in number over time. 16 It is, as Ludz suggests, the supreme decision-maker "in all spheres of East German social life." 17

An East German writer succinctly describes the basic functions performed by this organ: "The Politburo involves itself with basic questions of politics revolving around the role of the Party, governmental leadership, and the economy. . . . Members and candidates of this organ engage themselves in the job of making sure that decisions by the Party and government within these task areas are carried out." 18 The writer goes on to note, however, that the Politburo cannot perform such tasks without the assistance of organs placed under its direction. Of particular significance in this regard are the (1) Bureau for Industry and Construction; (2) Bureau of Agricultural Economics; (3) Ideological Commission, entrusted with the task of making Politburo decisions immediately comprehensible to party and nonparty members; and (4) Agitation Commission, called upon to develop communication policies for the television, radio, and newspaper industries. 19

Working directly with the Politburo is the Secretariat, which handles its on-going work. As of August 1974, it consists of a first secretary, who is always the head of the Politburo and the Central Committee, and 10 adjunct secretaries. 20 As a coordinator of work jointly involving the energies of the Politburo and Central Committee, 21 the Secretariat is an indispensable executive organ. In this regard, one writer observes that "the Secretariat normally meets at least once a week—it has access to a well-coordinated and expert staff; its comprehensive bureau apparatus controls contact with the Central Committee technical sections [Fachabteilungen] and their linked regional counterparts; inevitably, those individuals involved in its daily operation are substantially more influential than those Politburo members and candidates who are not simultaneously members of the Secretariat." 22

Central Committee

The Central Committee has become an increasingly significant decision-making organ in the GDR, especially since the late 1950s and early 1960s when the party began to change recruitment criteria for membership in this organ. From a "purely acclamatory and declamatory assembly it is increasingly undergoing change to an active coordinative and transforming body, in which Politburo decisions are objectively discussed by party functionaries and experts and prepared for transmission downward." 23

As of August 1974, the Central Committee was composed of 135 full members and 46 candidates. While a body of this size cannot exercise the kind of power and influence held either by the Politburo or its Secretariat, the visibility of the Central Committee cannot be underemphasized, especially in terms of its role in the decision-making process. From this angle, the Central Committee performs the key task of publicizing decisions and general guidelines emanating from the Politburo, as well as publicly evaluating the progress of various party programs enunciated at the congresses of the SED. Regarding these last-named functions, a number of plenums are held—they must take place at least once every six months—for the purpose of airing SED policies in light of the most recent conditions at work within the society at large and the decision-making process more specifically.[24] Though the realities lying behind the real exercise of political power strongly contradict official Party literature (which states that the committee is the highest "organ of the SED between Party Congresses"), there is little question that it plays an important role in the political process.[25]

In terms of social representation, the Central Committee is perhaps the most reliable indicator of change within the GDR. Even considering the fact that the SED has made ambitious attempts to fill elite party organs with representatives of the working classes, the general occupational makeup of the Central Committee conforms with overall contours of change that have transformed East Germany from a system staffed by party bureaucrats, with little or no formal education, into a system peopled by individuals and groups boasting advanced degrees in the fields of applied mathematics, organizational theory, and engineering (as noted in Chapter 4). In short,

the Central Committee of the SED is no longer an organizational focal point for the "old guard" of Communist functionaries, whose political mores were established in the struggles of the 1920s and 1930s and who were therefore frequently unable to adapt themselves to the reality of a highly mobile industrial society. New and younger groups of functionaries are entering the Central Committee, mostly via key positions in the state apparatus. They have considerably altered the profile of the leading groups in the party apparatus.[26]

Party Congresses

The Party Congress of the SED occupies an elevated position in official East German literature dealing with the organization of political authority in the GDR. A glance at the organizational chart

(Figure 2, p. 147) places the Party Congress (or "Party Days," as the
SED refers to them) at the pinnacle of the authority pyramid, with the
Central Committee, Politburo, and its Secretariat, resting directly
beneath it. It would be easy to argue that the facts contradict reality
since, as previously mentioned, a large body of individuals, called
together once every four to five years, cannot possibly exercise
dominant authority over the conduct of politics on a daily basis. Just
as the English queen does not really occupy the number-one political
slot in the British political system, neither does the Party Congress
stand at the peak of the East German authority structure.

The significance of the Party Congress lies not in its organizational visibility, but in its ability to broadly outline, and articulate,
the goals of the party. Thus, while the Politburo, the Secretariat,
and, to a lesser degree, the Central Committee, are held responsible
for the performance of the East German polity, the Party Congress
represents an important stock-taking effort on behalf of the party.
From this vantage point, the intricacies and nuances of daily political
affairs are glossed over in the attempt by the party to sketch the
broad dimensions of policy that have been articulated since the last
Congress, on the one hand, and a package of issues that remain to
be acted upon in the future, on the other hand. Thus the Party
Congress plays an important, albeit symbolic, role in the policy-
making process.

Combining a description of stock-taking activity with practical
aspects of Party Congress activity, specialists feel the SED Congresses

> invariably play an important role in the GDR: within
> their structure, political changes within the single
> authoritative state party become recognizable.
> Officially, the SED is constructed according to the
> principles of democratic centralism. As its highest
> organ, the Party Day thereby determines the political
> line for the next four years and chooses the leader-
> ship. . . . They provide general information about the
> adopted direction of change taken by the Party, while
> also allowing one to identify areas of structural influ-
> ence within its leadership. . . . [27]

These last items deserve additional comment.

The selection of leaders at Party Congresses is a reflection of
earlier decisions made within the confines of the Politburo and its
Secretariat. The Party Congress simply ratifies, and subsequently
publicizes, those decisions. More specifically, the Congress chooses
the new Central Committee, both members and candidates, as well

as the "Central Revision Commission," an organ entrusted with the
oversight and evaluation of party business from the national through
the district, regional, and city levels of SED organization. (As of
August 1974, this body consisted of 1 president, 23 full members, and
5 candidates.)[28] At least for the Central Committee, the change in
membership from one Congress to another is slight, though as in the
case of party elections, such events nonetheless provide an opportunity
for the SED to cleanse its ranks of members who are either unable
to perform executive functions or who have been removed by the
party hierarchy due to unacceptable political deviation, a consideration
dominantly mirrored in the SED's treatment of dissidents during the
purges of 1953 and 1957.

The study of politics is in part an examination of decisions and
how they have been arrived at.[29] Very little is known about how the
Politburo, the Secretariat, and the Central Committee behave in this
area. Party Congresses do not supply additional insight into this
process, though they are capable of supplying general profiles of
SED commitments to particular goals that, in turn, supply content
and direction to subsequent policies undertaken by the regime. Two
Congresses, the VI and the VIII, are especially significant in this
regard.

The VI Congress of the SED (January 15-21, 1963) represents
an important turning point in the party's definition of policy questions.
To be sure, the SED had begun to change the relationship between
party and state apparatuses by the late 1950s as a new generation of
technically trained groups began to make their entrance into both
structures. Nonetheless, it was not until the Berlin Wall was constructed in late summer 1961 that the party felt itself able to relax
the degree of control it had exerted on all levels of the governmental
apparatus. Without giving up ultimate control of the governmental
structure, and especially the economic and finance ministries, the
SED announced at the Congress that economic development would be
allowed to follow the dictates of technical and local (district, regional,
and, to a lesser degree, communal) reality instead of being forced
to operate within the somewhat rigid, and overly centralized, framework of official Marxist/Leninist categories applied to the operation
of the economic system. Large industrial combines (Volks Vereinigte
Betriebe, VVB) "would now be held responsible for technical and
sales development," so the Congress decided.[30] By the end of these
proceedings, the by-now famous "New Economic System" had been
launched.

While the VI Congress of the SED signified a fundamental change
in regime policy on the economic front, the VIII Congress represented
a mixture of continuity and revision within the official policy structure
of the SED. On the one hand, the party did not announce any intention

to drastically revise the elemental assumptions of economic planning
and decision-making that had been given official blessing at the VI
Congress. On the other hand, the formal proceedings (June 15-19,
1971) highlighted party dissatisfaction with some aspects of Walter
Ulbricht's social and economic policies that had increasingly tended
to neglect the interests of the working class. In this latter vein,
Honecker, Ulbricht's chosen successor, touched upon four specific
goals that were to be fully realized between the VIII and IX Congresses.
To begin, he called for an increase in real income of 4 percent per
annum for the working population. With particular emphasis given to
the inadequate condition of housing for the working classes, he then
called for the construction and refurbishing of 500,000 new dwellings—
the challenge of "improving the living conditions of workers in the
main industrial centers" was given strong emphasis more generally
within this specific context. Third, problems of environmental control,
which had elicited little concern at the VI or VII Congresses, were
now given prominence.* Finally, and most broadly, a list of social-
political measures were announced, all of which directly committed
the SED and the socialist state to the improvement of daily living conditions for the mass population. [31]

Basic Organizations

        The SED is divided into 54,000 primary groups, composed of
no less than 3 and no more than 15 members. [32] The rationale behind
organizing such groups is that despite an aura of centralization,
party work is ultimately carried out by small groups of individuals
who concern themselves with such problems and tasks as: (1) whether
a given factory can fulfill a specific production quota, (2) whether an
errant member of the party is deserving of one more chance before
being publicly disciplined by the local organization, and (3) whether
enough party members can be organized on the weekend to build tents
for a circus soon to visit the community.
        Predictably, basic organizations are located along all points of
East German society, a reality that does not come as a surprise in
light of the ambitious tasks the party has assigned itself within East
German society:† As one analyst describes its role, "The foundation
of the Party rests on its basic organizations."[33] The SED's Statute

----

        *As the world's ninth largest industrial system, East Germany
has unfortunately imitated other societies in its neglect of the environment.

        †Refer to page 181 for a short discussion of this phenomenon.

correspondingly lists a variety of functions that must be performed
by it:

>   1. Explanations of political affairs and organiza-
> tional work within the working class and other working
> strata [wertätigen Schichten] in city and country. . . .
>   2. The organization of systematic political schooling
> for members and candidates; exploiting all possibilities
> for the acquisition of Marxist/Leninist theory and its
> application in the practice of socialist construction.
>   3. Active participation in political, economic, and
> cultural life within the German Democratic Republic.
>   4. The selection of the best people for entrance
> into the Party as members and candidates, and their
> subsequent political education.
>   5. The scrupulous and timely fulfillment of
> practical tasks which have been decided upon by the
> Party leadership.
>   6. The mobilization and organization of the masses
> for the fulfillment of state, economic, and cultural tasks.
>   7. Leading the struggle to make sure that every
> member and candidate accepts socialist laws, morals,
> and ethics, as the foundation for his deeds and behavior. . . .
>   8. Struggling against the miseducation of members
> in the realms of bureaucratism, maladministration, and
> carelessness, as well as exercising implacable and
> revolutionary watchfulness toward the enemies of the
> Party and people.
>   9. The development of criticism and self-
> criticism. . . . [34]

State

The theoretical and practical relationship between party and
state in communist systems is an uneasy one.[35] Ideologically, the
Communist party is supposedly moving toward a society that obviates
the need for a governmental apparatus. This apparent paradox is
solved, as already noted, by the establishment of what Lenin calls a
"transitional" stage, or the dictatorship of the proletariat (see Chapter 1 for a discussion of this phenomenon). Under the circumstances
within which the GDR finds itself developmentally, the following
description of the socialist state appears to reflect the SED's conception of how governmental authority should be used in the pursuit of
Marxist/Leninist goals of social and political development:

The socialist state is the power instrument of the
working class and its allies in developing socialist
society. It is chiefly through the state that the working
class accomplishes its historic mission of building
socialism completely and definitively. This assignment
from the working class is carried out by all organs of
state power, each of them making a specific contribution
to the solution of the tasks facing the community and the
state as a whole. They are all under the same constitutional obligation to work for the welfare of the people.
The working class also draws its allies into the activities
of the organs of state power. Hence the socialist state is
the highest form of the alliance that the working class
establishes with all social forces and it is at the same
time the highest embodiment of socialist democracy. 36

On the level of decision-making, the socialist state is given the
task of implementing the SED's policies that have been formally
announced at various Party Congresses. Thus, "Through the agency
of the state the working class implements all the measures outlined
in principle in the decisions of its party. In the shape of laws and
decrees they become the basis for the action of the whole community. ²
Thus, while the party sets the general policy guidelines, the state is
expected to fill in the necessary administrative details as well as
playing a supportive role in the mobilization of public support. As
East German society has become increasingly diversified in an
occupational sense, and as the general and specific tasks of political
leadership have continued to become increasingly complex over time,
the art of administration has elevated the socialist state within the
GDR into a permanent policy-implementing role, at least for the
immediate future.
In view of the growth of state influence within the policy-making
realm, the SED has devoted serious attention to the roles and responsi
bilities of state organs in the GDR. At the outset, one analyst of
party-state relations notes the traditional problem facing government
structures in political systems operating according to Marxist/
Leninist concepts of decision-making and rule-making:

The activity of the socialist state is not considered to be
something which is "peculiar," isolated, or independent
from the working class and its Marxist/Leninist Party,
involved in the execution of social functions. Instead, the
[state] is directly engaged in the work of helping to realize
the leading role of the working class and its Marxist/
Leninist Party. Its peculiarity is located in the application

of specific means and methods with which the socialist
state operates in attempting to realize the historical
mission of the working class. In their application and
content they are determined by the leading role and
social function of the working class. [Further on, it
is asserted that the] Socialist State is above all the
creative organizer of social progress as it is reflected
in objective demands. These demands, in turn, are
mirrored in the decisions of the Party of the work
class [the SED].[38]

Returning to the crucial work relationship existing between
party and state organs, another analyst makes these concluding points:
"There is between Party and state a functional division. The Party
leadership makes the basic decisions, which the organs of the state
apparatus concretize and then execute. Control of the execution phase
is normally undertaken by the Party."[39]

The functions and responsibilities of four basic state organs
are significant, beginning with the Minister Council, extending through
the State Council and People's Chamber, and ending with an examination of local representative bodies.

Minister Council

The Minister Council [Ministerrat] is the most important
governmental organ in the GDR. Until the spring of 1971, when Walter
Ulbricht passed from the leadership of the SED, the State Council
was the authoritative governmental influence within the GDR, but
changes at work within the state apparatus have transformed this
relationship. This evolution has been given constitutional legitimacy
as seen by the alterations in the GDR's most important legal document,
which were approved by the People's Chamber on September 27,
1974.[40]

The Minister Council performs the following functions: In the
most comprehensive sense, it is the government (Regierung) of the
GDR. In domestic and external affairs it leads the way by dint of its
direct control over governmental ministries. Thus, "the Minister
Council creates the guidelines for the activities of Ministries and
other state organs, determines their areas of competence, and
exercises control over them. It coordinates their activities with
those of other governmental organs, as well as performing the same
coordinative tasks at lower levels of government.[41]

As with the Politburo and Central Committee, membership on
the Minister Council has fluctuated over the years, although a mean
figure appears to be 40. Directing the work of the Minister Council

falls within the purview of a special executive organ, the Presidium, composed of a chairman and 11 subordinate members.[42] Although the Politburo and Central Committee are also involved in numerous aspects of governmental activity in the GDR, the Minister Council is especially committed to the job of ensuring that economic performance is maintained at politically acceptable levels. The projected goal between 1972 and 1976 is 5 percent growth per annum. In terms of economic competence and administrative responsibility, the following description outlines its specific areas of concern: "Greatest significance is given to the Minister Council in the realm of economics. Among other considerations, it is responsible for long-range economic planning; the State Planning Commission, as a special planning organ, works closely with it. The Presidium of the Minister Council is responsible for the task of economic coordination. . . ."[43]

Questions of membership selection are difficult to answer with any degree of precision, although the official claim that the People's Chamber creates the Minister Council is a slight distortion of reality. In a formal sense, the People's Chamber does ratify the Council's membership, including its chairman, but the real personnel decisions are made in the Politburo and the Central Committee. While the last two chairmen of the GDR's leading economic organ have been members of the Politburo, Willy Stoph (until October 1973) and Horst Sindermann, research by Ursula Hoffmann leads to the conclusion that a "fusion of memberships on the Minister Council, Central Committee, and Politburo" has begun to take place. Regarding the Central Committee, she notes that almost half of her research sample (N = 55) were either past or present members of the Central Committee while simultaneously serving on the Minister Council.[44] Drawing on a slightly smaller percentages of individuals serving simultaneously on the Central Committee and Minister Council between 1954 and 1966, the overlap between party and governmental membership is as follows, 41 percent, 48 percent, 50 percent, and 39 percent.[45]

The involvement of the Minister Council in East German society extends beyond the realms of state-party affairs, however. In view of the party's developmental goals, especially within the area of economic growth, the engagement of the GDR's most important governmental structure in all phases of social life within East Germany is not surprising.

State Council

The State Council (Staatsrat) has experienced a loss of symbolic and real authority over the past several years as previously mentioned. From a structure that occupied a supreme and unchallengeable position in the areas of domestic and external affairs, the State Council has been stripped of its most important functions, a condition most cogently manifested in recent constitutional changes that removed it from all spheres of authoritative rule-making.[46] As an official description clearly underlines, the State Council occupies an increasingly marginal position within the East German state apparatus. "The main functions . . . are the following: Its Chairman represents the GDR under international law, appoints and recalls the GDR's diplomats and receives the credentials and letters of recall of foreign diplomats accredited in the GDR."[47] Because the State Council has exercised far-reaching influence in the governmental sphere until quite recently, however, some observations on its previous role and function follow.

The State Council was formally proclaimed in October 1960. In a "programmatic declaration," Walter Ulbricht described the functions the new organ was expected to perform. At the outset, the new structure was to operate as a small working panel capable of fulfilling the "basic tasks" growing out of the laws and decisions of the People's Chamber.[48] On this institutional foundation, the State Council was expected to develop "the foundations of 'socialiststate leadership activity,' especially the integration of the population within the processes of governmental activity."[49] Over time, the definition of the State Council's realm of competence became increasingly ambitious. By 1968 it had become the "de jure 'Organ' of the People's Chamber," thus arrogating to itself the job of "fulfilling the basic tasks set forth by the People's Chamber as they were mirrored in its laws and declarations."[50]

Along with an increase in decision-making authority, the State Council also attempted to weaken the authority of the Minister Council. As chairman, Ulbricht gave himself the responsibility of explicitly naming those functions to be performed by the Minister Council. By the late 1960s the practical result of these actions meant that the latter had become an executive organ of the former.[51] Thus, not only was the State Council able to directly control the activities of the Minister Council, but it also was in the position of being able to engage in the following activities touching upon important areas of domestic and international politics (especially national defense): structural aspects of the state apparatus, citizen petitions, administration of justice (Rechtspflege), educational and cultural politics, youth politics, questions of national defense (especially treaty ratification and the accreditation of diplomats serving in foreign countries), and the handling of legal drafts.[52]

Currently the State Council is made up of 25 members consisting of a chairman, Willy Stoph, 6 subchairmen, 18 regular members, and 1 secretary. As with other party and governmental organs, membership figures fluctuate slightly, though 25-28 appears to be the

norm. Though State Council representation on the Central Committee
is not high—no more than 8 of its membership have served on the
Central Committee at one time; between 1958 and 1963 the number
was 6—the number of SED members on this organ has always been
substantive (as of August 1974, 18 out of its 25 members are in the
SED).[53]

People's Chamber

In a manner analogous to the formal authority vested in Party
Congresses in the political area, the People's Chamber is considered
to be the GDR's top governmental organ. The East German Constitution is clear on this point: "The People's Chamber is the supreme
state organ in the GDR. In its plenary sessions, basic questions of
state policy are decided. The People's Chamber is the single constitutional and legal organ in the GDR. No one may abrogate its rights."[54]
Constitutional alterations, approved by the People's Chamber on
September 27, 1974, contain the provision for an extension of the
elected term of office to the Chamber from four to five years.[55]
The socioeconomic and political composition of the People's
Chamber suggests the following characteristics:

> The GDR parliament, the People's Chamber, consists of
> 500 deputies elected for a (five) year term. The parlia-
> mentary groups are as follows, with the number of
> members in parentheses (as of October 4, 1972):
> Socialist Unity Party (127); Democratic Peasant Party
> (52); Christian Democratic Union (52); Liberal Demo-
> cratic Party (52); National Democratic Party (52);
> Free German Trade Unions (68); Democratic Women's
> League (35); Free German Youth (40); German League
> of Culture (22); 159 of the deputies, or almost 32 percent
> of the total, are women. The others, rather obviously,
> are men. A breakdown according to age-groups shows
> 6 percent of the deputies aged 21 to 25; 6 percent aged
> 26 to 30; 20 percent aged 31 to 40; 43 percent aged 41 to
> 50; 16 percent aged 51 to 60; and 9 percent over 60. A
> social analysis shows that about 44 percent of the deputies
> are (or were) workers; 15 percent work in agriculture or
> fisheries; 20 percent are office workers; and another 20
> percent come from the intelligentsia; one deputy is classi-
> fied as "other." 53 of the deputies—just over 10 percent
> of the total—were active in the antinazi struggle from
> 1933 to 1945.[56]

Structurally, the People's Chamber consists of one president, one acting president, and an additional nine members, each of whom represent the dominant socioeconomic and political groups that operate within the larger legislative body. As an important consultative organ, the chamber is made up of the following committees: Foreign Affairs, Industry, Building and Transport, Budget and Finance, Labor and Social Policy, Education, Culture, Petitions, and Youth Affairs.[57] While generalizations are subject to change in this area, it appears as if the party has decided to make the People's Chamber and the State Council parallel in terms of governmental influence, a consideration strongly undergirded by the realization that both organs display an unaccustomed number of representatives from the "bloc-party system," middle class political organizations that operate within the centralized framework of SED direction and authority.

Within the People's Chamber, the representation of social groups loyally conforms with the overall design of East German society—with strong support given to the seating of workers, women, and people between the ages of 21-50. In this sense, the GDR's social structure has begun to display corporatist tendencies.

Local Representative Bodies

Along with their counterparts, the basic organizations, local representative bodies supply a necessary element of personal and group initiative to the decision-making process on the local level. On each level of geographic-political organization, beginning with the GDR's 15 districts, extending through its regions, cities, and local community units, local representative bodies play important roles in various aspects of the decision-making and rule-making processes.

There are approximately 200,000 representatives active within all four levels of state government in the GDR. Additionally, there are 1,000,000 honorary functionaries who assist in the running of various government levels. Regarding the significance of local representative bodies, Friedrich Ebert, member of the SED's Politburo and party spokesmen on issues relating to local government, makes these observations:

Local representative bodies and their organs carry a large responsibility for the direct shaping of working and living conditions of the working people; they are largely responsible for the direction of our economy, such as the administration of the district-industry directorate, the locally controlled building industry,

the local supply economy, locally directed communications
systems; in large degree these bodies are responsible
for the direction of country, forest, and food supply
industries.[58]

From all levels of state organization the role of local representative bodies is crucial in the realm of mass mobilization. Thus, along
with the SED's basic organizations, local bodies attempt to provide
a measure of individual and group impetus into decision-making and
rule-making. The refurbishing of old dwellings in local communities,
voluntary work done by citizens interested in cleaning the main
streets of a given community, and a myriad of related activities fall
within the province of these bodies.

The function of local representative bodies on the city and
communal levels is particularly important in the GDR. Generally
speaking, the party is committed to the improvement of relations
between the two levels of government. As one spokesman expresses
it, "For the fulfillment of our tasks, local state organs [cities and
communities] must develop socialist cooperation. . . . Proceeding
from the Basic Task laid out at the VIII Party Congress, progress
will be attained through the cooperation of cities and communities.
Of special relevance in this regard is the growing development of
communal assemblies." Turning to some specific considerations
attached to this particular hope, this spokesman goes on to argue
that "it now lies within the broad social interest, as well as within
the direct interests of citizens living in small cities and communities,
to intensify the level of community cooperation. This development
will then be able to liberate important reserves, thereby contributing
to an increase in the material and cultural living standards within
these two entities, and thus narrowing the gap between themselves
and the larger cities."[59]

The structure and functions of local representative bodies fit
into the following pattern:

1. District Councils are chosen from assemblages of between
160 and 200 representatives who are selected by the voters on "District
Days." These representatives, in turn, determine the composition
of the council. In terms of function, District Councils are expected
to realize the decisions of the People's Chamber and the Minister
Council. Of special importance is the successful implementation,
and continuous administration, of the party's five-year plan.[60]

2. Regional Councils are chosen in the same manner as their
larger counterparts: Between 45 and 120 delegates are elected by
citizens within a given region. These delegates, in turn, choose a
council of the region that is called upon, in a manner similar to its
larger relative, to implement the decisions of the party. Unlike

District Councils, however, the regional organization is expected to involve itself with the "dwelling and living conditions of the population in cities and communities."[61]

3. Communal Councils are directly chosen from local assemblies themselves. Though exact numbers for a given communal council are lacking, their basic function is to galvanize the population behind the most pressing daily tasks, running the gamut from attempting to improve working conditions in local industries, to providing improved means of distributing food products within the community.[62]

4. City Councils occupy an intermediate position between regional and communal councils. The general electoral arrangements are as follows: A conference of "city representatives" (Stadtverordnetenversammlung) is convened for the purpose of electing a new City Council. Once this is accomplished, the council, in turn, is expected to administer to the daily and long-term needs of the city.[63]

As with higher organs on the party and state levels, there is a strong, and predominant, representation of SED members on all four levels of electoral organization. Figures taken from the GDR's 1973 Statistical Yearbook provide the following information:

	Representatives of the SED	Total Membership
District day	722	2,840
Regional day	4,463	17,214
Communal day	60,382	180,890
City-county assemblies	819	3,000

Without exception, the SED has a 2-1 plurality over any other single group represented on these various electoral committees, though it should also be noted that party membership also overlaps with such aligned organizations as the Free German Trade Union Organization, the Free German Youth, and the Democratic Women's Federation. If these groupings are added to the existing percentage of direct SED representation, the degree of formal and informal party influence within such assemblies would undoubtedly be even higher.[64]

Individuals serving in local representative bodies perform crucial communication tasks within their respective communities (Chapter 8 discusses political communications generally). From this angle, the key role is performed by the deputy (Abgeordnete), who is called upon to create a spirit of citizen initiative. In fact, over the past several years the SED has devoted increased attention to the functions performed by the deputy.

For instance, calling upon individuals serving in local representative bodies to develop an activist concept of public duty means that deputies are expected to strike out on their own in attempting to

determine the needs and problems of their local community. As one
manual on the subject asserts, deputies must not wait for the public
to contact them during official office hours. Instead, the deputy is
urged to make the first move by engaging constituents in conversation.
"Why is it necessary—so one might ask—for the deputy to wait until
citizens come to him? Why doesn't he go to where they are? Examples
of this attitude are seen in home meetings, presentations at veterans'
clubs, parent gatherings at schools, trade union gatherings or work
consultations in the factory. On such occasions, directed discussions
offer the deputy an outstanding opportunity to come into contact with
many citizens."[65]

Pedagogical considerations become especially important in
examining the relationship between deputies and constituents, a subject touched upon in terms of "persuasion and activation." As one
official manual contends, "Speaking ability is unimportant without
(a) the possession of relevant knowledge at the outset by the deputy,
and (b) the ability to persuade oneself as well as others."[66] Above
all else, the deputy must be able to make himself understood within
the community, a requirement at least partially satisfied by the
individual deputy's ability to pose the following queries to himself
before and after communicating with the public: "What is to be done?
Why is it necessary to do it? How it is to be accomplished? What
conditions must be observed? With whom must these tasks be performed?"[67] During presentations, the deputy is urged to be especially
sensitive to the application of simple pedagogical devices that can be
employed to highlight important examples and general points for the
audience. The use of numbers can be important, for example. Thus,
"When the audience is not in the position of being able to take extended notes . . . the speaker must be able to display the most per-
tinent argument and the most persuasive statistics. Frequently the
use of comparative numerical displays is more effective than an
absolute value."[68]

Flowing out of this activist concept of public service, decision-
making and rule-making considerations tend to be dominantly reflected in the ability of deputies to initially gauge the depth and content
of public opinion within their constituency while carrying out various
aspects of party and governmental policy in their work. Within the
organizational framework of "conferences," the policy- and rule-
making demands of society and the needs of the local constituency are
brought into line with each other. As one source notes in this regard,
"Conferences are the basic organizational-legal form which calls an
assembly [District, Region, city, community] into session. Within
these forums, political experience and factual knowledge of deputies
is enriched by the facts and ideas which they have acquired in their
work with laboring people."[69] In summation, there is little question

that local representative bodies perform crucial tasks in the mobilization of public support for party and governmental policies, though
certain problems facing them on the decision- and rule-making levels
will be examined later on.

POLICY-MAKING

All political systems must formulate policies that find resonance
within the broad population. In constitutional democracies, the number
of actors publicly involved in the process of formulating policies is
normally quite large, though the final decision-makers may constitute
an extremely small group of people. In communist political systems,
the search for viable public policy is no less important, although these
regimes devote considerable effort to masking such efforts in a cloud
of secrecy. Only when policy choices are arrived at does a communist
system normally begin to publicize its policy-making process.[70]
Two general considerations surround the making of policy choices
in the GDR.

On the one hand, the party considers itself to be an agent of
sociopolitical modernization. Though it considers itself to be an
integral—the determinant—aspect of East German society, it also
reserves a sphere of "marginality" for itself. From an organizational
vantage point, "marginality" allows the SED to partially remove itself
from the clamor of partisan, that is, self-interested and "subjective,"
conflict in the search for scientific answers to what it defines as
pressing social, economic, and political issues. At least in theory,
this conception of marginality easily fits into the Leninist conception
of vangardism and its accentuation of secrecy and combat readiness.
In terms of SED politics, this stance is a natural one for a party
reared in an environment of struggle, illegality, and repression.
Thus, Politburo policy deliberations are kept away from the reach
of direct public scrutiny, only surfacing when the SED's most elite
cadre strata has made a necessary bow to the requirements of masking
decision- and rule-making processes within an aura of secrecy.

On the other hand, the party and state apparatuses exist in an
atmosphere that demands frequent consultation of affected interests
at all levels of social interaction. Thus, despite the requirement
that policy- and rule-making processes unfold within an aura of
secrecy, East German society is increasingly called upon to process
the public demands of organized groups (as seen in Chapter 4). The
result of this apparent dilemma is that policy-making has increasingly
become a "group" process in the GDR, albeit one kept within the
general auspices of SED direction and control.

The SED has always been policy conscious. In the broadest
sense, a Marxist/Leninist party attempting to engineer successful
political and social revolution cannot ignore the ramifications of the
most obscure party or state program. Nonetheless, it has become
increasingly obvious, and especially so since the VI Party Congress
of the SED, that the party has become progressively aware of its
policy-making role.

As previously discussed, the party has been involved since the
early 1960s in the task of stabilizing its authority within all sectors
of the population. While not eschewing an occasional resort to selective coercion when confronted by group and individual opposition to its
policies, there are convincing indications that the SED has come to
place main reliance on a wide variety of techniques and methods that
underline the influence of consensus-building mechanisms. The SED's
continuous attempt to present its program of social and political
modernization in terms of "collective self-interest" certainly expresses this conception of nonviolent consensus-building. As Erich
Honecker stated the SED's position at the VIII Party Congress, "We
know only one aim that pervades the whole policy of our party: to do
everything for the well-being of man, for the happiness of the people,
for the interests of the working class and all working people. This
is the nature of socialism. This is what we are working and struggling
for."71 Beyond this somewhat vague conception of social interest,
and the party's attempt to define it in line with its goals of social and
political change, there are a number of practical considerations that
give meaning to the policy process within the framework of party
decision- and rule-making activities.

                                Party Congresses

Although Party Congresses have already been touched upon
(see pages 183-186), attention is now given to how they reflect significant decisions of the SED in the realms of politics, economics, and
society most generally. As one official description of the SED's
Congress suggests,

> Party Days elaborate the course of development in all
> phases of society within the GDR. The leading role of
> the working class in the GDR is incorporated within its
> decisions. Given an existing level of social development,
> the Party Day answers complex and crucial questions
> about politics, economics, ideology, culture, and organi-
> zational activity. Thus, Party Days are high points in the

life of the Party as the working people of the GDR
increasingly come to make their decisions a matter of
personal concern. [72]

These occasions are significant for at least two reasons. One,
they represent important stock-taking efforts on the part of the SED.
From this perspective, the party critically reviews the course of
progress, and resulting difficulties, between the last Party Day and
the current one. While no attack is made on the general orientation
of the political system, and the function of the SED within it, criticism
and overall evaluation of past activity are made within a Marxist/
Leninist context. Proceedings of various Congresses lead to the
conclusion that the SED takes the job of criticism and evaluation
seriously.

Plans and Measures

Party Congresses lay down the general ideological and programmatic directions that the SED wants East German society to travel
toward over the next several years, but it is the plan and a related
body of concrete measures that give party commitments their operational meaning. As the VIII Party Congress illustrates, both sets of
practical considerations are important for the SED.
In the first case, the party has developed a general set of
economic, political, and social goals that must be realized between
Congresses. Once these goals have been reduced to a set of operational guidelines, the importance of planning processes becomes
obvious. Thus, in regard to the agreed-upon plans emanating from
the VIII Party Congress, the official list of commitments is seen in
the following description:

On the basis of the successes achieved by the working
class party, as the leading force of socialist society,
the following priority tasks for the various fields of
national life are outlined: Industry: further development and perfection of the material and technical basis
of the national economy, increase in the technical
standards and efficiency of production, a growth of the
produced national income by 26 to 28 percent, of industrial goods production by 34 to 36 percent, and of the
labour productivity of workers (manual and nonmanual)
by 35 to 37 percent by 1975; Agriculture: ever better
supply of the population with foodstuffs and of the industry

with raw materials from domestic resources through large-scale intensification and the gradual transition to industrial methods of production; Education: continued improvement of the uniform socialist system of education, full introduction of ten-year general education for all children, increase in the number of kindergarten places; Health system: intensified and continued reconstruction and modernization of hospitals, out-patient centers and departments, priority implementation of preventive measures for preserving and promoting health and combating widespread diseases; increase in the number of places in creches to 290-300 per 1,000 children under three years of age; Culture: close cooperation between cultural facilities, factories, organizations and cultural workers to satisfy the intellectual and cultural demands of all citizens.[73]

Following almost directly upon the announcement of these general plans came a list of specific policy commitments, or measures, that represented specific allocations of public resources (money, time, official publicity, administrative effort—coordination of policy) for the realization of the agreed-upon planning targets. Of special significance in this vein has been the linking of comprehensive social planning with the promulgation of "Social-Political Measures" explicitly geared to the pursuit of the SED's planning goals announced at the VIII Party Congress.

Plenums

Plenums are forums that allow the party and state a public opportunity to evaluate the degree to which plans and measures have been actualized over specific periods of time. Called into session at least once every six months, they normally last between three and four days. For the party, these sessions faithfully reflect the centralized and hierarchic structure of the SED's authority pyramid. Thus, plenums begin with an announcement that the report of the Politburo, the SED's top decision and rule-making organ as previously noted, has been accepted by the Central Committee. Always emanating from decisions and goals outlined at Party Congresses or Party Conferences (these are rare events, normally called together to deal with a crisis in party leadership), Politburo reports are enlarged upon by Central Committee announcements during plenums. Because these occasions are always employed as a means of gaining widespread public support for the plans and measures announced at Party Congresses, the participation of individuals and groups within lower levels of the SED's apparatus, mass organizations (especially the Free German Trade Union Association, FDGB), state and economic organs, "as well as technical personnel from separate areas of society," is strongly encouraged. [74] In a similar manner, plenums are also called into session for the socialist state by the People's Chamber, though it is clear that plenums within the SED are more important in the determination of what policies are to be given main attention by East German society. For party and state organs, decisions of plenums are binding upon all levels of subordinate organization.

In line with new directions in party decision- and rule-making practices since the coming to power of Erich Honecker, two plenums have substantively contributed to the making of SED policy since the last Party Congress. [75]

The 5th Plenum of the SED (spring 1972) is an extension, and elaboration, of Honecker's original declarations made at the VIII Party Congress. As a forum in which practical aspects of policy-making can be fleshed out for public inspection, this plenum dealt with the following issues: increases in social security and social services for retired people (65 and above); alleviation of difficulties facing working mothers, [76] and the encouragement of young couples (people under 26) to marry and have children;[77] a reduction, or stabilization, of rents in all newly constructed dwellings for the working class. [78]

While the 5th Plenum outlined those arenas of policy to which the SED was committing itself, the 8th Plenum (fall 1972) provides a fuller elaboration of how these goals were given more precise definition by the party. Beginning on a sober note, Honecker opened the meeting with the admission that the calculation of retired people had been in original error: "Not 3.4 million retirees, as originally calculated, but 3.9 million invididuals can expect their incomes to be increased."[79] With this item disposed of, a number of related considerations were then presented.

The condition of the working mother was initially touched upon. The emphasis was placed on reducing the amount of weekly labor to no more than 40 hours and an increase in vacation time. Shifting attention to the working population in general (men and women of all ages), attention was given to the securing of pay increases for key occupational groups: foundry workers, individuals holding jobs in the coal and energy industries, communications (including railways, post, and telephone sectors), industrial craftsmen, food processors, the police force, social health and popular culture. [80] For the year 1972, Honecker announced a rise of 11 percent in wages across all

occupational sectors, with a combined national income of 86.5 million
Deutsche marks.[81]

Consumer issues occupied an important position at the 8th
Plenum, a subject Honecker dealt with by declaring that goods and
services had increased 3.1 percent in 1971 (in comparison with 1970,
Ulbricht's last full year of office), and around 7 percent for 1972,
if all indicators were to be relied upon. Finally, the housing question
was touched upon:

> The increase in housing construction has affected the
> material and cultural position of the working people.
> In 1971 and 1972, 189,000 dwellings were either built
> or refurbished. Of special significance is the fact that
> we have built 105,000 dwellings this year, of which
> 69,000 were newly constructed. . . . In terms of 1971
> and 1972, taken together, the living conditions of
> 570,000 individuals have been improved. In every
> single case, this means an advance for the family, the
> environment within which children grow up, and finally,
> for the design of free time activity.[82]

Policy Coalitions

As has already been discussed (see Chapter 4), East German
society is characterized by the activities of numerous interest groups
within various phases of the decision- and rule-making process.
This does not mean the existence of interest group "autonomy," as
that concept is applied to the operation of pluralist systems, though
it strongly suggests that organized groups are called upon to play
active and supportive roles in the overall policy-making process by
the SED. Given the ambitious tasks the party has set itself through
the GDR's history, especially since the VIII Party Congress, the
symbiotic relationship between the SED and organized groups is an
understandable one.

In line with a gradual rise in the policy-making influence of
the Minister Council since 1971, the emergence of a policy coalition
in many areas of decision- and rule-making has taken place in the
GDR. This coalition is made up of the Politburo and its Central
Committee, the Minister Council, and the Free German Trade Union
Association. There are a number of cogent reasons justifying this
particular alliance, in view of developmental trends at work in East
German society. Thus, in the first case, it is clear that all three
groups are dominantly concerned with improving the material

conditions of the working population, manifested in the promulgation
of social-political measures. Second, there is a general overlapping
of leadership perspective uniting these three groups, although the
degree of parallelism on the personnel level is most strongly pro-
nounced when comparisons are drawn between the Central Committee,
Politburo, and the Minister Council (see Chapter 3). Regarding complementary leadership groupings uniting the FDGB (aside from political
ideology) with elite party organs, the GDR's single trade union has
one member on the Politburo (its chairman, Herbert Warnke), while
the Central Committee holds three FDGB members (Warnke once
again, and the association's two acting chairmen, Wolfgang Beyreuther
and Jōhanna Tōpfer). [83] Finally, and in line with a rise in the status
of the Minister Council, the role of the FDGB in the policy-making
process has continuously expanded in terms of the association's
participation within the state apparatus. While numerical representation does not, in itself, guarantee a requisite degree of decision-
making input, the marked shift in SED policy toward the working class
since Honecker came to power may indeed point to an increase in
policy-making latitude for the GDR's official trade union association,
and in this vein it should be noted that "in the People's Chamber,"
as one official handbook remarks, "the parliamentary group of the
trade union confederation with 68 MPs is second in size only to the
SED."[84]

POLICY PROCESSES

Decision- and rule-making involve the party and state in an
extended process of deliberation, planning, and consultation. A
brief description and analysis of this process is necessary, though
it should be kept in mind that many aspects of this dynamic are not
amenable to observation in the West. At the outset, some general
aspects of the process are traced out, followed by an elaboration of
one particular situation that involved policy-making concern within
a local elected assembly.

National Policy-Making

On the national level—starting with Berlin and extending down
into the smallest elements of party and state organization—there are
five general activities making up the policy-making process in the
GDR:

1. <u>Initiative</u>: The "Basic Direction" contained in four- and five-year plans is supplied by the SED's Party Congress. However, as earlier points in this discussion have already demonstrated, the ultimate decision-making point lies within the councils of the Politburo, its Secretariat, the Central Committee, and their resolutions (see pages 180-82). While economic plans do not represent the only focus of policy-making attention, they are clearly one significant arena within which authoritative activity occurs, especially in terms of promulgating important plans.

2. <u>Confirmation</u>: Once the plan has been announced at the Party Congress, it is then confirmed (that is, accepted) by the People's Chamber. During the period in which legislative examination, and subsequent confirmation, is taking place, the "Basic Direction" is publicly discussed within organized group meetings that are placed under the leadership of the GDR's network of mass organizations (see Chapter 4). Regarding economic matters, the FDGB undoubtedly plays an important role in this area. Although official accounts are not precise on this matter, this initial phase of opinion-formation appears to be a preliminary attempt by the party to determine the level and intensity of organized public feeling on a variety of goals contained within the forthcoming plan.

3. <u>Draft</u>: Once the People's Chamber has confirmed the plan, it is sent back to the Central Committee (and the Politburo), in "draft form."

4. <u>Public Discussion</u>: The draft form of the plan is submitted to all party organizations of the SED, all trade union assemblies, and other "meetings of the working people" organized under the auspices of the National Front. Thousands of "proposals" (<u>Vorschläge</u>) and "guidances" flow out of these public discussions. They, in turn, are examined by the party (special commissions being specially established for this overview purpose) and subsequently considered in terms of whether they conform with the general direction of policy earlier articulated at the Party Congress. Undoubtedly a large amount of public participation is symbolic, not only because the SED believes that it must act in the most "objective" interests of the public given the GDR's level of social and political development, but the large numbers of people involved in the interest articulation and aggregative processes inevitably means that individual contributions are apt to be glossed over as they are communicated upward in the communications process. At the same time, there is every reason to believe that the party is increasingly sensitized to the nuances of public opinion in the GDR, and for this reason alone undoubtedly pays strict attention to popular mood as it is reflected in mass solicitations for proposals and guides.

5. Legislation: Once the directive has been exhaustively scrutinized by the leaders and members of organized groups, it is subsequently reexamined by the Central Committee and the Politburo, reformulated in line with its perception of what constitutes "constructive" suggestions emanating from the public, and finally returned to the People's Chamber where it is accorded Legal Power. At this point the directive is transformed into a law, thereby demanding complete acceptance by all elements of the population in line with the general requirement of democratic centralism.

Undoubtedly, the policy-making process does not unfold in the orderly fashion described above. Rather, the party constantly attempts to keep itself informed about the status and effectiveness of various laws promulgated in the GDR since the SED came to official power in late 1949. Thus it is entirely possible—as recent changes in the GDR's second Constitution demonstrate—that new policy processes will be set into motion when the party decides that changes within existing legal procedures and assumptions must once again be brought into line with broader elements of sociopolitical change. (In this sense, then, laws in the GDR, as elsewhere, are provisional.)

In order to supply an air of decision- and rule-making reality, this extended process is described in terms of one example that focuses attention on how the GDR's first five-year plan was drafted, discussed, evaluated, and finally accepted:

The basic direction contained within the first Five Year Plan for the development of the economy in the GDR between 1951-1955 was prepared during the III Party Day of the SED (1950). In line with the great significance accorded to the Plan for the progressive development of society in the GDR, its confirmation by the People's Chamber was accompanied by a scientifically thorough preparation and a comprehensive discussion of its contents within the population. The draft of the Plan directive was confirmed by the Central Committee of the SED, and thoroughly discussed in gatherings of Party organizations, trade union assemblies, and other meetings of the working people. The proposals and directives of the working people were evaluated and considered during the advanced preparation of the Plan. During the evaluative process, past economic performance was analyzed in line with the goals for the progressive social development of the GDR as contained in the new 5 Year Plan. The Plan directive was binding on all state and economic organs and laid the foundation for the preparation of the 5 Year and individual 1 Year Plans.

The legal drafts for the 5 Year Plan were the result
of a comprehensive effort given by factory and agricultural collectives. . . . These efforts were carried
out under the leadership of the SED and government,
in close cooperation with the FDGB, FDJ. . . . The
People's Chamber administered the legal drafts, then
granted them legal force. [85]

Local Policy-Making

Local representative assemblies are called upon to deal effectively with problems that arise during the course of daily communal
affairs. Accordingly, they are expected to make numerous decisions
on how party goals can be fitted within the specific circumstances at
work within the local community. One illustrative example of how
local assemblies attempt to meet such obligations is provided by the
experiences of the Karl Marx city council:

At the first meeting of the city assembly
[Stadtverordnetenversammlung, see p. 195], the
occasion on which the Plan document for 1972 was
decided upon, some problems relating to the preparation of a construction area in Markersdorf-Helbersdorf
arose. To begin, the airplane landing ground for the
Society of Sports and Technology (GST) would have to be
shifted. Additionally, tenders of small gardens did not
wish to give up their patches in this area. They rejected
the [assembly's] proposal for a settlement based upon
the commitment to provide them with another growing
area. The city council informed the deputies in an
open manner about this situation and the possible implications: If the garden patches remained, some 613
fewer dwelling units would be constructed; additionally, the cost per constructed dwelling unit
[Wohnungseinheit] would be increased by 3,500 marks.
This situation would contradict the interests of the
worker and all working people. The deputies quickly
empowered the council to clarify this matter. In this
particular case, the deputies were subsequently informed
by the council regarding various alternatives available.
Every deputy was given the opportunity to acquaint
himself with the problem, to argue about it, as well as
to propose one solution over another. At the same time,

it was also necessary for the tenders to search for an
acceptable solution to the problem. [Finally] the council,
its deputies and the Alliance of small garden tenders,
arrived at one: On the edge of the new construction area
stands a new small garden installation. [86]

SUMMARY AND CONCLUSIONS

Decision- and rule-making dynamics in the GDR are strongly
related to a number of other functions performed by the East German
political system. In the first case, it is clear that the kinds of policies
decided upon by the SED invariably reflect the kinds of values and
norms contained within the political culture of the GDR. Indeed, the
successful promulgation of a five-year plan, a revised Constitution,
or a new Youth Law (as occurred during the summer of 1973),
directly reflects upon the ability of a regime to actualize and strengthen
various elements of the political culture that it is committed to maintain and extend. Certainly for the SED, the direct relationship between
policy-making and political culture within the GDR is clear. Second,
and more directly, the effective operation of decision- and rule-making
processes strongly depends upon the ability and willingness of trained
personnel within the party and state apparatus to act effectively upon
the general plans and directives provided by their leaders. Thus,
political recruitment, selection, and training processes are inextri-
cably bound up with the operations of the decision- and rule-making
system in the GDR. This consideration has become increasingly
important on the community level where the work of cadres in the
party and state organization can make or compromise the SED's
plans for wide-reaching social and political change. Finally, the
willingness of the mass public to support regime decisions and rules
is intimately linked with the operation of the GDR's communications
media (see Chapter 8 for a fuller elaboration of this phenomenon).
One indication of the importance given to the role and impact of the
media in this area is that on every occasion where the SED has felt
it necessary to involve the broad public in discussions of major social
concern—Labor Code (1961), Socialist Education Act (1965), Family
Code (1965), Constitution (1967-68), Local Government Act (1973),
Youth Act (1973), Constitutional Revision (1974)—the involvement of
East German radio, television, and press organs has been massive.
As already noted, the party has activated itself "from the ground up,"
so to speak, in attempting to provide maximum ideological and
organizational impact behind these media campaigns.

Along with the obvious areas of interrelationship that bind the decision- and rule-making processes directly to the operation of the GDR's political system, there is the more subtle element of changed political style that has come into prominence since Honecker succeeded Walter Ulbricht just prior to the VIII Party Congress of the SED. In this vein, the new SED chief seems to be reacting against the increasingly autocratic style of political leadership that characterized the last years of Ulbricht's tenure as SED chairman, as well as attempting to recreate a spirit of revolutionary vitality within a new and emerging generation of East German youth. Perhaps the most important aspect of this concern lies in Honecker's penchant to define problems immediately in terms of simple language, demanding prompt and effective results. Since he has been in power there has been a more open atmosphere within most levels of the SED and state apparatus. This accomplishment, in itself, is not to be underemphasized.

Given the complexities and challenges facing the GDR in its attempt to meet new decision- and rule-making demands, it is not surprising to encounter weaknesses within these areas. A look at some of these problems follows, beginning with an elaboration on a variety of selected difficulties facing deputies active in local representative assemblies, and ending with some remarks on general decision- and rule-making styles within the party and state apparatus.

Problems of the Deputy

Members of local representative bodies are faced with a variety of problems in the conduct of their work. For example, there is the problem of time that inevitably complicates the effective conduct of legislative duties in all societies including the GDR. Narrowing this issue down to its essential element, there seems to be a general feeling held by many deputies on the city and communal (Stadt and Gemeinde) levels that their occupational (deputies serve part-time only) and political (deputy-centered) activities leave them insufficient time for a careful perusal of legislative business. A questionnaire distributed to 100 members of the Rostock city-delegate assembly posed the question, "Whether it was possible for the respondent to effectively comprehend the draft outlines of decisions made at the assembly?" Of the respondents, 65 answered with "partially," 13 with "no." Reasons given for the two answers were grouped into several areas: 67 respondents said their partial lack of preparation had to do with time problems; 17 criticized the large work load; 16 responded by saying they had received legislative drafts too late to enable them to act effectively upon them. The questionnaire's author concludes on the sober note that "the situation is in need of improvement."[87]

Closely related to the dilemma of not feeling capable of effectively dealing with legislative affairs because of competing time
pressures (because of the heavy legislative work load, sloppy administration of legal drafts, the general lack of preparation by deputies
prior to acting on legislative matters), is the fact that many deputies
are simply overcommitted in too many areas of social life. In the
city of Rostock, 110 deputies of its city-delegate assembly were
asked how many social (that is, public) functions they were currently
involved with aside from their work as deputies: 31 said 1, 34 answered with 2, and 37 answered with 3 or more. [88]

Aside from the pressures of time, two additional difficulties
stand in the way of optimal decision- and rule-making performance.
In the first case, the routine conduct of their duties is complicated
by the fact that their obligation to keep themselves informed about
local community affairs is not always honored by their counterparts
in the occupational world. Thus one observer remarks that "unfortunately there are still examples where factory executives, or presi-
dents of agricultural collectives, do not have time for the deputy." [89]
Second, there appears to be some confusion about provisions for
"released time," which allows the deputy time off from his normal
occupational duties in order to participate in legislative affairs. As
one observer of this problem remarks,

> In many factories there is some confusion regarding the
> participation of deputies in the meetings of local assem-
> blies, as well as important consultations and investigations
> of commissions, and other kinds of activity. It must be
> recognized that release from occupational work (by the
> work leader) is especially necessary for deputies active
> in the higher levels (District, Region, and big city assem-
> blies), while members of assemblies within the smaller
> cities and communities are normally expected to fulfill
> their duties during free time in the evening or over the
> weekend. [90]

General Problems

Two interrelated issues related to the exercise of decision-
and rule-making processes deserve attention. To begin, there is
some question whether the regime, party and state, is making the
best use of its considerable intellectual reserves within the mass
population. The problem does not lie with the general level of popular
education in the GDR, considered to be one of the world's highest,

but with the official leadership's propensity to equate—if only for public consumption—symbolic with real participation in decision-making activities. Thus, the SED invariably justifies its mode of centralized decision-making not only in terms of the ideological and scientific validity of democratic centralism, but also in terms of a participatory rhetoric that asserts that average persons enjoy direct influence within the decision-making process as evidenced by the number of proposals and petitions gathered at various meetings of organized groups on those occasions when the SED feels itself called upon to gain public support for making alterations in legal documents, such as the Constitution or the Youth Law. The difficulty in making the argument that "participation" in itself is equal to the exercise of effective influence has little to do with the real value gained by the regime in its ability to elicit a degree of mass symbolic support for party policies, but with whether the SED is unconsciously deluding itself into believing that its participatory concepts make the most effective and creative use of the intellectual abilities of the East German population.

Not unrelated to this initial problem is the realm of secrecy that pervades a large part of the decision- and rule-making dynamic within the party and state apparatus. Seen from this point of reference, there is some question whether the SED's conception of revolutionary vanguardism (see p. 197), and its emphasis on maintaining a degree of "marginality" for itself in dealing with the broad public, is reconciliable with a rational and pragmatic decision- and rule-making process. While there is every reason to believe that the SED makes continuous efforts to inform its membership (it possesses the highest party-to-population ratio, 1-6, in the socialist camp) of new trends within the thinking of its leadership core—especially through the communications structure of the basic organization—there is still some doubt as to whether its exertions have resulted in a substantive growth in policy consciousness within its lower ranks, or the larger population more generally.[91]

The dilemma facing the SED in the future is that the goal of building political legitimacy in the GDR flies in the face of official secrecy. If the regime—party and state—is committed to the task of developing a socialist nation in East Germany, it may be called upon eventually to place greater trust in the abilities of average citizens to make up their own minds about the direction and content of socialist policies. The rhetoric of participation undoubtedly has helped make many individuals in the GDR more sensitive, and generally aware, of what the SED wants to accomplish. Nonetheless, and some alterations in party leadership style since Honecker came into power tend to support this statement, the SED must make additional efforts to provide the mass population with increased influence in the decision and rule-making process.[92]

Predicting future political developments in the GDR is not an easy task in general: Determining whether the party will be able to shed some of its authoritarian tendencies in the realm of decision- and rule-making behavior is especially difficult. There are so many considerations that must be examined, not least of which is the evolution of the party apparatus itself. Thus, while the Honecker regime appears to be concerned about the general problem of decision- and rule-making, even going to the point of criticizing party and state organs for their insensitivity to the feelings of the membership, there are few indications that the SED is prepared to make substantive changes in its style of rulership. As a Marxist/Leninist party, it continues to insist upon the uncontested validity of its leadership role, simultaneously denying other parties or groups the right to publicly challenge even the smallest of oversights. Seen from the vantage point of decision- and rule-making dynamics, the important issue is not whether the party should become increasingly tolerant of "pluralist" tendencies choosing to operate outside the framework of SED authority, but whether a new generation of political leaders within East Germany's leading political organization can begin to shed their ingrained suspicion about opening up the policy-making process to the broad population. If the party ever decides to become more tolerant in this ideologically sensitive area, it will only be the result of a long-term process of domestic and international stabilization, developments that might convince the SED's cadre apparatus that it has little to fear from loosening its authoritative hold on the general population. While there are some indications—witness the relatively free exchange of opinion that was allowed during the tenth Youth Festival in Berlin, and the gradual blossoming of a more self critical artistic style—that the SED is becoming aware that a more open atmosphere contributes to the development of socialism generally, there is serious question whether the party apparatus is prepared to introduce similar changes within the recesses of its decision- and rule-making practices. Unless, and until, such changes are initiated, however, the ability of the party to make sound policy decisions will continue to be placed in doubt.

NOTES

1. Fundamentals of Marxism-Leninism. (Moscow: Foreign Languages Publishing House, 1963).
2. Ibid., p. 525.
3. I. Slepov, Pravda, 4/16/53, translated from Current Digest of the Soviet Press, 5/9/53.

4. Statute der SED (Berlin: Dietz Verlag, 1972), p. 24.

5. V.I. Lenin, Collected Works, Vol. 10 (Moscow: Foreign Languages Publishing House, 1962), p. 443.

6. Horst Dohlus, Der demokratische Zentralismus-Grundprinzip der Fürungstätigkeit der SED (Berlin: Dietz Verlag, 1965), p. 9.

7. Ibid., pp. 9-10.

8. Samuel Huntington, Political Order in Changing Societies (New Haven, Conn.: Yale University Press, 1968), p. 1.

9. Michael Gehlen, The Communist Party of the Soviet Union: A Functional Analysis (Bloomington: Indiana University Press, 1969), p. 10.

10. For two fine treatments of these issues, see Thomas Arthur Baylis, "The Technical Intelligentsia in East German Politics," Ph.D. dissertation, University of California, Berkeley, 1968, and Peter Christian Ludz, The Changing Party Elite in East Germany (Cambridge, Mass.: MIT Press, 1972).

11. See Thomas Arthur Baylis, "East Germany's Rulers," M.A. thesis, University of California, Berkeley, 1961, pp. 84-85.

12. Introducing the GDR (Dresden: Verlag Zeit im Bild, 1974), p. 82.

13. Heinz Lippmann, Honecker, trans. Helen Sebba. (New York: Macmillan, 1972), p. 13.

14. Ibid., p. 229.

15. Hans Beyer et al., Die politisch Organisation der socialistischen Gesellschaft (Berlin: VEB Deutscher Verlag der Wissenschaften, 1973), p. 44.

16. See Ludz, op. cit., pp. 453-552 for change within the SED's elite organs; also see Fred Oldenburg, "Information uber die SED," Deutschland Archiv, January 1973, p. 50.

17. Ludz, op. cit., p. 123.

18. See Otto Schön, Die höchsten Organe der Socialistischen Einheitspartei Deutschlands (Berlin: Dietz Verlag, 1965), p. 23.

19. Ibid., pp. 27-33.

20. Staats- und Parteiapparat der DDR—Stand, August 1, 1974, pp. 26-27.

21. Schön, op. cit., pp. 26-27.

22. Ernst Richert, Macht Ohne Mandat (Cologne & Opladen: Westdeutscher Verlag, 1963), p. 32.

23. See Ludz, op. cit., p. 409.

24. See Kleines Politisches Wörterbuch (Berlin: Dietz Verlag, 1973), p. 982.

25. Ibid.

26. Ludz, op. cit., p. 323.

27. See Hermann Weber, Von SBZ zur DDR (Hannover: Verlag für Literatur und Zeitgeschehen, 1968), p. 194.

28. Staats- und Parteiapparat Der DDR, op. cit., p. 30.

29. See Robert Dahl, Who Governs? (New Haven, Conn.: Yale University Press, 1961) for an examination of decision-making on the domestic level. For a study of decision-making variables in the GDR policy, see Anita Mallinckrodt, Wer Macht die Aussenpolitik der DDR? (Dusseldorf: Droste Verlag, 1972).

30. Peter Christian Ludz, Parteielite Im Wandel (Cologne and Opladen: Westdeutscher Verlag), p. 66.

31. Protokoll die Verhandlungen des VIII. Parteitages der SED (I) (Berlin: Dietz Verlag, 1971), pp. 561-64.

32. Oldenburg, op. cit., p. 50.

33. Statute der SED, op. cit., p. 73.

34. Ibid., pp. 75-81.

35. Ludz, The Changing Party Elite in East Germany, op. cit., pp. 155-78.

36. Introducing the GDR, op. cit., p. 73.

37. Ibid.

38. See Wolfgang Weichelt, Der socialistische Staat-Hauptinstrument der Arbeiterklasse zur Gestaltung der sozialistischen Gesellschaft (Berlin: Staatsverlag, 1972), p. 29.

39. Bericht der Bundesregierung und Materialien zur Lage der Nation 1972 (Bonn: Gesamtdeutsches Institut, 1972), p. 41.

40. Siegfried Mampel, "DDR-Verfassung fortgeschrieben," Deutschland Archiv, 11/74, pp. 1155-57.

41. See, "Gesetz über den Ministerrat der DDR von 16/10/72," in Die staatliche Leitung noch enger mit der Masseninitiative verbinden (Berlin: Staatsverlag 1972), p. 54.

42. Richert, op. cit., p. 97.

43. Bericht zur Lage der Nation, op. cit., p. 42.

44. See Ursula Hoffmann, Die Veränderungen in der Sozialstruktur des Ministerrats der DDR 1949-1969 (Dusseldorf: Droste Verlag, 1971), p. 68.

45. Ludz, The Changing Party Elite, op. cit., p. 296.

46. Mampel, "DDR-Verfassung fortgeschrieben," op. cit., pp. 1155-56.

47. Introducing the GDR, op. cit., p. 78.

48. See Peter Joachim Lapp, Der Staatsrat im politischen System der DDR (1960-1971) (Opladen: Westdeutscher Verlag, 1972), pp. 30-31.

49. Ibid., p. 31.

50. Ibid., p. 36.

51. Ibid., p. 47.

52. Ibid., p. 70.

53. Staats- und Parteiapparat der DDR, op. cit., pp. 3-4.

54. Verfassung der Deutschen Demokratischen Republik, Art. 48.

55. Democratic German Report, 10/9/74, p. 142.

56. Democratic German Report, 10/4/72, p. 143.

57. Introducing the GDR, op. cit., pp. 76-78.

58. See Friedrich Ebert, Der VIII. Parteitag der SED über die Entwicklung der sozialistischen Demokratie. Die Aufgaben zur Erhöhung der Rolle der örtlichen Volksvertretungen (Berlin: Dietz Verlag, 1973), p. 16.

59. Ibid., pp. 22-23.

60. Kleines Politisches Wörterbuch, op. cit., p. 115.

61. Ibid., p. 467.

62. Ibid., p. 258.

63. Ibid., p. 836.

64. See Statistisches Taschenbuch der DDR (Berlin: Staatsverlag, 1973), p. 19.

65. Opitz Brendel, Sternkopf, Zur Arbeitsweise der Mitglieder örtlicher Volksvertretung (Berlin: Staatsverlag, 1974), p. 49.

66. Ibid., p. 84.

67. Ibid., p. 87.

68. Ibid.

69. Werner Sternkopf, Der Abgeordnete der örtlichen Volksvertretung (Berlin: Staatsverlag, 1974), p. 35.

70. See Chapter 4 in this text for further elaboration.

71. Introducing the GDR, op. cit., p. 29.

72. Kleines Politisches Wörterbuch, op. cit., p. 643.

73. Introducing the GDR, op. cit., pp. 29.

74. Kleines Politisches Wörterbuch, op. cit., p. 652.

75. See Was der VIII Parteitag Beschloss wird sein! (Berlin: Dietz Verlag, 1972).

76. See Peter Christian Ludz, "Politische Ziele der SED und gesellschaftlicher Wandel in der DDR," Deutschland Archiv, 12/74, p. 1267. Ludz notes that with the inclusion of retired people who continue to work (mostly parttime), fully 81 percent of the GDR's women are in the labor force.

77. Ibid., p. 1267. Ludz notes that since 1964 population growth in the GDR has stagnated, and since 1973 has indeed fallen below the 17 million level.

78. Erich Honecker, Neue Massnahmen zur Verwirklichung des sozialpolitischen Programms des VIII. Parteitages. 5. Tagung des Zentralkomittees, 28/4/72, p. 6.

79. Erich Honecker, Das Volk der DDR kann mit Zuversicht die Schwelle zum Jahr 1973 überschreiten. 8 Tagung des Zentralkomitees, 6/7/12/72, p. 10.

80. Das Volk der DDR, op. cit., p. 10.

81. Ibid., pp. 10-11.

82. Ibid., p. 11.

83. Staats- und Parteiapparat der DDR, op. cit., pp. 37-38.

84. Introducing the GDR, op. cit., p. 50.

85. Kleines Politisches Wörterbuch, op. cit., pp. 244-45.

86. Sternkopf, op. cit., p. 43.

87. Ibid., p. 38.

88. Ibid., p. 60.

89. Ibid., pp. 83-84.

90. Ibid., p. 86.

91. See Peter Christian Ludz, Deutschlands Doppelte Zukunft (Munich: Karl Hanser Verlag, 1974), pp. 80-86.

92. Ludz makes the argument that the GDR has faced a paradox of sorts since the Wall was built in August 1961: On the one hand, dynamics of change characteristic of all modern societies have been set into motion—modernization of industrial equipment, social mobilization of various populations of administratively and technically trained occupational strata; on the other hand, information blockages, bureaucratic controls, etc., continue to exist. See pp. 86-91 in ibid.

THEORETICAL FRAMEWORK

Marxism/Leninism

Ultimate Absence of Social Control

As noted in previous chapters, Marx conceived of a society ultimately free of social control, of administration by a bureaucracy. Communism would be an administration of "things," not of "men." In fact, as Marxist scholars unceasingly point out, the problem of bureaucracy was one of the most important factors in the development of his sociological theory: Not only was he the first to see that state administration was a distinct and separate apparatus, but he further showed "that certain mechanisms had developed within the state which were inseparable from it and which proved resistant to all rational argumentation."[1] Carrying this line of analysis a bit further, Marx himself asserted that

> due to its bureaucratic essence, administration was <u>unable</u> to grasp the reasons for the misery in the sphere of administration and could only see the reasons in the spheres of nature and private citizens, outside of the sphere of administration. Even with the best of intentions and devout humanism, highest intelligence, the administrative authorities were unable to do more than solve instantaneous and transitory conflicts and were incapable of eliminating the permanent conflicts between

reality and principles of administration, partly because
such measures or activities were not included in the
tasks of their positions and partly because even the
best intentions were bound to fail in breaking through
a substantive relationship or, in other words, destiny.
This substantive relationship was the bureaucracy, both
within the body of administration and in respect of the
body managed.[2]

In short, the bureacuracy was a self-contained, independent power.

As Lenin, too, saw it, the bureaucracy as a state apparatus
was to be eliminated. In State and Revolution he wrote,

The workers, after winning political power, will smash
the old bureaucratic apparatus, shatter it to its very
foundations, and raze it to the ground; they will replace
it by a new one, consisting of the very same workers
and other employees, against whose transformation
into bureaucrats the measures will at once be taken
which were specified in detail by Marx and Engels:
(1) not only election, but also recall at any time;
(2) pay not to exceed that of a workman; (3) immediate
introduction of control and supervision by all, so that all
may become "bureaucrats" for a time and that, therefore, nobody may be able to become a "bureaucrat."[3]

New Kind of Bureaucracy in the Transitional Period

Recognizing, however, that a transitional period (dictatorship
of the proletariat) was necessary, Lenin felt that the interim bureaucratic structure would, nevertheless, take on new characteristics:
"Abolishing the bureaucracy at once, everywhere and completely, is
out of the question. It is a utopia. But to smash the old bureaucratic
machine at once and to begin immediately to construct a new one that
will make possible the gradual abolition of all bureaucracy—that is
not a utopia, it is the experience of the Commune, the direct and
immediate task of the revolutionary proletariat."[4] Thus, in the
period of the dictatorship of the proletariat, the bureaucracy would
be seized and turned against former exploiters.

But, specialists suggest, Lenin's practical problems apparently
overcame his theoretical intentions. Since trained administrators,
loyal to communism, were in short supply, Tsarist bureaucrats were
needed—they would be kept in line through administrative controls,
that is, the bureaucracy. In short, Lenin used bureaucratic solutions
to solve the problem of increased bureaucratization.[5]

As the challenge of "state-building" continued to push earlier theoretical commitments to the background, Lenin opted for bourgeois industrial technology as a means of speeding up and completing the transitional period:

> The task that the Soviet government must make the people
> see in all its scope is—learn to work. The Taylor system,
> the latest word of capitalism in this respect, like all
> capitalist progress, is a combination of the refined brutality
> of bourgeois exploitation and a number of the greatest
> scientific achievements in the field of analyzing mechanical
> motions during work, the elimination of superfluous and
> awkward motions, the elaboration of correct methods of
> work, the introduction of the best system of accounting
> and control, etc. The Soviet Republic must at all costs
> adopt all that is valuable in the achievements of science
> and technology to this field. The possibility of building
> socialism depends exactly upon our success in combining
> the Soviet power and the Soviet organization of administra-
> tion with the up-to-date achievements of capitalism. We
> must organize in Russia the study and teaching of the
> Taylor system and systematically try it out and adopt it
> to our own ends. [6]

Naturally enough, this type of borrowing ultimately led to the adoption of hierarchic bureaucratic procedures.

Leading Role of the Party

The next step in Lenin's theoretical development, as has been noted on various occasions already, was to accord the Communist party a leading role in state administration. As a result, party functionaries, or bureaucrats, supervise state bureaucrats at all levels of government. Side stepping the question of whether the Communist party could have developed an effective governing apparatus without having introduced a massive system of duplication, in which party and governmental structures have tended to unnecessarily ape the work of the other, the end result, once again, was a further retreat from theoretical principle.

Role of the State

It comes as no surprise that contemporary Leninists see the predicted "withering away of the state" far down the road of socialist construction. Thus, in the meanwhile ("inevitably," loosely defined), the state has increasingly become important as a "means to an ideologically legitimate end," namely the completion of "socialist construction" and the subsequent achievement of communism. This tendency is mirrored in the development of every governmental apparatus lying within the radius of Soviet direction and control.

Functional

Functionalists generally agree that the bureaucracy is (1) essential, (2) large and complex, at least in modern industrial societies, and (3) growing ever larger. In terms of its essentiality, it is pointed out that bureaucrats possess the technical and administrative proficiency that is needed in the daily and long-term conduct of public affairs, that they have intimate contact with specialized (and therefore esoteric) areas of public policy, and that "they are in possession of information which is essential to the making and enforcing of public policy."[7] (The function of the bureaucracy within the political communications process will be examined in Chapter 8.)

Bureaucratic size—probably the number-one characteristic of bureaucracy and that which receives the most criticism—is seen by some functionalists as almost unavoidable. As Almond and Powell remark:

> As a political system expands in size, or faces an
> increasingly complex environment or a widening range
> of tasks, the pressures to develop specialized rule
> application are inexorable. The sheer volume of rules
> to be enforced, resources to be gathered, and informa-
> tion to be processed and transmitted, requires the
> rule-making structure . . . to seek assistance in
> application. It becomes imperative that the system
> develop capabilities to meet new goals or pressures;
> effective rule application is a necessary prerequisite to
> such development. [8]

Indeed, the writers estimate further that in the modern state, "bureaucrats outnumber judges on the order of more than a thousand to one."[9] Functionalists who have focused on the behavior of communist systems make similar observations, as Barghoorn does about the development of complex bureaucratic structures in the Soviet Union:

> One reason why there is in the Soviet Union a formal
> government with authority to employ force if necessary

to secure obedience to its commands, is that the
communists early found that neither ideological
conviction nor sheer force would alone enable them
to do the positive and negative work of governing a
complex, rapidly modernizing, society. It was found
almost from the first days that a legitimate authority
was also necessary, namely, the "state," endowed with
the symbolic majesty of a duly constituted and publicly
acknowledged agency for social control. [10]

Building on early developments in the Soviet Union, communist
systems in Eastern Europe have been called upon to build a comprehensive administrative structure capable of processing the complex
problems of the societies over which they rule. Commenting on the
administrative functions allocated to party and state organs in the
postwar era, another observer comments that

the commitment to directed growth and societal change
requires the creation of an administrative structure
extending throughout the society which is responsive to
the demands of central authorities. Communist systems
are composed of essentially two system-wide structures:
the organization of the Communist Party and the organization of the state or government. The Party is the decision-
making and supervising organization of the society, and
the state or governmental organization implements and
coordinates Party policy. It is the Party's role that tends
to distinguish Communist systems from other societies
undergoing directed social change. [11]

As a final consideration, because Communist parties view
themselves as revolutionary agents of guided social change, the
working class, or proletariat, is called upon to join both systems of
bureaucracy: Since the revolution has been made in their name and
interests, it is only logical, and pragmatic, that the working class
become members of the administrative order. Events and developments in the GDR illustrate the existence of all these elements.

SITUATION IN THE GDR

The destruction of the Third Reich, and the subsequent division
of Germany, created the foundations upon which political authority
was to be built in the German Democratic Republic. In light of vast

destruction in its part of Germany—then named the "Soviet Occupation Zone"—one of the first tasks facing East Germany's future political rulers lay in the area of administrative reconstruction.

Developmental Circumstances

The nationalization of agricultural and industrial enterprises by the SED in 1946 and 1947 created, as has already been seen (see Chapter 2), the preconditions for the development of socialism in East Germany. At the same time, however, the party was aware that the breakdown of traditional forms of economic and social authority could not substitute for the fact that public authority had yet to be created. Seen from this vantage point, the gradual development of an administrative apparatus became necessary. In its continued absence, the party would not be able to realize its long-run designs for wide-reaching political change. Thus, in line with Leninist conceptions of political development, the creation of a bureaucracy by the party in East Germany was to serve the state- and nation-building goals of the SED.

Numerous difficulties faced the emerging leadership group in its attempt to establish a base for administrative operations. In the first place, the scope of economic destruction meant that a future bureaucracy would be forced to cope with giant problems of industrial renovation before a solid foundation for economic growth, and the generation of an acceptable standard of living for a traditionally middle class society, could be guaranteed. Second, and as an extension of this initial consideration, the Soviet Union placed a heavy financial burden on East Germany that helped contribute to the lateness of the GDR's eventual economic upswing. One observer of this phenomenon makes the following points:

> According to the Yalta Agreement of 1945 Russia was entitled to remove certain industrial plants, stocks and transport installations. She could use German labor in her own reconstruction efforts, and she had also the right to reparations out of current German production. . . . Till June 1948 a total of 1,372 plants were entirely or partially dismantled. Among the removed plants were, of course, all armament and airplane factories, also the Auto-Union works in Saxony and the Opel truck plant in Brandenburg as well as the Zeiss works at Jena. According to a U.S. source, East Germany lost about 45 percent of her industrial capacity as a result of dismantlings, as

> against a comparative loss of 8 percent by West
> Germany. . . . According to an official West German
> estimate, the pillaging of East German capital goods
> and the expropriations from current production had
> reached a total of approximately $11.6 billion by 1953,
> when this form of reparations was finally discontinued. [12]

As a final consideration, the interaction of economic difficulties, plus
the fear held by many of Germany's prewar administrative elite that
it would be dealt with harshly by Soviet occupation authorities and
their domestic communist allies, created a serious drain in the supply
of individuals capable of exercising bureaucratic authority in East
Germany during the immediate postwar era (1945-49). While the
party might have been able to console itself that the "foundations" of
socialism had been laid during this period, there are numerous indications that the evolution of a reliable and effective state apparatus
was seriously hindered. As another analyst notes in this regard, the
creation of the GDR's future "technical intelligentsia" did not take
place immediately. Citing one empirical source the following picture
emerges: "A refugee study from 1958 indicates that 40.3 percent
of the higher technical managers questioned (N = 528) had completed
no more than elementary school; the same was true of 50 percent of
the lower managers and engineers (N = 137), 38 percent of the sales
managers (N = 161), 45 percent of the administrative managers
(N = 70), and 79 percent of the 'political managers' (N = 86)—a figure
presumably including the factory directors." [13]

By the late 1950s, however, the establishment of a functioning
state apparatus, under the SED control, had become a reality.
Reparations to the Soviet Union had been discontinued by the early
1950s and a new generation of professionally trained groups was
beginning to enter the state and party apparatus. When the Berlin
Wall was built in late summer of 1961, the final hindrance to the
development of a functioning bureaucracy was removed. The VI
Congress of the SED (January 1963) represents an important bench-
mark of this trend as manifested in the fact that the party committed
itself not only to a more imaginative conception of economic performance, strongly mirrored in the recruitment of technically trained
managers to staff planning organs at all levels of the economic bureaucracy, but to "a basic organizational restructuring of all East German
bureaucratic institutions." [14] These changes, while not representing
a rejection of centralized economic planning and the primacy of the
SED within all phases of economic construction, did bring about an
increased emphasis on the constructive role to be played by the
socialist state in the realization of economic goals. Within the party
and state bureaucracies, more generally, the early-to-late 1960s

brought about a dramatic advance in "technocratic representation" within both organs of public power, a phenomenon most obviously seen in the evolution of overlapping elite groupings in the SED's Central Committee and the Minister Council (see Chapter 3).

VIII Party Congress and After

The basic direction of East German society has not been altered since the change of personnel at the peak of the SED hierarchy brought Erich Honecker in to succeed his long-time mentor, Walter Ulbricht. The increasing role of bureaucratic structures generally, and the growing role of the socialist state most particularly, has not been reversed. Furthermore, the tendency of the SED to make its appeals for popular support by pointing to the undoubted economic affluence it has been able to generate since the early 1960s continues to be a hallmark of party policy. Nonetheless, the newly chosen SED chief did outline a number of considerations that demanded increased attention by the party and state bureaucracy for the coming years. In terms of the economy, he called for greater demands being placed on administrative organs responsible for the "exact balancing and unified administration and planning of social development."[15] Within the realm of economic and financial relations in the socialist camp, an increase in "international cooperation and socialist economic integration within the Council for Mutual Economic Aid (RGW)" was tied to the successful performance of administrative tasks.[16]

Within this same Congress, the SED's chief also called for a series of social-political measures (see Chapter 5), which committed the party to an increase in old age pensions, more generous provisions for maternity leaves, and provisions for increased monetary aid for those families choosing to have one child or more. All of these considerations invariably mean a growth in the importance of administrative personnel within all levels of the party and state apparatus, especially in terms of their ability to work closely and efficiently together. Thus, while the overall authority of the SED in ideological and political affairs sets the framework within which administrative, or bureaucratic, issues are posed, the importance of rule-application processes within the GDR continues to grow.

STRUCTURE

Party Bureaucracy

As previously noted, the party has found it increasingly necessary to involve itself with rule-application questions. The role of the Central Committee is especially important in this regard.

Central Committee

The Central Committee is the GDR's ruling political structure between Party Congresses. While the Politburo is the real locus of final political authority, it is the Central Committee that is given the task of making public statements on the conduct of social, political, and economic affairs. Plenums are the most convenient means of fulfilling this task.

The Central Committee exercises administrative authority in the following manner. In the first place, it is the official party watchdog over the conduct of public affairs by the socialist state, a host of concerns that are mirrored in the following official description of its activities: "It represents the SED in the conduct of affairs with other parties and organizations, nominated representatives of the Party for the People's Chamber of the GDR and the highest administrative organs of the state apparatus and the economy. The Central Committee links the work of elected central state and social organs, and organizations, through its existing Party groups."[17] Additionally, the Central Committee has the authority to convene special conferences on matters relating to the successful functioning of the state apparatus, and especially the ability of this apparatus to meet current problems of economic modernization. In this vein, the Central Committee normally calls upon individuals and groups possessing expertise in areas of public affairs that touch upon the conduct of state work.

In an organizational sense, the Central Committee administers the operation of the national party bureaucracy. Consisting of 36 Sections and 5 Institutes for Social Science, they are listed as follows: Sections—1) agitation, 2) foreign information, 3) construction, 4) bureau of the Politburo, 5) the SED journal Unity (Einheit), 6) research and technical development, 7) women 8) health policy, 9) trade unions and social policy, 10) raw materials industry, 11) trade distribution and external trade, 12) international ties (Internationale Verbindungen), 13) youth, 14) cadre questions, 15) church questions, 16) culture, 17) agricultural economics, 18) light foodstuffs and district-directed industry, 19) machine construction and metallurgy,

20) the journal New Way (Neuer Weg), 21) parties and mass organizations, 22) party finance and operations, 23) party organs, 24) planning
and finance, 25) propaganda, 26) protocol 27) security questions,
28) socialist economic administration, 29) sports, 30) state and legal
questions, 31) transport and communications, 32) education,
33) Western affairs, 34) administration and economic operations,
35) sciences, 36) Zentrag; Institutes—1) Social Sciences, 2) Marxism/
Leninism, 3) Opinion Research, 4) Central Institute for Socialist
Economic Administration, and the 5) Party University "Karl Marx."[18]
As an organ of the Politburo and Central Committee, the
Secretariat deserves attention. Consisting of one first secretary,
Erich Honecker, there are nine regular members of whom only one
(Horst Dohlus) is not a member or candidate of the Politburo as well.
Each member is responsible for one general policy area, which in
every case is simultaneously mirrored in the activities of the Central
Committee section organization or within the state ministerial appa-
ratus. The following areas of concern are mirrored in the makeup
of the Secretariat: international ties (Hermann Axen), party organs
(Horst Dohlus), agricultural economics (Gerhard Grüneberg), culture-
science (Kurt Hager), trade and distribution (Werner Jarowinsky),
economics (Werner Krolikowski), agitation (Werner Lamberz), women
(Ingeborg Lange), propaganda-West (Albert Norden), security (Paul
Verner).[19]

District and region

While the Central Committee, and its Secretariat, attempts to
monitor and coordinate the activities of party and state structures on
the national level, District and Regional party organizations exist for
the purpose of keeping touch with the operations of state agencies at
lower levels of administrative, and especially economic, activity.
Regarding the operations of both party structures, crucial importance
is given to their ability to work closely with parallel organizational
units, the District and Regional councils, in the state sector in the
design and carrying through of short- and long-range economic growth,
and general performance, plans.
District leadership structures (Bezirksleitungen) are composed
of the same organizational elements as those possessed by the next
highest organ (the Central Committee). Led by 15 first secretaries,
each entity consists of its own Secretariat and two party-control
organizations (the District Party Control Commission, and the District
Party-Revision Commission). As District representatives, each first
secretary is located in one of the following urban centers—Berlin,
Cottbus, Dresden, Erfurt, Frankfurt, Gera, Halle, Karl Marx Stadt,
Leipzig, Magdeburg, Neubrandenburg, Potsdam, Rostack, Schwerin,

Suhl. Among this group, all members are listed as members of the
Central Committee, with one being listed as a Politburo member
(Konrad Naumann, Berlin), and two named as Politburo candidates
(Werner Felfe, Halle, and Harry Tisch, Rostock).[20] "As the
politically decisive organs," District leaderships are "responsible
for the unified administration of prognostic and perspective-directed
work in the district."[21]

Regional leadership organizations, totalling 252, are divided
into two general administrative categories: 215 are defined in terms
of territorial responsibility, with the remaining 37 being located in
large national factories (VEBs), universities, and technical schools.
In large- and medium-sized cities, such as Berlin (East), Karl Marx
Stadt, Dresden, and Leipzig, parallel administrative structures are
formed that essentially pursue the same goals, and perform the same
functions, as the Regional organization. Instead of bearing the name
of the former, however, they are labeled city organizations.

Regional and city administrations are called upon to perform
three main tasks, each involving the relevant party organ in administrative activity:

1. Innerparty and organizational functions—carrying through
of Central Committee decisions, leadership of party organizations,
finance administration, controlling the administration of decisions,
communication of information upward (Berlin) and downward, registra-
tion of party members, the drafting of proposals directed toward the
solution of political, economic, and cultural questions.[22]

2. Ideological and cadre-political questions—"the development
of systematic, political, and organizational work among the masses,"
the organization of ideological work, agitation and propaganda among
party members and nonmembers, administration of local press
organs as well as the staffing of their editorial offices, and cadre
work.[23]

3. Control and leadership activities directed outward—"Leadership of state organs, guaranteeing their support by lower organs of
state power (Staatsmacht); leadership of trade unions, youth and
women's organizations as well as all other social organizations
through existing Party groups."[24]

From an administrative standpoint, the District and Regional
organs of the SED are called upon to communicate important Politburo
and Central Committee directives to all inferior levels of party organization, especially the basic organizations. Special assemblies of all
basic organizations in a given city and/or District/Region fulfill this
communications requirement much of the time. Regular meetings
with members of the city or regional SED leadership group are
another way of meeting this obligation.

Regarding the coordination of party and state organs in the conduct of public affairs, district, regional, and city administrations are in daily contact with their opposite organizational number, the District, Regional, and city council. The most important dimension of this institutionalized relationship has to do with the combined ability of party and state organs to jointly fulfill their geographical division's part of the "Main Task," as the current five-year economic plan is called. Of crucial importance is the ongoing performance of socialist industrial and agricultural sectors within the perspective of one-year plans. Work groups representative of various layers of party and state administrative competence meet frequently in attempting to improve areas of difficulty that jointly involve the efforts of SED and state apparatuses.

Basic Party Organization

The heart of party administration rests with the smallest element of organization in the SED, the basic organization. Containing no less than three members, these elementary units are frequently aggregated into larger organizations called "Section-Party-Organizations." Depending on the size of the concern—hospital, factory plant, collective farm—the basic organization is called upon to form a larger body, the "Membership Assembly," at least once a month. On this occasion, general problems, running the gamut from topical political issues to questions of worker morale, are publicly discussed and resolved.

Though basic organizations perform a wide variety of tasks, their central purpose lies in their ability to provide individuals and groups with the opportunity to vent personal opinions on the role and responsibilities of the party in the occupational world, especially the production process. One party secretary on the county level focuses in on this activity in terms of regularly held "experience exchanges" that take place within the basic organization. Thus, in evaluating the impact of these sessions, he remarks that "much stimulation was supplied by one experience exchange in the People's Enterprise (VEB) Abus. Members of the Party leadership were able to inform themselves about the involvement of work-youth in political-ideological work, about the class-based education of the youth generally, their occupational demands, on the development of their creative powers and their contribution to the movement, the 'Fair for the Leader of Tomorrow' (Messe der Meister von Morgen)."[25] He then went on to describe another experience that occupies a crucial dimension of SED administrative effort on the local level. Commenting on the information transmission role of the party, he notes that

another experience exchange was involved with
information. Good methods were studied within the
Basic Organization in the VEB Junkalor. The leadership of the Basic Organization developed weekly
arguments which were later articulated upon by
agitators and leading cadres. Stationing themselves at
40 different important gathering places in the factory,
these comrades informed workers about the most
important tasks remaining to be accomplished there
as well as providing insights into newsworthy events.
In isolated spots, comrades collected tips, proposals,
and criticisms from the workers and entered them
into information books. [26]

Certainly one of the most important elements of activity
involving basic organizations has to do with their ability to engender
enthusiasm for economic programs developed by the party, and that
subsequently must be realized within the environment of agricultural
and industrial enterprises. Thus the current emphasis given to the
saving of raw materials and the ever-present campaign to increase
work productivity are directly related to the daily engagement of the
SED in all phases of the production process, via the basic organization.
From this vantage point, the party is expected to galvanize people
behind improvement programs by the application of their organizational and communications skills. In placing its stamp of legitimacy
on such varied enterprises, the SED is consistently able to identify
itself with the goal of economic modernization and, therefore, the
further development of socialism in the GDR. Alternatively, the
inability of the party to mobilize the public effectively behind economic
goals invariably means that it will be forced to shoulder responsibility
for failure, albeit of a temporary nature.

State Bureaucracy

State bureaucratic organs, as previously mentioned, are being
called upon to accept increasing degrees of administrative responsibility for the daily and long-term operation of the East German polity.
In this area, however, some governmental organs have been given
larger degrees of responsibility and influence than others. The
development of the Minister Council into the GDR's most important
agent of governmental authority represents the most significant change
in this realm of affairs.

Minister Council

This organ has become increasingly authoritative in the area
of economic planning, control, and administration. While it has
always been directly engaged in such tasks, events over the past
several years have increasingly propelled the Minister Council into
the status of becoming the GDR's "super economics ministry," as
one analyst expresses it.[27] The new Minister Council Act, passed
on October 16, 1972, has been given institutional legitimacy by recent
changes entered into the GDR's 1968 Constitution.[28]

While SED sources make an attempt to demonstrate that the
Minister Council is directly responsible to the People's Chamber,
the real source of administrative control over its operations lies
within the party, especially through the Politburo and the Central
Committee Secretariat. From this subordinated vantage point,
however, the Minister Council exercises two important kinds of
bureaucratic mandate.

In one set of circumstances, the Minister Council plays an
important role in the selection of personnel for individual governmental ministries, currently numbering 31. Of special significance
here is the influence of its most important consultative and decision-
making organ, the Collegium, which is normally composed of the
most important ministers, their immediate subordinates, and other
leading administrators. As a second order of consideration, the
Minister Council is expected to "coordinate" the work of individual
ministries. Though other state organs, such as the State Planning
Commission, play important roles in the realm of administrative
coordination, the Minister Council is given the responsibility for
successfully coordinating the whole complex of interrelated activities
that engage the energies of individual ministers. Thus, the Minister
Council is given the task of providing a long-run rationale for the
entire operation of governmental structures in the GDR. Even in light
of the fact that it is not strictly obliged to subordinate its operation
to the whims of the People's Chamber, this official account of its
general areas of administrative responsibility seems accurate:

> Under the leadership of the party of the working class
> [the SED] it defines the tenets of government home and
> foreign policy on behalf of the People's Chamber. It
> supervises and organizes the uniform application of
> government policy and ensures the concerted action
> of all authorities. The Council of Ministers guarantees
> the proportional development of the national economy
> to raise the population's living and cultural standards
> further. Its foreign policy activities are focused on

consolidating friendship and cooperation with the Soviet
Union and the other countries of the socialist community
and fulfilling the tasks arising from the economic integration of the socialist countries. . . . Following his election
(pro-forma via the People's Chamber) the Prime Minister
delivers a policy statement on behalf of the Government
in which he sets out the aims and basic lines of government policy. [29]

A critical function is performed by the Minister Council in the
realm of communication, whereby it is held responsible for the
explanation and carrying out of important party and state decisions
on the district, regional, and communal levels of government. This
obligation invariably becomes the direct responsibility of individual
ministers and their immediate entourage:

As determined in the Minister Council Act, all Ministers,
and other leading cadres in the central organs, are obligated
to elaborate upon the decisions of the Party of the working
class and the government before meetings of local elected
assemblies and their councils and in meetings with the
working people. . . . This circle of experienced functionaries within the central state apparatus is obligated
to provide support of all kinds to local elected assemblies,
as well as being active in the presentation of relevant
models which can be employed in attempting to carry out
directives. Last but not least, members of the government,
and their spokesmen, are called upon to carefully syn-
chronize central activities with local organs who are
sensitive to the impact of various policies. [30]

In terms of organizational structure, the Minister Council is
currently composed of 1 chairman, 2 first deputy chairman, 9 regular
deputy chairmen, all of whom carry ministerial portfolios and 29
regular members, each of whom represents a specific Ministry. [31]
Directly below this collective ministerial organ are the individual
ministries. As of August 1974 they number 30: external trade, external affairs, construction, district-directed industry and foodstuffs,
chemistry, electro-technics and electronics, iron, metallurgy and
potash, finance, geology, health, glass and ceramics, trade and
supply, university and technical schools, internal affairs, justice,
coal and energy, culture, agriculture-forest and food economics,
light industry, general land machines and vessel construction material
economy, national defense, postal and telecommunications, heavy
machines and equipment, state security, environmental protection

and water economy, traffic, public education, construction and manu-
facturing implements, science and technology.[32]

Administrative authority rests directly in the hands of individual
ministers, with the number-two person being either a state secretary—
responsible for all activities within the portfolio in the event of
ministerial absence—or an acting minister. For the ministries of
national defense, state security, and internal affairs, there are no
public provisions for the devolution of administrative responsibility
to either a state secretary or an acting minister. Within the ministerial hierarchy, the largest administrative staff is contained within
external affairs, which boasts 1 full minister, 7 acting ministers,
and 35 additional personnel who specialize in activities running the
gamut from cadre training to the conduct of official relations with
parliamentary bodies outside the territory of the GDR.[33]

Standing directly outside the ministerial hierarchy is the State
Planning Commission. Consisting of 1 chairman, 2 state secretaries,
and 14 acting chairmen, this organ is important for the work it performs in the areas of economic planning and administrative coordination. Most generally, these activities involve the commission in the
following task-related areas: "The commission and the relevant
ministries work together in perfecting the operation of a given set
of plans, balances them off against each other, and analyzes and
controls their execution."[34] With reference to a new Statute laying
out the realms of explicit administrative competence and responsibility,
the commission is given the authority to carry through plans as well
as being able independently to make the necessary decisions in
drawing up one- and five-year plans, which includes the appropriate
central balancing decisions. In discharging these duties, it is
"entitled and obliged to provide appropriate instructions to ministries
and directors of other central state organs."[35] Individual ministries
are expected to consult with the commission during all phases of
plan development, implementation, and execution. As one handbook
notes, the commission has become the central planning organ of the
East German government.[36] Only three of its members are represented in the highest organs of the SED, however: Gerhard Schürer,
its chairman, was elected to candidate membership to the Politburo
in October 1973; two other individuals on this body currently hold
candidate membership in the Central Committee.[37]

Below the State Planning Commission there are a number of
lesser administrative structures that work with it and various full
ministerial bodies—3 central organs for agricultural economics
(Zentrale Organe der Landwirtschaft); 1 research council (Forschungs-
rat); 5 state secretariats (Staatssekretariate); 9 state offices
(Staatliche Amter); 2 state committees for television and radio
(Staatliche Komitees für Fernsehen und Rundfunk); 4 state trusteeships
(Staatliche Verwaltungen); 3 state banks (Staatsbank).[38]

State Council and People's Chamber

The administrative competence of these organs is not especially great. Until late 1971 the State Council, among the two, had by far the most important administrative profile: Every subordinate branch of government, with the exception of the People's Chamber, was expected to submit regular performance reports to it. For the GDR's top legislative organ, it is provided with the formal status of being an integral aspect of the state apparatus; being consulted regularly by the Minister Council on various questions of economic and social policy, this organ possesses little direct or indirect administrative authority. Because the People's Chamber possesses 15 legislative committees, all of which tend to focus upon areas of bureaucratic activity engaging the attention of the Minister Council, the possibility theoretically exists for it to exert greater administrative influence sometime in the future. For the moment, however, neither it or the State Council find themselves in the position of being able to meaning-fully influence the operation of other state or party organs.

District and Regional Councils

District and Regional councils work closely with their parallel administrative organs in the party apparatus: On the one side, the party occupies the most authoritative role in the original articulation and carrying out of social and economic policy—basic organizations, and leadership structures on the district, regional, and city levels are carriers of responsibility; on the other side, the state operates as an ideological and subordinate institution in the practical realiza-tion of party programs. From this latter vantage point, questions of administrative success or failure turn on the activities of structures below the national level. District and regional councils (Rat des Bezirkes and Rat Des Kreises) occupy the center of attention in this regard. Some observations on their functions are followed by some examples of how they operate within the GDR.

In an administrative sense, District councils, of which there are 15, work closely with the SED district leadership organization in the realms of economic policy administration and decision-making. Not accidentally, each member of the state apparatus within this geographical jurisdiction is simultaneously a member of the party. Disagreements that might arise between these two administrative structures rarely, if ever, touch on ideology. As one example of how the two structures cooperate with each other, one analyst describes the following situation:

> Control and leadership of state organs by Party institu-
> tions can be demonstrated by an example which is typical

for the cooperative work which unfolds on the district,
as well as the regional level. The secretariat of the
district leadership organization carries out consultations
on all basic questions having relevance for the district;
during meetings of the district secretariat, members
of the district council [Rat des Bezirkes] are allowed
to participate—in most cases, the latter are members
of the SED. The secretariat of the district leadership
organization regularly evaluates the activities of Party
members active in district council meetings, as well as
within district days and its related institutions [see
Chapter 5]. Important decisions of the highest Party
organs [Politburo, Secretariat, and the Central
Committee] are personally interpreted by the district
Party secretary during meetings of the district day. . . .
Between the first secretary of the district leadership
organization and the chairman of the district council,
an on-going exchange of information and consultation is
normal. Members of the district leadership organization
of the Party work in commissions and work groups of
state organs, while members of the district council
work in various levels of the Party apparatus on the
district level. [39]

In terms of activities falling uniquely within the realm of state
competence on the district or regional levels, one SED functionary
makes the following observations in evaluating the functions of state
bodies within agricultural areas of the GDR:

The most important activities performed by members of
state organs are, (1) preparation and execution of the
harvest, (2) organization of socialist competitions,
and a rapid communication of the best performances,
(3) the ability to correctly organize the work force for
optimal results, (4) the ability to work directly with
cooperative farmers and country works in the mastery
of complex situations. . . . Regimentation is in all cases
out of order. The task of state organs is to help administer changes. [40]

Local Representative Bodies

Local representative bodies encompass two interrelated
groupings. On the communal level (Gemeinde Vertretungen), there
are approximately 180, 890 individuals serving as representatives;

on the City-Regional level (representatives serving within various cities which because of their size carry out regionwide activities— East Berlin and Leipzig are of special importance in this regard), there are 3,000 such individuals. Although important differences separate the functioning of small communal representative assemblies—between 500 and 1,000 people—from an assembly attempting to act in the interests of a large metropolitan area, the basic assumptions underlying their operation are generally the same.

What is the administrative importance of such assemblies? The following description supplies a large part of the answer:

> As elements of the uniform socialist state power the local authorities [local representative assemblies], acting in the interests of the state as a whole and within the framework of existing legislation and other legal provisions, decide all basic local affairs under their own authority. To this end they adopt decisions that are binding upon each and everybody in their territory. With their activity the local authorities make a specific contribution to the solution to the primary task defined by the VIII Congress of the SED. It is especially incumbent upon them constantly to improve local living and working conditions and thus to promote socialist patterns of behavior and ways of life among all classes and strata of the population. They are to ensure stable and continuous supplies for the local population, assume responsibility for housing including the construction and conversion of flats, provide new recreational facilities and further youth, physical culture and sports. The local authorities do much to promote citizens intellectual and cultural life and create ever better conditions for them to attain high educational and cultural standards. Social and health services as well as safety at work and the development of workers' occupational environment also come under their responsibility. They make use of whatever possibilities there exist to improve the human environment. For the solution of these tasks the local authorities have at their disposal extensive material and financial resources made up of local taxes they levy and of contributions from the national budget. [41]

In addition to these obvious considerations, there are two additional considerations that should be kept in mind in evaluating the impact and function of local representative bodies from the standpoint of administrative behavior. First, the SED is strongly committed to the belief that it cannot attain its social and economic goals without the full support of every available member of East German society. As things now stand, the GDR's population has been in a condition of numerical decline since 1973. Local representative bodies are seen as yet another means for the integration of individuals and groups into the realm of public affairs, and particularly rule-application activity, by the party. Second, one cannot lose sight of the SED's goals of building a socialist personality. One necessary component of this new identity structure strongly underlines the importance of individual and group activism, a consideration provided institutional reinforcement within the activities of local representative bodies. Pulling these two considerations into one generalization, this means that local representative assemblies are the repositories of party efforts to encourage average citizens to help run the daily affairs of their community with a minimal degree of interference from the party or state. While hardly suggesting laissez-faire administration, this commitment does suggest that the regime, party and state, wants East Germany's citizens to become more involved in the design of public life in the GDR.

Albert Norden, Politburo member, addressed himself to this challenge in the following problem-oriented manner. Taking public issue with an apparent disinclination on the part of the local population to spontaneously involve themselves with the tasks of municipal im-provement, Norden focused attention on one small sample community, Löwenburg. Having congratulated its citizenry for engineering long-overdue change in the physical profile of their community, he then went on to make these critical observations:

> Once a signal came from Berlin informing Löwenbergers
> how to formulate specific problems, their community
> became more attractive and pleasanter to be in. Its
> citizens have become intellectually and politically more
> mature. This situation helps bring with it greater
> happiness, clearer goals, more success. But why must
> it be necessary to wait upon a signal from above? We
> believe this is not necessary given the fact that what
> stands "above" us, the communal assembly and the city
> council, has been chosen by us, the electors. . . . Every
> community which believes it necessary to wait for a signal
> from Berlin is in error. [42]

The solution, in Norden's and the SED's view, is to convince local citizens that they are capable of taking a degree of independent initiative on matters relating to the improvement of their communities. Local representative assemblies should increasingly become the focal

point for mass involvement in such matters. Though it is difficult to
determine whether these kinds of admonitions bring about the desired
result, there is little question that the party continues to confront
the problem of mass passivity.

PROBLEMS

The bureaucracy problem in modern industrial societies is hard
to pin down with absolute precision. In some cases, nothing government attempts or accomplishes is right or adequate. Reducing these
problems into practical language, perhaps the biggest source of
irritation has to do with administrative insensitivity to the needs of
the broad population. Every political system has been forced to
grapple with these issues, and the GDR is not an exception. A list
of specific problems follows.

Inefficiency

At the VIII Party Congress of the SED, Erich Honecker made
a number of related points dealing with the general problem of
inefficiency:

> Out of this list of measures designed to further improve
> the living conditions of working people, let me bring
> one particular issue to your attention given its especially
> pressing nature. This has to do with the supply of daily
> goods to the population, such as consumption articles
> and social services. The gaps and inconsistencies in
> these areas are rightly criticized by the working people.
> We must not be rent asunder by our inability to give appro-
> priate attention to those so-called 1, 000 little things. . . .
> Manifestations of heartlessness and bureaucratism—
> wherever they appear—must be decisively fought against. [43]

Of greater significance to the party and state apparatus is the
rising number of industrial accidents. Public education drives, within
and outside of the work environment, have been undertaken in the
attempt to inform the working population about the dangers of not
exercising a proper degree of caution in the use of heavy machinery.
Local representative organs are important in this area given their
ability to work with basic organizations in joint campaigns to make
the industrial environment safer for employees. [44]

Information

Party and state organs are apparently encountering difficulties in the gathering and evaluation of information on the needs and feelings of the broad population. In this vein, the remarks of one SED secretary are enlightening: "The Party leadership is not interested in the diplomatic formulation of reports, characterized by the most-general of expressions. We say quite openly that we want to know about where specific ideological and factory problems arise within the twelve Party groups, and in what degree they have been able to clear them up with the help of the leadership."[45]

Collectivity and Personal Responsibility

Acceptable models of administrative behavior can generally be divided into two categories in the GDR. On the one hand, there is the expectation that members of the party and state apparatuses will comport themselves in a manner consonant with the precepts of democratic centralism. Individuals displaying excessive degrees of "egoism" in pursuit of their individual duties cannot be tolerated by a party bent on establishing its claims to complete political authority. The doctrine of democratic centralism mirrors this consideration. On the other hand, the SED is not insensitive to the challenge of building a spirit of "personal responsibility" within the consciousness of party and state officials. From this angle, the party is concerned with the relative disinclination of administrators to accept personal responsibility for decisions and actions that fall within their realms of competence. As one observer expresses this dual concern,

> Lenin placed great value on consultations which would result in a realistic formulation of basic questions, that debates in plenary sessions, assemblies, or meetings would not unfold in an artificial manner, but would instead be led in a constructive and creative manner. At the same time, he persistently fought against the degeneration of collectivity in the conduct of political work. . . . He repeatedly warned against manifestations of indecisiveness and irresponsibility appearing under the protective cover of collectivity. . . . We need personal responsibility: While it is necessary to employ the collectivity principle in dealing with the important questions, it is no less important for individuals to be able to exercise personal

> responsibility, including the ability to apply force, in
> order to prevent bureaucratism, in order to prevent
> individuals from avoiding responsibility. [46]

Thus, what the party would like ideally to achieve is an administrative synthesis of two models of behavior.

The dilemma in this domain is that the belief in collectivity makes it easy for individuals in the party and state apparatus to take refuge in what Graham Allison labels "standard operating procedures," or the propensity to define complicated problems, particularly human ones, in terms of automatic responses culled from rule books. The pursuit of personal responsibility, alternatively, runs against the grain of monolithic party authority, which the SED continues to insist upon within the framework of democratic centralism.

Responsiveness

Perhaps the most impressive development in East German bureaucratic practice over the last several years has been an official commitment to a more open airing of party and state problems within the public realm. Whether these changes can become institutionalized, however, depends upon the readiness of the party to extend greater amounts of unqualified trust in the broad population. For the moment, this can be said with some degree of confidence: Every indication suggests the existence of official concern on behalf of the regime that its slender margin of popular legitimacy, almost exhausted during the last years of the Ulbricht regime, be strengthened by meeting public demands. In this regard, there has been a partial retreat away from bureaucratic and "numerical" answers to fundamental human needs and issues. As one party secretary observes in this regard, "During basic discussions dealing with the production of consumer goods in our combine, diverse voices posed questions regarding the kinds of consumer goods we would be producing, where and how they would be manufactured. For us it is clear that this question could not be answered solely by a group of experts sitting around a 'green table.' It is important to develop an atmosphere of creativity and argumentation in all areas of our work. . . ."[47]

SUMMARY AND CONCLUSIONS

The study of bureaucratic structure in the GDR is unavoidably bound up with other functions of the political system. For example, an appreciation of bureaucratic oversight cannot be divorced from an analysis of political recruitment, leadership selection, and training. Further, and of equal importance, an understanding of administration cannot be divorced from the study of interest identification and agregation. Far from being carried out in a lifeless vacuum, as traditional theories of totalitarian politics have earlier (though no more) argued, administrative politics in a one-party system is the apparent result of temporary bargains struck by authoritative groups in the attempt to control and effectively regulate political conflict.

The problem facing the SED, and East German society more generally, is whether the new leadership group who have come into power with Erich Honecker are in the position to change some of the worst manifestations of bureaucratic behavior in the GDR. On this issue, several interrelated issues deserve mention.

At the outset, the VIII Party Congress of the SED, and subsequent plenums thereafter, did address serious attention to the issue of bureaucratic behavior in the GDR. In terms of some questions—the distribution of goods, an improvement in their quality—Honecker took economic functionaries to task for neglecting the material needs of the populace. In other cases, he rightly underscored the necessity of making elected officials integral elements of the interest articulation and aggregation process, if not directly influential decision and rule-making participants. Thus, he called upon local representative assemblies to improve their work, while simultaneously asserting that they needed more authority in the performance of assigned tasks.[48] Three years later at the 12th Plenum of the SED, this concern for improving the operation of these bodies was aired with the same emphasis it had been at the VIII Party Congress. As Hermann Axen, Politburo member, asserted on this recent occasion, "The local councils, and their organs, have exerted themselves in attempting to process the requests of the citizens, and the realization of their proposals. We should not attempt to push aside the fact, however, that not all of the interests, concerns, and complaints of citizens are being met in an appropriate manner."[49] As recently as the 13th Plenum of the party, Honecker made note of the fact that on-going effort and attention was being devoted to the creation of a "trusting atmosphere between the organs of socialist state power and the citizenry."[50] Running the gamut from general work conditions to the saving of scarce raw materials, there is little question that the SED is increasingly aware of the problems that plague a society characterized by such an abundance of bureaucratic structures.

The party's sensitivity to problems such as bureaucratic inefficiency, if not outright callousness, does not mean that serious difficulties do not continue to exist, however. Perhaps the biggest problem is that the SED apparently seems more inclined to take the state bureaucracy to task without coming to the public realization that the Party apparatus is also guilty of being occasionally insensitive to the needs and demands of average citizens. This particular issue has undoubtedly been talked about openly in private gatherings—from the basic organization upward—but there is little direct reference made to "bottlenecks" in party work, certainly not on the level, or with the intensity, at which official complaints are directed at state organs.

One important indication that the regime, both party and state, is taking the problem of bureaucratic insensitivity and general ineffi-ciency seriously is reflected in the SED's continuous effort to enlist the services of the mass population in the running of social affairs. This point is driven home with special vigor regarding the participa-tion of youth within the framework of party and state organizations. Revisions in Article 22 of the 1968 East German Constitution have now made it possible for individuals 18 years of age, instead of 21, to serve in the People's Chamber. As one official source highlights this general concern of the party in attempting to integrate ever-larger numbers of young people into the operation of socialist institutions in the GDR:

> . . . Now that the years of socialist construction have
> confirmed that more faith must give rise to broader
> rights and higher demands the law [Youth Law of 1973]
> defines the rights and duties of youth in all spheres of
> life. At the same time it lays down a variety of measures
> designed to guarantee the all-round development of the
> young generation. . . . A basic expression of socialist
> youth policy is the fact that young people are drawn
> into the running and planning of social affairs. They
> serve as deputies in all representative assemblies,
> as members of commissions and many other honorary
> bodies as well as of trade union branches in enterprises
> which enables them to take part in the discussion of the
> plan and in the preparation of other important decisions.
> Many young people hold posts carrying great responsibility
> in public and economic life. . . . [51]

Within the People's Chamber this general theme is reflected in the fact that nearly one-third of its membership consists of individuals between the ages of 21 and 40 years of age—163 seats, 32.6 percent of the total membership. If one relaxes membership rules somewhat, a more impressive statistic surrounds memberships (of June 20, 1971) in the Party's Central Committee, where 59.8 percent of its members and candidates (N = 189) lie between the ages of 21-50.[52]

Whether the participation of younger individuals and groups within the institutions of socialist society will bring about an improvement in the functioning of the party and state apparatus is open to question. For example, a highly centralized economy will continue to operate in a certain manner irrespective of the age groups who are active in its daily and long-term administration. There is little impressionistic proof that the traditional kinds of coordinative— cooperation between various branches of industry within a given VVB area—and production problems have been ameliorated over the past several years despite the party's strong attempt to engage the occupational interests of young people within the work force in the running of socialist concerns. Additionally, problems of chronic raw material shortages within socialist industry, though partially correctable through campaigns aimed at cutting down on wastage in the plant or agricultural section, are not immediately resolvable by the drafting of younger people into the occupational and social activity sectors. In a word, certain kinds of inefficiency, insensitivity, and ignorance— all quintessentially bureaucratic dilemmas in the GDR, as elsewhere— are environmental in origin.

Having made these observations, however, it is nonetheless clear that the Honecker regime has begun to come to realistic terms with the simple, and unavoidable, fact that the organs of public power have not always met the demands of the population of whom they rule. On this modest note, the study of East German bureaucratic behavior— especially the relationship between party and state organs, on the one hand, and the mass population, on the other—bears serious attention by students of the GDR's political system in the West.

In surveying future developmental trends within the party and state apparatus of the GDR, a student of Soviet bureaucratic behavior provides a concluding perspective:

> One senses that the most viable model for the Soviet system must somehow strike a balance between the populist and the bureaucratic formulas for rationalization. Public participation and institutionalization must figure as integral and inevitable features of the model. Having said this, however, we have already extended the scope and import of our analysis well beyond the rationalization of Soviet totalitarianism. Indeed, the persistent and baffling problem of properly mixing mobilization and organization is not peculiar to the rationalization of Communist and other authoritarian regimes, but is the basic dilemma constantly facing all developing political systems, Communist and non-Communist. Thus, in the final analysis, the choices and challenges involved in the

rationalization of totalitarianism must be viewed within
the broader perspective of comparative politics and
modernization theory.[53]

Given the obvious fact that the German Democratic Republic, like its
relative to the west, is in many ways a young and developing society,
it would be premature to assume easily that the SED and the socialist
state are not capable of effectively tackling the bureaucracy problem.
In the short term, and given the gigantic tasks the party has set for
East German society to accomplish, it is probably safe to conclude
that administrative bottlenecks, and popular dissatisfaction with the
operation of SED and state organs more generally, will continue to
exist in the GDR. On the basis of what the regime has been able to
accomplish in the realm of economic modernization and social integration since the early 1960s, however, there is some foundation in
believing that the "bureaucracy problem" may one day be ameliorated,
if not solved, in East Germany.

NOTES

1. Andras Hegedus, "Marxist Theories of Leadership," in
ed. R. Barry Farrell Political Leadership in Eastern Europe and
the Soviet Union, (Chicago: Aldine, 1970), p. 44.
2. Karl Marx and Friedrich Engels, Complete Works, Vol. I
(Moscow: Foreign Language Publishing House, 1961), p. 187.
3. V.I. Lenin, Collected Works, Vol. 25 (Moscow: Progress
Publishers, 1964), p. 481.
4. Ibid., p. 425.
5. Frederic J. Fleron, Jr. and Lou Jean Fleron, "Administrative Theory as Repressive Political Theory: The Communist Experience," Newsletter on Comparative Studies of Communism, 11/72,
p. 20.
6. Lenin, op. cit., p. 259.
7. Gabriel Almond and G. Bingham Powell, Comparative
Politics (Boston: Little, Brown, 1966), p. 153.
8. Ibid., p. 142.
9. Ibid., p. 152.
10. Frederick C. Barghoorn, The USSR (Boston: Little, Brown,
1966), p. 266.
11. Paul H.B. Hoodwin, "Communist Systems and Modernization:
Sources of Political Crises," Comparative Communism 6, nos. 1-2
(Spring/Summer, 1973), p. 112.

12. Karl Heinz Kahrs, "The 'Economic System of Socialism' in East Germany," Ph.D. dissertation, University of California, Santa Barbara, 1970, pp. 10-12.

13. Thomas Arthur Baylis, "The Technical Intelligentsia in East German Politics," Ph.D. dissertation, University of California, Berkeley, 1968, p. 43.

14. Peter Christian Ludz, The Changing Party Elite in East Germany (Cambridge, Mass.: MIT Press, 1972), p. 82.

15. Erich Honecker, "Die weitere Festigung der Arbeiter-und Bauern-Macht, die Entwicklung der sozilaistischen Demokratie," in Protokoll der Verhandlungen des VIII. Parteitages der SED (Vol I) (Berlin: Dietz Verlag, 1971), p. 84.

16. Ibid., p. 84.

17. Kleines Politisches Wörterbuch (Berlin: Dietz Verlag, 1973), p. 982.

18. Staats- und Parteiapparat der DDR, August 1, 1974, p. 31-33.

19. Ibid., pp. 26-27.

20. Ibid., p. 33.

21. Eckart Förtsch, Die SED (Stuttgart: W. Kohlhammer, 1969), p. 54.

22. Ibid., p. 50.

23. Ibid.

24. Ibid.

25. Willi Jost, "Erfahrungsaustausch in den Grundorganizationen nebenan," Neuer Weg, 10/73, pp. 447-48.

26. Ibid., p. 448.

27. Peter Joachim Lapp, "Zum Regierungssystem der DDR," Deutschland Archiv, 10/73, p. 1057.

28. Siegfried Mampel, "DDR-Verfassung fortgeschrieben," Deutschland Archiv, 11/74, pp. 1215-17.

29. Introducing the GDR (Dresden: Verlag Zeim im Bild, 1974), p. 78-79.

30. Friedrich Ebert, Der VIII. Parteitag der SED (Berlin: Dietz Verlag, 1973), p. 14.

31. Staats- und Parteiapparat der DDR, op. cit., pp. 4-7.

32. Ibid., pp. 7-18.

33. Ibid., pp. 8-9.

34. Kleines Politisches Wörterbuch, op. cit., p. 818.

35. Hannsjörg Buck, "Neues Statut starkt erneut Weisungsmacht der Staatlichen Plankommission der DDR," Deutschland Archiv 11/73, p. 1183.

36. Michael Benhamin, Harry Möbis, and Ludwig Penig, Funktion, Aufgaben und Arbeitsweise der Ministerien (Berlin: Staatsverlag, 1973), p. 30.

37. Staats- und Parteiapparat der DDR, op. cit., pp. 26-29.

38. Ibid., pp. 19-23.

39. Förtsch, op. cit., pp. 135-36.

40. "Unser Interview mit Wolfgang Lippmann," Neuer Weg 10/73, p. 446.

41. Introducing the GDR, op. cit., pp. 79-80.

42. Albert Norden, Miteinander und Füreinander (Berlin: Staatsverlag, 1972), pp. 15.

43. Honecker, Protokoll der Verhandlungen, op. cit., pp. 64 and 86.

44. DDR Report, No. 60, May 1973, pp. 291 and 240.

45. Wolfgang Schmidt, "Anliegen der Mitglieder behandeln," Neuer Weg, 9/73, p. 399.

46. Friedrich Ebert, Die Beschlüsse des VIII Parteitag der SED und die nächsten Aufgaben (Berlin: Dietz Verlag, 1973, p. 39.

47. Möbel aus Schwedt," Neuer Weg, 2/73, p. 71.

48. Honecker, Protokoll der Verhandlungen, op. cit., p. 85.

49. Dokumentation: "Die 12. Tagung des ZK der SED (I)," Deutschland Archiv, 8/74, p. 874.

50. Neues Deutschland, December 13, 1974, p. 6.

51. Introducing the GDR, op. cit., pp. 67-68.

52. Bericht zur Lage der Nation 1972 (Bonn, 1972), p. 30.

53. Paul Cocks, "The Rationalization of Party Control," in Change in Communist Systems, ed. Chalmers Johnson (Stanford, Calif.: Stanford University Press, 1970), pp. 189-90.

7

RULE ADJUDICATION
AND ENFORCEMENT

THEORETICAL FRAMEWORK

Marxism/Leninism

According to classical Marxism, coercive settlement of disputes and rule enforcement could be made unnecessary in a future society— since man was a product of nature and society, if society changed, so would human thoughts and behavior. Since the economic structure of society was the basis for social institutions, including law, one could change such sociopolitical structures by changing economic relations. Although there was feedback between the economic basis and the legal superstructure, in the last analysis economic conditions were decisive. Thus, it would be necessary to change the whole economy before fundamental legal reforms could be undertaken.

The change that Marx advocated, of course, was putting the means of production into the hands of the majority of the people, that is, the workers. This change, he felt, would come through the proletariat revolution. It would permit the establishment of a political system that, in turn, would lead first to socialism and ultimately to communism.

Thus, Marx did not suggest a new science of law. Instead, he saw law as a repressive institution of rule enforcement and social control that first was to be exposed, then under socialism changed, and finally abolished. For Marx, the key to the law's repressive nature was the fact that the rule-enforcement structure was controlled by the middle class, or bourgeoisie. Thus, for instance, the bourgeois protection of private property and private contracts had a higher priority than protection of the individual rights of those who owned no property. When such property relations disappear, and the working class is not subjected to the owning class, Marx believed there would be no need for state or law. Instead, men would freely obey rules because those rules would have been decided by them and would be in their best interests. In short, there would be free self-determination through contract and administration. A collectivist-oriented society of free and enlightened citizens could solve problems rationally, without resorting to coercion and compulsion.

Lenin, a lawyer by training, accepted Marx's idea of the coercive nature of the state and law as an institution of rule adjudication and enforcement and social control. In fact, the "withering away of the state" was a central Leninist thesis. At the same time, however, he argued for centralization of power in the immediate postrevolutionary period. A young revolutionary state, threatened externally (by noncommunist states) as well as internally (by remnants of capitalistic attitudes and behavior), and short of enlightened citizens as well as trained loyal communist leaders, at first needed a powerful state apparatus. This is the phase in which the states of Eastern Europe at present see themselves.

Thus, socialist law today is a legal system that aims at creating the sociopolitical foundations of communism, as well as the economic basis. Therefore the economic plan and law are interrelated, economic misdeeds are crimes, and laws of property and contract exist within a socialist context—that is, there are crimes against socialist property and the domestic economy as well as against personal and private property.

In this present phase of developing socialism, the communist political system demands that rule adjudication, enforcement, and social control be controlled by the Communist party. This role is derived from Marxist/Leninist a priori assumptions noted earlier regarding history, economic classes, and the leading role of the party. Indeed, the party's apparat itself has become a basic instrument of rule adjudication and enforcement, along with state organs. At each level, from the basic party unit up through the party hierarchy, disputes about rules are settled and rules are enforced according to decisions laid down by the party's top leaders. As will be seen, their decisions dominate a vast network of bureaucratic and administrative controls within the state structure, as well as in the formal legal structures. In addition, noncoercive adjudication, enforcement, and control are exercised by a host of special social structures created by the party.

Functionalism

When rules are written for a political system, the rule-makers assume there will be violations. Thus, provisions for penalties are included in the rules, so the system has the power to assure implementation of its political decisions and maintenance of social control. However, deciding whether or not a rule indeed has been violated is a cause for controversy and interpretation. Similarly, contention arises over the extent of the violation and the appropriate punishment. The resolution of such conflicts regarding the rules of the political system is the adjudication function.[1] It is the process of rule enforcement, that is, imposing authoritative restraints or obligations on individuals, classes or strata, or everyone.

People usually think of the rule- adjudication and -enforcement function in terms of police, courts, and judges, that is, "law enforcement." However, while it is conceded that such structures can contribute to impartial conflict solution, much more is involved. The rule-application structure, for instance the bureaucracy, may itself settle disputes and assess fines and penalties. Regulatory agencies do the same. And in some political systems arbitrary adjudication and coercive enforcement measures are taken by secret police, metropolitan police, or party officials. Taken together, the coercive forms of rule enforcement—fines, penalties, regulatory power, police power, and terror—are effective in securing short-term compliance. It is less effective, however, in securing subjective commitment over long periods.[2] Further, it is costly—more so, for instance, than normative power (such as socialization or persuasion) or material power (wages, rewards, bonuses, promotions). The problem of "mixing" these forms of coercion in carrying out the rule-enforcement function is an especially painful dilemma for a revolutionary government. It at first lacks a broad base of common values, for socialization and indoctrination take time. Yet it must assure survival and consolidate power—thus, it often resorts to coercion. On the other hand, overdoing the application of coercion may damage the potential system-identification of important groups within the system and lead to a minimal input of support.

SITUATION IN THE GDR

In its phase of developing socialism, the GDR's basic theoretical principles regarding adjudication and enforcement, especially in the case of crime, emphasize the following:

1. A society's superstructure lags behind the base, sometimes by as much as several decades; thus antisocial phenomena continue. Antisocial behavior is that which is detrimental to the interests of the socialist society and the state. It violates the written rules or unwritten moral code of conduct. The punishment is penalty or public censure. Such behavior is alien to the nature of the socialist system. That is, antisocial behavior is believed to be "leftovers" of capitalism, not the result of socialism itself. Hooligans, parasites, swindlers, thieves, bribetakers, speculators, etc., show habits of exploitation that are a legacy of capitalism. Similarly, disrespect for women, drunkenness, and similar misbehavior are seen as practices and traditions rooted in the past and not arising from the nature of socialism itself. Thus, a distinct line is drawn between individual antisocial acts and crime as a widespread social phenomenon.

While socialism creates the conditions necessary for producing a "new man" and a society free of crime, outside influences still hinder the process. For example, information regarding the affluence of the nonsocialist world confuses people regarding social standards relevant to revolutionary, "nation-building," societies. Thus, not every family or labor collective provides a true socialist context for behavior—"unenlightened" adults pass on unsocialist attitudes to children. Public ownership of the means of production is not yet complete; differences between classes and groups exist; differences between city and countryside, as well as between manual and mental work continue. The phase of socialism is a long, complicated one.

In short, crime is caused by the fact that consciousness lags behind social conditions, that the outside (capitalist) world is hostile to socialism, and that the continuing shortages of cultural and material services affect children and adults.[3] While individual psychology plays a role in crime, it is more affected by these social conditions under which the person lives and has been raised.

2. The continued presence of antisocial behavior, combined with the increasing significance of state power,[4] makes socialist law the "major method" used by the state leadership for guiding the socialist society: "Without law the socialist state can fulfill its class function just as little as socialist law can arise and become realized without the state."[5] For example, the new law concerning the Local People's Representations (Volksvertretungen) of July 12, 1973 (GBI I, S. 313) makes clear that rule adjudication, enforcement, and social control are increasingly a state responsibility. The new law, is said, articulates "anew the growing role of socialist law and the necessity for the steady solidification of socialist legality. . . . In the Rule of Conduct, Paragraph 2, Section 6, the strict standard of socialist legality, the maintenance of order and security, and the increase of state discipline are made a firm ingredient of state leadership at all levels."[6]

Law is seen as such an important instrument of state leadership because it contributes to the harmonious growth of all elements of socialism, including the development of socialist democracy and optimal conditions for economic production. The following comprehensive definition, therefore, is suggested for socialist law in the GDR:

> In the socialist social order of our Republic, it is the totality of all effective, generally binding behavioral demands (Norms) on the citizens, their collectives and social communities, state and economic organs, as well as their functionaries, which express the concrete social demands of the objective laws of development of the socialist society and its efficacy stipulations. [7]

3. In this present phase the use of coercive power in socialist rule enforcement is legitimized. GDR writers admit that because of the role allocated by Marxism/Leninism to the power of persuasion, "the argument for the application of coercion or force in the process of applying law presents one of the most difficult questions of the Marxist/Leninist theory of government." However, the writers continue, while one is patient and persuasive with citizens learning socialist consciousness, "at the same time those who threaten the life of our people, the stability of our nation, must be severely punished."[8] In other words,

> the socialist society cannot wait until its last member is persuaded of the correctness of behavioral demands necessary in the interest of social development. In the interest of further planned development of the socialist society, and thereby the overwhelming majority of the working people, it is also required through coercive means to lead every citizen, who has not recognized his responsibility, to a realization of the objective requisites and the society-wide wish for judicial behavior.

The use of coercion, thus, is in the interest of the great majority of citizens and will be used.

4. At the same time, however, coercion acquires a new quality in a socialist society in that its aim is its own abolition through its interrelationship with persuasion. In short, the use of coercion in the socialist society aims at

- realizing legally demanded behavior,
- making conscious legal behavioral demands and setting socially justified motives,

- introducing and realizing education and reeducation processes,
- creating an atmosphere of impatience vis-a-vis breaking the law, maladministration, and disorder,
- protecting effectively the socialist society, its state, and its citizens.[9]

5. Since wrongdoing is socially generated, emphasis is not on coercion through punishment but reeducation away from bad habits. Since wrongdoing is socially generated, the criminal in a sense is the innocent instrument of historical laws. Thus, he is not to be "punished," in the traditional sense, but reeducated away from his bad habits. He is to be helped to exercise conscious discipline over himself. However, although objective conditions exist that explain why he "went astray," the presence of these conditions do not excuse the socialist citizen from responsibility. A fatalist attitude toward crime is not acceptable. Rather, crime is seen as a combination of objective factors and the individual personality of the criminal himself. Both causes are the object of continued efforts of reform.

6. For rule adjudication and enforcement to be effective, the public must increasingly be brought into the process. In general, as seen in the preceding chapter on rule making, the GDR prides itself on the fact that the public does play a large role in making the laws, and that those laws are based on scientific inquiry and procedures that are up to date. Similarly, as will be shown in this chapter, thousands of GDR citizens are active in the rule-adjudication and -enforcement function.

In summary, the functions of the law in the GDR are (1) to suppress the enemies of the sociopolitical system, (2) to regulate the economic and organizational life of the society, and (3) to educate citizens to a "socialist consciousness."

COERCIVE POWER

Laws

The Constitution and other laws of the GDR cannot be adequately understood if they are viewed through the prism of Western constitutional democracies. In systems such as those of the United States or the Federal Republic of Germany, rights are written into law primarily as defense and protection against possible encroachment of state power. In short, the law is there primarily to protect the integrity of the individual by limiting the state.

That, however, is not the case in a system based on Marxist principles. There, state and society are not seen as two opposing interests, one of which has to be protected from the other. Rather, they are seen as an identity of interest. For instance, basic rights of citizens are matched by their basic duties to society—the right to work and education correspond with the responsibility to work and obtain an education (Constitution, Articles 24, 25). Thus, the law does not have the role of protecting citizens by limiting government, but rather by controlling social development. The rights prescribed by law describe and confirm already achieved social developments of the society—as the development progresses, laws reflecting the new stages are passed. As Robert Sharlet notes, the constitutions of socialist systems therefore usually make clear the achievements of the first phase of revolutionary political development—nationalizing private property, extending legal protection to the newly acquired public property, secularizing marriage and divorce—that appropriated the economic base, consolidated it, and created the possibility for mobilizing society by making social relations more fluid and releasing the social energy of the individual. [10]

Next, the constitutions reflect the mobilization phase of political development marked by the transformation of the environment, maximization of power, and harnessing of energy. This is seen in the legal role of central planning, the priority of public property and crimes against it, the control of social forces, and the strengthening of the family structure.

Thus, the legal system of the GDR can be understood only within its specific political times. For instance, during the initial phases of the construction of socialism (1949-61), the enforcement of rules was strict, that is, relatively more coercion was applied than in the later phase, where persuasion could be used more since the political basis of the GDR had been secured. That the political context influences the degree of coercion found in the GDR's rule-adjudication and -enforcement measures is reflected clearly in the minister of justice's explanation that

> at the apex of the "Special Part" of our criminal code offenses against the sovereignty of the GDR, peace, humanity, and human rights are regulated. . . . In the criminal code we also always have to take into account that imperialism . . . will still and increasingly attempt to prepare and carry out barbaric strikes of different kinds against peace and the GDR. In the future we also will counter such offenses with all decisiveness and with the appropriate firmness of our laws and our justice. [11]

In light of the importance of the political context for the GDR's legal system, it thus is interesting to note that a new judicial organizational law (Gerichtsverfassungsgesetz), which went into effect November 1, 1975, apparently gives the Ministry of Justice greater possibilities to influence directly the administration of justice than it previously had. While this fits in with the general development in the GDR to strengthen state institutions, it also may be seen as possibly limiting the independence of judges. For example, the Justice Ministry now is responsible for the guidance and control of the administration of justice, whereas the old law called for "firm ties to the people" and a "democratic system of guidance and control" for the judicial system. Further, the ministry is given responsibility for overseeing District and Regional courts and, along with the Supreme Court, the implementation of the courts' tasks. Still another change may prove to be significant: Instead of making its educational function top priority for the judicial system, the new law names protection of the socialist state and social system as the number-one task. [12]

Also important in the GDR's Legal System is the codification of fields of law (Gesetzbücher). They are considered of "fundamental significance" because they (1) give revolutionary governments an opportunity to publicly proclaim their goals and to ideologically and organizationally achieve them, (2) are expression of a certain maturity and consolidation of social relations, (3) provide an overview of existing laws, (4) help to make the law comprehensible for the public, and (5) abolish outdated and irrelevant legal requirements. Thus, the GDR published the Work Law Code in 1961, the Educational Law in 1965, the Family Law Code the same year, and the Criminal Law Code and Rules for Criminal Proceedings in 1968. These codes are integrated, one with the other, and thereby provide coordinated regulation of interrelated social relations.

A Civil Law Code is still necessary, for it would give legal expression to the new position of GDR citizens in their developing socialist society. In addition, economic law, too, is to be further developed and perhaps eventually also codified. Problems that such a legal code would have to cope with include "the treatment of scientific-technological progress, increase of discipline and responsibility, self-responsibility of enterprises within the context of central leadership and planning of the domestic economy, and the relations of the enterprises to the territory." [13]

Constitution

The GDR's first Constitution, of 1949, reflected primarily the antifascist nature of the new German state that was set up in what

then was known as the Soviet Zone of Occupation. By 1951 the character of that new state was described in the following way:

> The abolition of the reactionary class of Junkers [big
> landowners, primarily in Prussia], the removal of
> the big industrialists from their positions of power,
> made possible the development of a peace economy free
> from crises. The democratic reform of the schools was
> a decisive factor for the erection in Germany of a new
> social order. This is an antifascist democratic order
> in which the united working class holds the decisive
> positions of power. [14]

Political conditions had changed by 1968 when a new Constitution
was adopted. The GDR now was called "a socialist state of the
German nation," rather than merely a "democratic Republic," and
its power was derived not just from "the people" but from "the
working people" (Article 2). Article 1, further, made clear that
"the working people" were under the leadership of the "Marxist/
Leninist party"—in short, the leading role of the SED was fixed in
the Constitution. Thus, it was clear that the initial political stages
of revolution, the gaining and consolidating of power, were past.

Organizationally, too, the new constitution reflected the GDR's
changed context. The legal system, for instance, was given greater
attention: The socialist society had proceeded far enough so that the
people themselves could carry out some rule-adjudication and
-enforcement activities.

Similarly, the economic changes were spelled out in the Constitution. The old constitution had called for an economic system
based on "principles of social justice [to] ensure an adequate standard
of living for all." The new Constitution made clear that these goals
were to be achieved through socialism (Article 9). The GDR's
continuing economic problems, resulting from its inadequate man-
power base, also were reflected. The old Constitution had guaranteed
the right to work. The new one said: "The right to work and the duty
to work form a unity" (Article 24). A work right that completely
disappeared from the new Constitution was the right to strike. The
explanation was that since the time the old Constitution was written
the means of production had come into state hands, that is, the state
of the working people, and so the workers would be striking against
themselves. Instead, their grievances now could be handled through
trade union representatives.

Socially, the new Constitution also reflected the growth and
continuing problems of the GDR. While extending family rights, it
at the same time, because of continuing feelings generated during the

Nazi oppression, renewed restrictions against preaching racial hatred, militarist propaganda, and incitement to war. The right to travel was significantly changed, again a reflection of the political context of the nearly 20 years through which the GDR had passed between its initial and new constitutions: The old document guaranteed "the right to choose one's place of residence"; the new one merely granted all citizens "the right to move freely within the state territory of the German Democratic Republic within the framework of the laws" (Article 32).

In the 1970s it was felt the GDR had changed so much that it was necessary to again update the Constitution so it would more accurately reflect the times. Thus, a new Constitution was adopted in October 1974, on the 25th anniversary of the establishment of the GDR. [15] The most important changes were found in Part I of the 1974 Constitution, "Principles of the Socialist Community State System." Here were reflected the short but decisive 25 years of GDR history. First of all, the idea of the GDR being part of a "German nation" was stricken, as well as the concepts "Germany" and "unification of both German states." Instead, it was said the GDR is "a socialist state of workers and farmers" (Article 1) and the National Front was changed from "of democratic Germany" to "of the German Democratic Republic" (Article 3). Further, the position of the GDR in the socialist family of nations was made precise—that is, an "inseparable part"; and the relationship to the Soviet Union was separated from that of the other socialist states and expressed with unmistakable firmness—that is, the GDR is allied with the USSR "forever and irrevocably" (Article 6). The clarity of these positions reflected the GDR's view that it had reached a decisive point in its historical development and foreign relationships.

The economic changes in the GDR since the last Constitution also were reflected. The present phase of economic development was said to be the "creation of the developed socialist society." Thus, the new Constitution reflects the fact that all industrial enterprises are now state property, and that the economic system of central management and planning is to be increasingly tied to the initiatives of the workers, rather than just to producers and state organs (Article 9, Paragraph 3).

Organizationally, too, there were significant changes in the 1974 Constitution, with more power being given to the People's Chamber and the Minister Council and less to the State Council. This was said to reflect the experience the GDR had gained in strengthening the role of state power and in developing socialist democracy. There were no changes that would make the role of the party in the political system more precise.

Socially, the new Constitution contained few changes, as in Part II concerning "Citizen and Community in the Socialist Society." One rather significant change, however, was made in Part I—the Ulbricht concept of "socialist human community" was changed to "socialist society" (Article 18) because it was felt that the former was not exact vis-a-vis the present phase of development and its continuing existence of class differences.

In the case of the GDR, the Constitution as the core of the legal system not only contains such legal rights of citizens and state organs, but it further specifically binds those organs to work out new, relevant laws on the basis of the Constitution itself. Thus, the Constitution is especially influential in codification of various fields of law: "The Constitution contains the basic assumptive norms in the form of important principles for all significant branches of our legal system, especially for constitutional law, economic law, labor law, agricultural collective law, land law, family law, as well as criminal law."[16] In short, in addition to containing the political system's norms, the GDR's Constitution sets standards for rule adjudication and enforcement and rule application, as well as further rule-making. The Constitution is simultaneously a program for the further development of the socialist legal system and for unifying law and law application.

Work Law Code (Gesetzbuch der Arbeit—GBA)

Based on the Marxist thesis that work is the most important form of individual and social self-realization, a Code of Work Law was issued in 1961. It unified the then-existing labor laws and made clear that such laws no longer were part of the private sphere. With the elimination of private ownership of the means of production, labor law no longer was a means of solving contradictions between capital and labor. Rather, work law was to be the basis of common work among free producers. Further, the new law was to make clear that citizens, through their work and use of their right of codetermination, exercised power.[17] Another goal of the new law was to solve the contradictions (seen as surmountable) between production and consumption and the resulting conflicts between personal and social interests.

In short, the Work Law Code regulated:

1. Rights and duties of enterprise leadership as well as the participation of workers, especially in and through the trade union;

2. The conclusion and suspension of work contracts, as well as determination of wages and bonuses;

3. Job training and advanced education;

4. Health and work protection, as well as work discipline;

5. The caring for cultural and sport activities of workers through enterprises;

6. The special support of working youth as well as women.

The fact that the enterprises have steadily increased their number of libraries, books, nurseries, vacation homes, and sport organizations[18] is evidence that points 4 to 6 above, as guaranteed in the Work Law Code, are more than mere theory. On the other hand, there seems to be a contradiction in point 1 between the right of workers to take part in planning, leadership, and organization at all levels of an enterprise and the leadership hierarchy's present rights to make decisions without significant interference from the trade union leadership. The question often is asked whether the prevailing principle of centralized decision-making leads to the evolution of a so-called new class of managers, or whether it is primarily a tactic for solving problems arising from the demands to increase work productivity.

Meanwhile, there is discussion in the GDR about revision of the Work Law Code. It is pointed out, for instance, that there are, as supplements to the GBA, some 400 laws, resolutions, regulations, and ordinances, 150 collective contracts, and about 220 labor protection ordinances and standards. These various forms of the law are not adequately coordinated, summarized, and available to workers.[19]

Nevertheless, the present Work Law Code is seen by the GDR as having "historic and national significance," for it is based on man's relationship to the material production conditions of a socialist society. Further, it contains the basis of "socialist work morality" (Arbeitsmoral), works out the position of trade unions as an organization of the working class, and supports socialist "teamwork" (Gemeinschaftsarbeit) as the key to solving tasks.[20]

Family Law Code (Familiengesetzbuch)

A proposal for a Family Law Code was introduced at the beginning of 1965 and discussed for nearly a year. More than 23,000 petitions, or suggestions, were offered, resulting in several hundred changes in the proposed law.[21] The final law was announced the end of 1965 and went into effect April 1, 1966.[22]

It contains several innovations over the previous law:

1. Marriage rights no longer are seen as private rights, and the institution of marriage is no longer seen primarily as one of care and welfare (Versorgung). Instead, in it man and woman are equal, in terms of work, choosing a name, and divorce grounds.

2. The concept "illegitimate" for a child is replaced through "not legitimate," and equal rights are guaranteed for those children, as well as for children born within the institution of marriage.

3. Special attention is given families with numerous children and also single-parent families.[23]

Three years later, in 1968, the equality of men and women, as well as the position of marriage and family, was further enunciated and fixed in the Constitution. And on March 9, 1972, abortion was made legal.

The Family Law Code is significant in GDR legal developments in that it "makes possible, for the first time, the realization of the thoughts and forecasts of Marx and Engels concerning the development of the family in a community of equal people, free to decide for themselves."[24] It also set moral standards for the society and its rule-adjudication and -enforcement function.

Criminal Law Code and Criminal Law Procedure (Strafgesetzbuch und Straffprozessordnung)

Once the important areas of social life concerning work and the family had been newly codified, the GDR could take up revision of the nineteenth-century criminal laws on the books. Thus, the preparation of the Criminal Law Code was undertaken simultaneously with preparation of the new Constitution of 1968. The aim was "to develop state power so that it would become effective as an active instrument of social progress even under the new economic conditions." Further, this law was not seen as relevant for the final phase of socio-economic development, that is, "communism," but rather "a law for the present and the foreseeable future."

New in the Criminal Law Code was the distinction between criminal acts against personal and private property and against public property and the domestic economy. The protection of the latter, as already noted, is seen as the primary aim of GDR criminal law—the uninterrupted construction of the socialist economic system and further development of its productivity are seen as basic to the all-around strengthening of the GDR which is necessary for the happiness of all its citizens.[25]

The proposal for the new law was worked out in a commission of jurists, social scientists, workers, and managers. Some 35,000 copies of the proposal were distributed for discussion, resulting in more than 8,000 suggested changes, many of which were incorporated. The revised proposal then was again considered by the State Council and committees of the People's Chamber and finally unanimously passed by the Supreme Court.[26] It was the first time in GDR history that criminal law had as its stated goal not punishment but rather crime prevention:[27] "It protects the socialist society and state order, its political and economic bases, for the people's wishes. . . . Punishment in the socialist GDR is not an act of revenge and not an outlawing of the culprit."[28]

Youth Law

The GDR has modernized its youth law, along with the other fields of law discussed above. The first Youth Law (Jugendgesetz) was passed in February 1950. It guaranteed the younger citizens of the new German state political rights, the right to work and recreation, the right to education, and the right to happiness. In 1964 this law was expanded to take into account youth's active participation in the system's "construction of socialism" phase. At that time all state and economic organs were directed to support the initiatives of youth, in profession, school, culture, and sport.

Then in 1973 the public was presented with a third Youth Law to be debated before final adoption. It took into account "the developed social possibility for many-sided support of the youths' socialist personality development."[29] Thus, the newest law was seen by the GDR as a logical next step in a continuously developing program of care for the interests of youth. The new law proposes, among other aims, four major ones:

1. Socialist education of youth is a top priority, for socialist class consciousness is neither inherited nor developed spontaneously; every new generation has to develop it.

2. Individual responsibility of youth for the development of their socialist personality is emphasized. Therefore, society is to give youth meaningful tasks. Further, society is to support youth collectives and cultural, sport, and social activities for the young.

3. Increased attention is to be given to leisure-time opportunities of youth. Not necessarily the quantity of such opportunities is to be increased, but rather the quality, so that leisure-time activities lead to the development of socialist personalities.

4. The rights and influence of the FDJ on the life of youth in the GDR are to be significantly increased. Other state organizations are responsible for cooperation with the FDJ.[30]

During the public discussion of this proposal (thousands of meetings attracting 5.4 million citizens), many problems, contradictions, and obstacles to implementation were discussed. Some 4,821 suggestions for improvement of the proposed law were received; 200 changes were made;[31] and the new law went into effect in February 1974.[32]

Economic Law

According to the VIII Party Congress, the economic law now will be gradually organized. Whether it will be codified is not yet clear. But that it is a crucial aspect of the GDR's rule-adjudication and -enforcement system is clear:

> In clear contrast to capitalist law, social law contributes
> directly to formation of all significant relations of
> socialist property, the forms of production within
> socialist enterprises and cooperatives as well as between
> them. In closest cooperation with planning it regulates
> the normal routine and constantly expanded reproduction
> of economic and total social life. Thereby it directly
> effects the fundamentals of social life, namely work of
> people and production of material and spiritual values.
> At the same time, it helps to create prerequisites for
> comprehensive participation by all workers in manage-
> ment of the production of their enterprise, their domestic
> economic branch, and the over-all domestic economy. [33]

Or, put another way, "the economic law as an instrument of the
socialist State has to look after the interests of the working class
and, as part of this task, help organize the activity of the State
agencies and give full scope to the allaround initiative of the working
people."[34]

While the Constitution provides flexibility for stricter centralization or decentralization it also requires efficient production
(Article 2). Economic laws on the books define the competence
limitations of the state organs, enterprises, and the workers themselves. [35]

Of key importance in the GDR's economic law are the economic
contracts that the enterprises draw up to carry out their economic
activities. These contracts spell out in detail the relations between
the enterprises in their activities aimed at fulfilling the State Planning
Agency's guidelines. Formerly the contracts outlined the tasks of
the economic plan; now they are a means for working out the plan
itself.

The watchdog agency controlling these contracts is the State
Arbitration Board. Its general task is

> to ensure and watch over the observance of official
> directives in the negotiation and execution of economic
> contracts through the settling of disputes arising
> between the contracting enterprises as to what
> constitutes performance regarding the exact quantity,
> schedules, variety, quality and price of the commodity
> or commodities in question. [36]

In short, the Arbitration Board is interested in guaranteeing fulfillment of the plan and increasing work discipline.

The Arbitration Board is not a court in the conventional sense. It deals with independently responsible economic units operating on the basis of the overall state plan; the court's competence concerns relations between and among individuals. Thus, the board's main task is to ensure proper functioning of the economic contract so that the aims of the state planning and management authorities are met.

Courts

The highest court, the Supreme Court, is responsible to the People's Chamber and between sessions to the State Council. Beneath the Supreme Court of the GDR are District Courts (Bezirksgericht) and 249 Regional Courts (Kreisgericht).

In addition to being the final court of appeal, the Supreme Court directs the jurisdiction of the other courts. It exercises this guidance function (Leitungsfunktion) in that it formulates guidelines in plenary sessions of the court, as well as through resolutions of its Presidium.

These suggestions, and those of the General State Prosecution, make possible the change, dissolution, and reform of legal regulations through the various courts and state prosecution. For instance, in 1970, when the legal principles involved in the material responsibility of the workers were unclear, the Supreme Court published a guideline on the subject.[37] (The next step to bring existing laws into conformity with the present phase of social development would be passage of a revised law incorporating the essence of the guidelines.) In short, the Supreme Court does not create new laws, but rather sets rule-enforcement norms. This is unlike the precedent decisions of courts in the Anglo-Saxon system of law, whose basic decisions create completely new legal norms.

In addition, the Supreme Court carries out court criticism (Gerichtskritik) when charges are brought against lower courts, other judicial organs, as well as state and social organizations. The criticized organ is duty-bound to respond to the court criticism within two weeks, reporting whether it accepted the criticism and what it intends to do about it.

Reportedly, 75 percent of the court criticisms were accepted by those charged with breaking laws, and steps were taken to correct the conditions criticized. A study of six Bezirks showed that in 1971, 63 percent of the Court's critique resolutions concerned criminal proceedings, 3 percent civil cases, 4 percent family matters, and 30 percent work laws. These legal cases concerned problems of hiring and firing conditions, work time and vacation, disciplinary responsibility, use of alcohol on the job or served to youth, inadequate leadership regarding general security and order, unsafe construction sites, failure to cooperate in rehabilitation of former convicts, etc.[38]

Judges

The GDR's judges are not career civil servants who are appointed for fixed terms. Rather, through the election of all judges and lay judges the GDR "guarantees that justice will be administered by men and women of all classes and groups of the people," (Article 94, Constitution).

All judges are elected for a four-year term by the People's Chamber if they are Supreme Court judges (or jurors), by the District (Bezirk) legislatures for the District Courts, and by Regional (Kreis) Councils and the public in the case of Regional Courts. The party, of course, exercises an influence on the nomination or election of the judges in that party members are active at the levels where the nominations first are made. In making decisions to settle disputes, the judges are influenced in their interpretation of the law by, as has been seen, the guidelines of the Supreme Court, party resolutions, preambles to laws—in short, the norms that correspond to the present phase of social development.

Public Prosecutors

According to Article 97 of the GDR Constitution, the General Procuracy (Generalstaatsanwaltschaft) is charged with securing the socialist social and political order and leading the struggle against crime. It carries out its work through District and Regional, as well as military, prosecutors who work closely with the local public representative bodies (Volksvertretungen).

The job of the state prosecutors is more than that of representing the prosecution. Rather, they lead and counsel the social courts and at the same time control the execution of punishment and influence the general legal atmosphere. They watch over the observance of laws and other legal decisions through state organs, social institutions, trade unions, and enterprises.[39]

In recent years the state prosecutors have been urged to increase their cooperation with local state organs in order to improve the combatting and prevention of crime. According to General State Prosecutor Josef Streit, the effectiveness of information passed on by state prosecutors to state organs had to be significantly increased. In fact, new regulations to this effect were in the process of formulation. Especially necessary was a constant coordination between the local state organs and state prosecution, and also between state security organs and the courts. The state prosecutors were to pay special attention to the causes and conditions of criminal offenses, as well as to regular analysis of the results of measures taken to curb crime.[40] Further, according to Streit, crime is only one of the current concerns of the public prosecutors—they also emphasize "socialist legality," that is, rules and regulations with economic implications (work attitudes, health and traffic conditions, concepts of ownership, work discipline, production accountability).[41]

Lawyers

Private legal practice, as it is known in Western constitutional democracies, is not known in the GDR. There are only 630 lawyers for the 17 million population, although plans call for an increase to 1,000. This small number, as will be seen, arises from the fact that the GDR has evolved other forms of conflict settlement and rule enforcement that function without professional lawyers. For instance, "social courts" decide more than 60 percent of all criminal cases and more than 90 percent of the cases involving labor laws.[42] Furthermore, most GDR lawyers are not private (only 174 of the 630 in 1964),[43] but are organized into cooperatives, a kind of multi-member law firm.

To understand this aspect of GDR life, as all others, it is necessary to go back into the political history of the state, to the postwar period. At that time there were two overriding concerns in the GDR: (1) to establish a socialist form of judicial administration and (2) to exclude from it lawyers tainted by membership in, or association with, the Nazi regime. Therefore a lawyers' college (Anwaltskollegien) was established as early as 1953. It was to train lawyers who would not serve isolated private interests, as had been the case under capitalism, and whose collective strength would be greater than the sum of its members. They would be free of the economic "strings" of private interests and so could help solve conflicts in the interests of the total society's development. Since the founding of the college, no lawyers have been admitted to legal practice who have not attended this school.

The conflicts that the lawyers were to deal with were in most cases not seen primarily as juridical ones, but rather as social and human problems, that is, a question of the development of the

consciousness of the citizens. Thus, in the early postwar period, the
goal was to develop "antifascist-democratic" consciousness; then
after 1950 a "people's democracy" attitude; and in the present period
a "socialist personality."

This role of lawyers vis-a-vis GDR citizens stemmed from the
Marxist/Leninist thesis discussed earlier that man is a social creature
and that the state (including its judicial system) is an expression and
instrument of the unity between collective and individual interests.
Marxism-Leninism concedes that for some time there continue to be
contradictions between social and individual interests but contends
that these can be overcome with time. The process of "overcoming"
calls for efforts on the part of the total society, including lawyers
and the legal profession. Guided by the party, the lawyers are to
apply legal norms reflecting the stage of development in which the
society finds itself. Individual interests are to be represented and
defended by lawyers as long as they do not oppose party and state
guidelines at a particular time. As Lenin wrote,

> One cannot build communism out of anything else and
> not other than out of and with the human material which
> capitalism has created; one cannot expel and destroy the
> bourgeois intelligentsia, rather one must conquer, reform,
> change, and reeducate it, exactly as one in long struggles
> must reeducate the proletariat itself on the basis of the
> dictatorship of the proletariat. [44]

In short, the social administration of justice aimed at (1) supressing
forces opposed to the new system ("antifascist democratic revolutionary" phase, 1948 until 1949), (2) regulating the economic and
organizational life of the society ("construction of socialism" phase,
1949-60), and (3) since then educating citizens to a new socialist
legal consciousness ("developing socialism" phase, 1961-62 until
the present). [45]

In this present phase, the lawyer is to use all his personal
contacts with clients as opportunities for such education. Similarly,
he engages in public education in that he lectures on the nature of
socialist legality to meetings in enterprises, collective agricultural
units, and residential groups. In this and all his other activities, the
lawyer is guided by the Ministry of Justice. In addition to the time
spent educating the public to legal matters, about 15 percent of the
lawyer's time is used counseling enterprises and institutions regarding
problems of economic law. [46]

The work of the lawyer as spokesman for the defense was
considerably reduced when the new institution of social defender was
introduced in the GDR in 1963. The social defender represents the

opinion of the collective in which the accused lives and works—he is
seen as the public's participation in specified criminal procedures
where the background of the accused and mitigating circumstances
are considered especially significant. Thus, the social defender is
seen as a meaningful supplement to the legal profession as such.

Jurors

There are 48,733 GDR citizens who serve the courts of their
country as jurors (Schöffen).[47] The jurors who are elected usually
are party members (in the Bezirk of Dresden, for instance, 60 percent
of the 4,600 jurors are SED members).[48] In 1974 jurors were elected
at the same time as district and regional representatives. Two jurors
serve equally alongside the judge in all Bezirk and Kreis court cases
involving criminal, family, and civil matters. They also serve in
criminal cases as collective representative, public defender, or
social prosecutor.

Their specific responsibility, as delegated to them by a work
collective or residential collective (Hausgemeinschaft), is to inform
the court, the state prosecutor, and the defense of the crime, of its
causes, conditions, as well as the personality of the accused.[49]
They present evidence and may express an opinion regarding the
kind or severity of punishment. In more than 85 percent of the cases
there are representatives of collectives who express a view; there
also are social prosecutors or defendants participating in every
fourth case—thus, they carry out the responsibility of the society for
the organization of legal relations in the GDR.[50]

For instance, the duties of the jurors in the cases of family
conflicts may reach from counseling with the plaintiffs to cooperation
with state organs and work collectives. This may include finding a
job, suitable housing, or a vacancy in a nursery.[51]

To carry out their many-sided rule-adjudication tasks, the
jurors are specially trained. Such training consists, for instance,
of a study course including emphasis on (1) the leading role of the
party in organizing the developing socialist society, (2) the growing
role of the socialist states in further development of socialist democracy, (3) the necessity for realization of socialist legality, and
(4) the responsibility of jurors in implementation of the socialist
law.[52] To further help the jurors in these and other respects, the
Ministry of Justice publishes a monthly 32-page magazine for them,
Der Schöffe.

Naturally the training of lay persons to act as jurors has not
been easy for the GDR and it has not occured overnight, especially

since the inclusion of a large proportion of workers and women is stressed. It is an ongoing learning process, with many problems remaining. For instance, the party feels that the ideological training of jurors needs to be improved, they should play a larger role in the legal education of the public, their effectiveness should be increased by organizing themselves into cooperatives, and greater effort should be made to help them exchange experiences which have proved to be useful. [53]

Fines, Penalties, Amnesties

Observers feel there is a double tendency in the coercive measures used to achieve rule adjudication and enforcement in the GDR. For instance, concerning violent criminal or politically criminal acts, the punishments are harsh—the death sentence can be applied in cases of murder or planning an aggressive war. [54] Other kinds of crimes, however, are dealt with in a much more differentiated manner, with priority given to education and resocialization. For instance, prison sentences can run from 6 months to 15 years, can be for life, or as short as 6 weeks.

In addition to prison sentences, probationary sentences and public rebukes were introduced in 1957. These were cases where a law was found to be broken, but no punishment was designated. Instead, the wrongdoer was put on one to three years' probation (while he "made good" his wrong) and therefore it did not appear on his records as a sentence. [55]

However, concerning probation, special emphasis is placed on exact determination of the positive as well as negative factors. Sometimes measures beyond mere judgment are not felt necessary. But this does not apply if the wrongdoer "finds himself in an especially deep conflict with the society, doesn't show insight into his criminal act, is unstable, lacks will, or is a recidivist."[56] Under GDR law, it also is possible to put a wrongdoer under a guardianship, to make a public announcement of the judgment regarding his offense, to impose limitations on his residence, to issue taboos against certain activities, to deprive him of property, or to withdraw citizenship rights. The social courts, on the other hand, as will be seen, are limited to educational measures, such as public apologies, restitution of damage, fines of 5 to 150 marks, or administration of rebukes. [57]

These possibilities of differentiated punishment "naturally set very high challenges, especially for judges, state attorneys, and lawyers. An additional guarantee for optimal use of all these possibilities is the direct inclusion of broad circles of the population in the administration of justice."[58]

Sometimes, too, amnesties are granted. This was the case in October 1972 when the State Council announced that on the 23rd anniversary of the founding of the GDR the state would amnesty the largest number of prisoners in its history. Both political and criminal prisoners were included. According to SED chief Honecker, they numbered 25,060 under sentence and 6,261 in presentence detention.[59] Not included were persons who had tried to flee the GDR or who had aided attempted escape. This is still seen by the GDR as a major crime.

Crimes and Rehabilitation

The effectiveness of a rule-adjudication and -enforcement system can be seen in the crime rate and trends. Thus the GDR prides itself that (1) there has been a significant reduction in crime as a whole (54.1 percent reduction from 1950 until 1965); (2) there has been significant reduction in isolated criminal phenomena; and (3) there has been almost total suppression of certain kinds of crimes that remain typical today for nonsocialist societies: narcotics offenses, counterfeiting of paper money, bank robberies, armed robbery, forgery, and illegal sale of art objects. This process of crime reduction has come about, the GDR feels, because of (1) the active creation of optimal social relations in the work and everyday life of the citizen and (2) the educational/preventive nature of the socialist criminal law.[60]

Statistics show that the GDR, indeed, has a relatively low crime rate, 640 offenses per 100,000 population in 1970. And of those, traffic offenses made up about one-third and property offenses about one-half.[61] (Interesting, because of the differentiation between crimes against public and private property, is the fact that the frequency of offenses in both categories was about the same for 1970.) Among the remaining criminal acts registered for 1972, only 136 were premeditated murders and attempted murders, 324 robbery and blackmail, 763 rape, and 9,855 premeditated bodily injury.[62] Further, the crime rate has steadily dropped. In 1946, for instance, there were 500,000 criminal offenses committed, 230,000 in 1959, and 110,000 in 1970.[63] About 40 percent of civil suits brought before the courts concern cases involving housing rent relationships (of these cases, some 42 percent involve claims for unpaid rent).[64]

A special note, too, should be taken of the GDR's efforts toward rehabilitation. As the GDR minister of justice says,

Our basic attitude toward a legal offender is in its
nature positive and optimistic. In the interest of the

individual, and also in the interest of the socialist
society, the efforts of all involved state and social
forces are directed toward educating an offender in
order to reintegrate him firmly into the society.
That means also in the case of punishment by
imprisonment to quickly win back the offender for
society and to help him in a directed fashion to
again become, through restitution and proof in
daily work, a completely worthy member of society. [65]

In practice this means, for instance, that prisoners are paid
normal wages while "doing time," although about 80 percent is held
back to cover the costs of incarceration. State organs are ordered
to provide the released prisoner with a job and dwelling, in case his
old job no longer is available. Enterprises and social organizations,
too, are instructed to contribute to the prisoner's reintegration into
society. Apparently this emphasis is not without results, for only
20 percent of the GDR's criminals are recidivists. [66]

Some of the kinds of crime in the GDR deserve special comment.
There are, for instance, the "antistate," or political, crimes. All
nation-states protect themselves against revolutionary elements,
espionage, and treason, and opposition groups seen as dangerous to
the established system. The GDR is no exception. Because of the
emphasis on the securing and preserving of the socialist order in
the GDR—and the fear of forces continuing to try to undermine the
relatively new sociopolitical system—the GDR makes the death sentence available in 11 kinds of political crimes. In nonpolitical crimes,
the death sentence can be used only in murder cases. [67]

Such "antistate crimes" include instigation to boycott, instigation
to war, instigation to murder and genocide, endangering the peace,
disaffection, terrorism, fleeing the republic, industrial sabotage,
and diversionism. ("Diversionism" is an economic crime, defined
as "destruction, damage, or rendering inapplicable of machines,
technical installations, transportation and traffic equipment or other
objects vital to the economy and defense.")

Juvenile crime poses a special problem. Its rate has remained
constant; but in light of a reduced general crime rate, juvenile crime
is reflected in the statistics as having increased slightly. While
Western countries are registering increases in the proportion of total
crimes committed by youthful offenders, the proportion in the GDR
has remained constant. [68] Further, the GDR sees the criminal offenses
of its youth as "not significantly socially hostile." Most cases involved
simply theft of objects of minimal value. [69]

Alcoholism, and crimes committed under its influence, apparently are a significant problem for the GDR. In journal articles

calling attention to the problem, it is quickly pointed out that if a drunk is ordered to leave his job, according to the law the enterprise's responsibility does not end there. Rather, it is responsible for seeing that no injury to life and health occurs. The enterprise is told, for instance, to keep the drunken employee until he sobers up, to have someone take him home, to notify his family, and to deprive him of his automobile keys.

Apparently a new kind of crime is troubling the GDR: group theft of public property, which results in big material and financial damage. [70] That this is considered a serious offense in the GDR is clear, because of its fundamental Marxist/Leninist orientation to public property.

Because of a kind of "division of labor" within the theft groups, it is difficult to apprehend the wrongdoers. Some members are apparently responsible for the collection of material to be stolen, others for its transportation, and still others for its "sale." There was the case in a <u>Kombinat</u> where several of its members in two years' time made off with special pipes, radiators, and tin—valued at 67,000 marks—which they sold to "interested citizens." Thus, a group theft is seen as one in which the participants have joined together not only among work colleagues, but where "outsiders," as from other enterprizes are involved. "Fences," who take the stolen property, are included among such "outsiders" if they are part of an organized plan.

One explanation suggested for this increase in group theft of state property is that since more consumer goods now are available, the earning of extra marks through sale of stolen property makes sense: "Why earn money by stealing if there is nothing to buy with the money?" was the previous deterring rhetoric. Furthermore, as in the West, it is believed that some thefts of materials are for the robber's own use—as the common practice of office employees in the West who "help themselves" to office supplies, etc.

Police

Maintaining public order is the responsibility of the People's Police (<u>Volkspolizei</u>) under the control of the minister of interior. This police force numbers about 40,000 men and women. [71] As a national police, they are responsible to Berlin and not to the district county levels where they are organized. They cooperate internationally with other police forces of socialist countries in preventing and fighting crime. [72]

In addition, there are 8,500 transport police (Transport-polizei), [73] 10,000 customs police, [74] and 4,500 troops of the Ministry for State Security. [75] Also included among the police forces are the approximately 350,000 militiamen organized within factories, called Betriebskampfgruppen. [76] At one time there also was a special Grenzpolizei, or border police, which consisted of about 45,000 officers and men. They were absorbed into the national army in autumn 1961.

The secret police (SSD, Staatssicherheitsdienst) had its beginning in the postwar days when cooperation with the Soviet secret police was close. It is assumed, however, that the SSD now has evolved into a force of its own—it surely was not without good reason that the SSD's boss, Cd. Gen. Erich Mielke, in 1972 became a candidate member of the GDR's Politburo. (He is now, however, a full member, as is his Soviet counterpart Andropov.)

Civil Liberties

After all the discussion about how rule adjudication and enforce-ment is carried out through coercive measures, the big question arises: "And what's with civil liberties in the GDR?" But the question cannot be asked or answered in the same way that it would be in a Western constitutional democracy. First of all, as already noted, in a society that assumes that personal and social interests are identical, one does not think of freedom from the state, but freedom to the state—that is, freedom to play a meaningful role in society, for the citizen is seen not just as an "individual," but rather as a social individual (gesellschaftlichen Individuum).

Secondly, while the classical rights to freedom of speech, press, assembly, and association are guaranteed by the GDR Con-stitution, they can only be exercised "in accordance with the spirit and aims of this Constitution." That obviously means, as is true of every state, that such rights cannot be exercised to overthrow the existing, constitutionally guaranteed, socioeconomic political system.

But even granted this context, a goodly number of GDR citizens are critical about their civil liberties. They feel they should be allowed to travel outside of Eastern Europe, that their press should be more open, that the bureaucratic restrictions of their political system should be less stringent. A leading GDR natural scientist and philosopher, who is a socialist but critical of the present regime and not published in his country, has said,

In connection with the national recognition [of the
GDR] many feel increasingly the confinement of
delimitation. One simply says to himself that he
would like to be able to travel, anywhere, as other
people, too. Perhaps not so many people would then
travel if it were possible. One only wants the security
that one can. That, namely, is a question of trust. . . .
    The freedom which the people here want is
undoubtedly not the often illusory freedom of the
bourgeois society, that is, more freedom for the
exploiter than for the exploited. No, the people here
want to have freedom of will, not less but more
freedom that past social forms of their society could
guarantee. . . .
    [the socialist state] is still threatened absolutely
only by the circumstances under which it now exists.
The only threat to socialism is the present state form
as it rules here. . . .
    In all socialist countries this possibility [for
liberalization] exists and it is really a historic necessity.
Without such a change ultimately the great undertaking
of socialism is in danger of failing. . . .
    I believe that one cannot foresee in detail the
process of change. But one thing can be foreseen:
it will change.[77]

Party functionaries of the SED, too, apparently think the situation
will change, especially as it concerns travel possibilities. They
recognize that this is one of the "stickiest" domestic problems of
the GDR. However, the measures they forsee will allow more, but
not completely open, travel by GDR citizens to the West. Possibilities of increased group travel, for instance, are discussed. At the
same time, SED spokesmen point out that other states, including
so-called free countries, also have travel restrictions about which
Western governments do not become unduly agitated. Furthermore,
SED functionaries feel the FRG's citizenship laws make it uniquely
difficult for the GDR to take broad steps toward relaxing its travel
restrictions—that is, the FRG grants citizenship almost automatically
to GDR citizens crossing the borders, whereas other countries have
more complex immigration procedures. Also it is pointed out that
the FRG provides special housing and employment assistance to GDR
"border-crossers." Given the continuing discrepancies in standards
of living between the two German states, such financial aid tempts
GDR citizens to leave their country. Other peoples of the world who
contemplate emigration often are deterred from doing so by their

awareness that it will be very difficult for them to get a start in another cultural, language, and employment context.

Some day, however, the GDR will have to deal with this domestic problem, for it will not just go away. The moral and morale aspects of the pressure for relaxation will have to be balanced against pragmatic reasons for continuing strict controls, such as loss of trained personnel and prestige.

PERSUASIVE POWER

As already has been noted, coercive measures of rule adjudication and enforcement in socialist political systems are combined with persuasive measures. Thus, one of the most important tasks of socialist law is seen as

> education of the person to a socialist personality.
> That is the significant content of the ideological
> and organizational function of the law, to educate
> the person in the spirit of socialist progress, the
> socialist organization and discipline, and deep
> respect for the regulations of the socialist com-
> munity life. Thus, the law functions as an instru-
> ment with which the individual consciousness is
> lifted to the niveau of the social consciousness. . . .
> Differences between individual and social conscious-
> ness are completely overcome. The law must help
> to overcome the contradictions between them.

Specifically, this means "to lead the people to firm, basically social-istic influenced habits in their relations among themselves, to their collective, to the society, and to the state."[78] The legal and moral persuasion to this attitude, as has been seen, comes, in the opinion of GDR legal specialists, through the practical participation of citizens in law making and law application. The point is that a law lives and is effected only when it is accepted (that is, "obeyed"); that, in turn, happens only when people are convinced (through persuasion and participation) that the law is "right."

Thus, a period of persuasion is necessary before rule-making, application, and enforcement take place, as well as simultaneous with those functions. This is based on the accepted concept that formulation of morals progresses more rapidly than law—laws usually come only after an accepting climate already exists, for otherwise the law would be powerless. (An illustration is the 1972 law permitting

abortions in the GDR. It was passed seemingly quickly, but in reality
was based on decades of education and persuasion regarding the rights
of women.)

Education

As has already been noted, Marxists/Leninists hold that with
continuing social development, including a larger role of the state
and law, the socialist legal consciousness (Rechtsbewusststein)
becomes increasingly important. However, it is conceded that the
problems and development of this consciousness is "a complicated
process." Furthermore, it is an interrelated process, of education
and experience in which the development of consciousness, or attitude
formation, goes through at least three phases: (1) becoming acquainted
with present legal norms or norm complexes; (2) recognition of the
necessity and correctness of the legal demands; (3) recognition of
these legal demands as also binding on one's self and personally
worthy of effort. In each phase, legal education (Rechtspropaganda)
is crucial and is combined with practical experience. The definition
of such legal education is clear: "We understand by legal propaganda
the goal-oriented and systematic dissemination and explanation of
legal attitudes, legal principles, and concrete knowledge about legal
norms, as well as their realization in social life. That includes the
propagation of legal application and the realization of socialist law."
Dissemination of this legal education is the responsibility of
all social organs, organizations, and institutions. Especially responsible, however, are (1) state organs with legal responsibilities,
(2) state organs with economic responsibilities, (3) trade unions and
other social organizations, and (4) state and social institutions,
especially the mass madia. Channels used by these organs and
institutions for the dissemination of legal education are numerous. [79]
Among the various information channels, a high priority is
attached to the potential for legal education of institutions dealing
with youth, local state organs, and the personal examples of state
and economic leaders. Trade unions, too, are especially called
upon to acquire and disseminate information about labor laws.
Admittedly problems exist in this respect because university and
trade-school education regarding work laws are inadequate, advanced
education in enterprises is inadequate, and work supervisors put
economic decisions ahead of legal ones. [80]
But among the various information channels available, the
mass media generally are held to have top priority. Thus there has
been much discussion about how the media can best fulfill its task.

For instance, legal institutions warn that the work of the mass media cannot be limited to purposeless reporting of crime, but rather should contribute to an understanding of the motives of the criminal. Thereby positive lessons could be learned. [81] For instance, the use of "case studies" is urged, that is, examples provided by workers who are involved in social groups working with rule-enforcement problems. [82] Also, court reporters are encouraged to emphasize the reason for legal decisions, for in such reporting legal education is significantly furthered. [83]

Many more problems were touched on when radio and press journalists, along with the leader of the Department of Public Information of the General State Prosecutor's office, took part in spring 1973 in a roundtable discussion in the official magazine of the Organization of German Journalists (VDJ). Among the problems highlighted in this published discussion were: (1) abstract, conventional, and, therefore, irrelevant court reporting, (2) inadequate expression of impatience with crime, (3) paucity of examples of effective law implementation, (4) need to increase emphasis on civil (rather than criminal) legal aspects of economic, cultural, local problems, (5) unbalanced emphasis on readers' need for information vis-a-vis need for analysis of the wider context of socialist legal consciousness, (6) inadequate cooperation with courts, and (7) inadequate attention to problems of prisoner reintegration. [84] To cope with some of these shortcomings and to further improve the quality of legal reporting, the VDJ then organized a four-week study course for journalists specializing in legal reporting. [85]

One practical example of how the press has come to grips with such challenges is especially interesting—GDR television has introduced a program entitled, "Ask Professor Kaul." Produced by the editorial division for legal policy, it is the first TV attempt to deal with legal questions concerning everyday life. Questions of work law were given priority, as were housing problems, debt law, and family law. Professor Kaul, well-known lawyer and radio author, answered questions in these areas, as well as all other queries submitted by listeners. Furthermore, the editorial staff forwarded viewer complaints to the relevant officers or institutions for study and action. [86] Newspapers, too, have begun making more use of legal news columns.

Normative Structures

Particularly significant in the GDR's efforts to expedite the rule-adjudication and -enforcement function through persuasive means are the social institutions that have been especially created for this purpose.

Worker-Farmer Inspection (Arbeiter- und Bauerninspektion, ABI)

On May 26, 1970, the SED Central Committee and the Minister Council passed a resolution concerning the goals and procedures of the ABI. This institution of the SED and state, organized along both territorial and enterprise lines, is responsible primarily for contributing to enforcement of economic rules, but also general discipline and legality: "to contribute to the completion of planning and leadership and state discipline, as well as to confirm socialist legality."[87]

In further implementation of rules, the ABIs have the right to gather information and take part in consultations of enforcement organs. This is carried out through 9,700 commissions and 5,200 control committees.[88] As Honecker said at the VIII Party Congress about this form of "people's control" involving more than 177,000 volunteer citizens: "The Party in the future will also struggle so that the Leninist idea of strict accountability and control will be consistently realized among us."[89]

Commission for Order and Security in Residential Areas (Kommissionen für Ordnung und Sicherheit in den Wohngebieten)

These commissions, made up of representatives of the National Front, enterprises, Conflict Commissions, Jurors Commission, Youth Aid Commission, and others, are responsible for campaigns against rowdyism, misuse of alcohol, crime against property, school negligence, reintegration of prisoners, and support of work groups for traffic safety. In carrying out these duties, they have a right to be given periodic estimates from the police concerning crime development.

The persuasive nature of their work is shown in a report from Berlin where commission members were able to talk with a youth group repeatedly engaged in disturbing noise and improper behavior toward girls and women. The group was persuaded, without resorting to criminal law means, to change its behavior. Other commissions have worked with cases of misuse of property by school children in department stores.[90]

Trade Union Legal Commission (Rechtskommissionen der Gewerkschaften, RK)

Legal Commissions must be formed in enterprises with more than 500 members. Called for in a 1969 law, the commissions' responsibilities include advice and suggestions for solution of legal problems, such as wages, work suggestions, year-end bonuses, disciplinary and material responsibilities, work protection, etc.—in short, legal advice aiming at fuller understanding of the Work Law Code. Other problems dealt with include social insurance, civil law, family law matters, and crime.[91]

Social Courts or Tribunals

As already noted, the GDR has many social forces available that persuasively work toward rule adjudication, enforcement, and social control. Primary are the 28,000 social courts, or tribunals (Gesellschaftlichegerichte).[92] Of these courts, 23,000 of them are called Conflict Commissions (Konfliktkommissionen), found primarily in the enterprises, and 5,300 are Arbitration Commissions (Scheids-kommissionen), organized in communities, cities, and city regions, as well as productive collectives.[93] Staffed by fellow citizens and work colleagues, the social courts cannot hand out legal punishments. Instead they rely on effective educational measures and concentrate primarily on the social causes of offenses, such as family, work, or leisure-time situations.

According to the Penal Code, this is the role of the social courts:

> Lesser crimes are discussed and decided by the social courts, if in view of the consequences of an offense and the guilt of the offender the offense is not too injurious to society and if, taking the offense and the personality of the offender into consideration, an effective educational influence is expected to be brought about by the social court.[94]

They are called "social" courts, rather than state agencies, because they are staffed by volunteers and because they concentrate on persuasion rather than coercion. Persons coming before them—and they must, if so ordered—are not called the "accused"; the hearings are informal; lawyers usually do not take part; the judges are fellow neighbors or work colleagues; the court members are elected. The punishments they may impose include the following, according to the Penal Code,

- A citizen is ordered to apologize to the aggrieved party or in front of a collective body.
- The undertaking of a citizen to repair the damage caused by him and other pledges are confirmed.

- A citizen is ordered to repair the damage caused
  by him through his own efforts, or should this not
  be feasible, to pay indemnity.
- A citizen is ordered to retract an insult in public.
- A citizen receives a reprimand.
- A citizen is ordered to pay a fine between 5 and 50
  marks, or in case of minor crimes or petty offenses
  against property a fine up to three times the value
  of the damage caused by him but never more than
  150 marks. [95]

In many cases the offenders themselves suggest what they might do
as restitution for damages they have caused. Such obligations undertaken or imposed are voluntarily implemented. Decisions can be
appealed to Kreis courts, but seldom are.

According to the GDR minister of justice, the social courts
handle 100, 000 cases per year. These consultations include more
than 90 percent of all work law controversies and nearly 40 percent
of all legal offenses. Further, the social courts serve as a kind of
inferior civil court in that they deal with disagreements among workers
and neighbors and regulate debts and disputes over money, not ex-
ceeding 500 marks. In addition, a third of all criminal law offenses
are dealt with by these social courts[96]—which is not surprising in
light of the already noted general decrease in crime, which means
the criminal cases coming before the social courts are relatively
minor. In general, if a case brought to the social courts is so serious
that sentences or probation seem likely, it is referred to regular
courts.

In addition to efficient conflict settlement, the social courts
are significant in that they contribute to the development of the
education of the nearly 250, 000 citizens who volunteer their work. [97]
That the institution of the social court's work is effective is suggested
by the fact that only 1 out of 20 persons coming before such a tribunal
ever appears a second time. [98] Further, the educational value of the
social courts is felt to lie in the fact that neighbors or colleagues of
an offender, not unknown lawyers and judges, discuss his case in a
friendly though critical manner, reminiscent of court social work
practices in noncommunist countries.

Among the substantive areas that the social courts at present
seem most concerned about are (1) housing problems, (2) work
discipline, and (3) economic crimes. Rent cases represent the
largest class of civil procedures and are a special concern of the
social courts. Most such cases involve demands for unpaid rent,
charges against abrogation of rental conditions, and charges concerning repairs. The problem of unpaid rent has increased signifi-

cantly in recent years. The reasons cited by judges are the absence of a sense of responsibility and discipline, inefficient economic practices, as well as the nonsocialist practice of thinking of one's own individual gain. Apparently this behavior also manifests itself in nonpayment of public utility bills and repayment of loans.[99]

Work discipline problems that come to the courts' attention usually involve absenteeism, alcoholism, faked illnesses, tardiness for work, etc. The economic crimes, however, are the most troublesome. For instance, nearly half of all the Conflict Commission consultations in the area of labor law involved the question of the material responsibility of workers. In fact, the protection of public property was one of the primary concerns of the spring 1973 plenary session of the Supreme Court.[100]

The crimes against property reach from antisocial offenses to serious crimes resulting in damages of several hundred thousand marks. One such case involved an employee working in the area of investments; through falsification of documents and fraud she had taken about 137,000 marks and deposited them to her own account. Another case concerned two construction engineers who were charged with fraud because they misused a gasoline credit card and split the profit. The loss to public property was set at 4,244 marks. And a Leipzig case involved the theft of meat, calling for erection of protective fences and reorganization of the storage room. Especially disturbing are cases in which several persons work together in an organized form of theft, such as noted above, where the loss was 67,000 marks in pipes, radiators, and tin.[101]

Among the procedural problems causing concern for the social courts is the question of when to assess a fine. The practice had been to go easy with penalties involving money, but the Supreme Court in mid-1971 called for more careful consideration of the economic conditions and the loss involved in the crime. Thus, in the case where a Conflict Commission handed out a reprimand for a theft involving 320 marks, it was felt, because of the sum involved, that a fine should have been assessed. In the case where one citizen fractured another's nose, a fine also would have been necessary, in light of the seriousness of the injury. In a third case, however, where a woman, divorced and caring for five children, stole 70 marks worth of panty-hose, a fine would have been too harsh. In short, "fines are to be primarily used when the deed rests on disrespect for values created by workers or their personal property, on greed or disrespect of property rights duties."[102]

Another problem of the social courts—a psychological one—is that of their acceptance by economists and engineers: "An economic functionary still too often does not feel responsibility for the observance and application of legal regulations."[103] Apparently they are more concerned with fulfilling economic goals than making sure that workers' rights are observed at the same time.

Conflict Commissions. Nearly 200,000 workers, employees, and intellectuals are involved in the GDR's 23,055 Conflict Commissions.[104] They decide some 90 percent of all cases in the GDR involving work-law affairs[105] and deal primarily with offenses against property, labor safety, health protection, and petty offenses.

Set up in 1953, the Conflict Commissions exist in enterprises of more than 50 persons and include between 8 and 15 members. They are nominated by the trade union leadership of the enterprise (BGL) and elected by the total personnel for two years.[106] Their procedures are public, but since they take place in enterprises it is not always possible for citizens to attend. Furthermore, persons who are not members of the enterprise can be invited to the consultations.[107]

The growth of the Conflict Commissions has been steady. In the Halle Bezirk, for instance, there were only several hundred by the end of 1953. By 1963 they had increased to 2,470 and rose steadily to 2,739 in 1972, with 24,220 members. Their importance is further reflected in statistics: 93 percent of all work law cases in the Halle Bezirk were decided by Conflict Commissions.

Their case load also grows. Again using the Halle Bezirk as as an example, its Conflict Commissions carried out 3,075 consultations in 1963 and 6,463 in 1971. In addition, in 1971 they handled 2,300 consultations regarding criminal cases, 373 concerning civil law, and 70 cases of school truancy.[108]

The Supreme Court, recognizing this increasing role that the Conflict Commissions have played in GDR society for two decades, in spring 1973 devoted its seventh plenary session to new problems of the commissions. One such problem was the necessity for dealing with crime to public property and the other was for closer cooperation with the trade unions. According to a resolution of the Supreme Court, the commissions are required to support the right of the trade unions to participate in their proceedings.[109] The point is that the Conflict Commissions can provide the trade unions with information necessary for an analysis of the overall experiences of the commissions in a given area of rule enforcement.

In addition, the Conflict Commissions are concerned with the problems of youth—more so, in fact, than are the Arbitration Commissions. Together they handle about a third of the cases involving youthful offenders. Of such cases, 32 percent involved theft of state property, 20 percent theft of personal property, 20 percent unallowed use of vehicles, 4 percent physical injury, and 3 percent fraud against public property. One problem in settling such conflicts is that until now the commissions have not included in their consultations those responsible for the youths' education. Ideally, parents, youth workers, school representatives, representatives of the enterprise, and the FDJ are invited. In dealing with the cases, the primary educational measure used is a reprimand and, in second place, a fine. [110]

The members of the Conflict Commission receive specialized training for fulfilling their duties. For instance, judges working with labor law take part in their instruction; and commission members are supplied with study materials intended to improve the efficiency of their work. For instance, in 1973 the trade union publishing house published a 362-page handbook for Conflict Commission members. It contained discussions of various areas of commission competence, as well as relevant laws and resolutions. [111] The daily trade union newspaper, Tribune, publishes a weekly supplement, "The Conflict Commission." It features a case study article concerning a commission consultation and decision, a feature story about a commission member, publication of new laws, discussion of the theme being taken up in the formal study course for commission members, and background material for kinds of cases coming before the commissions. The latter, for instance, in the first half of 1973 included discussions of school truancy, differences between physical and psychological damages, use of fines, sick-leave rights, salary or bonus calculations, use of educational recommendations, and conflicts between work rights and management decisions. The case studies featured on page 1 of the supplement during the first half of 1973 included, for example, thefts, mismanagement, work discipline, human relations, record falsification, vandalism, and absenteeism.

Arbitration Commissions. In the GDR's 5,267 Arbitration Commissions (Schiedskommissionen) about 55,000 citizens voluntarily take part (of which 37 percent are women). They represent residential areas and production groups: about 3,700 in the countryside, 1,400 in towns and cities, and 200 in socialist production cooperatives. [112]

Annually the commissions carry out about 29,000 consultations: the average is about 800 criminal cases, 13,000 Verfehlungen (offenses that are not criminal acts), 7,000 civil cases, 400 violations of regulations, 550 school truancies, and 300 cases involving work behavior. [113] The procedures are public, but individual citizens can be excluded if that furthers conflict solution.

Existing since 1963, the commissions' members are nominated by the National Front and elected by the Local Peoples Representations. The commissions were founded after the Conflict Commissions, operating in the enterprises, had shown a decade of success.

Because of the increasing trust of the public in the work of the Arbitration Commissions, their work load has increased significantly. For example, in one residential area of Berlin, an Arbitration

Commission reported that it handled a yearly average of 26 consultations (Beratungen) and 60 discussions (Aussprachen) with citizens; in 1972, the discussions increased to 82.[114] The primary areas dealt with are the handling of misdeamenors (Vergehen), offenses that are not criminal acts (Verfehlungen),[115] and civil rights controversies.

Using one Arbitration Commission as an example, it is interesting to note what kind of measures were recommended during its consultations. In 99 Beratung, the Berlin Commission in 88 cases recommended one or two educational measures. Of the total 142 educational measures recommended, 44 called for an apology, 33 for related responsibilities, 31 were reprimands, 12 called for restitution of damages, 8 for fines, 8 for a public "taking back" of insult or defamation, and 6 for publication of the decision. In 94 percent of the cases the offender voluntarily fulfilled the decision.[116]

An Arbitration Commission in Karl Marx Stadt provides a case study of the specific measures recommended in the case of a youth who mishandled another youth. Recommendations were sent

- to the school leadership, to undertake in an appropriate form an assessment of the circumstances of the case and deliberation with the pupils in order to prevent further beatings of this kind;
- to the department of residential management to direct, as soon as possible, the accused's father, who despite divorce still lived in the dwelling and exercised a bad influence on the youth through frequent beatings, to another dwelling;
- to the youth aid official to check whether it was permitted that the youthful accused played in a dance band for money and in how far that was a cause for his poor school performance.[117]

Another commission provides statistics concerning the results of its work: in Kreis Weissenfels the commission undertakes 80 Beratungen per year. On the average, in 62 percent of the cases the parties come to an agreement, in 9 percent the commission makes a decision, in 12 percent of the cases the charge is taken back, and 8 percent of the cases are set aside because no agreement can be reached.[118]

In carrying out such work, the Arbitration Commissions also make use of outsiders, that is, nonjurors. In the Berlin Commission referred to above, some 3 to 4 (and in 1972, 5) additional citizens took part.[119] And in cases of residence problems, more than 60 percent of all Beratungen included outsiders.[120] As a further act of public accountability, the Arbitration Commissions prepare an annual report that is presented to the residential committees of the National Front for its analysis.[121]

Despite such positive achievements of the GDR's Arbitration Commissions, they have their problems, too:

1. The commissions frequently are presented with cases outside their competence because citizens do not yet understand the territorial and functional responsibilities of the commissions.[122]

2. Commission jurors must improve the quality of their work. Specifically, what should be accomplished is that "they understand better to differentiate noncriminal offenses from misdeamenors, exert more effort to uncover causes and conditions of conflict, and use educational measures in a significantly more differentiated fashion."[123]

3. The leadership the commissions receive from the <u>Kreis</u> Courts must be improved. It is hoped this will be achieved through the new Advisory Councils (<u>Beiräte</u>), which were created in spring 1973.[124]

4. The commissions' work with the schools is not seen as adequate: "In the struggle against school truancy, the Arbitration Commission is totally inadequately used. It has been shown that the Arbitration Commission's own efforts for overcoming this condition are inadequate."[125]

5. Commissions must deal increasingly with economic crimes. And those cases, the chairman of an Arbitration Commission concedes, are difficult to understand: "Brain-racking for us are the many thefts in the self-service shops, carried out by citizens who are not in financial need."[126]

6. Commissions must find positive means for dealing with the numerous housing conflicts. For instance, an Arbitration Commission in Halle in an analysis of 10 years of work in this area found that the major causes of the housing conflicts it had to cope with were

- housing of numerous families in divided, formerly one-family units
- egotistic, uninsightful, and thoughtless behavior of lessor or lessee
- excessive demands of lessors
- negligence of house order
- inadequate condition of rental objects
- inadequate legal knowledge of participants
- errors of superficial formalization, for example, of written rent contracts or contract applications
- uncomplete or unclear allocation through the housing guidance organs

Interestingly, in 21 of 29 cases involving housing controversies, rental questions were combined with defamation, for instance, insult. Some of the typical housing controversies that came up involved use of basement rooms and laundry drying areas, the keeping of animals in apartments or houses, parking of baby carriages, bicycles, and motorcycles, late payment of rent, noise-making, postponement of urgently need repairs, and restitution for damages.[127]

Social Rewards

Among the persuasive means a political system uses to obtain rule adjudication, enforcement, and social control there are, in addition to education and normative structures, positive social rewards. These include social recognition in the form of titles, medals, awards, etc. The prestige of such recognition frequently is adequate to produce efforts and attitudes necessary for effective rule adjudication and enforcement. The political system of the GDR shows numerous such examples, especially in the fields of economics, law and order, and social service rule enforcement.

1. Since enforcement of the economic rules of the society is given a top priority, the news is not surprising that "there will be an unprecedented flood of medals and distinctions for individuals and work teams who distinguish themselves in GDR socialist emulation contents during 1973." These medals, totaling 27,500 (including 500 "Karl Marx Orders," the top distinction of the GDR, and 5,000 "Medals for Distinguished Achievements in Emulation") went to individuals and work teams in industry, transport, construction, trade, agriculture, education, health, and the military forces "for outstanding services in organizing and implementing socialist emulation contents for the fulfillment and overfulfillment of the 1973 Economic Plan."[128]

Almost all these rewards included prizes of money as well as the medal. In fact, a total of 50 million marks were involved for the year 1973. Specifically, to be awarded were:

> 500 Karl Marx Orders—individual award, 20,000
>   marks tax-free
> 1,000 honorary titles "Hero of Work" (Held der
>   Arbeit)—up to 10,000 marks tax-free
> 1,000 Fatherland Service Orders in Gold
>   (Vaterländische Verdienstorden)—up to 1,000
>   marks annually
> 5,000 Banner of Work Orders (Banner der Arbeit)—
>   up to 5,000 marks

5, 000 Distinguished Worker Orders (Verdienter
   Aktivist)—up to 1, 000 marks
5, 000 Medals for Distinguished Performance in
   Competition (Medaillen für Ausgezeichnete Leistung
   im Wettbewerb)—up to 1, 000 marks
10, 000 Meritorious Medals of the GDR (Verdienstmedallien)
   —no money prize[129]

The number of such awards to be made in 1973 was greatly increased
over the previous year. For instance, in 1972 the "Hero of Work"
title had been awarded only 41 times; the "Banner of Work" Order to
62 individuals, 65 collectives, and 71 enterprises; the "Distinguished
Worker" orders to 1, 717 persons.[130] While 45, 172 workers were
rewarded in 1949 for being outstanding activitists, they number
188, 861 in 1972. Meanwhile, work collectives rewarded for their
socialistic work increased from 59, 364 collectives with 706, 657
members in 1959 to 200, 537 collectives with 3, 412, 291 members in
1972.[131]

   2. In order to further order, discipline, and security, special
awards were made available to industrial and agricultural enterprises,
trade and health organizations, cities, communities, and neighbor-
hoods. The title for which they compete, first awarded in March
1973, is called "Area of Exemplary Order and Security" (Bereich
der vorbildlichen Ordnung und Sicherheit). According to the journal
for legal affairs, the awarding of this title has demonstrably led to
the fulfillment and overfulfillment of plan tasks in the reduction of
law breaking. Thus order, security, and discipline were decisively
supported.[132]

   GDR citizens involved in the field of rule adjudication and
enforcement directly are rewarded normatively, too. For instance,
in 1973 on the tenth anniversary of the establishment of the Arbitration
Commissions as a social institution, a dozen chairmen of such commissions were awarded the "Medal for Merit in the Service of the
Law" (Medaille für Verdienste in der Rechtspflege).[133] In addition,
the National Front and legal organs of the state award pins of honor
to individual members of the Arbitration Commissions, as well as
the commission collectives. And the Ministry of Justice awards a
certificate of honor.[134]

   3. Social service fields, too, have their social rewards. The
field of medicine, for example, uses this means to promote enforcement of rules intended to improve GDR medical care. New laws were
passed for awarding honorary medical titles and medals for special
services—for instance, the "Hufeland Medal" was made available in
gold, silver, or bronze. Such awards are announced on "Health
Affairs Day."

SUMMARY AND CONCLUSIONS

It has been seen that rule adjudication and enforcement in the GDR has as its primary goal the solution of political, economic, and cultural conflicts and violations that impede the development of socialism. For instance, with the increasing importance of the state, legal codification of the sociopolitical norms has become more important, and along with it the effectiveness of rule-adjudication and -enforcement structures and institutions. At the same time, because of the state's growing maturity, it is necessary to bring existing laws and regulations into conformity with existing conditions, through interpretation or revision. Thus, laws concerning work conditions, family life, and the role of various state organs have in recent years been revised.

Further, it has been shown which legal and social organs in the GDR play a role in determining whether or not a rule has been transgressed and what is to be done about it. If, as Almond says, the demands reflected in the conflicts coming before the rule-adjudication agencies are of sufficient quantity and quality, they may find their way to the rule-making centers through interest articulation, interest aggregation, and feedback. This could be the case, for instance, with the GDR's housing conflicts. If, however, the conflicts do not reflect new demands, as in the case of traffic offenses, they perhaps can be handled by the rule-adjudication and -enforcement function.[135]

At the same time it is interesting to note how this function interrelates with the other functions. For example, it is directly related to the rule-application function, for, as has been shown, many conflicts involve the administration and realization of laws and regulations on the books. At the same time, the rule-adjudication and -enforcement agencies participate in political communications, as when they declare the meaning of a rule, and as articulators and aggregators of interests when they interpret the rule-makers. And, obviously, the application of legal standards of judgment contributes to and enforces the political culture. Thus, the interdependency of the functions of the political system, as both functionalists and Marxist/Leninists view it, is illustrated.

A final point, however, needs to be made. A society is not limited to the use of coercive and normative power to bring about social control and rule enforcement. It also uses material power: wages, rewards, bonuses, bribes, promotions, etc. As GDR writers put it, the sanctions of a society indeed include "financial gifts, such as performance subsidies, premiums, but also promises of a prospective promotion or other privileged positions with financial improvement, old-age care, and other improvements of the living standard or living conditions (so-called positive sanctions)."[136] However, because of space limitations and the relatively nonunique application of this power in the GDR, a detailed discussion will not be undertaken.

NOTES

1. Gabriel A. Almond and G. Bingham Powell, Jr., Comparative Politics (Boston: Little, Brown, 1966), pp. 158-59.

2. Alexander Dallin and George W. Breslauer, Political Terror in Communist Systems (Stanford, Calif.: Stanford University Press, 1970), pp. 2-3

3. Neue Justiz, 5/1973, p. 130.

4. Protokoll der Verhandlungen des VIII Parteitags der SED, Bd. 1 (Berlin: 1971), p. 83 ff.

5. Reiner Arlt and Gerhard Stiller, Entwicklung der sozialistischen Rechtsordnung in der DDR (Berlin: Staatsverlag, 1973), pp. 11-12.

6. Neue Justiz, 15/73, p. 435.

7. Arlt and Stiller, op. cit., p. 32.

8. Ibid., pp. 49, 57.

9. Ibid., pp. 221-23.

10. Robert Sharlet, "Law in the Political Development of a Communist System," in The Behavioral Revolution and Communist Studies (New York: The Free Press, 1971), pp. 259-77.

11. Die DDR—Entwicklung, Probleme, Perspektiven (Frankfurt/ Main: Verlag Marxistischer Blätter, 1972), p. 295.

12. Informationen (Bonn: Bundesministerium für innerdeutsche Beziehungen, No. 22 [1974]), pp. 7-8.

13. Arlt and Stiller, op. cit., pp. 134-43.

14. The Development of the German Democratic Republic (Dresden: German National Preparatory Committee for the 3rd World Festival of Youth and Students for Peace, 1951 [?]), p. 21.

15. For text, see GBl 1, No. 47 (September 1974), and for Honecker's remarks to the new Constitution see Neues Deutschland September 28, 1974.

16. Arlt and Stiller, op. cit., pp. 128-29.

17. Gesezbuch der Arbeit der Deutschen Demokratischen Republik vom 12 April 1961 (GBl I S. 27).

18. Statistisches Jahrbuch 1973 der Deutschen Demokratischen Republik (Berlin: Staatsverlag, 1973).

19. Alfred Baumgart, "Uberlegungen der Arbeitsrechtswissenschaft zur Neugestaltung des Gesetzbuches der Arbeit," Staat und Recht, April 1973, pp. 656-63.

20. Arlt and Stiller, op. cit., p. 138.

21. Ibid. p. 139.

22. For text of GDR Family Law and discussion in English see, Law and Legislation in the German Democratic Republic (Berlin: Lawyers Association of the GDR, 1973), pp. 19-78.

23. Das Familienrecht der DDR: Kommentar (Berlin: Staatsverlag, 1970).

24. Arlt and Stiller, op. cit., p. 139.

25. Hilde Benjamin, Strafrecht der DDR: Lehrkommentar Bd I (Berlin, 1970).

26. Die DDR—Entwicklung, op. cit., p. 287.

27. Staat und Recht, 10/1970, pp. 1616 ff.

28. Arlt and Stiller, op. cit., p. 140.

29. Einheit, 9/1973, p. 1033.

30. Ibid.

31. Einheit, 4/74, p. 423.

32. Neues Deutschland, February 2, 1974.

33. Arlt and Stiller, op. cit., pp. 28-29.

34. Uwe-Jens Heuer and Günter Klinger, "Foundations of Socialist Economic Law," in Law and Legislation in the German Democratic Republic, op. cit., p. 8.

35. Deutschland Archiv, 1/73, p. 44.

36. Gerhard Walter, "Status and Terms of Reference of the State Arbitration Board of the German Democratic Republic," in Law and Legislation in the German Democratic Republic, op. cit., pp. 75-86.

37. 25. März 1970, Entscheidung des Obersten Gerichts der DDR in Arbeitsrechtssachen, Band 6, 1971, pp. 46-62.

38. "Die Rolle der Gerichtskritik bei der Festigung der sozialistischen Gesetzlichkeit," Der Schöffe, November 1972, pp. 375-80.

39. Rüdiger Thomas, Modell DDR (Munich: Carl Hanser Verlag, 1972), p. 47.

40. Neue Justiz, No. 16 (1973), pp. 465-69.

41. Informationen, op. cit., pp. 7-8.

42. Hans-Henning Bruhn, Die Rechtsanwaltschaft in der DDR (Cologne: Verlag Wissenschaft und Politik, 1972), p. 158.

43. Ibid., p. 27.

44. V.I. Lenin, Ausgewählte Werke, Bd. II, p. 755.

45. Beiträge zur Geschichte der Arbeiterbewegung (BZG), 3/1973, pp. 415-38.

46. Gerhard Häusler, "Die Entwicklung der sozialistischen Rechtsanwaltschaft in der DDR," Neue Justiz, No. 12 (June 1973), pp. 340-44.

47. Einheit, 4/1974, p. 423.

48. Der Schöffe, 3/1973, p. 73.

49. Die DDR—Entwicklung, op. cit., p. 294.

50. Thomas, op. cit., p. 47.

51. Der Schöffe, Nr. 2, February 1973, pp. 44-46.

52. Ibid., p. 73.

53. Ibid., p. 77.

54. Die DDR—Entwicklung, op. cit., p. 294.

55. Thomas, op. cit., pp. 48-50.

56. Neue Justiz, No. 5 (1973), pp. 134-37.

57. Thomas, op. cit., pp. 48-50.

58. Die DDR—Entwicklung, op. cit., p. 295.

59. "Interview des Kolumnisten der New York Times C. L. Sulzberger mit dem Ersten Sekretär des ZK der Sozialistischen Einheitspartei Deutschlands, Erich Honecker," Neues Deutschland, November 25, 1972.

60. Arlt and Stiller, op. cit., pp. 44-45, 140.

61. Die DDR—Entwicklung, op. cit., p. 291.

62. Statische Taschenbuch der Deutschen Demokratischen Republik 1972 (Berlin: Staatsverlag, 1972), p. 164.

63. Die DDR—Entwicklung, op. cit., p. 291.

64. Arlt and Stiller, op. cit., p. 207.

65. Die DDR—Entwicklung, op. cit., p. 290.

66. Thomas, op. cit., pp. 48-50.

67. Strafgesetzbuch, "Besondere Teil."

68. Deutschland Archiv, 5/1973, p. 519.

69. Neue Justiz, 23/1973, pp. 702-706.

70. Der Schöffe, 4/1973, pp. 146-147; Neue Justiz, 16/1973, pp. 474-77.

71. Staatslexikon: Recht, Wirtschaft, Gesellschaft (Sonderdruck) (Freiburg: Verlag Herder, 1970 [?]).

72. Democratic German Republic, February 28, 1973, p. 31.

73. Zahlenspiegel (Bonn: Bundesminister für innerdeutsche Beziehungen, 1973), p. 8.

74. Staatslexikon, op. cit.

75. Zahlenspiegel, op. cit.

76. Ibid. See also Heinz Marks, Die Kampfgruppen der Arbeiterklasse (Cologne: Markus Verlag, 1970).

77. Interview with Robert Havemann, Frankfurter Rundschau, December 6, 1973. Reprinted in Deutschland Archiv, 1/1974, pp. 46-49.

78. Arlt and Stiller, op. cit., pp. 46-47, 53.

79. Ibid., pp. 237-43.

80. Die Arbeit, February 1973, pp. 61-63.

81. Neue Justiz, March 1973, pp. 129-34.

82. Neue Deutsche Presse, 10/1973, p. 5.

83. Neue Deutsche Presse, 17/1973, pp. 6-7.

84. Neue Deutsche Presse, 3/1973, pp. 2-4.

85. Neue Deutsche Presse, 10/1973, p. 5.

86. Neue Deutsche Presse, 1/1973, pp. 20-21.

87. GB1 II, S. 363.

88. Statistische Jahrbuch 1973, op. cit., p. 522.

89. Honecker, Bericht des Zentralkomitees an den VIII Parteitag der SED (Berlin: Dietz Verlag, 1971), p. 66. See also Neuer Weg, 13 (1974), pp. 587-89, for a discussion of ABI's intensified activities since the VIII Party Congress.

90. Neue Justiz, No. 3 (February 1973), pp. 70-73.

91. Der Schöffe, March 1973, pp. 83-86.

92. For a detailed English-language discussion of the nature and problems of the social courts see, Law and Legislation in the German Democratic Republic, op. cit., pp. 5-15.

93. Statistische Jahrbuch 1973, op. cit., p. 522.

94. Democratic German Report, June 6, 1973, p. 78.

95. Ibid.

96. Die DDR—Entwicklung, op. cit., pp. 48, 292-93.

97. Statistische Jahrbuch 1973, op. cit., p. 522.

98. Die DDR—Entwicklung, op. cit., p. 293.

99. Der Schöffe, 10/1973, pp. 342-44.

100. Der Schöffe, 8/1973, pp. 274-75.

101. Ibid., pp. 146-50.

102. Der Schöffe, 1/1973, pp. 19-20.

103. Ibid., p. 66.

104. Statistische Jahrbuch 1973, op. cit., p. 522.

105. Die DDR—Entwicklung, op. cit., pp. 292-93.

106. Gesetz über die gesellschaftlichen Gerichte der Deutschen Demokratischen Republik vom 11, Juni 1968 (GB1 I, S. 229).

107. Konfliktkommissionsordnung, 13, Abs. 11.

108. Der Schöffe, 8/1973, pp. 277-78.

109. Arbeit und Arbeitsrecht, No. 24, December 1972, p. 762.

110. Der Schöffe, 1/1973, pp. 18-26.

111. Die Konfliktkommission (Berlin: Verlag Tribune, 1973).

112. Statistische Jahrbuch 1973, op. cit., p. 522.

113. Der Schöffe, 4/1973, pp. 113-14.

114. Der Schöffe, 3/1973, p. 88.

115. See Die Konflikt Kommission (Berlin: Verlag Tribune, 1973), p. 108, for detailed definition of each.

116. Der Schöffe, 3/1973, pp. 90-91.

117. Der Schöffe, 1/1973, p. 20.

118. Der Schöffe, 5/1973, p. 181.

119. Der Schöffe, 3/1973, p. 90.

120. Der Schöffe, 5/1973, p. 182.

121. Der Schöffe, 3/1973, p. 87.
122. Ibid., p. 189.
123. Der Schöffe, 4/1973, p. 115.
124. Der Schöffe, 10/1973, pp. 351-52.
125. Der Schöffe, 3/1973, p. 89.
126. Der Schöffe, 4/1973, p. 127.
127. Der Schöffe, 5/1973, pp. 173-76, 183.
128. Democratic German Report, January 31, 1973, p. 14.
129. Neues Deutschland, January 12, 1973.
130. Statistische Jahrbuch 1973, op. cit., p. 72.
131. Neuer Weg, 19/1973, p. 913.
132. Neue Justiz, No. 11 (June 1973), pp. 312-15.
133. Der Schöffe, 5/1973, p. 172.
134. Der Schöffe, 6/1973, p. 208.
135. Almond and Powell, op. cit., pp. 159-61.
136. Arlt and Stiller, op. cit., p. 130.

PART

III

FEEDBACK

As noted earlier, the communications feedback process tells authorities what kind of and how much output is needed to satisfy the demands and to maximize the support being put into the system. Thus, feedback enables a political system to correct its behavior. A following question, then, is whether the communicated supports and demands will continue to balance, that is, whether public opinion shows patterns of conflict or consensus.[1]

Levels of opinion and their roles must be clearly delineated. For instance, from a political science point of view, opinion is divided between what commonly is referred to as mass and elite. The mass opinion is that of the great majority of politically uninvolved people who set broad outlines of policy while elite, or leadership, opinion determines day-to-day decision-making. A dominant set of attitudes and expectations within the population (the political culture) generally permits a government to operate as if a real consensus exists while what is relatively more crucial is the common set of values and habits of action among the leadership group.

The dynamic relationship between the two levels of opinion remains largely a mystery, V. O. Key, the public opinion specialist, says, primarily because all too little is known about elite opinion. But, as already has been suggested, in all systems mass opinion has some impact on the demand, support, and apathy inputs that decision-makers must consider.

On the one hand, an opinion distribution may indicate consensus, or support, to decision-makers. Frequently it is assumed that such patterns of consensus reflect a general acceptance of "the rules of the game." However, there is a different view. Key says such assumptions are too sweeping because of the scarcity of reliable information of precisely what basic political attitudes do prevail. While it does seem that there are characteristic attitudes, beliefs, and behavior that distinguish national populations (political culture), the identification of those characteristics is not scientific.

Therefore, consensus may not be as much a general acceptance of values, goals, or rules of the game as a reflection of basic psychological and attitudinal factors—ethnocentrism, low level of expectation of government action, lack of intense concern about political issues, disposition to accept or tolerate the majority or authority view, tendency to repress private opinions that would cause conflict, etc. (what systems analysis calls cultural restraints on demand input).

In other words, as Key says, "the probability seems to be that consensus must be found in large measure in these characteristics of the
people rather than in any strong and widespread attachment to fundamental principles explicitly political in their content."[2]

Or, as Key says, a consensus reflects opinions that perform
supportive, permissive, or demand functions within a political system.
For instance, major continuing services (social welfare measures,
for instance), general rules of government (such as elite or majority
decision-making), or concrete and broad questions of public policy
(international cooperation) are backed by supportive opinions. These
are the "going operations" that long ago won acceptance. These
opinions give decision-makers a wide range of discretion. A consensus of permissive opinions reflects a general support and may
mean that dissent will not be widespread if a given action is taken.
This may be especially the fact regarding foreign policy that a people
generally entrust to a relatively small group of decision-makers.
Here, too, government is relatively free to work out a solution or to
take or avoid an action. The function of the opinions in this case is
to endow government actions with a general sense of legitimacy.
Thus, leaders feel they may say, for instance, that belligerent foreign
actions are "in the name of the people."

Thus, Key comes to the same input function of support as the
systems analyst. However, he does it more as a psychological
process of conditioned behavior rather than a communications feedback process that includes responses to specific outputs. Regardless
of whether one sees support resulting primarily from childhood
political socialization or from day-to-day response to output situations, the patterns of political behavior that result in the GDR seem
to suggest that (1) consensus is real and (2) communications plays
a major role.

One could suggest then that support and apathy together have
not been outweighed by demand in most cases. In other words, there
is what we might call a consensus of acceptance with a few dissenters
scattered in both directions along the attitudinal scale.

On the other hand, decision-makers may be confronted with an
opinion distribution, or support/demand constellation, which reflects
a conflict. In nearly all communist countries active opposition, as
publicly observable, seems quite small, although conflict is known
to be intense. Thus, it seems that in communist political systems
political attitudes/opinions predominantly fall into a middle range,
that is, a pragmatic mixture of criticism and passive support,
rather than active support or active opposition. One, indeed, is
struck by the absence of publicly articulated antisystem protest,
especially by students and intellectuals. Rather, much of the so-
called protest seems to be more a matter of "loyal opposition," that

is, criticism of a particular administration or regime. A major
quarrel seems to be with "means" rather than "ends."

But a more differentiated way of viewing the "opposition" suggested here is provided in a study by Skilling.[3] He contends opposition
in so-called closed societies always existed and does so now but in
forms different from those recognized as constituting "opposition" in
constitutional democracies.

For instance, in communist political systems the opposition
may be integral, factional, fundamental, or specific, representing
phases of a continuum. Integral opposition opposes the <u>system</u> itself,
either in conspiracies or in the more inchoate fashion of youth's
apolitical attitudes and alienation. Factional opposition, while not
opposing the system, represents <u>ideological rifts</u>. Fundamental
opposition also does not reject the system but rather criticizes a
<u>series of key policies</u> because of differing standards of value. Spe-
cific opposition is neither a rejection of the regime, the leaders, or
basic policies, but rather of <u>specific policies</u>.

Conceding the inability of measuring existing opposition, Skilling
nevertheless poses two conclusions: First, he says that the opposition
now seen in communist political systems of Eastern Europe is "loyal
opposition," seeking changes within the system, either in leadership
or in policy, but not replacement of the system per se. Second, he
says, "No doubt there is widespread disaffection, and even rejection
of the system as such, expressing itself in apathy, in disobedience
to the regime and its requirements, and to some degree in passive
resistance."

The unanswered problem of deciding how much of which type of
opposition is present is not eased by the fact that there is, obviously,
not an abundance of empirical data available on GDR views of political
questions. However, the overall opinion pattern, or input, seems
to be one of consensus, or support, made up of long-range acceptance
of values and short-range apathy, along with opposition of the "loyal"
variety, or legitimate demands. But one is left, as before, with the
problem of how much. How much of the support/consensus is active
or how much is natural apathy and conformity (a la Key's guidelines)?
How much of the demand/opposition is "loyal" (a la Skilling's four-
fold breakdown)?

These are among the concerns of those responsible for the
political communications described in the following pages.

NOTES

1. V. O. Key, <u>Public Opinion and America's Democracy</u> (New York: Knopf, 1961).

2. Ibid., p. 50.

3. Robert A. Dahl, ed., <u>Regimes and Opposition</u> (New Haven, Conn.: Yale University Press, 1973).

8

POLITICAL
COMMUNICATION

The lifeline that ties together a political system is that of communications. It is a necessary prerequisite for all other functions discussed thus far and accounts for the dynamics of political change, as well as the interdependence of functional performance. As Almond says, communications "holds the entire governmental structure together and makes possible coordinated implementation of laws and the mobilization of societal resources."[1] However, this function of communications and its organizational forms in communist political systems is only understandable if one proceeds from the principles of Marxism/Leninism.

THEORETICAL FRAMEWORK

Marxism/Leninism

According to Marxist/Leninist theory (as already noted in Chapter 4), the transition from capitalism to socialism includes the transition from merely spontaneous development of social progress to that of conscious guidance. The revolutionary party is the only institution capable of carrying out this conscious guiding of social progress. Thus, it is the party that will guide the constant education and persuasion necessary in the transitional phase:

Therefore for the Marxist/Leninist party realization of its leading role means persuading the working masses of

the correctness of the Party's policies, to lead the masses
to the Party's position and to the level of consciousness
of Party members and candidates and to directly include
the masses in the struggle to achieve the historic mission
of the working class. Therefore the method of persuasion
is one of the most important for leading the masses
through the Party. [2]

This guidance is necessary since consciousness does not develop
spontaneously and overnight; neither does it develop equally in all
social groups. Rather, residual forces, which hold back progressive
ones, remain present for some time. For instance, bourgeois influences are still present among certain groups within the population and
and they also penetrate from the outside, that is, from the surrounding capitalist world. Furthermore, even if this were not the case,
social development goes on without pause, thus creating a constant
need for the educational and persuasive work of the party: "The
political-ideological persuasion and educational work of the Party is
a constant struggle for the brains and hearts of people for socialism."[3]
Thus, communications are the party's decisive instrument for the
unending process of educating, training, leading, and controlling.
Or, as the SED puts it, the party's communication (Parteiinformation)
takes on increasingly greater meaning: "It is an important instrument of political leadership activities and includes all areas of social
life." Or, as the SED quotes Lenin, "It is the consciousness of the
masses which makes the state strong. It is strong when the masses
know everything, can judge everything and do everything consciously."[4]
    In addition to the special channels of communications created
by the party to further the educational and persuasive process, the
mass media also have a special role in Marxist/Leninist theory.
Clearly, the formal communications structure, that is, the mass
media, cannot be private property and cannot represent individualistic
attitudes. Rather, they are seen as collective organs of the party,
along with mass organizations or social institutions, which were
created to realize a socialist social order.
    Specifically, according to Lenin, the communications media are
(1) collective propagandists, (2) collective agitators, and (3) collective
organizers. As propagandists the media shall disseminate Marxism/
Leninism among all groups of the population; as agitators they shall
activate, or mobilize, the people for the fulfillment of goals set by
the party; and as organizers they will participate in the leading and
controlling of the political, economic, and cultural developments
planned by the party.
    Thus, in contrast to noncommunist systems, mass communi-
cations based on Marxist/Leninist principles are instruments of the

state and party, rather than independent mirrors of events. They are to be closely integrated with other instruments of state power and party influence to provide a unified force of persuasion, rather than to be a means of checks and balances. Publication of information, then, is according to its relevance to the current situation within the communist country and its phase of social development—it is not "news for news' sake." Each bit of information transmitted is aimed at promoting the ideological development of the people.

Contemporary Marxist/Leninists hold that this educative role of communications is especially crucial in the present transitional period between socialism and communism: "In the process of over-all socialist construction, the socioformative role of the socialist state defines itself increasingly clearly as the scientific leadership instrument of the working class and its Party as this side of its activity becomes increasingly central." And, they further contend, this specific period is marked not by a bypassing of the state or minimization of its rule—that is, its "withering away"—but developing socialism precisely through the state: "By this time the socialist state concentrates all powers on the many-faceted development of the advances of socialism. That means the socially formative and consciousness-training role of the socialist state, its creative and organizing character, wins increasing importance."[5]

Furthermore, that work of the state emphasizes increasingly persuasive, rather than coercive, means: "The role of persuasion, explanation and education of people through all means and all links of the state apparatus is growing, not to mention the activity of public organizations. . . ."[6] Or as the SED puts it, "Increasingly Party persuasion gains significance. Convinced people act with greater understanding in solution of tasks, approach creatively their realization, and develop a greater personal initiative to further develop the socialist society."[7] Among the persuasive themes to be emphasized are those concerning labor efficiency, attitudes toward consumption, safeguarding the public order, responsibility of people to state, and development of socialist consciousness.

But all of this communications effort is not a one-way street. Rather, the flow of communications back to the central regulatory apparatus is a central focus of Leninist concepts of communication, for a Leninist party has an intense interest in what the public is thinking. As Lenin said, "So that the central authority can really direct the orchestra it is necessary that one know exactly who plays the violin where, where and how he learned or is learning to play which instrument, who plays badly where and why . . . and who has to be transferred, how and where, in order to overcome the dis-harmony."[8] Or, as Der Parteiarbeiter tells its GDR readers, "The information from top to bottom, and from bottom to top, form a whole."[9] It is reported, for instance, that even during the time of Stalinism, channels were kept open for a flow of communications from the bottom up.[10]

Communist leadership seeks to assess mass feeling in order to determine whether there is support for party programs. Therefore, at every level of communist territorial-administrative structure, down to the factory or collective farm, each party unit has a communications section whose workers convey the state of popular thinking to party leaders. An extensive reporting system and a network of agitators, for instance, as will be shown, serve as constant sources of information on attitudes and opinions at the local level. Accounts are kept of questions asked and problems in which citizens show special interest. In fact, some observers see this corps of agitators and party reporting system serving as a substitute for modern public opinion polling organizations.[11]

Similarly, the Marxist concept of self-criticism underlies the feeding of information back to decision-makers. Marx, in fact, said that proletarian revolutions differed from capitalist or bourgeois revolutions in that the former continuously criticize their own mistakes and weaknesses.[12] Lenin, in turn, in 1921 made it a principle for the Communist party—the party was to permit and encourage popular exposure and criticism of defects in the functioning of communist institutions and personnel:

> Criticism of the Party's shortcomings, which is absolutely necessary, must be conducted in such a way that every practical proposal shall be submitted immediately, without any delay, in the most precise form possible for consideration and decision to the leading local and central bodies of the Party. Moreover, everyone who criticizes must see to it that the form of his criticism takes into account the position of the Party, surrounded as it is by a ring of enemies, and that the content of his criticism is such that, by directly participating in Soviet and Party work, he can test the rectification of the errors of the Party or of individual Party members in practice. The analysis of the general line of the Party, the estimate of its practical experience, the verification of the fulfillment of its decisions, the study of methods of rectifying errors, etc., must under no circumstances be submitted for preliminary discussion to groups formed on the basis of "platforms," etc., but must in all cases be submitted for discussion directly to all the members of the Party.[13]

Within the party itself the self-criticism was to take oral, as well as bureaucratic reporting, forms. And for the public a major channel of formal communications for expression of criticism "from below" was letters and contributions to newspapers.

Functional

Seen functionally, then, political communications within a communist political system operate at two major levels: (1) flowing from the party elite to party members and on to the public in general and (2) flowing from the public through party members back to the party elite. The latter includes elements of "feedback," that is, goal-correcting information, while the former includes the "interest aggregation" function, as discussed in an earlier chapter.

In a period of sociopolitical development, as in the case of a revolutionary country, the political elites use communications to further a new kind of political culture. To put it another way, the elites are involved in a process of "system establishment," while in developed countries communications serve to promote "system maintenance."

As Pye puts it, a political system uses communications to establish rules of political causality and to define the domain of the possible. [14] Specifically, the communications process (1) helps people who can personally observe only small segments of the political process to comprehend the overall substance of politics; (2) magnifies individual action so that they are felt throughout the society, thus creating politics that span a nation; (3) provides the common fund of knowledge and information people need to make political decisions; (4) gives people a basis for calculating the nature and likely behavior of other people and for interpreting events, that is, provides a basis for comprehending political motives; and (5) provides understanding and interpretation of interconnections between events.

In the case of a communist political system that considers itself revolutionary, this might mean, for instance, in terms of Pye's functions as listed above, that the communications process would (1) explain the relationship of the party's use of power to basic Marxist/Leninist tenets; (2) make clear the difference between private and public affairs and the citizens' responsibility regarding the latter; (3) disseminate the views and policies of the party so that the citizens could judge the validity of their leaders' actions; (4) clarify the extent to which citizens can and should question the motives of their leaders; and (5) establish the framework of party considerations and goals regarding the future against which the people would measure achievements and formulate anticipation. In the case of communist political

systems, the tight lines of command of the party structure and a network of intraparty communications systems makes this sociopoltical
development aspect of communications efficient. As already noted,
the mass media are seen instrumentally and guidance, therefore, is
highly centralized to achieve the desired unified effect.

Furthermore, communist communications tradition calls for a
combination of oral persuasion (agitators) and mass media. This
combination has many advantages. For example, specific, as well
as generalized, messages of mobilization can be effectively transmitted, one orally, one via the mass media. Further, oral agitation
and propaganda can be quickly turned on—and off—as the situation
demands. Additionally, the relatively limited number of professional
communicators are concentrated in the mass media, while thousands
of nonprofessional, yet relatively effective, communicators work in
the countryside and enterprises as agitators.

In short, political communications at the party-to-people level
in a communist system implement a cardinal rule of modern Western
communications research: The greatest effect is achieved when a
generalized message is reinforced through personal involvement (as
in conversation or through action). Thus, it might be fairly suggested
that a key to the successful mobilization efforts of communist-rule
states lies in their use of persuasive communications.

This "peculiarly intimate relationship" between communications
and the political process long has intrigued scholars.[15] As noted
above, systems-functionalists see it as the lifeline that "holds the
entire governmental structure together and makes possible coordinated implementation of laws and the mobilization of societal
resources."[16]

Deutsch, however, added another dimension: He saw communications as the self-correcting factor of the political organism. Relying on cybernetic terminology, Deutsch called the communications
network, which produced action in response to an input of information,
feedback. It included "the results of its own action in the new information by which it modifies its subsequent behavior."[17] Thus, Deutsch
moved away from equilibrium analysis, which was essentially static
in that it assumed a political system would balance output against
input to maintain a status quo, that is, that the system would return
to a particular state. Instead, Deutsch's approach enables one to
evaluate the efficiency of a feedback process in terms of the under-
or overcorrections it makes in reaching the goal.[18]

Moreover, the feedback concept allows the analyst to focus on
growth, evolution, and sudden changes. It highlights readjustment of
goals and internal conflict resulting from established working pref-
erences and the impact of new information. It points up the problems
that result when a system cuts itself off from information concerning

the world outside, from information about itself and its own parts and its past. In short, controlling the political system on the basis of <u>actual</u> performance rather than <u>expected</u> performance is feedback, that is, the reporting back to the central regulatory apparatus.

Few will dispute the contention that a ruling communist party, as well as any other governing elite, therefore needs dependable information in order to rule effectively. While some specialists feel this information comes primarily through elites (technocrats, scientists, managers) reporting upward about interest groups of which they are members, it generally is felt that the upward flow of communications from local levels of operations leaves something to be desired. On the other hand, it is widely accepted that the ruling communist parties of Eastern Europe are becoming increasingly aware of the need for a more full flow of communications from top to bottom. Without that, decisions may not achieve the desired results.

Clearly, then, information from below must come from (1) specialists at the local level involved in particular decisions, (2) implementors at the local level responsible for putting the decisions into effect, and (3) those affected by the decisions. Only with such multilevel reporting can those "on top" be sure that their output has satisfied the demand input.

In order to get that kind of broad upward reporting, the communications network has to allow for a certain amount of flexibility It clearly cannot be repressive, or the messages will not get through. And that, in turn, ties in closely with the question of how "open" or how "authoritarian" the party is. Simply put, with the growing need for two-way communications, the party can hardly afford the dysfunctional effects inevitably resulting from a rigid communications system. Equally as clear is the other side of the coin—the more flexible the communications system, the more demands it generates to be fed into the decision-making center. Thus, the task of sorting out the output priorities is complicated immensely. These, then, are the aspects of the GDR's political communications to be examined in the following sections.

SITUATION IN THE GDR

Background

Given its Marxist/Leninist theoretical base and the "developing nation" character of the GDR, it is obvious that political communications play an important role in the thinking of its leaders. Since the founding of the GDR, the communications function has never been neglected. There have, of course, from time to time been different degrees of emphasis on varying aspects of communications or on its overall intensity.

One such development, affecting present communications policies, came in 1967. At that time the VII Party Congress resolved to "form the developed social system of socialism" and called for new communications efforts. It was said that in this new phase of building socialism it was necessary to meet the people's need for information at the local level. The State Council, to implement this concept of local informational work, passed a resolution that emphasized communications' practical results—that is, higher production.[19] That resolution apparently had been based on careful research and an evolving concept called Offentlichkeitsarbeit, or public information work. It was an action-oriented concept, leading to increased citizen participation and activity. In that sense it was not entirely new, for it clearly went back to Lenin's "organizational" role as one of the three basic functions of the press.

In 1970 a research group of the DASR (German Academy for State and Legal Science) took up the theses that first articulated this concept and discussed them with practitioners (state functionaries, scientists, and journalists). Repeatedly the practical results of improved communications were emphasized. Further, an appeal was made to regularize communications and to avoid its past "campaign character."[20]

A confirmation of the GDR's emphasis on local-level information came in spring 1971 when Brezhnev told the 24th Party Congress of the CPSU that it was necessary

> to strengthen the overall ideological work and above all
> to propagate more actively and resolutely the communist
> ideals and the concrete tasks of our development. . . .
> Our chief tasks in this respect are to really understand
> how to communicate to the broad working masses the
> entire strength of our ideological convictions and how to
> correctly and really creatively approach the communist
> education of the Soviet people.[21]

For the GDR this communications guideline from Moscow was still further underlined by foreign policy developments in Europe. By this time it was clear that the growing detente efforts of the Soviet Union and the Ostpolitik of the Federal German Republic would push the GDR into a period of growing international contacts. That meant comparisons between political and social systems would be more readily seen by GDR citizens. Thus, communications had to cope

with this international situation on the one hand, as well as the growing domestic demand and need for more open and lighter forms of
communications on the other. From the party's point of view, this
need had to be satisfied in a manner that stabilized, rather than
unsettled, the society. Specifically, this meant tying the public
closer to the party rather than alienating it. And that had to be
achieved within the context of increasing Western contacts, above
all from West Germany. That, of course, was viewed as ideological
competition.

VIII Party Congress

Thus, it was no surprise that at the VIII Party Congress of the
SED, held in Berlin, June 15-19, 1971, Honecker characterized the
ideological work of the party as the key issue—and he spelled out the
guidelines for political communications in the GDR. The term
Offentlichkeitsarbeit no longer was stressed, but rather "ideological
work," the traditional Leninist term. Although the term "public
information work" continued to be used for some time by scholars,[22]
the term appeared less frequently in official party pronouncements.

Instead, toward the end of his lengthy report on behalf of the
Central Committee, SED First Secretary Honecker said "the theoretical activities of the Party must be lifted to a higher niveau
because the structuring of the developed socialist society of the
German Democratic Republic is constantly introducing new questions."[23]
In this transition from socialism to communism, he continued, there
was no strict line of demarcation. Rather, theory concerning this
process had to take into account the specific conditions of the GDR,
that is, its position vis-a-vis the FRG. This meant the party was
assigning social scientists and propagandists significant and responsible new assignments. Specifically,

> The entire Party, its agitators, propagandists and social
> scientists are responsible for protecting the working
> class and all citizens of the GDR from the poison of anti-
> communism and to remove them from the scene through
> our superior spiritual weapon. One should always keep
> in mind that the development of the socialist conscious-
> ness must be constantly related to the struggle against
> bourgeois ideology, against imperialism, which shies
> from no means in order to damage the construction of
> the socialist society in our republic.

In order to carry out this struggle, Honecker cited as especially useful communications channels the Party Study Year, new learning aids
for agitation and propaganda, and the personal political discussion
and conversation. "We don't need high-sounding words," he said,
"rather convincing arguments. We reject generalized political declarations and instead give understandable answers. Only thereby will
our correct policies also lead to correct effects." Additionally, he
cited the increase in GDR newspaper circulation, ownership of television sets and availability of programs, as well as radio ownership,
as positive facts in the intensified communications that was necessary.
Thus, the journalists were challenged to find more effective forms
and methods of communications in order to make the reporting of the
development of the socialist society more exciting and relevant to
listeners and readers.

Following this clear indication that ideological work would be
the major emphasis of the party leadership, the Secretariat of the
Central Committee in July 1972 announced that an Agitation and Propaganda Conference would be held in autumn. Its purpose would be
"to analyze, generalize, and consult concerning the new agitation
and propaganda goals needed to achieve the resolutions of the VIII
Party Congress."[24]

In early November, therefore, the Politburo formulated 15
goals to be discussed at the conference. They took into account the
new foreign policy situation confronting the GDR, the resulting
domestic communication needs, and the communication structures
to be emphasized. Specifically, the goals were contained in the first
five points: firmer anchoring of the GDR in the socialist state community, realization of the main tasks set forth at the VIII Party
Congress, developing socialist personalities, confronting imperialism,
and strengthening the influence and effectiveness of agitation and
propaganda. The next nine points enumerated communications means
for achieving these goals: membership meetings, Party Study Year,
party schools, political conversations, socialist mass competition,
mass work, press/radio/televistion, agitators/propagandists/jour-
nalists, and social science research. And the final goal was to keep
the guidance of the communications efforts in the hands of the party:
"Ideological activity is the core and chief content of Party work. The
leadership of agitation and propaganda belongs in the hands of elected
leadership."[25]

1972 Agitation and Propaganda Conference

Shortly after the publication of this resolution, the Central
Committee's Agitation and Propaganda Conference was held in

Berlin, on November 16-17, 1972. In opening the conference, Honecker again emphasized that it was necessary to strengthen the population ideologically because this was the period of "confrontation between socialism and capitalism." Politburo and Central Committee Secretary for Agitation and Propaganda Lamberz later put it specifically: "We do not have the intention to export revolution, but the import of counter-revolution certainly will absolutely not be permitted." Or, in other words, "peaceful coexistence is not ideological coexistence." Thus it was clear that one of the major reasons for the renewed ideological campaign in the GDR was the new political situation vis-a-vis the Federal Republic of Germany—with the possibility of increasing East/West contacts, it seemed necessary for every citizen of the GDR to have "a clear national consciousness [Staatsbewusstsein] in order to always and in every question represent the standpoint of his state and his society clearly and unmistakably."[26]

A more domestic goal, however, also was involved, Honecker said, to create within the workers a trust and conviction that the party's proposed solutions to present and future problems were the right ones. What was meant, of course, were the party's economic goals that called for still more production efforts from already hard-pressed workers. What the workers needed was basic information about concrete economic and political problems and goals, said Honecker. What was especially wished was that communications would be used to combat "appearances of bureaucracy, heartlessness, soulless administration, inattention and irresponsibility toward needs and initiatives of workers, corruption and arrogance, veiling of shortages and dishonesty."[27] Thus, indirectly, Honecker was listing some of the socioeconomic problems that hindered the party's efforts to meet increasing consumer demand through more efficient production.

While the foreign and domestic policy reasons for the intensified campaign of political communications at this time thus seemed clear to the party, Einheit, its theoretical monthly journal, acknowledged in its March 1973 issue that there were some questions about it outside of the GDR. Quite simply, said Einheit, it was a matter of an all-around strengthening of the GDR. That meant more effective agitational and propagandistic activities among party members. And that, in turn, called for increased theoretical-ideological work in the circles and seminars of the Party Study Year, as well as other educational centers for Marxist/Leninist study. The goal of all such efforts, according to Einheit, was to increase citizen initiatives for improving the standard of living in the GDR through an increase in work productivity. A second purpose was to meet the increasing informational needs of GDR citizens. Old tested media of communications were to be improved and new ones tried out.[28]

COMMUNICATIONS STRUCTURE

Basically, there are two structures available to the SED to carry out the essential function of political communications: the formal structure, using organized forms of communication, and the informal structure, relying on face-to-face communications.

Formal

The organized channels for political communication from top to bottom, from the party to the people, seem practically endless, especially during a time when communications is a top priority.

Party Resolutions

As has been noted, Honecker, in delivering the Politburo's report to the Central Committee at the VIII Party Congress in June 1971, set the tone of future political communications. Ideological work, that is, agitation and propaganda, was listed as a top priority. (From what is known about Politburo decision-making, it may be assumed that this represented a consensus view of the party's top leadership.) The Party Congress, in turn, put the priority into the form of a resolution. In November 1972 an official resolution of the Politburo was made public to implement the early Party Congress resolution—it was this Politburo document that contained the 15 points of emphasis discussed above. The party's wide distribution of these Party Congress documents and the Politburo resolution may be seen as one of the first steps in its use of formal communications structure—in this case, issuing brochures through state publishing houses. As the SED itself explains:

> The policies of our Party, the resolutions of the Central Committee and the international communist and workers movement constitute the major content of Party information. . . .
> Therefore Party information [in the Basic Party Units] begins with an explanation of the resolutions in the membership meetings of the Party and in the Party groups. [29]

Central Committee Information

    In the ten-man Secretariat of the Central Committee programs are worked out for the implementation of Politburo decisions. In the case of political communication, Werner Lamberz is a key figure— he is the secretary responsible for agitation. Next in the chain of command come the leaders of divisions (Abteilung) within the Central Committee's apparat. Here Heinz Geggel is responsible for the Agitation Division and Kurt Tiedke for the Propaganda Division. These, then, were the units that after the November 1972 Central Committee conference had to chart plans toward implementation of the resolutions on the books.

    One of the first moves was to call a Central Committee Conference on Agitation and Propaganda in mid-November 1972. The calling together of specialists, delivering to them a major statement representative of Politburo thinking, and publicizing the conference by all available mass media, was an unusually intensive use of formal communications structure.

    Another aspect of the formal communications structure brought into play to achieve implementation of the party's decisions was the publication of a new magazine for agitators and propagandists. Issued the first time in January 1973 by the Central Committee's Divisions for Agitation and Propaganda, the new 48-page magazine was called Was und Wie (Who and What). It was described as giving "tactical suggestions" and was addressed to "the agitators and propagandists of the Party in the work collectives and dwelling areas, to the leadership of the basic organizations, the Party organizations of Kreis and Bezirk." In defining its goal, Was und Wie said:

> The routine issuing of this advice shall facilitate exchange of experiences and thoughts regarding how the Party's resolutions are realized, how the multitude of forms and methods of ideological work are best applied and further developed. It shall be shown how in the basic organization and in the district and regional leadership every question is answered which constantly arises anew out of the further formation of the developed socialist society, the many-sided socialist integration, and development of the international class struggle. [30]

Thus, in its first number, Was und Wie discussed how membership meetings, daily political conversations, lectures, the Party Study Year, and other forms of communication could be used effectively.

In addition, the Central Committee regularly issues its "Informationen." Sent to all party organizations, the publication informs the party leadership of Central Committee meetings and resolutions, as well as domestic and foreign policy problems. Thus, all party leaders are uniformly informed concerning the party's programs.[31]

The Central Committee's Department for Propaganda is also especially concerned with directing the Party Study Year, whose goals are laid down in the form of a Central Committee resolution. It affects the ideological training of the 2 million party members but especially the 80,000 trained propagandists. Over the years the changes of emphases in the curriculum have been suggestive of the GDR's major domestic political problems. For instance, the VII Party Congress, still under Ulbricht's leadership, had challenged propagandists to emphasize "The Basic Problems of Strategy and Tactics of the SED During the Establishment of the Developed Social System of Socialism in the GDR." In the 1973-74 Party Study Year, however, the emphasis was on strengthening the GDR's campaign of delimitation vis-a-vis the FRG and the new social concepts of the Honecker-led SED. And for 1974-75 there seems again to be a change—this time an emphasis on the moral superiority of socialism as a system. Thus, the economic competition with the West apparently has been subordinated to the ideological/moral aspect. As Honecker said,

> The niveau of life under socialism, the safety and security
> of people in our society, our moral and ethics, the prog-
> ress and grandiose perspectives of socialism—those are
> our strongest arguments against the propaganda slogans
> of the bourgeois ideologists. . . . We confront the bour-
> geois ideology not only with theoretical weapons; we
> defeat it above all with the practice of the real, existent
> socialism.[32]

Or, as Central Committee Secretary for Propaganda Kurt Tiedke said,

> The historic inability of capitalism to solve the basic
> questions [Lebensfrage] of mankind, becomes still
> clearer. . . . Therefore a top-priority task of our
> times is and remains also the ideological confrontation,
> the struggle against the varying brands of reactionary
> bourgeois ideology, above all against anticommunism.
> . . . In the confrontation with the bourgeois ideologies,
> we are successful the more we offensively propagate the
> ideas and advantages of socialism, if we proceed from

the firm positions of our socialist reality and from this
point of view treat the problems of socialism in our Party
Study Year. [33]

To accomplish these goals, the Party Study Year 1974-75 offers
a basic Marxist/Leninist education for candidate members of the
Party, a study circle of basic Marxism-Leninism, three specialized
seminars (history of the CPSU, political economy of socialism and
the economic policy of the SED, and scientific communism), and a
lecture series in theoretic base problems of the party's politics. In
the basic course for candidate members, the last topic on the curriculum is, "The major characteristics of the sharpening, general
crisis of contemporary capitalism: The aggressive politics of reactionary forces in the FRG and the role of social democracy." This
same topic appears in first place among those to be discussed in the
specialized seminars and lecture series, albeit worded slightly
differently: "The sharpening of the ideological struggle between
socialism and imperialism under the conditions of the realization of
a policy of peaceful coexistence between states with opposing social
systems." In following priority, then, are economic themes and
Soviet history themes. [34]

During the 1973-74 Party Study Year, about 2 percent of the
students took part in the basic course for candidate members, 28 percent in the study circle, 17 percent in the CPSU history seminar,
17 percent in the political economy of socialism seminar, 23 percent
in the scientific communism seminar, and 2 percent in the lecture
series (another 12 percent attend evening schools). [35]

Bezirk Activities

From the Central Committee, guidelines are transmitted to the
agitation and propaganda divisions of the Bezirk, the district party
organization. At this level there are secretaries responsible for these
two communications functions. Among the formal communications
structures that they use are:

1. Training Centers (Bildungsstätte): One such center in Suhl
offers propagandists three-year courses, shorter intensive courses,
lecture series, meetings, and seminars for Kreis leaders.

2. Newspaper: When the Bezirk of Gera wanted to carry out a
communitywide action campaign to improve housing, it used the
party's district newspaper, Volkswacht, to involve readers by presenting them with questions concerning ways to improve the area
through reconstruction and renovation of existing structures. [36]

3. Special "Propaganda Days": The secretariat of the Bezirk
in Neubrandenburg held special days to discuss ideological and

practical problems and exchange experiences gathered at the Kreis
and basic organizational level. [37]

4. "Tradition Room" (Traditionskabinette): In order to disseminate a sense of history, the Bezirk leadership in Rostock initiated
"a new form of political-ideological work." Using a Soviet tradition,
it organized a so-called tradition room in the big harbor-related
industries of Rostock. The rooms featured pictures and documents
of how the new Rostock harbor was built. Also included were honors,
medals, documents, and flags of the harbor enterprise that over the
years had developed into a sizable fleet. Pictures of outstanding
workers were included, as well as documents attesting to the mutual
cooperation among the fishermen of the East European countries. [38]

Kreis Activities

The next level of formal communications structures used in
political communications are those guided by the Kreis, or regional,
party leadership. Here consultation and advising of party, as well
as mass organization, leadership takes place. The Kreis leadership
for Potsdam, for instance, used the materials of the 8th Plenum of
the Central Committee as a basis for its organizational plan for the
basic organizations, including points to be emphasized, study sched-
ules, and means for study. Further, the Kreis leadership in Potsdam
calls together its agitators from the various Kreis party organizations
once a month and briefs them on central questions that will be crop-
ping up in daily life. In addition, Kreis party leaders appear at
innumerable local meetings to articulate the Kreis point of view. [39]

Some of the other specific activities they encourage are:

1. Days of Rural Agitation: A Kreis leadership apparently has
unusual difficulties in coordinating the party's work in rural areas.
Thus in Pritzwalk, for instance, a monthly meeting, called the Day
of Rural Agitation and Propaganda, was organized. Representations
from the Kreis, the basic organizations of the state and collective
farms, community councils, and local committees of the National
Front were invited. Agitator groups were then formed, which, in
turn, could guide the community discussions held in the various work
brigades and production collectives. [40]

2. Rural Consultation Points: These are used as centers of
disseminating ideological and practical information to rural people.
One such center in Dedelow, Bezirk NeuBrandenburg, for instance,
emphasized the development of industrialized agricultural production
methods and the development of community organizations. Farmers
not only were told of the necessity and need for such methods, but
the reasons why. It was reported that about 4,500 people from collective farms, schools, and youth organizations, plus others, visited
this center. [41]

3. Agitators Day: Once a month the Kreis party leaders at Marienberg hold an "Agitators Day." To it are invited representatives of the basic party organizations in industry, construction, agriculture, forestry, and state organs. They discuss a specific theme that the Kreis secretariat has worked out (based on party resolutions, specific Kreis assignments, or resulting from the party's membership meetings or Party Study Year). The information is taken back to the agitators' collectives in their basic organizations and enterprises.[42]

4. Urania: An apparently especially effective communications instrument of the Kreis is its Uranian organization. This is an organization of lecturers who are available to party leaders for purposes of political communication. Thus, for instance, in 1972 Urania conducted more than 77,000 gatherings for workers, or 30 percent more than the year before. It plans to form membership groups in the large enterprises that will feed it with lecture ideas.[43]

Basic Party Unit (Grundorganisation)

The next level in the transmission of guidelines and implementation of communications plans is the Basic Party Unit, the heart of the party. They are found in industrial, handicraft, and agricultural enterprises, in units of the People's Police and the National People's Army, in administrative offices, scientific and educational institutions, in mass organizations, in dwelling places, and finally in the party apparat itself. Three party members are needed for a Basic Unit. And by 1974 there were 54,000 such units in the GDR.[44] Some of the communication activities carried out at the initiative of the Basic Party Unit include:

1. Membership Meeting (Mitgliederversammlung): Great emphasis is placed by the Basic Party Unit on its membership meeting. It is seen as an opportunity to disseminate information, check on the mood of the members, and to deal with troublesome questions. Central Committee Secretary for Agitation Lamberz has said,

> The most important forum for processing and disseminating arguments for the daily persuasion work of all comrades is the membership meeting. In it we mold the Party's forces for successful realization of the resolutions of the Central Committee. It is the school for Marxist/Leninist training and education for all comrades.

Going on, Lamberz called for an "openness" about these meetings. Every comrade, he said, should be able to present his questions and problems in a candid fashion. Every kind of formalism, he warned, was damaging.[45]

2. Party Study Year (Pateilehrjahr): According to Lamberz, the Party Study Year creates the prerequisites necessary for the daily ideological work among party members. It holds "a central place in inner-Party life."[46] It is both a school of Marxist/Leninist theory and of practical experience, conducted through study circles and seminars.

According to party statutes, every member and candidate member is duty-bound to pursue, continuingly and systematically, his knowledge of Marxism/Leninism. Therefore, all are expected to take part in the Party Study Year, conducted by trained propagandists who are held accountable to the party leadership for the success of their instruction. The propagandists take up themes suggested by leaders of the Basic Party Units; since these themes also are being discussed through other forums, a coordination is possible. The Basic Party Unit, of course, stresses that the study room is not the only place where the learning goes on—every party member, or Comrade (Genossen), is encouraged to do his "homework," that is, what is called "self-study" in preparation for his circle meetings.

3. Propagandists: Clearly the role of propagandists is important to the Basic Party Unit. The Wismut party organization provides an example: It arranged 26 short courses, taking in 80 percent of its propagandists, to prepare them for the Party Study Year. In addition, more propagandists are slated to study at the Party School; they are encouraged to continue their self-studies; and they are brought together in the "Day of the Propagandist" to exchange experiences.[47]

4. "Argument of the Week": For years in the VEB Repair Works at Neubrandenburg, 80 members of the enterprise's Basic Party Unit have come together 30 minutes before beginning work to take part in what they call the "Argument of the Week." The members who come include leading functionaries of the enterprise, departmental chiefs, group leaders, and master craftsmen. After discussing their theme of the week—for instance, concerning cultural or production problems—the members go back to their work collectives and discuss the topic with their fellow workers.[48]

5. Specialists: The party leadership often makes use of specialists to supplement regular propagandists and agitators. For instance, in a Dessau VEB which makes gas apparatus, groups of specialists were formed that would be responsible for printed agitation and propaganda concerning such themes as foreign policy, economic policy, cultural policy, imperialism, etc.[49] Further, party leaders make a special effort to supply small Party Units with lectures specialists.[50]

6. State Organizations: Party organizations at the state level also get into agitation and propaganda work. For instance, in autumn 1969 the Party Unit within the city leadership for Magdeburg

opened an "Academy for Propagandists." Within two to three years
at least 800 propagandists were trained here, whereas previously
they had taken part in special classes at the Kreis School of Marxism/
Leninism. The study plan, lectures, seminars, etc., were patterned
after that of the Kreis School. Those now attending the academy come
primarily from a newly formed VEB and other small Basic Party
Units, meeting weekly for half-day instruction. After the first several
years of training only new propagandists, the school brought back the
already trained for refresher courses in preparation for the Party
Study Year. Further, a special lecture series, related to the Study
Year, was begun. Professors from the party units of the Technical
University, Pedagogic University, Academy of Medicine, and Trade
School for Chemistry are also invited to help with the continuing
education of the propagandists, especially in courses dealing with
Marxism/Leninism.[51]

    7. Mass Organizations: Since all party members are also
members of one or more social organizations, the Basic Party Unit
leadership is responsible for inspiring members to do their bit off
the job, as well as on. Thus, for instance, if they are active in the
women's or youth organizations, they are responsible for emphasizing
in those organizations the same points they do in their on-the-job
activities. This contributes to unified and effective political communications.

    8. Youth Work: In the membership meeting of Basic Party
Units of a Berlin-Friedrichshain High School, the role of agitation
and propaganda in respect to preparation of FDJ members for the
Tenth Youth Festival in summer 1973 was a special concern. Thus,
it was proposed that older party members should meet with FDJ
members in what was called a "Red Meeting" (Roten Treff). There
a specific theme was discussed, and experienced comrades would
show, in a kind of role-playing situation, how one argues convincingly and parteilich (partyish). In every class, agitator groups of
three to five persons were formed so that the agitators could conduct
political discussions during class breaks, as well as in FDJ membership meetings.[52]

    9. Schools: In the party organization of a high school in Bran-
denburg, the emphasis on ideological work meant, for instance,
strengthening instruction that pointed up the relationship between the
natural sciences and their visible consequences.[53]

    10. Special Tasks: The Basic Party Unit is also the logical
instrument for carrying out special political communications tasks.
For instance, there were the cases of firms converted from semistate status (including private interests) to VEBs, or state enterprises, after the 1970 party decision calling for such a change.[54]
The problem was that only a fourth of the formerly semistate firms

had Basic Party Units. Therefore, the Kreis leadership of the party decided to send 2,000 experienced workers and functionaries out of bigger state enterprises to the new VEB to carry out political-ideological work. In addition to explaining the reason for the national-ization of the firm, these experienced party members founded new Basic Party Units. Members of these organizations were then sent to numerous short courses organized at <u>Bezirk</u> and <u>Kreis</u> levels. In fact, 20 percent of the leadership personnel of the new VEB com-pleted the Kreis school for Marxism/Leninism. Thus, in the member-ship meetings of their basic organizations they were able to share what they had learned. For example, they were trained to coordinate their mass political work, to hold educational membership meetings, to lead the campaign for plan fulfillments, to exercise party control over activities undertaken to fulfill the plan, and to guide the trade union and mass organizations related to their enterprise. Further-more, they went out to talk with women who did cottage work at home for the industry, in order to draw them closer into the life of the industry. [55] Within the factories themselves, the Basic Party Units used work breaks and shift changes as opportunities to discuss political topics and to give pointers for work emphasis. [56]

Another example of the essential role played by agitators and propagandists in the transition from semistate to state enterprises comes from a tin enterprise in Scheibenberg. There, eight agitators were selected and divided among individual trade union groups that had the most influential personnel in work collectives. They then were able, through their personal authority, to convince workers of the necessity to increase production. [57]

That progress has been made in the political communications work of the Basic Party Unit seemed clear to top-level party leader-ship by mid-1973—a <u>Neuer Weg</u> editorial described the progress as "clearly recognizable." At the same time, the continuing problem was that of "development of mass initiatives among the workers." Thus, the goal remained the same: "Increase the effectiveness of political ideological work."[58]

BPO (Betriebsparteiorganisation, or enterprise party organization)

The Basic Party Units are further divided into BPOs. At this level, too, a party member is responsible for agitation and propa-ganda work.

1. <u>Work with Trade Unions</u>: In any enterprise one of the major channels of communication through which the party organization can work is that of the BGL (<u>Betriebsgewerkschaftsleitungen</u>), the enter-prise trade union leadership. The BGL has a commission for agitation and propaganda that works through groups concerned with trade union

agitation, training functionaries, and education of trade union members, that is, the Schools of Socialist Work (see item 2 below). In addition, the commission supports the BGL to increase the effectiveness of its membership meeting, considered the basis of trade union activities. To aid in agitation, the commission, among other activities, provides printed materials in the form of brochures, posters, cartoons, clippings, etc. It also publicizes relevant television and radio programs.[59]

2. Schools of Socialist Work (Schulen der sozialistischen Arbeit). What formerly were called "activist schools," a form of political mass work of the trade unions within enterprises, are now taking a new form as Schools of Socialist Work. According to the Politburo's report to the 8th Plenum of the Central Committee, these new schools will affect the work process and the work collective, those areas where the best possibilities exist for influencing the attitudes of workers.[60] Within the past several years the number of these schools has increased significantly—from 14,000 schools with 300,000 participants at the end of 1972 to 51,220 schools with 1,041,949 participants at the end of 1973.[61]

An example of how these schools operate comes from a machine industry enterprise in Berlin. Eight separate work collectives, or teams, took part there in discussions meant to lead to suggestions for improving leadership quality and increasing work productivity. The discussion leader is a member of a work collective—for instance the master craftsman—who then can make the connections between the theoretical context and the practical results for the work of the individual collective.[62] Other enterprise Schools of Socialist Work use the Lektorat, or organized lecture forum, as a special communications form for dealing with economic problems. The Ernst Thälmann Works in Magdeburg, for instance, uses some 300 lecturers, trained in a centralized study course. Leading functionaries take part in these courses.[63]

3. Membership Meeting: The BPO membership meeting is very significant to the party leadership. It is felt that in such meetings party members develop their capabilities and willingness to represent the policies of the party in a convincing and disciplined fashion. At such meetings all party members receive an orientation that is unified and goal-oriented in content. Frequently party leaders find it necessary to talk first personally with members and candidates in order to arouse their interest in the meeting and to draw out the opinions they would wish to articulate. Within such a context, a party secretary in the tire works and the VEB pipe kombinat in Riesa then proudly reports that, for instance, an average of 85 to 88 percent of the Genossen attend the membership meeting of the BPOs.[64]

4. _Enterprise Newspaper_: The enterprise newspaper is considered one of the most effective agitational media because it is timely and reaches a large audience. In fact, it is held to be so important to the party's political communication program that the Central Committee's Division for Agitation holds a special study course leading to qualification as enterprise newspaper editor. The editors meet weekly with party leadership and party functionaries to discuss points of emphasis for the week. The purposes of the newspaper include: disseminating regular information about production plans and progress, praise of the best workers, medium of exchange of experiences and performance, support of worker initiatives, reporting on all aspects of collective life.[65]

For instance, a big machine construction VEB found a "Consultation Corner" in its plant newspaper a useful forum for answering current political questions. The mass organizations and plant agitators supplied the arguments for the editors to use in their column. In addition, social scientists were approached to take up the questions, opinions, and moods of the workers and comment on them.[66]

A plant newspaper in Rostock used satire to increase its circulation and to point up unsolved practical problems in the plant. The workers developed the feeling that the satirist was on the side of "the little man," so to speak, and therefore provided him with tips for stories. According to the newspaper, satire is "the most appropriate cloth against moral dust which clouds consciousness. . . . There are no taboos, but breath-fine limits."[67]

An interesting insight into the effectiveness of these plant newspapers comes from Karl Marx Stadt. There the party leadership and editorial staff of a plant newspaper resolved to circulate a questionnaire about the effectiveness of the newspaper. Especially wished were the opinions of the Party Unit organizers, trade union leaders, and master workers in the most important work collectives. While 90 percent of the respondents said the plant newspaper was useful, 13.7 percent of them combined their response with critical comments and suggestions. It was further clear from the questionnaire that almost everyone read with great attention critical contributions in the paper. All questioned state functionaries were particularly interested in criticism, and the workers, too, listed critical contributions as the most-read newspaper item (94.2 percent). Meanwhile, cultural articles were least read by both workers and intellectuals.[68]

Seen from the point of view of the editor, the major problem of putting out a plant newspaper is to make its political-ideological themes relevant to the readers: "The reader must be able to identify at once with the theme of the discussion. It must interest him from the first moment on, challenge opinions, and mobilize thought and action. It must not only explain and convince, but rather also lead people to action." Success then is measured, according to the editor, if the workers develop good ideas and initiatives leading to increased work production. For instance, the paper commented on every answer from a reader to an "Open Letter" from the enterprise's leaders calling for suggestions for improvement. Through cooperation with the work groups, the newspaper then organized a control—it interviewed people to see whether the suggestions were really put into effect. They found that of the 1,300 answers received, nearly half from workers, more than 1,000 suggestions were usable. And by year's end about 75 percent of all those suggestions had been put into practice. Thus, the editor concluded, the newspaper had played its role as collective agitator and organizer.[69]

APO (Abteilungsparteiorganisation)

Where the enterprises are large, the BPOs referred to above are again subdivided into divisional, or departmental, party organizations, the APOs. At this level, too, a party member is responsible for agitation and propaganda work, that is, local-level political communications.

1. Meetings: APO leaders meet regularly to study party guidelines from higher echelons, to organize lectures on these themes for membership meetings, and to pass on suggestions to APO agitators and propagandists.[70]

2. Workers' Discussions (Arbeiteraussprachen): In a big machine-building enterprise in Ilsenburg, the APOs formed a collective among their 70 agitators. Among other activities, the collective is responsible for conducting bimonthly worker discussions, which long have been a tradition in this enterprise. Agitators go among the workers, especially during breaks in the work routine, and discuss the work of the enterprise and the newest daily political questions. If the agitator is particularly trusted, the workers use this opportunity also to discuss personal problems with him. Discussions in such small groups have been found to be an effective form of agitation in the enterprise.[71]

3. Lectures: Because of its crucial contribution to the GDR's economy, the engineering enterprise Hermann Schlimme in Berlin places great emphasis on its APOs. The party secretary for the enterprise reports that all APO secretaries are given a short lecture every six weeks about a theme important in party propaganda, for instance, the dollar crisis. Representatives of all APOs attend these meetings and report back to their membership. Also every two weeks an advisory meeting of the central agitators' collective is held, led by the secretary of the Basic Party Unit.[72]

4. Printed Material: Some APOs rely especially heavily on printed agitational materials. For instance, in a Dessau VEB, not only is the bimonthly plant newspaper published, but also an informational sheet published by the party leadership; it is meant to provide quick comment on daily problems that come up in conversation. The sheets are prepared by a specialist group working with the agitators. [73]

5. Party Study Year: The APOs in the Kali works in Bleicherode are interested in having every party member participate in the Party Study Year and in "homework." Thus, the APOs report that in the Party Study Year circles almost every comrade receives a specific personal assignment to speak on some ideological problem under discussion. They thereby improve their persuasive abilities as agitators and propagandists. [74]

Party Press

All of the units of the party make use of the voluminous output of the party publishing houses in their political communications work. At the top of the press pyramid is the official party newspaper, Neues Deutschland; down to the Basic Party Units there are publications at every level of the party's organization—Bezirk, Kreis, city, local—with more than 1 million circulation. Next there are 14 Bezirk SED newspapers, with special editions for the various Kreis. Together these 15 major SED daily newspapers have more than 5.3 million circulation, [75] or nearly three-fourths of the total daily circulation in the GDR. In addition, there are about 600 weekly plant newspapers, with over 2.7 million circulation, [76] and another 100 Kreis weeklies, with 1.5 million circulation. [77] In addition (as seen in Chapter 4), there are hundreds of publications of the mass organizations, state ministries, party and state institutes, professional organizations, etc. All of these serve as useful published background and reference material for the ideological work of party communicators. (Naturally they make use, too, of information presented by the electronic media, especially TV.) In fact, there is a special job for literature dissemination, called the Literaturobmann, as prescribed in a Central Committee resolution of 1965. It is his responsibility to inform himself through the party organizations, book lists, literary newspaper supplements, etc., as to new material available. [78]

In addition, the units of the party make use of varied special communications media. Brochures, fliers, wall newspapers, plant newspapers, and exhibits are some of the common ones. [79] In some cases even negative communication is used—such as a wall newspaper listing the names of workers who have wasted the most work materials; this is contrasted to photos and production rates of "The Month's Best," shown at the top of the page. [80]

In the various study groups, Marxist/Leninist literature is disseminated, as well as documents and resolutions of the SED, of the communist world movement, and of the CPSU. Dozens of other special publications, such as The Party Worker, The ABC of Marxism/Leninism, Actual Politics, and World Politics Viewpoint are used. [81]

Elections

The Central Committee resolution calling for party elections in 1973 made it clear that another of their purposes is to increase the effectiveness of political-ideological work. A major part of this communication should be clarification of the problems of the GDR's policy of delimitation from the FRG and the "nationality question" in general. Thus, the election directive said that the GDR's policy of peaceful coexistence was a "hard class struggle, a global confrontation with imperialism" that called for "Marxist/Leninist principledness, ideological alertness and the active participation of all members and candidates of the Party." [82]

Another communications task of the party elections is to mobilize the masses, specifically for carrying out the "Main Tasks" (Hauptaufgabe) of the current five-year plan. Thus, in the Central Committee resolution regarding the last party elections it was said that the purpose of the elections was to carry out the resolutions of the VIII Party Congress (that is, to improve the material and cultural niveau of the people on the basis of increased production tempo as well as scientific-technical progress).

State elections serve a similar communications function. They involve a vast propaganda campaign that gives the party a forum for explaining official policies and highlighting achievements. An army of agitators is sent into the society to disseminate the party view at study circles, discussion groups, campaign meetings, house-to-house canvassing, and organized demonstrations, all intended to educate the citizens—and, of course, to persuade them to vote.

Mass Media

As seen at the beginning of this chapter, Marxism/Leninism places great emphasis on the role of the mass media in the entire political system. Its role in the party's interest aggregation function has already been discussed (in Chapter 4). In addition, the mass media have a key role in the political communications process that ties all the other functions together. Thus, Secretary for Agitation and Propaganda Lamberz, for instance, stressed the concept that mass media were instruments of political leadership of the party and described them as the "fastest and most immediate tie to the masses."[83] Recognizing that the political persuasion work—which presently is a top priority of the party—consists of combining many media, the party now insists on "the coordinated effect of press, radio, and television with oral agitation and propaganda."[84] Thus the mass media, together with the party's formal communications structure, are seen as a whole. And both are to be improved. An improvement in the quality of mass media output, Lamberz said, means an improvement in the quality of political information and argumentation—specifically, less one-sided information and more exact and timely reporting of the political nature of developments.[85]

Thus, the mass media are trying to meet the party's goals of political communication, as newly defined. Specifically, as the party puts it, this includes

● deepening the unity between citizens and state, thus strengthening the socialist state;

● providing the information necessary for developing socialist democracy: awareness of everything, responsibility for the whole;

● meeting the workers' growing need for more information;

● putting political communications work on a regular basis;

● avoiding the pessimism and paralysis of initiative that is produced by illusionary goals.[86]

For journalists, the professional group most directly concerned, the new political communications emphases mean for the mass media,

● as collective agitator, to increase the liveliness and daily relevance of the press' work; to answer the workers' questions more concretely; to use offensive argumentation against bourgeois ideological attacks;

● as collective propagandist, to go more deeply into theoretical Marxism/Leninism; to exercise greater understanding and practicality in the communication of socialism's scientific Weltanschaung; to carry on thorough, persuasive, and telling confrontations against all oppositional theories, from the construction of the industrial and postindustrial society, to revisionism and social democracy, to Maoism;

● as collective organizer, to study more thoroughly the life of the workers, especially their progressive experiences in production work, in political struggles, and in the formation of social relations; to communicate progress in education and culture; to assist the exchange of experiences; to develop criticism and self-criticism; to increasingly support the development of the personality and to always give the work of the individual more expression.[87]

Practically, the journalists see their goals as the use of the mass media to help workers become more effective in their orientation to the complexities of present life—to help them to understand

so that they can react. Journalists must take up the real questions of
the workers and answer them in such a manner that that which hinders
progress and the fulfillment of resolutions, and that which citizens
rightly criticize, will be changed. Further, workers are to be shown
how work policy is made. Differences between country and city, and
between mental and physical work, are to be overcome. Information
leading to activity is to be disseminated so effective implementation
of decisions is possible.[88] And for the journalists themselves, as
a profession, the goals include (1) overcoming specialist thinking in
editorial offices and instead practicing socialist collectivity, and
(2) working together closely with party functionaries, mass organizations, and state leadership, but at the same time always pushing,
in a friendly fashion, for that which journalism is and can give.[89]

The problems existing, or expected, in working toward these
goals are freely admitted. One candid expression of the overall
problem came in the statement of a party leader who said, "The
public should not say, 'What do you want to talk with us about now?
You already have decided everything.'" In this respect, journalists
admit that their publications have been too dry and that workers too
seldom have had a word. Party theoreticians scold that on the TV
screen life has been shown very one-sidedly—human relations need to
be presented in a deeper, many-sided fashion. The real problems
of people had been ignored. The legitimate need for relaxation and
entertainment, too, had been overlooked.[90] In short, the major
problem was seen as one of inferior-quality communications. Communicators did not speak and write so people could understand.
Officials standing for election were not shown doing their jobs after
elections took place. Letters to the editors were not taken seriously
as citizens' initiatives. Neither were they seen as barometers of the
atmosphere throughout the country. Results were presented rather
than processes.

Organizational problems, too, have drawn their share of
attention. For instance, "partner relationships, too, especially
between state and economic organs and editors" are called for,
along with further development of press centers in economic organs,
state enterprises, etc.[91]

However, by early 1973 the Central Committee leader for
agitational work could say that this question of quality mass media
political communications "had come a good step forward" since the
challenge of the VIII Party Congress.[92] Evidence of the changes that
were achieved include: a looser style in Neues Deutschland, the
central party's newspaper; livelier new radio programs that emphasize
sports, youth, and interviews with well-known personalities; more
modern themes in weekly and illustrated press; "problem articles"
in weekend editions of regional newspapers; a more lively reader

discussion in newspapers about the problems of socialist life and art; appearance on TV of state leaders to answer public questions, etc.

One of the special problems continuing to bother the GDR press is what might be termed the general communications gap. As the Neue Deutsche Presse explained it and its ramifications:

> By 1975 the number of citizens in the GDR who have spent the greatest part of their life in a socialist social system will be the majority. The generation grown up in the GDR no longer has experiences of direct struggle with the capitalist class and its exploitive methods.
>
> However, under the conditions of sharpened ideological aggression of the opponent, the factor of individual experience becomes more important in formation of socialist consciousness, for experiences determine attitudes and serve to internalize behavioral norms.

Therefore, the foreign news editors working with GDR television emphasize reports about daily life in the FRG and other capitalist countries to show how the system there affects workers. By presenting such material, GDR journalists hope that younger listeners and viewers will see the contrast between the two sociopolitical systems.[93]

Another special problem of the mass media is to meet the party's challenge for a better presentation of the so-called new socialist man. Thus journalists have attempted to define more specifically than in the past the concept of "socialist personality." Specifically, they say, reports about the new socialist man should include:

1. Vital statistics: name, age, profession, function, social organizations.

2. Physical appearance: body build, gestures, face, manner of speaking and dress.

3. Development: social background, political Weltanschaung, social involvement, professional training and responsibility, experiences in the trade union movement, anti-fascist resistance, World War II experience, meeting with Soviet comrades, successful experiences in profession, culture, or sport, and outstanding social achievements.

4. Personal characteristics: honesty, thoroughness, modesty, justice, sensitivity; qualities of will, such as ambition, perseverance, decisiveness, independence, self-control, discipline, courage; capabilities, such as for leadership, study, practical scientific knowledge, recognition of newness, collective work.

5. Individual thoughts and feelings: breadth and depth of "scientificness," independence, flexibility, accurateness, alertness; socialist thought patterns, such as class-consciousness, state-consciousness, sense of responsibility and defense; emotions, such as happiness, gaiety, sorrow, pain; moral qualities, such as love for fatherland, pride in the GDR, joy in its achievements, joy in work, feeling of friendship, camaraderie, and responsibility.

6. Behavior: relationship to work, such as involvement in fulfilling plans and willingness to accept new ideas and methods; relationship to other people, such as a sense of collectiveness and internationalism; relationship to himself, such as willingness to learn, to educate himself.

7. Motivation: for exemplary work achievement, desire for knowledge, for completion of tasks, for maintenance of his own health, and for efforts toward socialist collectivity in work, at home, and in husband-wife and parent-child relationship.[94]

Clearly the point made here, and elsewhere, reflects the need to show that the wishes of the workers do count in bringing about change; that people can and do work comradely together; that they do have weaknesses as well as strengths; and that that which is new is not only attractive but understandable. But problems remain, as for example within the medium of television. But as the deputy chairman of the State Committee for Television wrote, exchange of timely programs with other socialist countries should be better utilized; the news should be more carefully selected, better formulated, and prepared especially for the television screen (that is, immediate information and interpretation); and documentary films devoted to political analyses should be used.[95]

Informal

Social science research has shown repeatedly the persistence and potential of face-to-face contacts. For instance, in modern political systems it has been found that personal communications frequently can penetrate the growing selective inattention resulting from oversaturation of communications. Then, too, personal conversations and experiences sometimes are able to loosen attitudes on which prejudices and stereotypes are based. And, of course, face-to-face communications interpret information received through mass media. Einheit, the SED party journal, puts it this way: "After all, life everywhere has shown that the mass media . . . even with its powerful mass effectiveness, cannot replace the living word of the agitator, the dialogue with a conversation partner."[96]

Taking into account these findings, the SED pursues two basic forms of informal communications. First, it encourages all party members to engage in face-to-face communications with fellow citizens in what it calls "political conversations." Second, it organizes thousands of members to do this in an official capacity, that is, as party agitators. As Lamberz said,

> If the broad effectiveness of our <u>oral agitation</u> depends on every comrade in daily conversation with non-Party people knowing how to represent the standpoint of the Party and truly doing so, so on the other hand it has been shown that the Party needs <u>agitators</u> to guarantee the impact of oral agitation—as it needs propagandists for dissemination of theory.[97]

Political Conversations

"The personal political conversation, the discussion, the exchange of opinion and idea" was said by Honecker at the VIII Party Congress to be "irreplaceable" in the persuasive work necessary for explaining the party's policies and answering the multifaceted questions of the people. This personal conversation, he went on to explain, is a matter

> for the entire Party and every single comrade and not just the assignment of some specialists. It is a tested Leninist principle that every Party member daily feel totally responsible for political conversation with non-Party people in his immediate work and living environment, sensitively and patiently relate to events and practical experiences of his colleagues and fellow citizens, and spread and deepen our socialist persuasion.

According to the party, through such conversations the fundamental prerequisite for a relationship of trust between it and all people is deepened. The fact that citizens who are not members of the party come to those who are with their questions, problems, and even difficulties is proof of the increasing maturity of this trust.[98] Thus, in instructions for party secretaries, the first source listed for getting party information to the leadership and the membership is the "personal conversation of comrades with colleagues at work and citizens where they live."[99]

But despite this theoretical priority, it is clear from the party press in the GDR that the actual practice did not always measure up. As the first party secretary for a major city wrote, "After all, it is really not that long ago that political conversations were neglected in many areas of our social life." Therefore, he went on, if the "daily conversation with the workers on a broader basis" was carried out, and thereby trust deepened and initiatives developed, "then we consider that as something qualitatively new."[100] Further evidence that it takes more than a party resolution to bring into being effective political conversations is found in the statement of a party group organizer in a textile VEB in Niederschmalkalden. She says, "Proceeding from the work proposal of our Basic Party Unit and the Party group, we seek to have every comrade daily lead a political conversation. But there are still great differences—some comrades have already been helped to independently take standpoints on contemporary political problems, but others wait for guidance."[101]

Apparently there are special problems, too, in communicating with nonparty colleagues. For instance, a member of the party's city leadership group in Dresden wrote that it had proved useful for the most politically experienced party members (emphasis added) to converse with a set circle of nonparty colleagues.[102] Seemingly such special rapport is necessary for effective communications between the two groups.

Thus, to help its members carry out such conversations effectively, the party publishes many aids. For instance, in an issue of The Party Worker devoted to the topic, "The Political Conversation in the Party Study Course," much attention was paid to elementary techniques of oral communications.[103]

Agitators

According to the party, agitators shall have (1) party experience, (2) solid knowledge of Marxism/Leninism, (3) ability to relate easily to people, (4) capacity to argue convincingly, and (5) ability to listen to others, to understand them and relate to their questions.[104] A party member of the Kreis leadership, who is secretary of the departmental party organization (APO) in his hydraulic construction firm, explained it this way:

To perform political persuasion work, that is expected of all comrades . . . for instance, in the membership meeting we have worked out for the entire departmental Party organization which ideological questions have to be explained by all comrades. We cannot and may not delegate the responsibility for persuasion work to several comrades, for it is a cause of all Party members. . . .
We agree that permanent agitators can be a great help.
Therefore we selected comrades who can explain clearly

the standpoint of the Party, who "make it" with their
colleagues. These comrades inform themselves independently, always bring something back from guidance,
and are in a position to relay it well.[105]

As has been seen, many of their guidelines start at the very top of
the party apparat. They are passed on from the Central Committee
Department for Agitation and Propaganda, to the Bezirk party leadership, then to the Kreis, and from there to local-level agitators.

Propaganda and agitation are not seen as goals in themselves.
Rather, they are to increase the effectiveness of social, economic,
and cultural processes. Such mass political communication cannot
be limited just to answering questions but, suggests the Leipzig
Bezirk secretary, lead to a higher quality of membership meeting
where party members can demonstrate their own maturity.[106] Specifically, in the GDR's present stage of economic development, it is
the purpose of every party organization to use agitation and propaganda
work to increase economic efficiency—to rationalize work so that
jobs are reduced and more employees thus made available for achieving a higher level of technocratization.[107] At this local level agitators
are selected by the Basic Party Unit. They operate at their place of
work (factories, offices), where they live (apartment units), and
where they serve in volunteer capacities (mass and social organizations, school councils, etc.).

The example of a beverage kombinat in Berlin illustrates how
many-faceted the organization of the agitator's work is. The kombinat
is made up of several branches located in different places, without a
factory newspaper or radio network to tie them together. Yet,
according to the view of the party, it is necessary that the workers
be daily informed. Verbal agitation is the solution. Thus the party
leadership in the kombinat first selected Genossen (party members)
from among the branch directors, departmental secretaries, functionaries from the youth organization, etc. They were responsible,
in turn, for communicating to the brigades and collectives within
their divisions. Later they added agitators from individual work collectives on the assembly line and from administrative units. The
total agitators' collective finally consisted of 150 Genossen and
Kollegen (colleagues, that is, nonparty persons). They met every
two weeks and were instructed by the party leadership regarding the
important topics to be discussed. If only one departmental agitator
could be spared from work time, he was responsible for passing the
guidelines along to the others. For really important topics, however,
the party leadership called all agitators together. The agitators then
returned to their departments and passed along the information about
the problems discussed at the meeting. This was especially

important, for instance, when the factory was going over to a three-shift system and problems were resulting. [108]

Another example of the use of agitators comes from the VEB Locomotive Construction and Electrotechnical Works in Henningsdorf. The VEB's problem was that of increasing work productivity. In addition to using many other means of communication, the party leadership of the factory established an agitators' group. It consisted of one agitator from each of 11 party groups, plus several other experienced party members. The leader of this new agitators' group, who was also a member of the APO leadership, disseminated guidelines, verbal and written, to the agitators every 14 days. He, in turn, had gotten these from the leadership of the BPO. In fact, at every level agitators are aided in their work by the party. [109]

But there are problems. As has been noted, the party has selected its agitators in part on the basis of how well they get along with people. It is felt that an agitator has an advantage if he or she knows the audience. It is in a sense, however, at the same time a disadvantage—if the agitator is known, colleagues will have less inhibitions about expressing to him their reservations and misgivings about political development and party policies that the agitator is supposed to explain to them. In fact, the agitator often becomes the scapegoat for the frustrations of his fellow citizens. As one agitator reported, after years of agitating for higher work productivity, "The idea can surely come up about how long this is to continue."[110] Furthermore, with the increasing complexity of political life, the agitator finds it difficult to have answers to all questions. Therefore, he is encouraged to call on the help of specialists.

Allied Parties

An especially interesting case utilizing informal communications media involves the so-called bloc or allied parties in the GDR, that is, the four non-Marxist parties. As has already been pointed out,

> All allied parties enable those citizens of the GDR, who
> approach socialism from bourgeois-democratic positions,
> who possess special traditions and experiences and who
> would not be in a position to obtain or exercise the high
> obligations of membership in a Marxist-Leninist party,
> to consolidate their positions within socialist society. [111]

However, while these non-Marxist positions are recognized, they are not accepted as permanent. Rather, they are "relics of bourgeois ideology, elitist concepts and distorted historical viewpoints which must be rectified."[112] Specifically, leaders within the allied parties

are confronted with "very serious problems" in helping their members
fit into the scheme of society. They are faced with

> assisting craftsmen's cooperatives in recruiting new
> members for them and in mobilizing all individually
> operating craftsmen and tradespeople. . . . A party
> such as the DBD, which has firm roots in the village,
> sees its principal task in mobilizing its members for
> increased activity in the building up of co-operative
> relations, in the intensification of the agricultural
> production processes, in the stepping up of production
> for marketing and in the improvement of social life
> within the village altogether.[113]

Further, there is much to be done in the way of so-called internation-
alist education, that is, obligation toward class brethren and allies in
the other socialist countries. This kind of education, within a relatively hostile climate, obviously can be achieved best through informal
communications by non-SED members, just as party members are
effective within their own context (as shown in numerous examples
already discussed in this chapter).

FEEDBACK

        Having found feedback essential for political communications,
both in the theoretical context provided by Marxism/Leninism as well
as the systems-functional point of view, it then becomes necessary
to describe the feedback mechanism available to the GDR political
elites. If the function of feedback were absent, one could hardly
describe the GDR's communications practice either as really "functional" or as Leninist.
        Lenin often stressed that the leading party organs constantly
have to have an exact overview of the work of the basic party units,
as well as the mood and opinion of the workers. Specifically, he said
the party must be able "to precisely ascertain for every question in
any moment the mood of the masses, their real efforts, needs and
thoughts."[114] Or put another way, as seen earlier, he conceived of
the party leadership needing such information in much the same way
that an orchestra director needs information to be able to produce
harmonious sound. In less colorful SED terms, the importance of
feedback in the GDR today is described in this way: "A leadership
which wants to perform good political-ideological work must constantly be informed about what happens in its area of responsibility,

which opinions people have, which problems move them, and how they understand the policies of the Party."[115] Thus the party has organized numerous formal channels through which the desired feedback flows to the party leadership centers.

Formal Feedback Structures

Periodic Reports

The party leadership requires a monthly report from every Basic Party Unit regarding its innerparty life, development of strength, the Party Study Year, and mass political work.[116] The reports are intended to provide the party with an overview of the political activities of members and candidates, the effectiveness of political ideological work, and the mood and opinions of the people. As the party secretary at a Brandenburg high school put it, "The Party leadership wants to know how every Party member assesses his own political work with students, with the FDJ, in the Parents 'Aktiv,' etc., how he sees the effectiveness of the membership meeting, indeed, the entire Party organization."[117] This obviously covers a wide spectrum when one considers that every fourth adult GDR citizen is voluntarily active. For instance, 500 are active as representatives to the Volkskammer, 2,838 as deputies to the Bezirk assemblies, 190,895 in the local people's representative bodies, 335,000 in the committees and work groups of the National Front, 434,000 in permanent production consultation within enterprises, 660,310 in parent consultative councils and class groups of the schools, 177,100 in the ABI (Worker and Farmer Inspection), 254,941 in conflict and arbitration commissions, 50,194 as jurists (Schöffen), and 300,000 as members of consultative councils to HO (state shops) or sales committees of the consumer collectives (Konsumgenossenschaften).[118]

The monthly report, prepared on a standard form, is passed up from the Basic Party Unit to the Kreis leadership (or over the APO and BPO, if these units exist). The information includes answers to these questions: (1) What problems were taken care of in the leadership meetings and what resolutions were passed? (2) What was discussed in the membership meetings? (3) What questions and problems came up in the Party Study Year? (4) What moods and opinions concerning the party's policies exist in the area for which the Basic Party Unit is responsible? (5) What indicators, suggestions, and criticisms exist? In addition to these standard questions, statistics also are requested concerning the number of participants at the membership meetings and the Party Study Year. From an LPG (agricultural cooperative), for instance, the written monthly report takes this form: "On three to six hectographed pages the collective membership is informed about the status of plan-fulfillment and the performance of brigades is compared. Exemplary work is praised, the achievement of specialist or master's credentials is honored, shortages critically illuminated."[119]

The party further makes clear that not only its various units and leaders are to concentrate on such feedback information, but that the agitators and propagandists have a special responsibility to do so. A member of the party leadership in a VEB tool factory in Königsee summed up this viewpoint:

> The agitator surely does not wait for questions. Above all in conversation he daily seeks to be able to relate to questions and problems of people. Therefore he constantly needs much information. Thus for me the meetings of agitators are important, not only because of the guidance but rather because we can mutually counsel and inform ourselves.
>
> The feedback of opinions and arguments which the agitators have encountered is also very important for the Party leadership. I consider that a necessary condition so that the Party leadership can more exactly assess and influence the ideological problems in the enterprise.[120]

Other party group leaders emphasize that agitators need to report on their work with nonparty, as well as party members. This, says a party leader, "demands also the continuous feedback (Ruckinformation) about opinions, suggestions, and instructions to the party group organizer."[121] How the feedback is to be handled in the specific case of agitators was dealt with at length in the initial issue of Was und Wie, the Central Committee's special magazine for agitators and propagandists. The party secretary in a machine works in Ilsenburg reported that

> our Party leadership places great worth on learning how the people think, what they talk about. Point 1 for every leadership meeting is the information report. Similarly, point 1 for every agitator is information to the Party leadership concerning which problems were discussed, what suggestions were made, which questions were explained, which could not be answered adequately, to which specialists, for instance in foreign policy questions, one must give answers quickly, which directors are immedi-

ately responsible for changes concerning criticized work
and living conditions. The agitators give us this information in writing or orally.

These reports from the agitators then are evaluated by the central
party leadership and sorted according to responsibilities, for instance
the BGL, the FDJ, etc. But if the reports show that problems are
not being solved within the work collectives and perhaps cannot be
solved through delegation, the party then helps its agitators. It does
this by working out written argumentation with relevant background
material. [122]
    If such required lower-level reports are not forthcoming,
apparently the Kreis leadership has difficulty with the monthly assessment of party life that it, in turn, is expected to prepare. Thus a
Kreis secretary writes firmly, "It also cannot be tolerated if for several months absolutely no membership meeting is held or if the Party
leadership inadequately informs the regional leadership concerning
Party work and its results."[123] With increasing demands being
placed on the Kreis leadership, the reporting of information becomes
crucial. Clearly, information from below is necessary for realistic
estimates of the strength of the Basic Party Units, preparation for
collective decisions, control over implementation of resolutions, as
well as for analytical work. On the other hand, with adequate information it is possible "to take the right measures at the right time,
to recognize obstacles promptly and to correct them, and to deepen
the trust of working people, above all the worker, in the policies of
the Party."[124]

Specifically Requested Reports

    In addition to the standard monthly reports, party units also
have special long-range reports (Auftragsinformation) that they are
requested to turn in.[125] These are basic and multifactor estimates
of specific aspects of the GDR's program of building socialism and
developing consciousness among the workers. For instance, estimates
of the achievement of portions of the five-year plan (such as progress
in rationalization of the economy or in socialist competition) are
included, as well as estimates of the level of political awareness
among special groups, such as workers, farmers, intellectuals,
women, and youth. These themes that are required in the long-range
reports emerge from current party resolutions and the resulting work
plans for each level of party work.

Case-Study Information

Another form of required reporting is case studies (fallweise Information) concerning timely events—initiatives, positive experiences, opinion concerning political events. [126] Here the element of timeliness is crucial, and the reports are to be sent through channels immediately.

Initial Mood and Opinion Reports

Of special significance for the party leadership are reports that assess people's immediate reactions to political events. [127] These are called "first voices and opinions" (erste Stimmen und Meinungen) reports. Many Basic Party Units have the principle that members of the various party groups and the APO leadership at once go out to talk with workers in their area about political happenings and then give the party leadership the information they have gathered regarding the reactions. Differentiated opinion reports are not expected in this form of reporting; rather, rapid information is sought so that the party leadership can react quickly.

An example of how this works comes from a BPO leadership unit that says it has as the Number-one item on its meeting agendas the preparation of a "thorough estimate of the situation, the mood and opinions in the entreprise." This feedback information is organized through participation in the information support centers (Informationsstützpunken) of the enterprise. There leaders from enterprise and party members from state units are given the question for which the party leadership wants immediate answers in order to assess the situation in a given enterprise. [128]

"Consciousness Analyses"

For the more differentiated, basic assessment of the political mood of the people, the party leadership requires a regular "consciousness analysis." [129] The point here is to stress trends related to party resolutions, as well as general attitudes. Therefore, the reporting is broken into estimates concerning various classes and groups and individual areas and collectives of a firm or agricultural cooperative. The reports contain assessments of questions such as (1) What do the workers think of the policies of the party? Which questions are understood and where is there still unclearness? (2) Which supportive and inhibitive factors appear in the development of the socialist consciousness and what are the reasons? (3) Which means and methods of political educational work have proved to be especially effective in explaining the party's policies?

Clearly the point here is not only to determine basic attitudes and opinions regarding the important political questions of the day and the resolutions of the party, but to find ways to improve the party's educational/persuasive work. In order to keep the reports from becoming too tangential, the reporters are asked to limit their assessments to aspects related specifically to party resolutions: For instance, "What do the people say about the resolutions? And how do they translate the party's policies through their own behavior and attitudes?" In short, realities, not possibilities, are stressed. Admittedly, preparation of such reports is not easy for the party leadership, for it is difficult to coordinate information regarding opinions, behavior, and attitudes, which are locally influenced, with the resolutions of the party. But, as the party says, "Whoever wants to win people over to social participation must stimulate their understanding, awake their interests, satisfy their need for information, and simultaneously seek their advice!" (emphasis added).[130]

Group Discussions and Meetings

According to the party, group discussion of specific topics is the best method for gaining solid information quickly about the mood and opinion of workers.[131] In a relatively short time a large portion of the workers' opinions can be tapped. Further, such groups can be organized according to social or age factors, and thus be sampled rather effectively. Finally, if the discussion group is so arranged that it represents a good cross-cut of the workers, a relatively sound statistical assessment of mood and opinion can be gained.

But it is not always possible for the Basic Party Units to organize such specific goal-oriented group discussions. In such cases, on-the-spot meetings can be called, individual conversations can be conducted on the job, etc. For example, many Basic Units have a fixed group of experienced Genossen who are sent onto the assembly lines, for instance, to carry out just such discussions. In other Basic Units, immediate party group meetings are called to brief party members quickly for the political discussions they are to lead on given topics. These members then report back on a daily basis the results of their individual discussions or work brigade meetings.

Further, the party points out, this feedback from its members is especially sought out during membership meetings. Such party meetings should be "open" in the sense that all problems are discussed and that solutions are sought. There party leaders have to permit "all comrades to speak up."[132] To continue to underestimate the role of the membership meetings, and to substitute for them consultation within the basic party groups themselves, could not be permitted even though the necessary confrontations were indeed being carried out in the Basic Party Units and the APOs. The party guideline continues, "It absolutely must be achieved that the Party leadership regularly reports on its own activity to the membership meeting."[133]

A Bezirk party leader put the challenge to the membership meeting rather graphically when he wrote, "Here the 'hot irons' will not be avoided. Questions and criticism are answered concretely."[134] That this apparently takes place is suggested in a report from a departmental party secretary in the research center of a machine tool enterprise in Karl Marx Stadt. He says, "Increasingly an open atmosphere of criticism and self-criticism is developing here. The reality of the meetings was increased, as well as the comrades' willingness to discuss."[135] Another case comes from an LPG party secretary who reported that through membership feedback, in the form of questions addressed to the LPG leader or the party leadership, "public criticism contributed very much toward finding reserves within the brigades and overcoming shortages."[136] A feedback problem, however, seems to remain with the LPGs. There, according to a party secretary, party members too often confine their attempts at soliciting feedback to purely economic questions. Rather, political questions, too, need to be discussed and political reactions sought.[137]

Nevertheless, the party leadership at all levels is especially concerned with increasing the feedback concerning economic issues—after all, it was clearly said that the central point in political communications work was to strengthen the position of the GDR by increasing work production. Thus, a party leader in a coal mine enterprise belonging to a big gas kombinat reported that the working out of a clear political conception by the party leadership was made possible through consultation with all party members at membership meetings and in personal conversations. Innerparty democracy in action was seen in that "comrades present numerous suggestions for mastering the goals and properly allocating comrades. These were taken up by the leadership. So, with the help of all comrades, the basic organization worked out a uniform standpoint."[138]

Statistical Analyses

The party also requests from its various units statistical material and analyses of enterprises that can be used as sources for overall assessments of political work and development of political consciousness.[139] Statistics, for instance, concerning absenteeism, quality control, plan fulfillment, etc., are useful in this respect.

Reports of State and Mass Organizations

The party leadership of the Basic Party Units are requested in their assessments to make use of information to which they have access from the trade unions, the youth organizations, mass organizations, and state leadership.[140] This gives them a broad and important source of information necessary for judging the social development and thinking of the people in their area of operation.

Workers' Petitions and Suggestions

To supply the party with additional feedback, its leaders are required constantly to assess suggestions and criticisms from the workers.[141] These, too, provide an overview of "what is with" the workers, so to say. Further, if such communications from the workers find a positive reaction, they, in turn, will come to party members and leadership with more personal problems and questions. That, in turn, means the party has a better idea of public moods, can deal better with troublesome problems, and can increase its trust among the people by doing so.

Party Elections

Party elections play a role in feedback in that, for instance, SED members in 1973 were encouraged to articulate criticism at local levels. They were called upon to draw a balance, through "free articulation to test what we have achieved in fulfilling the resolutions of the VIII Party Congress."[142] The personal contribution of "every comrade and comradess to accomplishment" should be evaluated and resulting "conclusions drawn for future work." The point was repeatedly made that the criticism should concern how local-level leadership carried out the resolutions of the leadership (not the top-level decisions themselves). Thus, the election meetings were a big public opinion poll regarding the political and ideological niveau of the total party, a kind of reliability test. Further, party organizations were called upon during the election campaign to give accountability of how individual party members politically participated and how they "carry out daily conversations with nonparty workers in work and residential collectives, how they disseminate our socialist convictions and react patiently, empathetically, and simultaneously, consequently, to all questions."[143]

<u>Mass Media</u>

As already suggested, the party relies heavily on the mass media to help fulfill not only its interest aggregation function, but feedback as well. In the Politburo resolution regarding the intensification of agitation and propaganda, for instance, it was said that "Of primary significance is that the workers themselves, with their ideas, suggestions, stimulus, experiences, and critical directions increasingly have their say in press, radio, and television, and that the mass media thereby make better use of their function as tribune of socialist democracy." And in the Agitation and Propaganda Conference that followed, Secretary Lamberz named specifically those who "should themselves speak—workers, collective farmers, members of the intelligentsia, women, and youth." Further, they were to be encouraged to do three things: "share their experiences, articulate their suggestions, and give their critical instructions."[144] Examples of how this feedback function is operating in the mass media since the VIII Party Congress include:

1. <u>Petitions</u>: Five years ago the <u>Lausitzer Rundschau</u> formed Reader Advisory Councils (<u>Leserbeiräte</u>). They have taken over the petitions from citizens, which formerly the editors were expected to take care of. This is not a small task, for the number of such petitions increased from 29 in 1967 to 52 in 1972. They usually concern complaints about conditions in enterprises and local governmental offices. One council member reported that it at first was difficult to achieve a positive answer to such petitions. Now, however, public officials know him and he says, "I know of no recent example where I was not accorded the necessary respect."[145]

2. <u>Roundtable Discussions</u>: Some years ago when the Alexplatz was being built in Berlin, the newspaper <u>BZ Am Abend</u> began a new forum in which the goals and progress of the construction project were reported. Now the forum usually appears monthly, taking up entire page 3 for the discussion of a specific theme. For instance, when the topic, "The Berliner and his Postal Service" was discussed, letters were invited from readers. The journalists then gave the Post Office the possibility to answer the criticisms.[146]

3. <u>Community Actions</u>: To further the party's goal of more public information concerning local governmental affairs, the <u>Ostsee Zeitung</u> in Rostock began a community action called "Journalists Question Delegates." Problems of local government were the point of discussion between the journalists and city officials—such as vacation and medical services, the work of the Community Organizations (<u>Gemeindeverbandes</u>), etc. High points of the discussion were then published in the newspaper. Local officials also were invited to contribute articles and readers to send in questions.[147]

4. Solicited Letters: Sometimes the newspapers deliberately solicit letters from readers on a specific topic. This was the case with the Magdeburg Volksstimme, which wanted to take up the priority problem of cooperation between local journalists and state functionaries. It began the action with the question to readers: "According to your opinion, where would a push be necessary so that resolutions become facts; where do false methods of thinking and behaving inhibit us in further improving life in our city?" With the help of a work team assigned to the City Council to evaluate petitions, it was possible to evaluate the more than 300 letters that were received. One common complaint came from readers in the Heumarkt section of the city—they had to go long distances to buy meat. The newspaper then ran a comment with which the City Council was displeased, despite the fact that a constructive suggestion accompanied the complaint. The problem was finally solved after the newspaper and the party leadership on the city level publicized the problem. Another example was when readers reported to the newspaper that the housing office conducted its relations with the public in a most unfriendly manner. After newspaper comment and report, editors were invited to a City Council meeting. There they defended their criticism, and again city authorities mended their ways. [148]

In Halle, the editors of the Freiheit asked their readers what possibilities existed for improving cultural life. Among the responses was a letter suggesting that a former laundry be turned into a youth club. It was done. [149]

Before the meeting of the City Council, the Ostsee Zeitung in Rostock asked readers to send in their questions and problems concerning the improvement of household and city services. Party and city representatives were asked to cooperate in the newspaper's action by holding forums and consultations with workers and citizens in the various housing areas. Grass roots suggestions were then reported in columns, news reports, or interviews. Some 200 responses were received. Additionally, a "telephone-in" was held shortly before the City Commissioners meeting—more than 70 calls came within two hours, with suggestions for the city council, various commissions, and directors of the major service enterprises. The result was a close cooperation between city officials and journalists. Although the editor reported that there was still a shortage of informational activities concerning city affairs, "the previous situation cannot be compared with the present." [150]

5. "Wish List": The Märkischen Volksstimme monthly circulates a flier called the "Wish List" (Wunschzettel). Sometimes it goes to mayors, sometimes to all institutions that have information centers, sometimes to photo correspondents. The recipients are

asked for certain information that the editors wish, relevant to the party and state resolutions they are trying to implement.[151]

People's Correspondent Movement
(Volkskorrespondentenbewegung, VK)

Another of the structures presently advocated as a means of achieving more relevant political communications and feedback within the mass media is the increased use of the People's Correspondent Movement. This movement is not a new idea. As long ago as 1924 at the first conference of the KPD's (Communist Party of Germany) worker press correspondents, it was emphasized that worker correspondents who reflected the working class were the best connecting link between the newspaper and the working masses. Then in East Germany in 1950, at the first press conference of the SED's party leadership, the significance of the VK movement again was emphasized, albeit with the criticism that the proportion of workers among the VK was to be significantly increased.

And more recently came the VIII Party Congress—it called for journalists "to further develop the people-related style" of their work and for the workers themselves, with the help of the mass media, to exchange their experiences. These goals, it was felt, could best be achieved by reactivating and intensifying the VK movement.[152] Obviously the aims were to give workers more opportunities to articulate themselves and their group interests and to give the media an idea of what people thought.

Pointing out the successes of such correspondents within the Soviet context, GDR spokesmen conceded that they had tried the movement themselves before; they now advocated that "the role and activities of the people's correspondents should be newly defined for our times."[153]

Since then, some changes are noticeable. The number of VK has greatly increased in (1) the party's central newspaper, Neues Deutschland, (2) the Bezirk party newspapers (72 percent of all editorial offices of these organs say they use VK information for editorial purposes), (3) the enterprise, or plant, papers, (4) trade union papers, and (5) the ADN news agency. In radio some reactivation of the VK movement also is noticeable (the Cottbus station, for example, reports that 19 percent of its news department reporters are VK),[154] but in television it is not quite as possible to use VKs. The development also is slow with illustrated magazines and the weekly press.

In the discussion since the VIII Party Congress, general agreement apparently has been reached on what a VK is and what his major responsibilities within the present situation are. The correspondents are to be seen as partners of journalists, not just helpers:

> People's correspondents are model workers of our
> Republic who, in the name of the working class and its
> Party, usually inform an editorial staff about social
> developments in their area of life and write contributions
> about them. They should for the most part be active in
> the area of material production. The people's corre-
> spondents are constantly guided by their editorial staff.
> They take on assignments and also <u>inform their editors</u>
> <u>about the effectiveness of publication</u> (emphasis added). [155]

He should be an "informer for the editorial staff, an organizer, and
alert, good conscience of the editors." Specifically, he is to be an
active advocate for realization of party guidelines in that he seeks
daily political conversations with workers, answers their questions,
and then feeds the information back to his editorial office. [156] Indeed,
this is the most important role of the People's Reporters, to provide
the mass media, and so the party, with feedback:

> The function of information about effectiveness of news-
> papers or radio is in part not yet even recognized. Many
> editorial staffs apparently have not even tried to tap such
> important information through their people's correspond-
> ents. This matter deserved great attention, because we
> generally know much too little about the effectiveness of
> our work. [157]

For instance, to some newspapers, the VK correspondence as a
source of feedback has become more important than letters from
readers—the VKs usually come up with more general problems,
that is, those bigger than a work collective or an enterprise. [158] For
instance, several years ago readers of the <u>Märkische Volksstimme</u>
in Brandenburg complained of a communitywide problem: While many
cultural events were reported, little was said about the reaction of
citizens to these offerings. The newspaper told its VKs this, since
they met monthly with the editors and supplied most of the information for the local pages. They then were assigned special areas of
cultural activities where they had the best contacts, such as theater,
youth clubs, museums, exhibits, etc., and reported on public
reactions. [159]

But there are problems with the VK movement and fulfillment
of its feedback role. For instance, the <u>Leipziger Volkszeitung</u>
reported that few party organizations support and inform the VKs.
The reason: "Not infrequently the People's Correspondent is a thorn
in the eye of state leaders because he could damage 'the external
lustre' of the enterprise." [160] Another example indicating that VKs

are not exactly the favorite people of an enterprise is found in a small
item entitled, "A Fable" in the journalists' journal: "Once upon a
time a People's Correspondent lived somewhere in the country. And
he had criticized his own enterprise. Thereupon he was ordered to
come before the Director—and he was praised."[161]

Thus, it is not surprising when the Märkische Volksstimme in
Potsdam reports that a problem with VKs is that they report too
positively! As the Potsdam newspaper representative said, "Many
People's Correspondents rely on the 'success report' because they
believe thereby they will avoid trouble." Since that will not do, the
newspaper uses "above all People's Correspondents who have the
necessary backbone to write about these questions. And I believe one
finds this backbone above all when they know that here are comrades
who advise me well."[162] In turn, the Organization of German Journalists (VDJ) said that "the unwritten law for every editorial staff
must be to place themselves protectively in front of all People's
Correspondents who have run into trouble because of justified criticism." Further, the journalists organization, at its May 1973 meeting,
included this "protection" aspect in its official resolutions: Resolution 5 said, in part, "In our society no one may encounter problems
because of justified criticism of conditions which hinder further
development."[163] Not long thereafter the editor of a plant newspaper
substantiated the resolution in an article in the Neue Deutsche Presse:

> I would like to contend that the work of a people's corre-
> spondent calls also for courage. Or one must have almost
> no courage when one writes an article . . . and to five
> major problems of our enterprise expresses one's open
> and honest opinion and puts it up for discussion. Or when
> the worker correspondent . . . writes about questions of
> work discipline in its leadership and states that precisely
> in the effective use of legal work time there still exists a
> great reserve for fulfilling the duties of our firm, in
> order to increase work productivity more than 1 percent
> above the plan, and proves it by example. I do think that
> something like that calls for courage.[164]

Another perhaps less critical problem of the VK movement is
that of recruiting more youthful correspondents. Youth are sought,
working women, collective farm women. This need for "new blood"
is illustrated by the fact that nearly half of the VKs are older than 45
and more than half have spent longer than 10 years in their VK
activities. Naturally if young VKs can be recruited, they are a
natural cadre reserve for journalism.[165] They, too, may have the
courage called for by the newspapers.

Feedback Problems

Obviously the feedback process has many problems.[166] For instance:

1. The party's reaction to workers' petitions and suggestions has been slow: For instance, workers often point out that the party leadership should be more concerned that the instructions and criticism of workers contained in reports, information, and petitions are more quickly taken up and answered.

2. The party leaders often are slow in assessing all the information that pours across their desks. Thus, the party suggests that such an evaluation of the incoming information be undertaken by a collective, rather than left to the party leaders alone. This would help overcome the fact that a one-man operation puts the brakes on a smooth and fast information flow upward as well as downward and thereby hinders lively political-ideological work with people.

3. Some Basic Party Units tend to overload their communications efforts, perhaps in part because of perceived pressure from above. They take the Information Plan provided for them by the Party's Central Committee and add numerous themes. This, suggests the party, should be reconsidered. Further, to cut down on the paper work involved in reporting, preliminary assessments can be made through regular consultation between the Basic Party Units and the party secretaries.

4. The Kreis leadership is faced with reporting gaps. This is a real handicap to the Kreis that is responsible for many Basic Party Units. If it does not receive reports from all of them, and regularly, its own assessments for the next echelon of party administration are inadequate.

5. What the party calls "formalism and bureaucratism" turns up in too many reports. Apparently many Basic Party Units still rely on a "plus and minus" point system for evaluating membership meetings, the Party Study Year, and leadership meetings. This gives the party leadership little insight into aspects it needs to understand in order to organize party affairs effectively.

6. Some indications have been noted that not all reporting is as honest as it should be. Apparently the admonition of Lenin that when criticizing one should take into account the fact that the party is surrounded by enemies is used as an excuse to cover up unfavorable factors which should be reported upward through party channels.

SUMMARY AND CONCLUSIONS

Thus it has been seen that political communications in the GDR involves an almost overwhelmingly comprehensive network of channels, both formal and informal. It reaches nearly every citizen, some would say to the point of "overkill," which results in selective inattention.

Especially significant in a "developing nation" context is the influence (and control) of this network in the direction of goal-orientation, specifically socialization of the citizenry into the political culture. Equally as important is the use of the network as a source of interest identification and its role in conditioning the demands and supports fed into the system. An obvious problem here, as noted in the chapter on interest identification and aggregation (Chapter 4), is the continuing dominant role played by the SED in communications vis-a-vis the desire of many GDR citizens for less "guidance" and more trust; they feel they have matured politically sufficiently to be allowed more individual communications expression.

On the output side, it has been shown that political communications are crucial to the making and implementing of political decisions. Rule-making, for example, depends on accurate and relevant information regarding factors involved in a decision (such as attitudes), and rule application calls for information regarding inefficiencies and trouble areas.

Thus, the communications network seems, indeed, to be the "nerves of government," as Deutsch says. That these nerves sometimes are raw and painful in the GDR is clear—complaints from citizens about the stodginess and saturation of the press are not accidental. But at the same time, as suggested in the foregoing pages, efforts apparently are underway to modify this situation.

Perhaps most significant, however, is the picture of feedback that emerges. Contrary to many assumptions, considerable evidence is available that suggests that political communication is not a one-way street in a communist political system. And therein lies the hope of those who champion responsive government and see in feedback the "self-corrective" mechanism of a political system.

NOTES

1. Gabriel A. Almond and G. Bingham Powell, Jr. Comparative Politics (Boston: Little, Brown, 1966), pp. 165-66, 168.
2. Die politische Organisation der sozialistischen Gesellschaft (Berlin: VEB Deutscher Verlag der Wissenschaften, 1973), p. 53.

3. Ibid., p. 54.

4. Walter Lorenz and Karl Gerber, "Die Parteiinformation in den Grundorganisationen," in Der Parteiarbeiter (Berlin: Dietz Verlag, 1972), pp. 7, 12.

5. Die politische Organisation, op. cit., pp. 63, 65.

6. D. Chesnokov, "The Educative Role of the Soviet State," in American and Soviet Society, ed. Paul Hollander (Englewood Cliffs, N.J.: Prentice-Hall, 1969), p. 95.

7. Erich Honecker, Die Vorbereitung und Durchführung der Parteiwahlen (Berlin, 1971), pp. 70 ff.

8. V. I. Lenin, "Letter to a Comrade on Our Organizational Tasks," in Collected Works, 6, p. 250.

9. Lorenz and Gerber, op. cit., p. 8.

10. Alex Inkeles, Social Change in Soviet Russia (Cambridge, Mass.: Harvard University Press, 1968), p. 265.

11. Ibid., p. 276.

12. Karl Marx, "The 18th Brumaire of Louis Bonaparte," Selected Works, Vol. I (Moscow: Foreign Languages Publishing House, 1962), p. 250.

13. V. I. Lenin, "Preliminary Draft of the Resolution of the Tenth Congress of the Russian Communist Party on Party Unity," Selected Works, Vol. 3 (Moscow: Foreign Languages Publishing House, 1961), pp. 627-28.

14. Lucien W. Pye, ed., Communications and Political Development (Princeton, N.J.: Princeton University Press, 1963), pp. 6-7.

15. Ibid.

16. Almond and Powell, op. cit., p. 168.

17. Karl Deutsch, The Nerves of Government (New York: The Free Press, 1966), p. 88.

18. Ibid., pp. 186-87, 191.

19. Gesetzblatt I, No. 10 (May 12, 1970): 39.

20. "Für eine wirksame kommanalpolitische Offentlichkeits-arbeit-Thesen," Beilage Sozialistische Demokratie, No. 32, 1970.

21. Rechenschaftsbericht des Zentralkomitees der KPdSU an den XXIV. Parteitag der Kommunistischen Partei der Sowjetunion. Referant: L. I. Breshnew, March 30, 1971, Moscow/Berlin 1971, pp. 122-23.

22. Karla Poerschka, "Uber Character und Aufgaben des sozialistischen Offentlichkeitsarbeit," Deutsche Zeitschrift für Philosophie, 3/1972, pp. 284-99.

23. Bericht des Zentralkomitees an den VIII. Parteitag der SED (Berlin: Dietz Verlag, 1972), pp. 93 ff.

24. Neuer Weg, 14/1972, p. 635.

25. Agitation und Propaganda nach dem VIII. Parteitag der SED (Berlin: Dietz Verlag, 1972), pp. 65-90.

26. Ibid., pp. 49-53.

27. Ibid., pp. 41-42.

28. Einheit, 3/1973, pp. 308-16.

29. Lorenz and Gerber, op. cit., p. 15.

30. Was und Wie, 1/1973, p. 3.

31. Lorenz and Gerber, op. cit., p. 19.

32. Neuer Weg, 22/1973, p. 1013.

33. Neuer Weg, 16/1974, pp. 721-26.

34. Neuer Weg, 8/1974, pp. 359-62.

35. Einheit, 10/1973, pp. 1189-96.

36. Sozialistische Demokratie, 47/1972, p. 5.

37. Was und Wie, 1/1973, pp. 8-9.

38. Ibid., pp. 17-18.

39. Neuer Weg, 1/1973, pp. 10-11.

40. Neuer Weg, 11/1973, pp. 517-18.

41. Was und Wie, 1/1973, p. 10.

42. Neuer Weg, 9/1973, p. 400.

43. Neuer Weg, 3/1973, pp. 132-35.

44. Einheit, 10/1973.

45. Agitation und Propaganda, op. cit., p. 56.

46. Ibid., pp. 56-57.

47. Neuer Weg, 2/1973, pp. 83-84.

48. Was und Wie, 2/1973, pp. 23-24.

49. Neuer Weg, 2/1973, p. 69.

50. Einheit, 3/1973, p. 313.

51. Neuer Weg, 6/1973, pp. 260-62.

52. Neuer Weg, 12/1973, pp. 546-47.

53. Neuer Weg, 1/1973, p. 14.

54. Neuer Weg, 4/1973, p. 158.

55. Neuer Weg, 2/1973, pp. 55 ff.

56. Neuer Weg, 10/1973, p. 472.

57. Neuer Weg, 5/1973, pp. 203-05.

58. Neuer Weg, 16/1973, p. 758.

59. Die Kommission Agitation und Propaganda (Berlin: Verlag Tribüne, 1973).

60. Die Wirtschaft, 50/1972, pp. 6-7.

61. Neuer Weg, 8/1974, p. 344.

62. Was und Wie, 1/1973, pp. 25-26.

63. Ibid., p. 35.

64. Neuer Weg, 10/1973, pp. 441, 448-49, 454-58.

65. "Betriebszeitung-Führungsinstrument der Betriebsparteiorganisation," Der Parteiarbeiter (Berlin: Dietz Verlag, 1972).

66. Neue Deutsche Presse, 3/1973, p. 10.

67. Neue Deutsche Presse, 5/1973, pp. 10-11.

68. Neue Deutsche Presse, 3/1973, pp. 8-9.

69. Neue Deutsche Presse, 7/1973, pp. 10-11.

70. Lorenz and Gerber, op. cit., p. 19.

71. Was und Wie, 1/1973, pp. 31-33.

72. Neuer Weg, 9/1973, p. 412.

73. Neuer Weg, 2/1973, p. 70.

74. Neuer Weg, 4/1973, p. 156.

75. Erich Honecker, Bericht des Zentralkomitees an dem VIII Parteitag der SED (Berlin: Dietz Verlag, 1971), p. 100.

76. Neue Deutsche Presse, 19/1974, p. 5.

77. "DDR-Presse," in Fischer Lexikon: Publizistik (Frankfurt: Fischer Lexikon, 1971), pp. 241-45.

78. "Handmaterial für den Parteisekretär," Der Parteiarbeiter (Berlin: Dietz Verlag, 1972), p. 118 ff.

79. Was und Wie, 1/1973, p. 26.

80. Was und Wie, 2/1973, p. 17.

81. "Handmaterial," op. cit.

82. "Direktive des Zentralkomitees der SED für die Durchführung der Parteiwahlen 1973," Neuer Weg, 15/1973, pp. 693-700.

83. Agitation und Propaganda, op. cit., p. 58.

84. Einheit, 3/1973, p. 316.

85. Agitation und Propaganda, op. cit., p. 59.

86. Neuer Weg, 14/1972, p. 632.

87. Neue Deutsche Presse, 4/1972, p. 2.

88. Neue Deutsche Presse, Theorie und Praxis Beilage, 13/1972, p. 1.

89. Neue Deutsche Presse, 4/1972, p. 4.

90. Einheit, 6/1972, pp. 722-24.

91. Neue Deutsche Presse, Theorie und Praxis Beilage, 13/1972, pp. 8-9.

92. Neue Deutsche Presse, 2/1973, p. 4.

93. Neue Deutsche Presse, p. 20.

94. Neue Deutsche Presse, Theorie und Praxis Beilage, 8/1972.

95. Neue Deutsche Presse, 7/1974, pp. 20-21.

96. Einheit, 3/1973, p. 313.

97. Agitation und Propaganda, op. cit., p. 57.

98. Bericht des Zentralkomitees, op. cit., p. 99.

99. "Handmaterial," op. cit., pp. 97-102.

100. Was und Wie, 1/1973, pp. 6-7.

101. Neuer Weg, 1/1973, p. 37.

102. Neuer Weg, 2/1973, p. 63.

103. Otto Ernst, "Das politische Gespräch im Parteilehrjahr," Der Parteiarbeiter (Berlin: Dietz Verlag, 1971).

104. Agitation und Propaganda, op. cit., p. 57.

105. Was und Wie, 2/1973, p. 3.

106. Neuer Weg, 10/1973, pp. 439-42.

107. Neuer Weg, 1/1973, p. 4.

108. Neuer Weg, 16/1973, pp. 748-49.

109. Neuer Weg, 7/1973, p. 300.

110. Was und Wie, 2/1973, p. 9.

111. Rolf Stöckigt, "Co-operation of the SED and the Other Parties of the National Front," German Foreign Policy, 2/1974, p. 183.

112. Ibid., p. 187.

113. Ibid., p. 186.

114. V. I. Lenin, "The Role and Functions of the Trade Unions," in Collected Works, 33, p. 192.

115. Lorenz and Gerber, op. cit., p. 31.

116. Lorenz and Gerber, op. cit., pp. 40-41.

117. Neuer Weg, 1/1973, p. 15.

118. Neuer Weg, 17/1974, p. 793.

119. Neuer Weg, 5/1973, p. 225.

120. Was und Wie, 2/1973, p. 4.

121. Neuer Weg, 2/1973, p. 63.

122. Was und Wie, 1/1973, p. 32.

123. Neuer Weg, 10/1973, p. 454.

124. Lorenz and Gerber, op. cit., p. 54.

125. Ibid., p. 41.

126. Ibid., pp. 41-42.

127. Ibid., p. 42.

128. Neuer Weg, 4/1973, p. 182.

129. Lorenz and Gerber, op. cit., pp. 43-45.

130. Einheit, 3/1973, p. 314.

131. Lorenz and Gerber, op. cit., pp. 46-47.

132. Neuer Weg, 6/1973, p. 273.

133. Neuer Weg, 9/1973, p. 388.

134. Neuer Weg, 11/1973, p. 487.

135. Neuer Weg, 7/1973, p. 326.

136. Neuer Weg, 5/1973, p. 225.

137. Neuer Weg, 7/1973, p. 326.

138. Neuer Weg, 2/1973, p. 78.

139. Lorenz and Gerber, op. cit., p. 48.

140. Ibid., p. 49.

141. Ibid., pp. 49-51.

142. Erich Honecker, "Interview zum Begin der Parteiwahlen 1973/74," Neues Deutschland, November 1, 1973.

143. "Direktiv des Zentralkomitees," op. cit., pp. 694-95.

144. Agitation und Propaganda, op. cit., pp. 60, 84.

145. Neue Deutsche Presse, 7/1973, p. 6.

146. Neue Deutsche Presse, Beilage, 2/1973, pp. 3-4.
147. Neue Deutsche Presse, 3/1973, p. 5.
148. Neue Deutsche Presse, 4/1973, p. 11.
149. Neue Deutsche Presse, 5/1973, p. 7.
150. Neue Deutsche Presse, 1/1973, pp. 22-23.
151. Neue Deutsche Presse, 3/1973, p. 14.
152. Neue Deutsche Presse, Beilage, 12/1973.
153. Neue Deutsche Presse, 14/1972, p. 12.
154. Neue Deutsche Presse, 3/1973, p. 3.
155. Neue Deutsche Presse, Beilage, 12/1973.
156. Neue Deutsche Presse, 3/1973, p. 2.
157. Neue Deutsche Presse, Beilage, 12/1973.
158. Neue Deutsche Presse, 3/1973, p. 3.
159. Neue Deutsche Presse, 5/1973, p. 7.
160. Neue Deutsche Presse, 4/1973, p. 5.
161. Neue Deutsche Presse, 6/1973, p. 3.
162. Neue Deutsche Presse, 3/1973, p. 4.
163. Neue Deutsche Presse, Beilage, 12/1973.
164. Neue Deutsche Presse, 13/1973, p. 2.
165. Neue Deutsche Presse, Beilage, 12/1973.
166. Lorenz and Gerber, op. cit.

9

Politics in the German Democratic Republic is a book that systematically examines the operation of the East German political order.
From this angle, two interrelated theoretical frameworks have been
employed. Marxism/Leninism has supplied a contextual element for
the study of politics in the GDR. While noting the obvious fact that
the teaching and doctrine of "M/L" cannot fit exactly within the contemporary circumstances surrounding development in East Germany,
there is little question that its central propositions are germane to
the study of the GDR. Systems-functional theory has been used in the
analysis as one means of adding a developmental perspective to the
study of politics in East Germany. It views the operation of a political
system in terms of central analytical categories: political culture,
recruitment, leadership selection and training, and interest articulation and aggregation. These, then, can be synthesized as input
functions. In terms of output functions, decision-making/rule-making,
rule application, adjudication and enforcement processes have been
analyzed. As a third analytical element, feedback processes, linking
output with input dynamics via the political communications process,
represent the concluding chapter within the framework of systems-
functional theory. Throughout the discussion, attempts are made to
synthesize the most obvious and relevant aspects of both theories in
terms of their central assumptions that can be applied to an understanding of East German politics. A brief review of how these two
theories highlight key aspects of GDR dynamics follows.

THEORETICAL FRAMEWORK

Marxism/Leninism

The writings of Karl Marx and V. I. Lenin have a general relevance for students of the German Democratic Republic. In the case of Marx, and to a lesser degree Friedrich Engels, the postwar evolution of East Germany falls within the historical and sociological profile that supplies dynamism to his conception of class struggle and revolution. Beginning with the "Anti-Fascist Democratic Order" and temporarily concluding with the most recent epoch, "The Comprehensive Building of Socialism," the evolution of East German politics and social structure falls within the general guidelines traced out by Marx in the middle nineteenth century. At least from the "official" standpoint of the GDR's ruling communist party, the SED, the society has faithfully stayed within the historical guidelines supplied by Marx, and now finds itself confidently moving into a socialist future whose end point is the "classless society," the final developmental phase into which all societies <u>must</u> pass. At the VIII Party Congress of the SED, Erich Honecker summed up the Marxist perspective by confidently assessing the present and future evolution of the GDR:

> With the socialization of the crucial means of production, with the victory of "socialist-production-relationships," a new social and economic foundation for society has been created. The socialist-planned economy has stepped into the place of capitalist anarchy and rivalry. Socialist society in the German Democratic Republic possesses a fundamentally new class structure. Under the leadership of the working class, amiably aligned classes and strata exist within a population which possesses socialist character traits. In the course of socialist development in our Republic, socialist ideology and a new socialist national culture—which has integrated all the humanistic traditions of the German past within it—has become dominant. [1]

Even the most cursory glance at the East German educational system, with its strong emphasis on training in the industrial and scientific areas, leads to the conclusion that Marxist perspectives on training and education (<u>Bildung und Erziehung</u>) of individuals, from the grade school to the university level and beyond, conform with the general outlines of his thinking, albeit within the contemporary

circumstances of modern industrial society. * Though private property
<u>still</u> exists in the GDR, recent measures taken by the SED have almost
extinguished the concept of private economic ownership in the GDR.
Thus, Marx's assertion that a communist society cannot be created
in the absence of a socialist "material" base is being honored in East
Germany. [2]

Lenin's ideological influence has been, if anything, more per-
vasive and intense than that of Karl Marx. From the SED's vantage
point, the systematic application of Lenin's conceptions of political
organization, running from the design of a modern "subject-participatory political culture," through the recruitment, selection, and
training processes, and ending perhaps most impressively with the
definition of mass media functions in a socialist society, permeate
the GDR. In terms of SED perceptions of political responsibility and
revolutionary political role, Lenin's early propositions about elite
political organization expresses the "vanguard" position of the SED
with special clarity:

> I assert: (1) that no revolutionary movement can endure
> without a stable organization of leaders maintaining con-
> tinuity; (2) that the broader the popular mass drawn
> spontaneously into the struggle, which forms the basis
> of the movement and participates in it, the more urgent
> the need for such an organization, and the more solid
> this organization must be (for it is much easier for all
> sorts of demagogues to side-track the more backward
> sections of the masses); (3) that such an organization
> must consist chiefly of people professionally engaged in
> revolutionary activity. [3]

Not surprisingly, the attempt to synthesize Marxism/Leninism
within the brief developmental experience of the GDR easily leads to
the critical observation that "pure" ideological doctrine cannot be
relevantly applied to the operative realities at work within a communist political system. The most usual form of observation, in this
vein, tends to suggest that communist elites most generally, and the
SED particularly, turn their backs on the teachings of their spiritual
fathers once the reins of state power have been placed in their hands.
These concerns, while valid, miss the point, however. At least
within the German Democratic Republic, the application of Marxism/
Leninism is not to be understood as a hopeless attempt to apply

---

* This is an evaluative observation, since some Marxists would
argue the opposite.

strictly ideological categories to contemporary dynamics in the GDR, but in terms of the justified effort to provide insight into some of the more general political motives underlying SED behavior over time. From this vantage point, there is every reason to believe that East German political culture, especially its tightly organized socialization process (see Chapter 2), recruitment, selection, training processes (see Chapter 3), and a host of other processes, bear a strong resemblance to many of the teachings of Marx and Lenin. If a strict, and therefore naive, application of Marxism/Leninism to the GDR does not recommend itself, a greater error would be made if the "internationalization" of "M/L" categories within the leadership and mass population were ignored. [4]

Functional

As Chapter 1 has already explained, the application of a systems-functional framework to the study of East German politics lends itself because it represents an effective means of isolating, and later synthesizing, the most important dynamics at work in the GDR polity. Reflecting a broader tradition of inquiry that rejects relatively static conceptions of politics in communist societies, the systems-functional framework implicitly rejects the "totalitarian" model of political development that has, until recently, been applied to the GDR. Without denying that the SED exercises monolithic authority within East German society, persuasive bodies of evidence, presented in systems-functional terms, suggest the existence of dynamic conflict within various subsystems of the political order. In general terms the systematic application of systems-functional categories to the GDR has resulted in the following division of analytical attention: [5]

1. Inputs—examined in terms of demands, supports, and apathy. Seen from the contexts supplied by political culture, elite recruitment, selection, training, and interest articulation and aggregation (Chapters 2-4, respectively), demands emanate from the political culture and "are transmitted through communications"; supports flow immediately from the articulation and aggregation processes, while apathy may be seen as continuing resistance to earlier socialization training and its emphasis on acting involvement.

2. Outputs—all political systems must be able to respond to inputs generating from the several input agencies. They do so in terms of decisions that reward and deprive various individuals or groups. Rewards are seen in the action and behavior of decision-making/rule-making agencies, as for example when the East German state grants "specific benefits to generate specific support" from

selected public clienteles. Recent sociopolitical measures of the
Honecker regime represent one significant attempt by the SED to
build diffuse support for itself by opting for "outputs" directed at
workers, employed women, and retired individuals.[6] Deprivations,
alternatively, may be perceived by intellectuals and others not bene-
fitting from a decision. Rule-adjudication and -enforcement agencies
in the GDR also play crucial roles in the reward/deprivation context,
as mirrored in the behavior of courts, judicial, police, and rehabilitation structures. The early years of East German sociopolitical
development (1945-61) witnessed frequent applications of coercion
against resistant members of society, especially groups within the
peasantry and bourgeoisie who were deprived of their traditional
positions of status and power in East German society by the SED.[7]
As the party gradually began to institutionalize its rule in the GDR,
however, applications of coercive rule have become increasingly
rare. As already noted in the Introduction to Part II, the SED has
opted for the employment of other means, such as the effective
employment of mass media propaganda and general information, to
secure compliance and support (see Chapter 7).

> . . . Reliance primarily on coercion as an output is an
> expensive proposition for a political system, more
> costly than, for instance, a national television address
> by political leaders who persuade citizens to accept and
> obey a decision for reasons of national interest. The
> ultimate aim is to turn "power" into "authority," that
> is, to gain the public acceptance which legitimizes a
> system and makes loyalty and obedience voluntary.
> Thus, in the case of the communist political systems
> of Eastern (including the GDR) Europe one in recent
> years has seen an increased reliance on persuasion and
> other forms of output.[8]

     3. Feedback—invaluable to political leaders in measuring the
impact of outputs on the mass population. Within the GDR this
dominantly involves the operation of the mass media, or formal communications structure, and the party's own communications system.
Running the gamut from party resolutions to informal communications
processes (political conversations and the function performed by
agitators), the extensiveness of interparty communications underlines
the degree to which the SED attempts to get its various messages
across to the population on the daily level. Similarly, feedback
processes logically involve communication structures through which
the regime taps public opinion in an effort to determine the degree
to which the party line is being selectively accepted or rejected by

the population. From the vantage point of systems-functional analysis, feedback processes are crucial in the regulation of relations between input and output processes. "Thus, feedback enables a political system to correct its behavior."[9]

Synthesis

The test of an analytical framework lies in its ability to provide intelligent descriptions and explanations of complex bodies of phenomena. The application of Marxism/Leninism and systems-functional theory should logically meet this intellectual requirement. Assumedly, normal reading of preceding chapters, especially their introductions and conclusions, has resulted in a general understanding of how various phenomena, such as political culture, relate to the operation of other processes—rule making and rule application, for instance. In the following pages, some crucial interrelationships existing between different processes will be drawn out for examination. While all possible combinations and permutations cannot be pulled to the analytical surface, some of the following commonalities clearly deserve attention.

Political Culture

Seen as a complex synthesis of basic political philosophies (Marxism/Leninism), systematic doctrines, traditional attitudes toward authority, and learning experiences taken from the political socialization process, the GDR's political culture provides a foundation upon which the political order has been developed from 1945 to the present. No one function on the input, output, or feedback side is inherently "more" or "less" important than another, given the obvious reality that all functions must be performed by a system in order for it to effectively cope with problems of stress. Nonetheless, political culture comes first.

Because political culture literally conditions the exercise of public authority in the GDR, giving it daily and long-term meaning, the relationship between it and the recruitment, leadership selection, and training process is strong. Thus, the political culture provides an overarching rationale for the functioning of the recruitment process into the SED. Leninism, with its conception of the revolutionary "vanguard" party, and Marx, with his belief in the historical role of the organized working class, are consequently taken from their doctrinal contexts and concretely applied to the operation of recruitment. When the party undertakes to train a special corps of activist elites, cadres, and propagandists, the linkage between political culture and selection becomes obvious as recruits are strongly encouraged "to acquire deeper insights into Marxist/Leninist theory so that they will be able to convincingly explain the scientific foundations—its germane strategies and tactics—to the working people."[10]

Interest articulation and aggregation are directly related to political culture in the GDR if only because the existence of formalized doctrines and values provides a general boundary within which groups—from elite bodies within the SED's Central Committee to broader social groupings—make known their specific demands. Because East Germany's political culture strongly supports the ideal of social equality, for one contemporary example, the Democratic Women's Association (Demokratische Frauenbund Deutschlands) has been able to effectively lobby for policies favoring the progressive emancipation of its members. In the spirit of the Constitutional Article 20, 2, which states that "men and women have equal rights and have the same legal status in all spheres of social, state and personal life. The promotion of women, particularly with regard to vocational qualifications, is a task of society and the state," the DFD has lobbied effectively for a generous system of maternity leave and abortion reform.[11] In light of their less-than-adequate gains within the party and state apparatuses, the continuing underrepresentation of women can be turned into a powerful appeal against political inequality by the invocation of egalitarian demands.

Decision-making/ rule-making dynamics are conditioned by the existence of operative political doctrines, especially those emanating from Lenin's conception of political discussion and "final" decision-making within a vanguard party organization. As the sole holder of what one observer calls "revolutionary legitimacy," the SED is able to apply the doctrines of political leadership, gained principally from Lenin, to the functioning of decision-making/rule-making operations. Hence, the broader cultural concept of "democratic centralism," which allows inferior organs of party and state power to discuss "democratically" general policy questions (abortion, Constitutional revision, production norms in socialized industries, to name some obvious examples) while calling upon them automatically to support the party's final decision, fits into the operation of decision and rule making processes.[12] Indeed, the SED legitimizes the monolithic role it has assigned itself here through an invocation of political culture principles!

Rule application and political culture also enjoy a close relationship in the GDR. Perhaps the most obvious manifestation of this interdependence lies in the ability of East German political culture to provide legitimacy to the conduct of administrative matters at all levels of the party and state apparatus. Admittedly, as an earlier

discussion has already noted (see Chapter 5), Marx's relative neglect
of bureaucratic issues in his analysis of future communist society
has contributed to a certain uneasiness in "M/L" elaborations on the
tasks and responsibilities of the "Socialist State."[13] This "special
apparatus," as Lenin referred to the fledgling Soviety bureaucracy,
continues to perform its routine and complex tasks under the watchful
eye of the SED, yet it would be absurd to suggest that a "withering
away" of the state—a cardinal assumption of Marx—is observable in
the GDR. Until that unlikely event occurs, the rule-application function is provided historical legitimation by East Germany's political
culture in terms of the party's ability to "chart" and "plan" the future
direction of the GDR en route to a communist society.

The building of political authority in East Germany has been
achieved in large degree. In this general sense, one might now be
able to argue that most elements of East German political culture
have been "internalized" within the population. As has been discussed,
this means that the SED is increasingly committed to the task of
eliciting spontaneous compliance to its demands. Since the GDR's
political culture has not been completely accepted by some elements
of the broad population, however, rule-enforcement procedures are
necessary. Thus, formalized rules mirroring coercive power (Constitutions, Work Law Codes, etc.) are combined with the activities
of courts, judges, jurors, and police forces in the defense of East
German political culture. "Love the GDR," one cardinal doctrine
of political culture in East Germany, is given coercive definition in
the practical application of "socialist legality" that

> articulates anew the growing role of socialist law and the
> necessity for the steady solidification of socialist legality.
> In the Rule of Conduct, Paragraph 2, Section 6, the strict
> standard of socialist legality, the maintenance of order
> and security, and the increase of state discipline are made
> a firm ingredient of state leadership at all levels.[14]

In linking coercive with persuasive power—the application of education
and normative structures—the regime undoubtedly wants to eliminate
the need to employ coercive measures in defense of East German
political culture. But until that time arrives, rule-enforcement procedures will continue to be integral parts of the SED's program to
safeguard its "revolutionary achievements."

Political culture and communication mutually interact with and
influence each other. Probably no other linkage within the East German
political system is so intimate or dynamic. From the communications,
or feedback, side the relevance of this dynamic in the strengthening
of socialist political culture is obvious. Seen within the context of

party activities in the broader society, the Soviet viewpoint has been
applied to the GDR as reflected in this observation on party responsibilities "to strengthen the overall ideological work and above all to
propagate more actively and resolutely the communist ideals and the
concrete tasks of our development. . . . Our chief tasks in this
respect are to really understand how to communicate to the broad
working masses the entire strength of our ideological convictions and
how to correctly and really creatively approach the communist education of the Soviet people."[15]

Staying within this communications emphasis, it is equally clear
that feedback processes, as reflected in the GDR's mass media, constantly raise issues and questions touching on the definition and reinforcement of political culture values and doctrines. Each time a
television program devotes attention to a recent SED plenum, on every
occasion when factory newspapers call for increased industrial and
agricultural output in order to contribute "to the many-sided strengthening of the GDR," the impact of communications processes on political culture is evident. Because the party cannot be sure that its definition of political culture is getting through to the population, a dynamic
system of elite-mass contact is put into operation. On the one hand,
communication structures (party resolutions, Central Committee information) are linked up with informal activities carried on by agents
of the party on all levels of social organization (agitators and propagandists). On the other hand, formal structures take the daily pulse
of East German society—group discussions and meetings, public
opinion surveys, party elections, etc.—in attempting to determine
whether the communication process's elaboration of political culture
is finding positive resonance within the population.

Shifting emphasis to the side of political culture and its impact
on communications behavior, one should not lose sight of the obvious
point that the general nature of feedback activity in the GDR, mirrored
in the operation of its mass media, is provided "instant" and "unassail-
able" ideological legitimacy by the existence of a Marxist/Leninist
political culture. "Partiality" (Parteilichkeit) in the handling of
domestic and international affairs is correspondingly legitimized in
terms of broader scientific-historical perspectives that "explain" and
"justify" the active role of the SED in the design and presentation of
public events. Typing the cultural activities of the SED into the mass
communications process, the use of the mass media as agents of
persuasion and education is provided the following obligation during
the "transitional" phase of development in which the GDR currently
finds itself

. . . For the Marxist/Leninist party, realization of its
leading role means persuading the working masses of the
correctness of the Party's policies, to lead the masses

to the Party's position and to the level of consciousness
of Party members and candidates, and to directly include
the masses in the struggle to achieve the historic mission
of the working class. Therefore, the method of persuasion
is one of the most important for leading the masses through
the Party.[16]

In summation, one can easily conclude that the dynamics of political
culture and the operation of feedback processes mutually influence,
as well as expand the range of, each other within the GDR.

Recruitment, Leadership Selection, Training, and Interest Articulation and Aggregation

These four functions are integrally linked with each other. In
the first place, input functions performed in the recruitment, selection,
and training processes carry over into the articulation and aggregation
areas in the sense that party leaders oversee, and participate in, the
routine conduct of interest group activity. Secondly the leadership
structures of official/bureaucratic, intellectual and broad social
groups are permeated with individuals and groups who have undergone
recruitment, selection, and training experiences within various levels
of the SED. As already touched upon (see Chapter 3), the reality of
elite "cooptation" in East German society tends to reflect a broader
pattern of institutionalized recruitment (in-house selection) within
all communist systems.[17]

Decision-Making/Rule-Making and Rule Application

These functions are related to each other in a pattern of organizational hierarchy that posits a leading influence for the party in all
interrelated phases of the three-part process. Thus, the SED defines
and articulates general policy directions for East German society,
especially through the mechanism of Party Congresses and plenums,
while the "socialist state" is given the responsibility of concretely
applying these directives in the daily administration of governmental
tasks. As in all communist political systems, the dichotomization of
authority and competence within both organizations is extremely
difficult to make for the obvious reason that elite groupings within
the SED are simultaneously present within leading branches of the
state apparatus. This consideration applies with special relevance
to the relationship between the Politburo and its Secretariat, on the
one hand, and the Minister Council, on the other.[18] Moving out from
the political center in Berlin, parallel and overlapping membership
groupings are reflected at all levels, from the District to the communal
division.

Rule Adjudication and Enforcement and Political Communication

These functions symbolize an especially important network of
interrelationships within East Germany's political system. In the
first place, the establishment of a "socialist" concept of law is
crucially dependent upon the ability of the SED to mobilize communications media in support of party conceptions of social justice,
equality, and deviance. Admittedly this consideration easily cuts
across different kinds of political orders, and within the communist
systems themselves the party's control of the mass media is an
established fact of life. In the GDR, however, there is little question
that the party is perhaps even more dedicated to the conception of
its "leading role" within the communications media, given the existence of a competitive German society to its west that has, until
recently, persistently challenged the right of the SED to speak for
17 million East Germans. In terms of rule-adjudication and -enforce-
ment considerations, this means that the regime must be especially
dedicated to the task of clearly defining what it wants coercive and
persuasive agencies to do. Building a "new society" within East
Germany has consequently involved legal entities, such as courts,
in the task of clearly delineating the manner in which GDR's legal
norms and values are different from, and antagonistic to, those of
the all-German past and the FRG. From this vantage point, communications media play an important role in articulating how socialist
values and norms are reflected in the progressive development of
East Germany into a socialist society. Secondly, one cannot lose
sight of important contributions made by the media in their ability,
and obligation, to underline and explain relevant questions surrounding
the development of an operative legal framework for the society. To
choose one of a number of examples, legal education (Rechtspropaganda) is regularly communicated to various segments of the public
by the mass media as seen in television programs involved with
problems of socialist administration of justice and legality. [19]
Moving beyond a discussion of specific kinds of relationships,
it should be clear that East Germany's political system is characterized by the existence of two important dynamics. In the first place,
an application of systems-functional analytical categories to the GDR
strongly suggests a growing interdependence of combined input, output, and feedback processes. From this vantage point, the "key"
role is played by feedback. While this observation should not be
taken to mean that East German society is so tightly organized that
breakdowns within one process, say rule application, will immediately be reflected in the behavior of another sector, it is to suggest
that each process cannot be studied in the absence of the others.
Secondly, it should be also obvious that a systems-functional

examination of East German politics appropriately underlines the
degree to which input, output, and feedback processes contribute to
the <u>maintenance</u> and <u>adaptation</u> of the polity as a whole. Seen from
this line of vision, system interdependence contributes to the ability
of East German society to cope with problems of stress. Because
the GDR, like the Federal Republic, is a comparatively new political
system, one cannot make easy predictions about how its regime will
handle future difficulties and challenges. But there is little question
that with gradual internal stabilization has come a growing confidence
that institutionalized methods of conflict control have taken root within
the broad population.

In systems-functional language, East Germany now finds itself
within the "nation-building" phase, the attempt by the SED to engender
feelings of spontaneous "loyalty and commitment" within the mass
population. Having accomplished the initial task of building effective
political authority in East Germany during the Ulbricht era, the party
evidently believes that the GDR must begin moving toward the goal of
nationhood, or some intermediate form of citizenship that effectively
distinguishes it from the Federal Republic. Because the SED is publicly committed to the goal of "separate national development,"[20]
perhaps some observations by a West German source are more
appropriate:

> . . . Apart from generational effects on long-range
> changes in attitudes, one must consider short-term feed-
> back effects. The international recognition of the GDR
> will change attitudes on both sides of the Wall by convinc-
> ing those who may not yet have realized it that the GDR
> is here to stay. Public opinion polls in West Germany
> reveal quite clearly such a short-term feedback effect:
> within the span of three years, the willingness to have
> the GDR recognized as a separate state increased from
> roughly 25 percent to over 60 percent. Ostpolitik, in
> fact, would not have been possible without this change in
> attitudes. Once the resulting political changes have
> taken place—most important here are the treaties with
> various East-Bloc countries—attitudes in this regard will
> become reinforced. Already both states have embarked
> on a program of giving their previously provisional
> capitals a permanent face; other changes of a symbolic
> nature will follow. All of these political and symbolic
> changes rest on changes in attitudes and in turn rein-
> force them. There is no reason to assume why such a
> process should not continue, in the Federal Republic as
> well as in the GDR. The movement towards nation-

statehood seems inevitable; the German Question appears
to have been answered.[21]

CURRENT DEVELOPMENTS

On the international and domestic levels, new events and processes have been set into motion involving the GDR. While this text
cannot avoid the problem posed by the infusion of new facts and dynamics into the analysis, some observations on recent developments
represent an attempt to redress it.

International Relations

East Germany's gradual emergence on the noncommunist diplomatic scene began in the early 1960s, accelerating dramatically in
the late 1960s when Ulbricht launched his diplomatic offensive within
the Third World.[22] With the signing of Four-Power Accords on Berlin
in late 1971, however, the most impressive movement toward complete international acceptance gained final momentum.[23] Especially
in terms of the GDR's longstanding goal of establishing de jure relations with the Western world, the NATO Communiqué of December
1972, authorizing all members to negotiate bilaterally concluding
protocols with East Berlin, appears to be decisive as the following
listing of governments now enjoying relations with East Germany
demonstrates: Australia: 12/22/72, Belgium: 12/27/72, Denmark:
1/12/73, France: 9/2/73, Greece: 5/25/73, Great Britain: 8/2/73,
Iceland: 12/1/73, Italy: 1/18/73, Japan: 5/15/73 non-NATO member,
but militarily aligned with the U.S., Lichtenstein: 6/28/73, Luxembourg: 1/5/73, Netherlands: 1/5/73, Norway: 1/17/73, Portugal:
6/19/74, Sweden: 12/21/72, Spain: 1/11/73, Federal Republic:
3/14/74, United States: 9/4/74.[24]
Other Western systems—some of whom are outside the alliance
framework, while others count themselves within other Western
alliance orders—who have entered into de jure contacts with the GDR
since December 1972 are: Finland: 1/7/73, New Zealand: 5/31/74,
Austria: 12/21/72, Switzerland: 12/20/72.[25] Having established full
diplomatic contacts with 112 governments over the last several years,
only Israel, a very special case,* and Canada stand outside the circle
which originally formed the "diplomatic wave."

---

*The GDR has yet to make restitution to Israel for the crimes
of the Nazi era, arguing that it has already fulfilled its obligations

In view of East Germany's entrance into the world of diplomatic and political respectability, certain elements of its international position should be gone into with some care.

Toward a "European" Identity

East Germany occupies an ambiguous status in East Central Europe. On the one hand, and especially since the spring of 1971, the SED has become the foremost champion of accelerated integration within the Soviet bloc, next to Moscow itself. Having abandoned the goal of making East Germany a "special" member of the Eastern European alliance order, post-Ulbricht SED leadership is now committed to the platform that the GDR is a coequal member of the Soviet bloc. On the other hand, East Germany's direct engagement with the Federal Republic across an entire range of economic-political and social issues has turned the GDR into a "transnational society."[26] By dint of its geographic position, the GDR is forced to be especially responsive to events and trends that flow into its domestic environment from West Germany and West Berlin. In this particular sense, then, East Germany is the most "Westernized" member of the socialist system in Europe. In line with these two realities—integration within the Eastern bloc and sensitivity to the West—the GDR has defined a somewhat unique foreign policy role for itself. One particularly interesting aspect of this role involves the element of multilateral engagement with Western Europe.

In line with its continuous support for various Moscow-sponsored forums dealing with military disengagement in Europe—The Conference on European Security, primarily, and to a lesser degree Mutual Force Reduction (MFR) and Strategic Arms Limitation Talks (SALT)—the SED has clearly had a special interest in the design and future outcome of these partially "linked" discussions. The 12th Plenum of the SED (July 4-5, 1974) laid appropriate emphasis on all three negotiations, albeit in an explicit descending order:

1. Support of policies favorable to a relaxation of international tensions via a successful convening of the European Conference on Security and Cooperation at the highest levels.
2. An expansion of trends leading toward political relaxation via measures favorable to military relaxation, especially in the area of troop and weapon reductions in central Europe.

-----

through massive indemnification payments to the USSR and the People's Republic of Poland.

3. Support for efforts directed toward reducing fears of
   nuclear war, and the development of agreements
   limiting the development of strategic arms.[27]

Regarding this conservative definition of MFR and SALT negotiations, the Politburo explicitly noted its opposition to any future
agreement that would work to the "disadvantage" (Nachteil) of any
state.[28] Some additional observations on the GDR's perception of the
European Security Conference follow.

The German Democratic Republic occupies one of the most
exposed positions within the central European military and strategic
environment. In the event of a conventional or nuclear exchange
between respective alliance organizations, it will be East Berlin that
absorbs the most immediate and frightening damage, a dramatic
change in strategic vulnerability that has traditionally placed Warsaw
in the direct line of military fire. Since the end of World War II it
is the GDR that must bear the brunt of a hypothetical thrust from the
West.

As with Ulbricht in the past, Honecker and the SED have developed two stances on matters relating to East German military security.
First, the GDR now devotes approximately 8 percent of its national
yearly budget to military security matters, including border patrols
and fortifications for East Berlin and the expanse of territory separating itself from the Federal Republic, secret police, and contributions to the Warsaw Pact Organization. At the SED's 10th Plenum
(October 2, 1973) these considerations were given additional representation in the Politburo with the promotion of Heinz Hoffmann,
supreme commander of the East German National People's Army
(NVA).[29] Second, East Germany has attempted to play an active role
in publicizing both phases of the Soviet-sponsored Conference on
European Security and Cooperation (formal title of the European
Security Conference cited above).

From the vantage point of East Berlin, a justified fear that
military tensions could undermine the GDR's sovereignty is combined
with the more focused anxiety that the Federal Republic has yet to
authoritatively renounce "peaceful" boundary changes in the future
within Germany. Thus, while the Soviet Union has used the conference
as a forum for the eventual legitimization of its hegemony in Eastern
Europe generally, the GDR has used the Helsinki gathering as one
additional means of thwarting its perception of an imagined or real
future challenge to its domestic authority on the part of Bonn.

From the East German vantage point, a reduction of military
and political tensions can be underlined in the following manner:

While the GDR does not have a different interest which
would presumably distinguish us from other socialist
states on these matters, we certainly do have a special
interest ["spezielle Interesse"]. This interest stems
from the realization that tensions within Europe invariably and directly affect the domestic situation within the
GDR. In terms of our geographic position and the common border we share with the Federal Republic, which
is also the border separating NATO from the Warsaw
Pact, questions relevant to immediate security . . .
involve us. [30]

Beyond direct participation within the Helsinki forum (Phase
1-2), East Germany has additionally attempted to develop a dialog
with what East Berlin refers to as the "positive neutral" systems that
fall within the GDR's range of geographic and political influence.
Finland, Sweden, and Austria most directly, Switzerland to a lesser
degree, and Denmark even less so given its membership in NATO,
have been the main recipients of attention. While the GDR has not
attempted to present itself as the future leader of a nonaligned bloc
within East Central Europe, it clearly has tried to generate a consensus with these systems on matters relating to military and political
relaxation. One should additionally note that the establishment of
these bilateral and multilateral contacts has been fruitfully employed
by East Berlin in the service of gaining diplomatic attention and subsequent recognition. Further, there is little question that the GDR's
ongoing dialog with "positive neutrals" fits into the broader Soviet
goal of gradually reducing the cohesion of the Western alliance system
in Europe by the support of neutralist sentiment.

A special aspect of the GDR's campaign to carve out a sphere
of influence within which its strategic and military concerns can be
pursued is most obviously reflected in yearly meetings of a North
European forum dealing with an array of regional issues, running
the gamut from military to environmental questions. Held in the
Hanseatic city of Rostock between July 8 and 15, the GDR's sponsorship of "North Sea Weeks" (17 such gatherings including 1974) represents an appropriate occasion for the SED leadership to articulate
its position on matters directly germane to regional security.

Aside from matters relating to military/strategic security for
the GDR, East Germany has also had an enduring interest in developing viable long-term economic relations with the Western European
community. While it already enjoys a privileged status in terms of
existing relations with the EEC, which the GDR has been able to join

as a "de facto" member under the sponsorship of the Federal Republic, East Germany has also been a supporter of economic cooperation between the Soviet-led Council for Mutual Economic Aid (CMEA) and the European Economic Community (EEC). One East German writer has made six general proposals in this area: (1) creation of an all-European infrastructure, especially in the realm of energy sharing and transportation; (2) substantial increases in all-European trade, and a simultaneous decrease in tariff and other "market restrictions" that allegedly discriminate unfairly against the CMEA; (3) long-term cooperative treaties in the field of technology exchange between the two blocs; (4) a common European market research system devoted to the gathering and analysis of data germane to the economic needs of the EEC and CMEA; (5) activation and extension of work done by international organizations <u>within</u> Europe, such as the UN-sponsored Economic Commission for Europe; (6) within a multilateral framework, the lifting of trade restrictions against CMEA products and the establishment of permanent agreements governing the purchase and delivery of industrial products between the two parts of Europe.[31]

In terms of economic and military/strategic issues, it is increasingly obvious—as well as encouraging—that East Germany has every intention of becoming an active member of the European community, viewed from the angles of limited engagement with the West and increased involvement within the Soviet bloc. In the wake of a long-delayed entrance into the world of diplomatic respectability, one might want to measure the degree to which the GDR has been able to move out of its ghetto of political illegitimacy since the appearance of one prophetic observation made in the wake of Honecker's succession to the top of the SED pyramid and the signing of Four-Power Accords:

> Probably the only way for the West to remove insecurity
> in East Berlin is to end the continuous challenges to the
> GDR's sovereignty and to treat it internationally on the
> same basis as the Federal Republic. It can then give
> priority to encouraging participation by East Germans in
> Europe-wide enterprises dealing with the many problems—
> from water pollution to mass tourism and from urban
> blight to technical education for industrial and post-
> industrial societies—with which European countries must
> deal individually in any case but could better cope with
> collectively. Honecker and his associates must be brought
> to see that a wide participation by East Germans in such
> projects will yield the GDR greater benefits and more
> real security than the rigidities, tension, isolation upon
> which it has had to rely so far. Then the skills, talents

and energies which the East Germans possess in no less
degree than their fellow countrymen west of the Elbe can
be enlisted in Europe's cause.[32]

The Dialog with Bonn

The discovery of an alleged East German agent within Willy
Brandt's coterie in the spring of 1974 once again underlines the
uneasy position of the SED in its conception of relations with the Federal Republic. For a regime that has strikingly attempted to cut
itself off from the path of all-German history, at least since the VIII
Congress of the SED, the GDR continues to be deeply involved with
domestic affairs in the Federal Republic. Obviously the paradox is
illusory in the sense that the SED's conception of "separate national
development," or delimitation, cannot be pursued successfully in the
absence of an effective policy for dealing with Bonn that continues to
pursue the goal of reunification via the network of intra-German
accords, put into operation several years ago.

In essence, and much to its discomfort, the GDR has been
forced to enter into a "special" dialog with its larger German neighbor
at the insistence of Moscow. Though the Soviet Union has continuously
demonstrated a degree of calculated indecision regarding the permanent form of its "German policy," swinging from all-German to
explicitly East German emphases, Willy Brandt's coming to power in
the fall of 1969 apparently persuaded Moscow that a new era in relations between the USSR and the FRG was at hand. In return for a
special channel of influence within West German affairs, including
provisions for wide-ranging economic and financial cooperation
between the two governments, the Soviet Union agreed to make East
Germany more cooperative in its dealing with the FRG, intent as it
was and is on multiplying contacts with the GDR. As one analyst
notes, in a content analysis of the East German press up to early
1971, this meant the GDR's grudging "acceptance—primarily in
response to Soviet pressure—of the necessity for modifying its
unbending position toward discussions with the Federal Republic."[33]

In the absence of Soviet prodding there is no evidence to suggest
that the GDR would have undertaken a commitment to expand dramatically the range and intensity of intra-German contacts even in
exchange for recognition by the Federal Republic. Among other considerations, it was established SED doctrine by the middle 1960s that
Bonn would eventually have to draw "the logical conclusion" and
recognize the de jure existence of East Germany. Whether this position took the form of "time works for us!" or the more catchy phrase
employed by some activists at the Erfurt Conference (March 19,
1970) that "with or without Brandt, the GDR will be recognized!"

(Mit oder ohne Brandt, die DDR wird anerkannt!), the East German
position was relatively clear on the matter. Thus, by forcing the SED
to be more flexible and cooperative in meeting Bonn's desire for
increased communication with the GDR, the Soviet Union had simply
pushed the historical process forward by a year or two. While this
interpretation is not the official SED standpoint, tending as it obviously does to define intra-German relations within the framework of
"peaceful coexistence" between societies encompassing two different
and antagonistic political orders, it is nonetheless clear that the East
Germans gained some additional diplomatic mileage and the burden
of carrying an unwanted "new" relationship with the Federal Republic.
Now that East Germany is involved with the FRG on a whole range of
issues, from sports competition to agreements on dispensing of
medical care to the nationals of each society, what will the SED's
policy toward the Federal Republic be in the future? Several dimensions seem significant.

In terms of human contact, the East German position has been
to accept an imposed fait accompli brought about in the wake of the
Four-Power Berlin Accords, the Basic and Transit Treaties. Following in their aftermath, some 10 million visitors from the FRG
and West Berlin had visited the GDR by the summer of 1974. The
SED has employed two obvious strategies in attempting to respond to
this massive influx of visitors. In terms of public officials, the
regime has strictly regulated the degree to which they can come into
contact with visitors. This hardly means an absolute "verbot" of
contact, since a requirement of that severity would be extremely
difficult to enforce, but it does mean that each public official and
his or her family is required to sign a Selfobligation certificate,
which reads in part that "I obligate myself to hold secret all those
facts and reports, coming out of my occupational or social work,
which touch upon the political or economic interests of the GDR and
aligned states. . . . I am aware that a carrier of secrets signifies
a position of great trust being invested in me. Because the socialist
society and state have placed great trust in me, I must justify this
grant of support daily."[34] Regarding contact between normal East
German citizens and visitors from the FRG and West Berlin, the SED
has apparently taken the position that regularized communication
between individuals is, in itself, not dangerous, and in any case cannot be avoided. As Werner Lamberz, minister for agitation within
the Politburo Secretariat, expresses it:

> The relationship between two states is clearly not deter-
> mined by the family relations of individual citizens and the
> length of their visits, but from their reigning social
> orders. . . . Whether Hans of the Heckert-Works in

> Karl Marx Stadt and Fritz von Conti in Hannover visit
> each other does not change power relationships (within
> the GDR) [emphasis added], Hans works within and for
> socialism, while Fritz remains exploited until the day
> the West German working class liberates itself.
>
> [Furthermore] Many of these visitors have become
> acquainted with the reality of our socialist state for the
> first time. As our citizens have shown them their social
> achievements with growing self consciousness and pride,
> West Germans will have to change their reportage about
> the GDR. [35]

While Lamberz is less-than-precise on his definition of "social
achievements," it appears to be the current SED policy—as articulated
at the 12th Plenum—to structure relations between its citizens and
their Western relatives in terms of moral dichotomies, with a corresponding deemphasis on the "economic" superiority of socialism.
Thus, the Politburo report heavily emphasized the necessity of making
the SED, and especially the cadre and propaganda apparatuses, more
sensitive to the role of "political moral categories" that distinguish
West Germany from the GDR:

> In our work, through our general bearing, by the con-
> scious engagement of our citizens with millions of
> visitors from the West, the oppressed majority of the
> capitalist world must be convinced that a fundamental
> change is in prospect for them. For those individuals
> who have spent time with us [from the West], we want
> them to return home with the following commitment:
> From this time onward, I will never again ridicule
> Socialism! [36]

From November 5, 1973 to November 15, 1974, the GDR
attempted to buttress its communications policy toward the FRG and
West Berlin by the imposition of sharp increases in the "minimal
exchange rate" incumbent upon all incoming visitors to East Berlin
and the GDR proper. Pegged at a 1 FRG to 1 GDR mark ratio,
required exchanges were raised from 5 to 10 marks for daily sojourns
in East Berlin, from 10 to 20 marks for 24-hour stays in the GDR.
One West German body of research reports that the impact on visitors
from the West in terms of raw numbers has been impressive. Focusing on the impact of such changes on numbers of West Berlin residents
traveling to the other part of the city or the GDR more generally, the
influx was reportedly cut back by a full 56.9 percent for one-day
sojourns in East Berlin, 31 percent for stays of 24 hours or more

within East Germany.[37] As of November 15, 1974, however, and in line with a growing desire to expand upon its range of economic options in bilateral dealings with the FRG, the East German Finance Ministry decided to roll back the November 1973 exchange hike in order to encourage tourism, on the surface something of an about-face if the official explanation is to be taken at face value. From 20 marks for stays in the GDR, FRG and Berlin residents are now required to exchange 13 West for 13 East marks, and 6.50 for one-day (and beyond) stays in East Berlin.[38]

While the SED has attempted to nullify the FRG's desire to gain a psychological foothold within the consciousness of the East German population via expanding human contacts between the two states, strong momentum is being given to an extension of economic and scientific-technical cooperation with Bonn. Simultaneous with the announcement of a cut in exchange rate requirements governing travel, the East German government made public an agreement signed between its Economic Ministry and representatives of the West German industrial firms of Krupp and Hoechst for the construction of factory installations in the GDR.[39]

By virtue of East Germany's special trading relationship with the Federal Republic, which currently makes up 10 percent of its entire trade portfolio, East German agricultural products are able to reach Common Market countries within the artificially high price mechanism set by Brussels.[40] As a de facto member of the EEC, East Germany has every material incentive to maintain its "special" tie with the Federal Republic despite the countervailing requirements of delimitation ideology. As if this special intra-German link needed to be strengthened by yet another economic advantage for the GDR, Bonn has once again extended a special "drawing credit" (Überzie-hungs-Kredit) to the East Germans that will allow them to purchase approximately 660 million marks from the Federal Republic at interest-free rates.

Perhaps the most complex dimension of East Germany's relations with the Federal Republic turns on the perennial Berlin question. While Honecker will probably not repeat Ulbricht's fatal mistake of being self-destructively inflexible on Berlin issues, there is every reason to believe that the recent uproar over the establishment of a West German "federal" environmental control agency in West Berlin outraged the SED more than it did the Soviet Union. The problem, viewed from this angle, is that Moscow now has a growing commitment to the maintenance of the status quo in both parts of the divided city, even at the potential expense of East German sensibilities that the Western part of the old national capital is being used for blatantly "political" purposes.

Rarely have the differences separating Moscow and East Berlin been articulated with sharper clarity than in a June 10, 1974 interview that Neues Deutschland, the SED daily, gave to the Soviet ambassador to the GDR, M. T. Jefremow. Responding to the leading question, "One often hears in West Berlin that the Soviet side ostensibly ignores events which take place there; are these reports true?" Moscow's representative in East Berlin went out of his way to express complete faith in the intentions of the Western allies and their administration of West Berlin in the "spirit" and "content" of the Four-Power Accords. [41] Instead of supporting the interviewer's indirect contention that the accords were being sabotaged, Jefremow reminded him that since the signing of these agreements in September 1971 the Soviet Union now enjoyed increased cultural and political entry in West Berlin.

West Berlin continues to be the GDR's most challenging security threat. Not only was the Berlin Wall constructed in August 1961 precisely because the outflow of East German citizens had reached flood proportions, but the role of this city in contemporary international history has consistently been a potentially destabilizing one. As one East German administrator was moved to remark when the subject of the Transit Treaties came up, jointly signed by the Four Powers and the GDR-FRG, the existence of an agreement guaranteeing "relatively" free and unhindered use of the autobahns meant that a "large hole had been dug in the GDR."[42] Regarding this last point, the official SED position was outlined with precision in an editorial carried in Neues Deutschland on August 10, 1973:

The GDR, as everyone can see, has done all it can to fulfill the agreement strictly, in accordance with the GDR policy of bringing about a basic and positive change in relations between the GDR and the FRG and the GDR and West Berlin. But at the same time, certain forces are at work which aim at undermining the transit agreement, forces operating in the FRG and West Berlin, those territories whose citizens enjoy the benefits of the agreement. In the recent period the transit agreement, which is applied by the GDR authorities in the word and in the spirit, is being increasingly abused by speculators. Criminal gangs, operating in the FRG and in West Berlin, charging fees of between 40,000 and 80,000 West marks, are misusing the transit routes in order to smuggle people across the frontier—people who dream of a life of luxury in the FRG or West Berlin, or scientists, doctors, and other specialists who even receive, from official quarters, promises of such a life of luxury. [43]

Under these unpleasant circumstances, the article went on to threaten counteraction against alleged official West German support for these efforts, albeit in highly vague terms. Thus, "it must be made clear that the continuing and increasing breaches of the transit agreement will have consequences—and consequences that will not be confined to those who organize such breaches of the law. At the appropriate time the GDR will take all necessary measures to prevent misuse of the transit routes."[44] As of August 9, 1974, East German legal authorities had sentenced 130 individuals to imprisonments running between almost three years and over ten years.[45]

Because West Berlin continues to be the GDR's most important security threat, albeit of a special kind, it is hardly surprising that the Honecker regime has been consistently opposed to even the barest hint of "additional" West German influence in West Berlin. To be fair, the Soviet-East German contention that only "links" can exist between the FRG and West Berlin, while the Bonn government, with varying degrees of public support coming from the Western allies, has argued that "connections" can be maintained, and indeed extended, confuses the matter on both sides. While "links" between the two entities would suggest a narrower vision of a West German presence in West Berlin, "connections" highlight something more ambitious, yet the concepts—by definition—are at best relative to the political and ideological belief systems of the contending parties. In a word, the SED wants Bonn's presence in West Berlin reduced as much as possible, while the FRG has every intention of maintaining, if not extending, the degree of influence it can wield in the noncommunist part of the divided city.

Honecker has implicitly abandoned Ulbricht's strict definition of West Berlin's status as lying directly on the territory of the GDR in favor of a slightly vaguer concept that holds that "West Berlin lies in the middle of the GDR, one hundred miles distant from the Federal Republic of Germany." At the same time, and in language highly reminiscent of the SED position in the middle and late 1960s, the SED chief refers to West Berlin as a "capitalist island, a special creature [Sondergebilde] in the midst of the German Democratic Republic."[46] As long as West Berlin represents a threat to the GDR's concept of sovereignty, there is little reason to assume a softening of the SED's position. In this regard, it may lie in the interests of the Federal Republic to make movements in the direction of calming East German fears over West Berlin, a proposition that certainly was not honored when the Schmidt/Genscher government decided that an environmental ministry should be established there as a demonstration of Bonn's commitment to their part of the divided city.[47]

Cooper and Sieber

On September 4, 1974, the United States and the German Democratic Republic agreed to establish normal de jure relations. From the vantage point of Washington, the relative lag in initiative to close negotiations with the GDR stemmed from a variety of sources. Relations with the Federal Republic and various "last-minute tangles" in the areas of financial compensation for American firms and property seized in the late 1940s, plus the effective lobbying of the American Jewish community (the peak organization being the Conference of Jewish Material Claims Against Germany based in New York), were the most important factors explaining delay. Additionally, the State Department was apparently persuaded that some calculated foot dragging by the U.S. would also make the East Germans more forthcoming in their future dealings with Washington. This strategy neatly complemented the realization that initial housing and general administrative difficulties confronting the already established French and British missions in East Berlin could provide Washington with a good idea of how to deal with similar problems in the future.

From the vantage point of the GDR, relations with the United States represent an important, and perhaps the final, symbolic victory for a regime that has spent its first 25 years as a relative outcast in the West. If the establishment of something close to de jure relations with the FRG meets the immediate strategic and political needs of the GDR, the fact of Washington's final decision to go ahead with concluding negotiations with the GDR signifies the virtual end of East Germany's contested status in central Europe.

Beyond the immediate ramifications of U.S. recognition of the GDR, perhaps the most significant long-range implication for East Germany lies in the realm of intra-German affairs. Having effectively removed itself from paying the barest amount of lip service to the goal of reunification, the Western allies, and principally Washington, have effectively "regionalized" the German equation, with the strong exception of Berlin where Three-Power responsibility for the Western part of the city remains in force. For Honecker and the SED, Washington's recognition of the GDR means a de jure acceptance of Germany's division. Certainly the party could not be happier now that East Germany has been sprung from the framework of Big Power politics, at least in terms of "ultimate" political questions. Regarding bilateral relations between the FRG and the GDR, these recent events mean that an important part of intra-German affairs has been directly transferred into the hands of the two German states. Given the proximity of West Germany, and its continued pursuit of reunification, the SED undoubtedly feels that its authority continues to be threatened, but Washington's decision to send former Senator John Sherman Cooper to East Berlin, and the GDR's establishment of a permanent diplomatic crew in the American capital under the administration of the East German ambassador, and former economist, Rolf Sieber, at least removes one massive obstacle from the GDR's long march toward uncontested sovereignty.

Toward a "Westpolitik"

In the wake of East Germany's entry into the United Nations on September 18, 1973 (the UN's 133rd member), it has become increasingly obvious that the GDR has developed a strategy, if not an articulated policy, of peaceful engagement toward the Western world. As already noted, it has played some part in creating a favorable environment for the convocation of the European Security Conference, given its "special" geopolitical situation within central Europe. Now that recognition has been achieved and the interrelated policy "baskets" representing negotiations on European security (ECSC), MFR, and SALT have been set into positive motion, is there an additional role to be played by East Germany within Western Europe? If the answer is positive, then it must be seen within the broader Soviet perspective on the evolution of political life in various West European societies, and especially within those systems, such as France and Italy and most recently Portugal, that have flourishing Communist parties. [48] Seen from this vantage point, the most important and durable linkage will undoubtedly involve the SED in an extension of bi- and multilateral relations with their counterpart organizations in the West.

Reporting on the outcome of a seven-day visit to the GDR by the head of the French Communist party, Georges Marchais (February 11-18, 1974), the official language of the SED does not obscure the obvious advantages to be gained in the furtherance of such contacts:

> Conversations between Erich Honecker, other members
> of the Politburo and Secretaries of the Central Committee,
> have led to the conclusion that the policies of both Parties
> toward the development of the communist world-movement
> and a more general evaluation of the international situation
> are aligned completely. The importance of the Brussels
> Conference of communist Parties in the capitalist nations
> of Europe was positively assessed as was the necessity
> for a new conference involving communist and worker
> parties in Europe as a whole. [49]

Given the sudden rise of Communist party power in Portugal, and to a lesser degree Greece, there is abundant reason to conclude that the

SED will ambitiously perform its obligation to extend Soviet foreign policy positions within its limited ability to do so. As a final note, however, it also should not be overlooked that the GDR's cultivation of relations with ideologically aligned parties in the West could lead to the infusion of more democratic orientations within the SED. Admittedly this possibility is extremely unlikely given the SED's continued preoccupation with maintaining its authoritative control over East German society. But the remarks of one comrade working for the Italian Communist party daily, Unita, on the occasion of Rome's recognition of the GDR (January 19, 1973) deserve mention:

> Along with other political forces . . . we have been consistently in favor of recognizing the GDR without being complaisant about the manner in which leadership was exercised by communists in Berlin. We are obviously satisfied that a socialist solution has been found within a society moving from a most difficult beginning to a system which has developed a positive answer to many of the important questions facing modern societies in their search for peace and security. The central purpose of the IKP has been to generate an Italian contribution to the goal of security and cooperation in Europe and in this regard recognition of the GDR was a necessary step.

Within this relatively positive context, the newspaper's foreign correspondent, in a separate article, voiced some concern, and guarded hope, in making the observation that the "GDR has yet to resolve the challenge of creatively involving its citizenry in the exercise of public authority, and in this vein, East Germany may learn something in its future dealings with the West."[50] Having experienced the temporary outbreak of democratic politics in Czechoslovakia several years earlier, the SED gives little indication that it is interested in, or can afford, experimentations with a more flexible—less monopolistic and bureaucratic—form of political leadership. In a more limited context, however, there is little question that East Germany has moved away from the isolated stances and perceptions that formerly characterized it. From this vantage point, then, it would not be inappropriate to assume that a limited degree of political flexibility will come from the GDR's new experience of being a transnational society.[51]

Domestic Affairs

Two recent developments are worthy of mention in attempting
to gain a final "domestic" perspective on the GDR. In the first case,
the regime has recently celebrated its first quarter century of official
existence. Some observations on the meaning of this anniversary are
in order. Secondly, a number of alterations have been made within
the 1968 Constitution. Because they reveal some important areas of
divergence, albeit moderate, from the intentions of the 1968 document,
attention is devoted to them.

The Twenty-Fifth Anniversary

On October 7, 1974, East Germany celebrated its twenty-fifth
anniversary, an occasion mirroring unparalleled international triumphs
for the GDR. In the Western press the dominant theme was on the
GDR's growing sense of confidence and pride in itself. As one account
notes in this general regard, diplomatic recognition, combined with
a general degree of economic well-being over the past several years,
has had a bolstering effect on East Germany:

> The effects on this Ohio-sized country of 17 million were
> underscored by today's spectacle of a seemingly endless
> wave of soldiers in rigidly disciplined ranks rolling down
> East Berlin's grand ceremonial avenue, Karl Marx Allee.
> On both sides, the avenue was packed with thousands of
> spectators who cheered and waved scarves of the black,
> red and gold national colors. Among the spectators were
> the country's top leader, Erich Honecker, first secretary
> of the East German Communist Party, and the chief patron
> of Honecker's regime, Soviet Communist Party leader
> Leonid Brezhnev. East Germany's new sense of assertive-
> ness was also symbolized by the list of those who did not
> attend the parade. Five years ago, when the country
> marked its 20th anniversary, almost all the ranking
> leaders of the European Communist bloc were on hand
> to demonstrate their solidarity with a regime then
> regarded as a pariah outside of Communist circles.
> Now, however, such backing is no longer considered
> necessary. Except for Brezhnev, who came in his sym-
> bolic role as leader of the bloc, the East Germans
> invited relatively low-ranking delegations from their
> Communist allies to participate in today's celebration. [52]

Moving beyond these general considerations, a number of interesting changes were reflected in the official party document commemorating the anniversary, Theses on the 25 Anniversary. [53] To begin, the relative absence of Walter Ulbricht's contribution to the development of East German social and political institutions was marked. Indeed, the process of neglecting the impact of Ulbricht has been in force almost from the time he was removed from the top post within the SED, yet his relative absence within the Theses tended to provide an impression markedly at odds with the fact that no one has been more important in turning the GDR into a functioning political system than the ex-head of the SED. In briefly summarizing the postwar history of East Germany from the end of World War II to the end of 1973, the following quotation accurately reflects this intention to play down the role in GDR affairs of "Comrade Cell," as Ulbricht used to be called by his party colleagues:

> The National Front, which had fought with all its strength against the division of Germany given its goal of erecting a unified democratic German Republic, gave the only answer it could to the creation of a West German state. On the 7th of October 1949, the National Front established the German People's Council [Deutsche Volksrat] and in universal, equal, and secret balloting procedures the highest organ of the anti-imperialist patriotic People's Movement, the Provisional People's Chamber, set the Constitution of the German Democratic Republic into effective action. Thus, the German Democratic Republic was created. Wilhelm Pieck, the fighting colleague of Karl Liebknecht, Rosa Luxembourg and Ernst Thälmann, was unanimously elected to the post of President. Otto Grotewohl—like Wilhelm Pieck, President of the SED—became Minister-President. After Wilhelm Pieck died, Walter Ulbricht served as President from 1960-1973, with Willi Stoph now occupying the executive post as President of the State Council. [54]

Aside from the more general observation that modern political systems rarely pay departed leaders great amounts of homage in the immediate aftermath of their demise—witness the neglect of Lyndon Johnson's role in the Democratic party during the 1972 convention—there are positive and negative aspects attached to this calculated slighting of the Ulbricht heritage. On the positive side, one analyst notes the following rationale:

> The repression of the Ulbricht-era in the historical con-
> sciousness of the GDR has less to do with a renunciation
> of the actual tradition [set by him] and far more to do
> with an attempt to conceal the less-pleasant aspects of
> actual history [Stalinism in the 1950's, movement away
> from the Soviet model toward the end of the 1960's] . The
> historical perspective of the SED is correspondingly
> defined with a new accent. [55]

The writer goes on to note that the contemporary historical perspective
of the party has increasingly been oriented toward a revival of older
traditions emphasizing the heroic figure of the pre-World War II
German Communist Party (KPD) and the role of Ernst Thälmann
within it. From this angle, the playing down of Ulbricht's place in
East German history can be seen as a reasonably healthy attempt to
introduce some of the more "heroic" and activistic dimensions of
communist party history in the GDR, albeit a history easily subject
to rigorous criticism by outside observers. On the negative side,
the official neglect of Ulbricht tends to underline the apparent
inability of the SED to "digest" its recent past, a problem that invariably highlights a broader dilemma as seen in the party's lack of
confidence in the broad population's intellectual capacity to arrive
at an independent judgment on the Ulbricht era. In this, the SED
faithfully has imitated the historical reflexes of its Soviet mentor,
which has yet to arrive at a balanced evaluation of Stalin's role in
the history of the USSR.

As a second consideration, and at partial variance with the
first tendency mirrored in the Theses, there has been an understandable tendency by the party to emphasize a powerful thread of historical
continuity in line with the larger claims of Marxism/Leninism and
its belief in scientific—step-wise—historical development. Thus,
the document states that

> we have used well these 25 years. Our road was right and
> is right; everyone feels this themselves. We built our
> Republic well and surely, and well and surely do we dwell
> in it. The GDR and its citizens are one, just as peace and
> socialism are one. We have reliable friends and allies.
> Our country enjoys international authority. Internationally
> recognized, as a member of the United Nations, the GDR
> makes a constructive contribution to the peace and security
> of the world. [56]

In anticipation of the obvious changes in domestic and international
affairs that have greeted the GDR since the departure of Ulbricht
from the scene, the continuity theme is subsequently watered down:

In the 25th year of the existence of our Republic we are
striding as never before along to peace and socialism,
together with the Soviet Union, the countries of the
socialist commonwealth, and the Communist world movement. Let us close the ranks yet more closely. Let us
combine our forces even more effectively, in the economy, in socialist economic integration, in the political,
ideological, cultural and military fields, and in the
struggle for the implementation of the principles of
peaceful coexistence, against the enemies of detente,
for the defense of peace. This should be our international
contribution to the 25th anniversary of our Republic
[emphasis added].[57]

Finally, and in line with stock-taking efforts made during
Party Congresses and regular plenums, the Theses outlines some of
the more important developmental trends at work in East German
society. Among the most significant are: the increase of the socialized sector within the economy—from 83.1 percent in 1971 to 94.9
percent; a rise in the number of universities and colleges from 21
to 54 by 1973, and a corresponding rise in educational expenditures
from 1.1 million marks for 1950 to a level of 6.8 million marks by
1972; increases in allocations for health and social services from a
base of 5.9 million marks in 1950 to 22.5 million marks in 1971; a
more than fivefold increase in national income, from a base of 22
million marks in 1949 to more than 126 million marks in 1973; finally,
a rise in the monthly incomes of individuals working full time, from
a base of 290 marks in 1949 to 814 marks by 1972.[58]

Constitutional Changes

On September 27, 1974, the GDR's legislature unanimously
accepted a number of long-expected alterations in the East German
Constitution of 1968. As an English language publication notes, "The
main changes in the Constitution dealt with the definition of the character of the state in the GDR, and its position as an inseparable part
of the socialist community of states. In addition there were more
technical changes, such as the alteration of the term of office of the
People's Chamber from four to five years, so that it shall in future
correspond with the five-year planning period, and also changes in
the rights and duties of the State Council and the Council of Ministers."[59] Within this generalized context, the following Constitutional alterations arc quoted in full:

Preamble: The amended preamble to the Constitution
states that "the people of the GDR, in continuation of the

revolutionary traditions of the working class, and basing themselves upon the liberation from fascism, have implemented their rights of socio-economic, state and national self-determination, and are shaping the developed socialist society. The people of the GDR will continue unswervingly on the road of socialism and communism, the road of peace, democracy and international friendship. . . ."

The 1968 preamble stated that the citizens of the GDR were "imbued with the responsibility of showing the whole German nation the road to a future of peace and socialism"; in addition it condemned "the fact that imperialism, under the leadership of the USA and in concert with circles of West German monopoly capital, split Germany in order to build up West Germany as a base of imperialism and of struggle against socialism;" this passage is omitted in the new version.

Article 1 of the amended constitution states: "The German Democratic Republic is a state of workers and farmers. It is the political organization of the working people in town and countryside under the leadership of the working class and its Marxist-Leninist party."

The equivalent passage in the 1968 constitution stated: "The German Democratic Republic is a socialist state of German nation. It is the political organization of the working people in town and countryside who are jointly implementing socialism under the leadership of the working class and its Marxist-Leninist party."

Article 2 of the amended constitution states: "All political power in the GDR is exercised by the working people. Man is the center of all efforts of socialist society and its state. The decisive task for the developed socialist society is the further increasing of the material and cultural standard of living of the people on the basis of high development of socialist production, increasing effectivity, scientific-technical progress, and increasing labor productivity."

The 1968 constitution contained the first two sentences quoted above, but the third sentence simply stated "The social system of socialism is constantly being perfected."

Article 6 was considerably revised by the new amendments. The new version reads as follows: "(1) The German Democratic Republic, faithful to the interests of the people and to international obligations, has eradicated German militarism and nazism on its territory. It pursues a foreign policy serving socialism and peace, international understanding and security."

   The 1968 version: "The German Democratic Republic,
faithful to the interests of the German people and the international obligations of all Germans . . . ."
"(2) The German Democratic Republic is allied for ever
and irrevocably with the Union of Soviet Republics. The
close and fraternal alliance with the Soviet Union guarantees the people of the GDR further strides forward on the
path to socialism and peace. The GDR is an inseparable
component of the socialist community of states. True to
the principles of socialist internationalism it contributes
to the strengthening of the community and fosters and
develops friendship, all-round cooperation, and mutual
aid with all states of the socialist community."

   The 1968 version: "The GDR fosters and develops all-
round cooperation and friendship with the USSR and the
other socialist states on the basis of socialist internationalism."

Article 7 of the amended constitution states: "The state
organs ensure the territorial integrity of the GDR and the
inviolability of its state frontiers, inclusive of its air
space and territorial waters, and the protection and
exploitation of its continental shelf."

   The 1968 version spoke of the "inviolability of the
state territory of the GDR."

Article 8 of the amended constitution was shortened by
the cancellation of paragraph 2. In the 1968 constitution,
Article 8(2) stated: "The establishment and cultivation
of normal relations and cooperation between the two
German states on the basis of equality are national concerns of the GDR. The GDR and its citizens strive in
addition to overcome the division of Germany imposed
upon the German nation by imperialism, and support
the step-by-step rapprochement of two German states
until the time of their unification on the basis of democracy and socialism."

Article 9 of the amended constitution states: "The economy of the GDR is based upon the socialist ownership of
the means of production. It develops in accordance with
the economic laws of socialism on the basis of socialist
relations of production, and the tenacious implementation
of socialist economic integration."

   In the 1968 constitution this paragraph omitted mention
of socialist economic integration and included a sentence on
"the struggle against the economic system of monopoly
capitalism, the aggressive and adventurist policy of which
has hitherto brought only disaster to the German nation."

Article 14 of the amended constitution states that private
economic associations for the establishment of economic
power are not permitted, and defines the status of small
craft undertakings "mainly based on personal work."

In the 1968 constitution this article also defined the
situation of private economic undertakings; this has been
cancelled in the amended constitution since all larger
private enterprises have in the meantime been nationalized.
Article 22 of the amended constitution reads as follows:
"Every citizen of the GDR who is 18 years of age on election day has the right to vote. Every citizen can be elected
to the People's Chamber and the local representative
bodies if he has reached the age of 18 on election day."

The 1968 constitution, and its predecessor, the 1949
constitution, gave everybody the right to vote at the age
of 18; but the right to be elected to the People's Chamber
was limited to persons over 21.
Article 54 of the amended constitution reads as follows:
"The People's Chamber is composed of 500 deputies who
are elected by the people for five years in free, general,
equal and secret ballot."

In the 1968 constitution the term of the People's
Chamber was set at four years.

Some other major amendments to the constitution deal in some
detail with changes in the rights and duties of the State Council (pres-
idential council) and the Council of Ministers (cabinet). Still other
amendments are mostly emendations of terminology. In Article 4,
the phrase "All power . . . guarantees a systematic increase in living
standards" has been amended to read "All power . . . guarantees a
socialist mode of living for citizens." In six different places the
phrase "planning and management" has been emended to read "management and planning." In Article 12, the 1968 constitution referred
to "larger industrial enterprises" which are nationally owned property;
the 1974 amendment strikes out the word "larger."[60] Focusing on
some relevant alterations in the functioning of the state apparatus, the
most important changes are found in the effort to downgrade the status
of the State Council, and the parallel effort to vest the Minister Council
with the "leading" role within the governmental apparatus. In this
vein, perhaps the most striking shift is found in a comparison of
Article 76 in the old (1968) and revised constitution. Whereas Article
76 formally made brief mention that the State Council initiates the
award of state orders—marks of distinguishment (auszeichnungen)
and honorable titles being presented by the president—the revised
article contains an elaborated description of the Minister Council's

expanded responsibilities without mentioning a word about the other structure. Thus,

> 1. The Minister Council is an organ of the People's Chamber of the German Democratic Republic. Under instruction from the People's Chamber, it is responsible for the unified administration of State politics and the organization, and fulfillment, of the political, economic, cultural, social, and relevant defense obligations. It is responsible and answerable to the People's Chamber.
> 2. The Minister Council directs the national economy and other social areas. It secures the plan-like proportional development of the national economy, the phased harmonious design of social categories and territories as well as the realization of socialist economic integration.
> 3. The Minister Council is responsible for carrying through the foreign policy of the German Democratic Republic in line with the basic clauses of the Constitution. It deepens the many-sided cooperation with the Soviet Union and the other socialist states and guarantees the active contribution of the German Democratic Republic to the strengthening of the socialist state-community.
> 4. The Minister Council, in accordance with its realm of competence, decides on the settlement and conclusion of de jure treaties. It is responsible for the preparation of state treaties.[61]

As an aligned matter, the organizational makeup of the Minister Council has been altered, as mirrored in the revision of Article 80. In the earlier version, "the President of the Minister Council is formally proposed by the State Council President to the People's Chamber (1)." The altered version of Article 80 (Sec. 1) now states that the "Minister Council is a collective working organ. All its Ministers carry responsibility for the Council's performance. Every Minister is held responsible for his field of responsibility."[62] Gone is all mention of State Council influence.

One final consideration should be mentioned in regard to constitutional revision in the GDR. The alteration in the relationship from the old status of linking "planning and management" to the new one of reversing them to read "management and planning" is perhaps of greater importance than the English-language report on constitutional revision suggests. Here one should realize that the shift in word order represents a more subtle change in SED leadership style in the aftermath of the Ulbricht era. While the former SED chief viewed political leadership as primarily a plan-centered activity, the

Honecker regime places stronger emphasis on the ability of individuals, especially within the party, to effectively manage human relationships. While the constitutional revisions do not pay implicit or explicit lip service to this value, the overall pattern of leadership in the GDR since the coming to power of Honecker strongly underlines a new bias in favor of more active, human-centered, modes of political leadership. Accordingly, these shifts in word order should not be underplayed.

THE FUTURE OF THE GERMAN DEMOCRATIC REPUBLIC

Traditional Western analyses of the GDR are increasingly united on at least two basic assumptions regarding the East German political system. In the first place, few observers question the long-run staying power of the SED within the GDR. Indeed, not since the publication of Brzezinski's Alternative to Partition in 1965 has there been a respectable argument made on the proposition that SED rule is transitory and will eventually decay of its accord.[63] Secondly, there is some degree of consensus on the proposition that while the SED's rule finally rests on a secure foundation of political support, there is still a marked absence of spontaneous trust in the mass population toward the ultimate purposes of the regime. This argument has most recently and effectively been made by Peter Christian Ludz who refers to this absence of support in terms of an alleged "legitimacy deficit" that confronts the SED in its attempt to build a pattern of affective loyalty in the broad population.[64] Some aspects of this position are examined below.

The core of Ludz's argument—his being representative—rests on a definition of legitimacy possessing three dimensions, of which the most important is framed in propositional form:

> To accept a government or regime as legitimate means to obey it because we feel that it speaks with authority that deserves to be obeyed even if we cannot ourselves test or judge its commands on their merits. Through the notion of legitimacy, we have linked our civic obedience to our own personality, to our respect and self-respect. If we fail to obey an authority which we have accepted as legitimate, we are likely to feel diminished or divided within ourselves. Legitimacy thus is also maintained by the automatic penalty of intrapsychic conflict—of a "bad conscience" in the event of disobedience.[65]

Among the various reasons given for the SED's current legitimacy deficit, two appear to be of elemental importance. On the one hand, the SED inherited the burden of reeducating millions of Germans who had been conditioned to look down on Slavic peoples in general, Russians in particular. Given the intensive propaganda of the Third Reich, this was a less-than-easy challenge to confront and master. On the other hand, the insecure—or provisional—nature of the East German regime, until the construction of the Berlin Wall on August 13, 1961 put an end to its "temporary" image, is also used by Ludz to carry a large part of the explanatory burden. [66] In response to these historical factors, and in light of a continued bureaucratization of political life in the GDR, the East German population behaves passively toward the SED "without according it legitimacy or taking an active part in its support." [67]

As long as the Berlin Wall performs the function of keeping at least some potentially errant groups within the borders of the GDR, there is no <u>direct</u> empirical test of the "legitimacy deficit" argument. One could easily make the counterargument that the FRG could materially force the GDR to run greater risks in trusting its population by suspending automatic grants of West German citizenship to individuals escaping to the FRG or West Berlin. In view of West Germany's rising unemployment problem, this possibility may be sooner at hand than most analysts think. Borrowing the language and thought of Charles E. Osgood, Bonn might be encouraged to develop a policy toward the GDR maximally geared to a "gradual reduction of international tensions" [68] (GRIT) in areas touching on West Berlin's relationship with the FRG and East Germany, especially those that arouse the anxieties of the SED and provide little, if any, benefits for the Federal Republic beyond the symbolic victories Bonn political leaders can point to when the domestic political debate forces West German leaders to occasionally use West Berlin as a "test" of FRG commitments to the maintenance of West Berlin as a bastion of resistance to the reality of national division. In the absence of this possibility, and in view of the SED's new perception of threat in the wake of massive infusions of German visitors from the West, an empirical test of legitimacy is unfortunately lacking.

If one is content to employ softer criteria as a means of critically examining this widely held thesis, however, a contrary image begins to emerge. From this angle, the dramatic rise of the GDR to third place in world sport competition on the amateur level suggests that certain critically significant groups—youth—within the East German population are capable of demonstrating an impressive degree of active enthusiasm for competitions ranging their society against an imposing slate of competitors, not least of which stand the Soviet Union, the United States, and the Federal Republic of Germany.

Perhaps the outstanding performance of East German athletes is directly traceable to the generous social and financial privileges given to its more successful competitors, though this argument is also applicable to the United States and West Germany where both amateur and professional athletes have been recipients of impressive amounts of money and social prestige. It should also be mentioned that the number of East German athletes who have chosen not to return to their homeland on those occasions when competitive meets in the noncommunist world were held is infinitesimally small. Beyond this specific consideration, there is also some question whether average East German citizens feel themselves coerced when called upon to display public support for the SED and the institutions and values it has created. Undoubtedly many individuals feel themselves put upon when they know that nonattendance at mass rallies is noted by party cadres, but given the traditional love of public display that marks the Prussian side of the German character, plus 25 years of uninterrupted political socialization, there is some reason to believe that growing numbers of East German citizens have come to accept passively the requirements of public life in the GDR.

NOTES

1. Erich Honecker, "Der Kampf für Frieden und Sicherheit und der Beitrag der Deutschen Demokratischen Republik," in Protokoll des VIII Parteitages, Volume I (Berlin: Dietz Verlag, 1971), pp. 56-57.

2. See "Constitutions-Old & New," Democratic German Report 10/9/74, p. 142.

3. V. I. Lenin, "The Urgent Tasks of our Movement," in Collected Works, Vol. 4 (Moscow: Foreign Language Publishing House, 1960), pp. 366-71.

4. Ideology is absorbed in varying degree within a society, depending upon the age group an individual is counted within, socio-economic status, etc. For the only quasi-systematic examination of this phenomenon in the GDR, see Hans Apel, Ohne Begleiter (Cologne: Verlag für Politik, 1965).

5. Refer to Part I: "Inputs: Demands, Supports, Apathy," in this text, pp. 15-18.

6. See Erich Honecker, Neue Massnahmen zur Verwirklichung des sozialpolitischen Programms des VIII Parteitages, 5. Tagung des Zentralkomittees, April 27-28, 1972.

7. See the discussion dealing with East Germany's "Anti-Fascist Democratic Revolution," Chapter 2.

8. See Part II: "Outputs—Rewards, Deprivations," p. 169, this text.

9. See Part III: "Feedback," p. 293, this text.

10. Der Parteiarbeiter: Aufgaben und Erfahrungen der Partei-und Massenpropaganda nach dem VIII Parteitag der SED (Berlin: Dietz Verlag, 1972), p. 80.

11. See Chapter 4, "Broad Social Groups," in this text for a fuller elaboration of these activities.

12. For a brief discussion of Democratic-Centralism, see "The Socialist State," Introducing the GDR (Dresden: Verlag Zeim im Bild, 1974), pp. 73-74. Also see "Demokratischer Zentralismus," Kleines Politisches Wörterbuch (Berlin: Dietz Verlag, 1973), pp. 148-50.

13. See Wolfgang Weichelt, Der sozialistische Staat (Berlin: Staatsverlag, 1972), p. 29.

14. Chapter 7, this text, p. 248.

15. Chapter 8, this test, p. 304.

16. See Chapter 8, this text, p. 297.

17. For a masterful treatment of SED recruitment practices up through the late 1960s, see Peter Christian Ludz, The Changing Party Elite in East Germany (Cambridge, Mass.: MIT Press, 1972).

18. See Chapter 3, this text, pp. 79-81.

19. See Chapter 7, this text, p. 272.

20. For a representative SED articulation of this position, see Hermann Axen, Zur Entwicklung der sozialistischen Nation in der DDR (Berlin: Dietz Verlag, 1973), pp. 10-13.

21. Gebhard L. Schweigler, "The Development of National Consciousness in the German Democratic Republic," a paper delivered at the 1973 Annual Meeting of the American Political Science Association, New Orleans, September 4-8, 1973, p. 17.

22. For a comprehensive treatment dealing with all phases of East German foreign-policy making, see Anita Dasbach-Mallinckrodt, Wer macht die Aussenpolitik der DDR? (Düsseldorf: Droste Verlag, 1972).

23. See Robert Gerald Livingston's thoughtful commentary on East Germany's international situation after the signing of the Four-Power Berlin Accords in "East Germany: Between Moscow and Bonn," Foreign Affairs, 1/1972.

24. Compiled from Staats und Parteiapparat der DDR, August 1, 1974, pp. 42-45.

25. Ibid., pp. 42-44.

26. See Ernst Richert's discussion of the "transnational" dimension in his "Zwischen Eigenständigkeit und Dependenz: Zur Wechselwirkung von Gesellschafts- und Aussenpolitik der DDR," Deutschland Archiv, 9/1974, pp. 956-58.

27. Dokumentation: "Die 12. Tagung des ZK der SED (I)," Deutschland Archiv, 8/1974, p. 881.

28. Ibid., p. 884.

29. See Karl Wilhelm Fricke, "Die Militärs in der DDR-Führung," Deutschland Archiv, 3/1974, pp. 231-34.

30. See Dokumentation: "Europäische Sicherheitskonferenz aus der Sicht beider deutsche Staaten," Deutschland Archiv, 1/1973, p. 86.

31. Jürgen Nitz, "Europäische Sicherheit und ökonomische Zusammenarbeit," in IPW Berichte, 1/1973, p. 6.

32. Livingston, op. cit., p. 309.

33. Mallinckrodt, op. cit., p. 333.

34. der Spiegel, December 18, 1972, p. 46.

35. Werner Lamberz, Agitation und Propaganda nach dem VIII Parteitag der SED (Berlin: Dietz Verlag, 1972), p. 49.

36. Fred Oldenburg, "Zum 12. Plenum des ZK der SED," Deutschland Archiv, 8/1974, p. 791.

37. Hans-Dieter Schulz, "Weniger Besuche-mehr Devisen Verdoppelung der Mindestumtauschätze," Deutschland Archiv, 12/1973, pp. 1241-48 covers the immediate impact of this East German decision.

38. der Spiegel, "An Tatsachen erinnern," 11/4/74, p. 49.

39. Ibid.

40. For a general treatment of this interesting three-cornered relationship, see Peter Scharpf, "Die Bedeutung des inner-deutschen Handels für die Beziehungen der EWG zur DDR," Deutschland Archiv, 3/1974, pp. 260-66.

41. "Vierseitiges Abkommen dient Frieden in Europa," Neues Deutschland, 6/10/74, p. 2.

42. der Spiegel, 20/8/73, p. 107.

43. Democratic German Report, 8/29/73, p. 107.

44. Ibid.

45. Dokumentation: "Verhaftungen auf den Transitstrecken und Urteile gegen Fluchthelfer," Deutschland Archiv, 9/1974, p. 1002.

46. Ilse Spittmann, "Die 9. Tagung des Zentralkomitees der SED," in Deutschland Archiv, 6/1973, p. 569.

47. der Spiegel, 7/29/74, p. 20.

48. For a recent example of this possibility, see Manfred Steinkühler, "Die SED zur kommunistischen Regierungsbeteilung in Portugal," Deutschland Archiv, 10/1974, pp. 1016-19.

49. Dokumentation: "Die 12. Tagung des ZK der SED (I)." Deutschland Archiv, 8/1974, p. 886.

50. Manfred Steinkühler, "Die Beziehungen der DDR mit Rom und Paris: Unerwartete Reaktionen von IKP und FKP," in Deutschland Archiv, 3/1973, p. 236.

51. See the late Heinz Lippmann's account of this phenomenon, and possibility, "X. Weltjugendfestspiele im Geist der Volksfront-politik," Deutschland Archiv, 8/1973, pp. 788-91.

52. "Goose-Stepping Pomp Marks East Germany's 25 Years," Washington Post, October 8, 1974, p. 14.

53. See Deutschland Archiv's account of this event, 10/1974, pp. 1062-80.

54. Ibid., p. 1066.

55. Consult Hermann Weber, "25 Jahre DDR-Kontinuität und Wandel," Deutschland Archiv, 10/1974, 1033.

56. Democratic German Report, 1/30/74, p. 10.

57. Ibid.

58. "Thesen zum 25. Jahrestag der DDR," Deutschland Archiv, 10/1974, p. 1072.

59. Democratic German Report, October 10/74, p. 141.

60. Ibid., pp. 141-42.

61. See Informationen-Bundesminister für innerdeutsche Beziehungen (Chronik Vom 23. September bis zum 6. Oktober 1974), p. 18.

62. Ibid., p. 19.

63. Zbigniew Brzezinski, Alternative to Partition (New York: McGraw-Hill, 1965).

64. Peter Christian Ludz, Deutschlands Doppelte Zukunft (Munich: Karl Hanser Verlag, 1974), pp. 80-86.

65. Karl Deutsch, "The German Federal Republic," in Modern Political Systems: Europe, ed. Macridis and Ward (Englewood Cliffs, N.J.: Prentice-Hall, 1972), p. 315.

66. Ludz, op. cit., p. 81.

67. Wolfgang Leonhard, Child of the Revolution (Chicago: Regnery Press, 1958), pp. 237-38.

68. Charles E. Osgood, "Calculated De-escalation as a Strategy," in Dean G. Pruitt and Richard C. Snyder, eds., Theory and Research on the Causes of War (Englewood Cliffs, N.J.: Prentice-Hall, 1969), pp. 213-16.

JOHN STARRELS is Assistant Professor of Political Science and International Affairs at the George Washington University. A specialist in comparative European political systems, he received his B.A. from the University of California at Berkeley, his Ph.D from the University of California at Santa Barbara. As a participant in the briefing of John Sherman Cooper, this country's first ambassador to the German Democratic Republic, Dr. Starrels is preparing a manuscript on intra-German relations.

ANITA MALLINCKRODT is Adjunct Associate Professor of International Affairs at the George Washington University and an associate of the "Deutsche Welle," the international radio voice of West Germany, broadcasting from Cologne. Additionally, she is a lecturer at the University of Cologne, Research Institute for Political Science. As a close follower of East German political affairs, Dr. Mallinckrodt has published two books on East German politics: Propoganda hinter der Mauer and most recently, Wer macht die Aussenpolitik der DDR? She received her Ph.D from the George Washington University.

EAST EUROPEAN PERSPECTIVES ON
EUROPEAN SECURITY AND COOPERATION

edited by Robert R. King and
Robert W. Dean

ENVIRONMENTAL DETERIORATION IN THE
SOVIET UNION AND EASTERN EUROPE

edited by Ivan Volgyes

MULTINATIONAL CORPORATIONS AND
EAST EUROPEAN ECONOMIES

Geza P. Lauter and Paul M. Dickie

PERSONAL AND SOCIAL CONSUMPTION IN
EASTERN EUROPE: Poland, Czechoslovakia,
Hungary, and East Germany

Bogdan Mieczkowski

POLITICAL SOCIALIZATION IN EASTERN
EUROPE: A Comparative Framework

edited by Ivan Volgyes

THE POLITICS OF MODERNIZATION IN
EASTERN EUROPE: Testing the Soviet
Model

edited by Charles Gati, with
introductory essays by
Vernon V. Aspaturian and
Cyril E. Black

TECHNOLOGY IN COMECON: Acceleration
of Technological Progress Through Economic
Planning and the Market

J. Wilczynski (available in the
U.S. only)